Jerusalem

written and researched by

Daniel Jacobs

ROUGH
GUIDES

www.roughguides.com

Contents

Colour section · 1

Introduction 4
What to see............................. 7
When to go 9
Things not to miss 10

Basics · 17

Getting there........................... 19
Arrival 23
Getting around........................ 24
City tours 28
Security and crime................... 29
Culture and etiquette 31
Gay and lesbian travellers........ 32
Travelling with children 33
Travellers with disabilities 34
The media............................... 35
Travel essentials 36

The City · 45

❶ Jaffa Gate and the Armenian
   Quarter............................ 47
❷ Via Dolorosa and the Christian
   Quarter............................ 55
❸ The Muslim Quarter 72
❹ The Jewish Quarter............. 84
❺ The Temple Mount 99
❻ East Jerusalem 108
❼ West Jerusalem................ 124
❽ Outlying areas.................. 144

Listings · 161

❾ Accommodation................ 163
❿ Eating.............................. 177

⓫ Drinking and nightlife 194
⓬ Entertainment................... 199
⓭ Sports and activities 205
⓮ Festivals and holidays....... 209
⓯ Shopping 216

Excursions · 229

Bethlehem and around........... 231
Hebron................................... 241
Jericho................................... 243
The Dead Sea and Masada.... 248
Heading west: Abu Ghosh 252
Tel Aviv and Jaffa.................. 253

Contexts · 265

A short history of Jerusalem ... 267
Religion.................................. 275
Books 284

Language · 291

Pronunciation, spelling and
   gestures.............................. 293
Useful words and phrases...... 294

Small print & Index · 301

The Holy City colour section following p.80

Colour maps following p.312

Jerusalem

3

Introduction to
Jerusalem

Ten measures of beauty gave God to the world: nine to Jerusalem and one to the remainder
Ten measures of sorrow gave God to the world: nine to Jerusalem and one to the remainder

The Talmud

Everybody's heard of Jerusalem (Yerushalayim in Hebrew, Al-Quds in Arabic), and most people have some image of it in their heads, but almost everyone who comes here is surprised at what they find. Sacred to three religions and once considered to be the centre of the world itself, the Holy City is, for all its fame, quite small, far from opulent and provincial in many ways. Yet it is undeniably a fascinating place, packed with museums, religious sites and ancient relics while still being a real, lived-in city, home to around 800,000 people.

Jerusalem is home to three of the world's most venerated places: the **Church of the Holy Sepulchre**, held to be the location of the crucifixion, and the holiest site in Christendom; the **Wailing Wall**, last remnant of the Second Temple and most sacred Jewish relic in the world; and the **Dome of the Rock** – third most hallowed location in Islam, and the spot from where the Prophet Mohammed made his ascent to heaven. But even without these monuments the city has much to offer – from the narrow alleys and vibrant **souqs** of the magnificent walled **Old City**, to the churches and tombs of the **Mount of Olives**, and the expensive shops and lively bars of downtown **West Jerusalem**. In fact, Arab East Jerusalem and Israeli West Jerusalem offer the visitor two worlds for the price of one: the tradition and relaxed pace of the Arab world and the cosmopolitan glitz of the West. And, in a city with an already diverse cultural mix, the assorted clergy from Christian sects worldwide, and the ultra-Orthodox of Mea Shearim in their eighteenth-century *shtetl* apparel, add further to the varied nature of the city's inhabitants.

Perched high in the Judean Hills, the city's **location** is equally captivating. The view on approach is dramatic, with even the modern city providing a magnificent array of white high-rises that gleam in the sunlight – an architectural legacy of the first British governor, who declared that all new buildings must be made from local limestone, a ruling that has continued to be observed to this day. To its west lie the fertile planted fields, olive groves and settled villages of the coastal plain and the Judean foothills, while to the east the harsh desert of the Jordan Valley stretches out to a horizon that, on a clear day, offers glimpses of the Dead Sea.

As far as **politics** is concerned, Jerusalem is at the heart of the Israel–Palestine question - hotly contested and deeply divided. It may be one city, but it's evidently in two countries. Israel has taken the position, since 1967, that Jerusalem is the single indivisible capital of the Jewish state, and it is the country's administrative centre, increasingly cut off from the West Bank by Israel's Separation Wall; but the Palestinians also consider Jerusalem their capital – however unrealistic that may seem – and it remains the

The four quarters

The four quarters of Jerusalem's Old City – Muslim, Jewish, Christian and Armenian – began to evolve after Muslim sultan Saladin's conquest of the city in 1187. Jews moved into the area around the Wailing Wall, Muslims into the area around the Dome of the Rock, and Christians into the area around the Church of the Holy Sepulchre; meanwhile, an Armenian

community had already established itself in the southwestern corner of the city around St James's Cathedral. The division of quarters was never rigid, and there were always Jews living in the Armenian Quarter, Muslims in the Christian Quarter and so on, but by convention, Souq Khan al-Zeit divides the Christian and Muslim quarters, Bab al-Silsila Street divides the Muslim and Jewish quarters, Habad Street divides the Jewish and Armenian quarters, and David Street divides the Armenian and Christian quarters. All four quarters meet at the southern end of the Central Souqs (see p.76).

focus of their culture and aspirations. The two halves live uneasily side by side, a tension heightened by the construction of new Jewish settlements encroaching upon Palestinian land.

All this can make Jerusalem a rather schizophrenic city, a frustrating and complex place that can seem overwhelming on a first visit. In fact such is the emotion it inspires in some visitors that it has its own (literally) schizophrenic mental disorder called **Jerusalem Syndrome**, whose sufferers believe themselves to be characters from the Bible – Jesus is the favourite, but others include Moses, King David, John the Baptist and the Virgin Mary. You might see them wandering the streets, dressed in the robes of their adopted persona. Other sufferers commit bizarre acts in their certainty of the imminent Second Coming: in 1969, an Australian tourist tried to burn down Al-Aqsa Mosque in preparation for Jesus's imminent arrival.

Despite its very real difficulties, Jerusalem is also a very beautiful city, teeming and alive. It's a historical location without compare, the backdrop against which the stories of three religions were acted out. It was from here that Mohammed ascended to heaven on his night journey, from the same spot where God tested Abraham by asking him to sacrifice his son. It was the residents of this city who welcomed Jesus by spreading palm leaves on the ground before him, along these streets that he dragged the cross, and here that he was executed upon it. Here, too, stood the capital of David and Solomon, home to the two Jewish Temples of antiquity, and this is the city for which the Jews, through all their centuries of exile and persecution, cried their ancient hope: "next year in Jerusalem". Little wonder that it inspires such dreams, such devotion, such love and such madness.

What to see

Jerusalem's key attractions are, of course, the big religious sites: the **Church of the Holy Sepulchre**, the **Wailing Wall** and the **Dome of the Rock**, all found within the walls of the labyrinthine **Old City**. A walk around the impressive Ottoman ramparts gives a wonderful introduction to the Old City, passing in turn each of its four traditional quarters. The **Muslim Quarter** holds some of the greatest treasures of Mamluk architecture, as well as much of the **Via Dolorosa**, along which Jesus is believed to have carried his cross. The **Christian Quarter** has some of the city's most important **souqs** or markets. The **Armenian Quarter** includes Jerusalem's citadel, known as the **Tower of David**. And the **Jewish Quarter** has been restored to preserve ancient remains like the old Roman **Cardo** or main street, as well as several old **synagogues**.

Outside the walls are **Mount Zion**, where the Last Supper is believed to have taken place, and where the Virgin Mary is thought to have resided after the death of her son. Nearby is the **City of David**, Jerusalem's original location, and to its east the ancient tombs of the **Kidron**

East and West

The 1948 Arab-Israeli War left Jerusalem divided, with West Jerusalem held by Israel, while East Jerusalem, along with the rest of the West Bank (the west bank of the River Jordan, that is), was taken by Jordan. The border between Israel and the West Bank – really an armistice line rather than a proper international frontier – is known as the Green Line after the colour of the ink used to draw it. In the 1967 Six Day War, Israel ended up occupying the West Bank, and unilaterally annexed East Jerusalem, but the two halves of the city remain very distinct. West Jerusalem, almost entirely Jewish, is the main commercial centre, and much like a European city, while East Jerusalem, including the Old City, remains largely Palestinian (though Jewish settlers are moving in too), and is a lot more Middle Eastern.

The Madaba map

In 1884, workers renovating an old church at Madaba in Jordan uncovered a sixth-century mosaic bearing a map of Palestine, and prominent in the middle of it is a depiction of the city of Jerusalem. Much of the city's geography is clearly visible, including the two main streets – the Cardo (Al-Wad Road) and the Cardo Maximus (Souq Khan al-Zeit, the central souqs and the "Cardo" of today; see p.92). The column at what is now the Damascus Gate (see p.72) is clearly shown, as are the Wailing Wall, the original building of the Church of the Holy Sepulchre, and the then new – now long gone – Nea Church (see p.98).

A reproduction of the Jerusalem section of the Madaba Map is displayed in Jerusalem beneath the Damascus Gate, and there are good reproductions of it online – one with the buildings labelled is posted on the city council's website at Ⓦwww.jerusalem.muni.il/english/map/madaba/cardo1e.html.

Valley. The **Mount of Olives** offers wonderful vistas over the Old City, and beyond it is the village of **Bethany**, where Jesus raised Lazarus from the dead. The downtown area of **West Jerusalem** includes the main shopping district, and the ultra-Orthodox neighbourhood of **Mea Shearim**, and spreads out to encompass Israel's parliament, the Knesset, as well as the excellent **Israel Museum** containing the **Dead Sea Scrolls**. Further out, you reach **Yad Vashem**, Israel's monument to the victims of the Holocaust, and the beautiful suburban village of **Ein Karem**.

If that isn't enough, there are a number of fascinating places easily reached on a day-trip. Of these, the ancient fortress of **Masada**, gets many a visitor out of bed for 3am for the ever-popular excursions to climb it at dawn and see the sun rise from the top before checking out that weird natural phenomenon, the **Dead Sea**. Nearer at hand, royal David's city of **Bethlehem**, the biblical birthplace of Jesus, is almost within walking distance, through a checkpoint just ten minutes away by bus. **Jericho**, whose walls came tumbling down, takes a little more getting to, but still lies only an hour to the east. Westward meanwhile, the village of **Abu Ghosh** attracts lovers of fine Middle Eastern food, while further west, on the Mediterranean coast, is Israel's commercial capital, **Tel Aviv** – the place to go for drinking and nightlife, but also for sightseeing, thanks to its wealth of Bauhaus architecture, and attractions such as the old city of **Jaffa**.

When to go

Spring (April and May) and autumn (Oct and Nov) are the ideal **times to visit** Jerusalem, when temperatures are agreeably warm, but not too hot. In summer, the heat can be uncomfortable though it's a dry heat, and the altitude makes it cooler than Israel's coastal plain, let alone Jericho where the heat can be oppressive. In winter, especially in January, Jerusalem can actually get pretty cold – even snow is not unknown – though it's still generally bright and even warmish during the day, with temperatures falling rapidly after sunset. At most times of the year, you'll want to wear loose-fitting cotton clothes, but you'll need to carry at least some which are sufficiently "modest" to visit religious sites (long sleeves, especially for women, long trousers for men, and long skirts for women; see p.31). In winter, you'll need at least a sweater or two as well, and in summer it's a very good idea to bring a sun hat to keep you cool and protect you from heatstroke (see p.38).

Climate

	Jan	Feb	Mar	Apr	May	Jun	Jul	Aug	Sep	Oct	Nov	Dec
Average daily temperatures												
°C (max/min)	11/6	15/7	16/8	21/12	25/15	27/17	30/19	31/18	28/18	26/16	19/12	14/8
°F (max/min)	52/43	57/45	61/46	70/54	77/59	81/63	86/66	87/64	82/64	79/61	66/54	57/46
Average rainfall												
mm	132	132	64	28	3	0	0	0	0	13	71	86
inches	5.2	5.2	2.5	1.1	0.1	0	0	0	0	0.5	2.8	3.4

23

things not to miss

It's not possible to see everything that Jerusalem has to offer in one trip – and we don't suggest you try. What follows is a selection of the city's highlights: spectacular religious sites, outstanding museums and the best excursions. They're arranged in no particular order in five colour-coded categories, which you can browse to find the very best things to see and experience. All highlights have a page reference to take you straight to where you can find out more.

01 Church of the Holy Sepulchre Page **63** • The holiest spot in Christendom, site of Christ's crucifixion and burial, a magnet for pilgrims from across the globe.

02 **Wailing Wall** Page **87** • The last remnant of the biblical Jewish Temples, and a magnificent sight, especially on a Friday evening when worshippers gather here to welcome in the Sabbath.

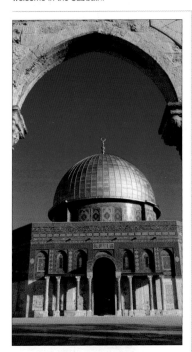

04 **Argila** Page **182** • The traditional Middle Eastern smoke, a hubbly-bubbly water-pipe, now undergoing a revival as young people try out newfangled fruit-flavoured tobaccos.

05 **Tomb of the Patriarchs, Hebron** Page **242** • See where the great biblical patriarch Abraham lies buried in a city rent asunder by the mortal struggle between descendants of his two sons.

03 **Dome of the Rock** Page **102** • Visible from across the city, this sublime masterpiece of Ummayad architecture houses the rock on which Abraham tried to sacrifice his son to God.

06 **Shopping in the Old City souqs** Page **225** • Test out your bargaining skills in Jerusalem's frenetic markets, particularly those in the Old City.

07 **Israel Museum** Page **144** • Apart from the world-famous Dead Sea Scrolls, this wonderful museum houses ancient and modern art, an outdoor model of Jerusalem and a reconstructed synagogue.

08 **Christmas mass in Bethlehem** Page **236** • Join Christians from around the world to celebrate Christmas where it all began, at the stroke of midnight in Manger Square.

09 **Day-trip to Jericho** Page **243** • The oldest city in the world, whose walls came a-tumblin' down, is home to the stunning Hisham's Palace with its beautifully preserved floor mosaics.

10 **Old Jaffa** Page **261** • Once Palestine's main port, Jaffa was the arrival point for the knights of the Crusades and departure point for the famous oranges; today it's a charming if rather twee artists' colony.

11 **People-watching in the midrahov** Page **128** • West Jerusalem's Ben Yehuda Street is packed with shops and restaurants and provides a European-style contrast to the rest of the city.

12 **Walk the Via Dolorosa** Page **58** • You can stop and pray at the site of each incident on this approximation of the very route along which Jesus carried his cross.

13 **Yad VaShem** Page **151** • Israel's mournful, grim but compelling national memorial to the six million Jewish people murdered by the Nazis during the Holocaust.

14 **Mea Shearim** Page **129** • The home of Jerusalem's ultra-Orthodox *Haredi* community, where black, eighteenth-century costumes and strictly observant piety remain the order of the day.

15 **Ramparts Walk** Page **50** • Circumnavigate the Old City on the magnificent ramparts commissioned by Suleiman the Magnificent after the Prophet himself ordered their construction in a dream.

16 Dead Sea Page **248** • One of nature's strangest phenomena, a super-dense salt lake set in a scorching lunar landscape at the lowest point on earth.

| ACTIVITIES | CONSUME | EVENTS | NATURE | SIGHTS |

18 Hezekiah's Tunnel Page **114** • Wade knee-deep in water through this tunnel whose construction, described in the Bible, saved Jerusalem from the invading Assyrians.

17 Tel Aviv Page **253** • Swap Middle Eastern piety for Mediterranean fun in Israel's dynamic commercial capital, the world centre of Bauhaus architecture.

19 Church of the Nativity, Bethlehem Page **235** • The exact spot in what was then a stable where Christ was born, laid in a manger, worshipped by humble shepherds and visited by great magi from the east.

20 **Banksy's murals, Bethlehem** Page **238** • Subversive murals by Britain's favourite graffiti artist, satirizing the Israeli occupation and the Separation Wall on which they are painted.

21 **Middle Eastern food** Page **177** • Specializing in Jewish and Palestinian cuisine and serving everything from *mezze* to hummus and falafel, Jerusalem has plenty of great places to eat.

22 **The Citadel** Page **50** • Dating from the second century BC, the city's stronghold has been fortified by almost every subsequent ruler, and makes the perfect setting for a sound and light show.

23 **Dawn at Masada** Page **250** • Watch the sun rise from atop the natural desert fortress where the last pocket of Jewish resistance held out till the bitter end against the might of imperial Rome.

Basics

Basics

Getting there 19

Arrival 23

Getting around 24

City tours... 28

Security and crime 29

Culture and etiquette 31

Gay and lesbian travellers.. 32

Travelling with children 33

Travellers with disabilities 34

The media 35

Travel essentials... 36

Getting there

Most visitors to Jerusalem arrive via Israel's international airport, Ben Gurion (officially Tel Aviv's airport), which is 45 minutes away from Jerusalem by bus or *sherut* (service taxi). A smaller number come by land from Jordan or Egypt.

Air fares tend to be higher in summer, and also for the main Jewish holidays of Passover (around April) and the Jewish New Year (around Sept), as well as Christmas and Easter.

If you're planning to stay at a four- or five-star establishment, it often makes sense to take a **package tour**, because of the huge discounts you can get on hotel rates. Very few firms offer Jerusalem city breaks as such, but any agent offering "tailor-made" tours can fix you up with a hotel and flight deal (specialist travel agents are listed on p.22).

Flights from the UK and Ireland

British Airways, BMI and El Al **fly direct** to Tel Aviv from London Heathrow, and El Al also run flights from Stanstead, as do Israel's no-frills domestic carrier, Israir (though their flights are rather often subject to delay or cancellation). British low-cost airline Jet2 run flights from Manchester, and Thompsonfly, affiliated to package holiday firm Thompson, sometimes run flights from Luton and Manchester. From elsewhere in the UK or Ireland, you'll need to take an **indirect flight** via London or a European hub such as Amsterdam, Frankfurt or Zurich. Indirect flights via Europe may also be a cheaper option from London. Expect to pay £240–375 including tax to fly to Tel Aviv from London in winter, £270–380 in summer. From Dublin, expect to pay €325–690/€375–760.

Flights from the US and Canada

There are **direct flights** to Ben Gurion from New York and LA (with El Al, Delta and Continental), Toronto (El Al and Air Canada), and Miami (Delta). From other North American airports, you'll need to fly to one of those for a connecting flight (American Airlines codeshares with El Al, so they can sell you a through ticket via New York, Toronto or LA), or else fly via Europe with a carrier such as British Airways, KLM or Lufthansa. Typical fares (including tax) will be around US$1200 in winter, rising to around US$1600 in summer from New York, US$1400/2000 from LA, C$1000/1500 from Toronto.

Flights from South Africa, Australia and New Zealand

El Al offer direct flights **from Johannesburg** to Tel Aviv, and South African Airways codeshare this flight, allowing you to buy through tickets from the other airports they serve. However, it may be cheaper to fly via Addis Ababa, which has direct flights to Tel Aviv with Ethiopian Airlines. Fares from Johannesburg to Tel Aviv are typically R10,000–15,000 in January, R7500–12,000 in July.

From Australia and New Zealand there are no direct flights, and Middle Eastern airlines such as Emirates do not serve Israel for political reasons, so your best bet is with

Airline security

Security on flights to Israel is always extra-tight, for obvious reasons. This is especially true on flights operated by Israel's national carrier **El Al** (who run their own security checks in addition to anything the airport may provide), but also applies on other airlines. As a result, you will almost certainly be required to check in around three hours before your flight departure time.

Qantas, Air New Zealand or a Southeast Asian airline in conjunction with El Al (whose services reach Bangkok, Beijing and Mumbai). Alternatively you could fly with South African Airways via Johannesburg, or even with a European airline via Europe. Typical fares from Sydney are A$2450–3000 in January, A$2500–3500 in July; from Auckland they are NZ$4300–9500 in January, NZ$3350–6050 in July.

By land from Jordan

The journey **from Amman** in Jordan to Jerusalem can take anything from two to five hours in total, and the earlier you start, the more likely you are to complete it quickly. The best option, especially if you do not want an Israeli passport stamp (see box opposite), is to travel via the **Allenby Bridge** (known in Jordan as King Hussein Bridge, or Jissr al-Malik Hussein). You can either take a service taxi (from the southern end of Abdali Bus Station) and stay on until you reach the foreigners' terminal at the bridge (not the terminal for Jordanians and Palestinians) or take a a JETT bus (6.30am daily, also from Abdali) all the way from Amman to the Israeli terminal. The first option means you have to take a bus across to the Israeli-held side – a ten-minute journey, but you can wait as long as two hours for the bus to fill up and go (you are not allowed to walk). If you're travelling by the JETT bus note that if you do not want your passport stamped you will need to take it to the immigration desk yourself (rather than let the driver take it along with everybody else's). Once through immigration and a security check on the Israeli side, you can pick up a service taxi to Jerusalem.

It is also possible to take a **direct bus** from Amman to Jerusalem, but it will use the Bet Shean crossing (so you'll get the border stamp in your passport) and it will take longer than coming via Allenby. Mazada Tours run buses whenever they have enough passengers (US$88 one-way plus US$10 border taxes, or US$33 on the way back plus US$15 for a Jordanian visa). For further information contact Neptune Tours (who run the tours in conjunction with Mazada) in Amman (☎06/552 1493, ✉info@neptune-tours.com) or Mazada direct in Jerusalem (15 Jaffa Rd ☎02/623 5777, ✆www.mazada.co.il).

By land from Egypt

At one time the most obvious route **from Egypt** into Israel was via Rafah in the Gaza Strip, but that border is currently closed, as are crossings from Gaza into Israel, so the only overland route at present is via Taba, near Israel's Red Sea port of Eilat. Taba can be reached by bus from Cairo or from Sinai beach resorts such as Dahab and Nuweiba, from which you may also be able to get a service taxi.

Once across the border at Taba, you can take local bus #15a (hourly 8.20am–6.20pm) or a taxi into Eilat, and pick up an Egged bus to Jerusalem (4 daily; 5hr), but note that the last departure from Eilat is at 5pm Sunday to Thursday, and 1pm Friday; buses on Saturday, on the other hand, do not run until nightfall to avoid the Jewish Sabbath – see ✆www.egged.co.il/eng for departure times.

More conveniently, Mazada Tours run **direct buses from Cairo** to Jerusalem, departing from the *Cairo Sheraton* hotel (Thurs & Sun 8am; US$145 one-way, US$165 return, including border taxes). For tickets and information, contact Misr Travel at the *Cairo Sheraton* (☎02/335-5470) or Mazada in Jerusalem (see above).

The only way to avoid getting an Israeli border stamp if coming from Egypt would be to take a boat from Nuweiba to Aqaba in Jordan and enter the West Bank via the Allenby Bridge (see above).

Airlines, agents and operators

Airlines

Aer Lingus Ireland ☎0818/365 000, ✆www .aerlingus.com.
Air Canada Canada & US ☎1-888/247-2262, ✆www.aircanada.com.
Air France US ☎1-800/237-2747, Canada ☎1-800/667-2747, UK ☎0870/142 4343, Australia ☎1300/390 190, South Africa ☎0861/340 340, Israel ☎03/755 5057; ✆www.airfrance.com.
Air New Zealand New Zealand ☎0800/737000, ✆www.airnz.co.nz.
Alitalia US ☎1-800/223-5730, Canada ☎1800/361-8336, UK ☎0871/424 1424, New Zealand ☎09/308 3357, South Africa ☎011/721 4500; ✆www.alitalia.com.
American Airlines US & Canada ☎1-800/433-7300, ✆www.aa.com.

Israeli passport stamps

At one time, an **Israeli stamp** in your passport would mean you were barred from entering most Arab countries, and to some other Islamic countries too. Although the number of nations refusing entry has reduced, those taking a hard line against Israel (notably Syria, Lebanon, Libya and Sudan) continue with the practice which can cause problems for onward travel.

In general, Israeli immigration officials will agree **not to stamp your passport** when asked, but do make this clear when you hand over your passport. Note that if you are coming to Jerusalem by land, Egyptian and Jordanian officials at borders with Israel will stamp your passport, and their stamps are as much evidence of a visit as stamps from Israel itself; the only way to avoid this is to enter and leave via the **Allenby Bridge** (see opposite). Note also that if you enter the West Bank and then come back to Jerusalem via an Israeli checkpoint with no Israeli entry stamp in your passport you may be subject to questioning.

Some travellers have tried to get round the Israeli stamps problem by obtaining a **new passport** in Cairo or Amman once they have finished travelling in Israel. However this will also raise questions at immigration as will the use of any visa issued in Israel.

Austrian Airlines US & Canada ☏ 1-800/843-0002, UK ☏ 0870/124 2625, Ireland ☏ 1800/509 142, Australia ☏ 1800/642 438 or 02/9200 4800, Israel ☏ 1800/444 777 or 03/511 5110; ☷ www .aua.com.

bmi US ☏ 1-800/788-0555, UK ☏ 0870/607 0555 or 0870/607 0222, Ireland ☏ 01/283 0700, Australia ☏ 02/8644 1881, New Zealand ☏ 09/623 4293, South Africa ☏ 011/289 8111, Israel ☏ 03/795 1588; ☷ www.flybmi.com.

British Airways US & Canada ☏ 1-800/AIRWAYS, UK ☏ 0844/493 0787, Ireland ☏ 1890/626 747, Australia ☏ 1300/767 177, New Zealand ☏ 09/966 9777, South Africa ☏ 011/441 6600, Israel ☏ 03/606 1555; ☷ www.ba.com.

Cathay Pacific Australia ☏ 13 17 47, New Zealand ☏ 09/379 0861; ☷ www.cathaypacific.com.

Continental Airlines US & Canada ☏ 1-800/523-3273, ☷ www.continental.com.

ČSA (Czech Airlines) US ☏ 1-800/223-2365, Canada ☏ 1-866/293-8702, UK ☏ 0870/444 3747, Ireland ☏ 0818/200 014, Australia ☏ 1800/063 257, Israel ☏ 03/516 5115; ☷ www.czechairlines.com.

Cyprus Airways US ☏ 718-267/6882, UK ☏ 020/8359 1333, Australia ☏ 03/9663 3711, Israel ☏ 03/975 4294; ☷ www.cyprusairways.com.

Delta US & Canada ☏ 1-800/221-1212, Israel ☏ 03/975 4058; ☷ www.delta.com.

El Al US ☏ 1-800/223-6700 or 1-212/852-0600, UK ☏ 020/7121 1400, Australia ☏ 03/9866 2755, New Zealand ☏ 09/308 5206, South Africa ☏ 011/ 620 2525, Israel ☏ 03/971 6111; ☷ www.elal.co.il.

Ethiopian Airlines South Africa ☏ 011/289 8077, Israel ☏ 03/510 0501; ☷ www.ethiopianairlines.com.

Iberia US ☏ 1-800/772-4642, UK ☏ 0870/609 0500, Ireland ☏ 0818/462 000, South Africa ☏ 011/884 9255, Israel ☏ 03/795 1920; ☷ www .iberia.com.

Israir US ☏ 1-877/477 2471, UK ☏ 0870/000 2468, Israel ☏ 1700/505 777; ☷ www.israirairlines.com.

Jet2 UK ☏ 020/3031 8103, ☷ www.jet2.com.

KLM US & Canada ☏ 1-800/225-2525 (Northwest), UK ☏ 0870/507 4074, Ireland ☏ 1850/747 400, Australia ☏ 1300/392 192, New Zealand ☏ 09/921 6040; ☷ www.klm.com.

LOT (Polish Airlines) US ☏ 1-212-789/0970, Canada ☏ 416-236/4242, UK ☏ 0845/601 0949, Ireland ☏ 1890/359 568, Australia ☏ 02/9244 2466, New Zealand ☏ 09/308 3369, Israel ☏ 03/510 4044; ☷ www.lot.com.

Lufthansa US ☏ 1-800/3995-838, Canada ☏ 1-800/563-5954, UK ☏ 0871/945 9747, Ireland ☏ 01/844 5544, Australia ☏ 1300/655 727, New Zealand ☏ 0800/945 220, Israel ☏ 1809/371 937, ☷ www.lufthansa.com.

Malev Hungarian Airlines US ☏ 1-800/223-6884, Canada ☏ 11-866/379-7313, UK ☏ 0870/909 0577, Ireland ☏ 0818/555 577, Israel ☏ 03/562 1100; ☷ www.malev.hu.

Qantas Airways Australia ☏ 13 13 13, New Zealand ☏ 0800/808 767 or 09/357 8900; ☷ www .qantas.com.

Singapore Airlines Australia ☏ 13 10 11, New Zealand ☏ 0800/808 909; ☷ www.singaporeair.com.

SN Brussels Airlines US ☏ 1-516/740-5200, Canada ☏ 1-866/308-2230, UK ☏ 0905/609 5609, Ireland ☏ 01/844 6006, Australia ☏ 02/9767 4305, Israel ☏ 1809/491 000; ☷ www.flysn.com.

South African Airways Australia ☏ 1300/435 972, New Zealand ☏ 09/977 2237, South Africa ☏ 011/978 1111; ☷ www.flysaa.com.

Six steps to a better kind of travel

At Rough Guides we are passionately committed to travel. We feel strongly that only through travelling do we truly come to understand the world we live in and the people we share it with – plus tourism has brought a great deal of **benefit** to developing economies around the world over the last few decades. But the extraordinary growth in tourism has also damaged some places irreparably, and of course **climate change** is exacerbated by most forms of transport, especially flying. This means that now more than ever it's important to **travel thoughtfully** and **responsibly**, with respect for the cultures you're visiting – not only to derive the most benefit from your trip but also to preserve the best bits of the planet for everyone to enjoy. At Rough Guides we feel there are six main areas in which you can make a difference:

- Consider what you're contributing to the **local economy**, and how much the services you use do the same, whether it's through employing local workers and guides or sourcing locally grown produce and local services.
- Consider the **environment** on holiday as well as at home. Water is scarce in many developing destinations, and the biodiversity of local flora and fauna can be adversely affected by tourism. Try to patronize businesses that take account of this.
- Travel with a purpose, not just to tick off experiences. Consider **spending longer** in a place, and getting to know it and its people.
- Give thought to how often you **fly**. Try to avoid short hops by air and more harmful night flights.
- Consider **alternatives to flying**, travelling instead by bus, train, boat and even by bike or on foot where possible.
- Make your trips "**climate neutral**" via a reputable carbon offset scheme. All Rough Guide flights are offset, and every year we donate money to a variety of charities devoted to combating the effects of climate change.

Swiss US & Canada ☎1-877/3597-947, UK ☎0845/601 0956, Ireland ☎1890/200 515, Australia ☎1300/724 666, New Zealand ☎09/977 2238; ⓦwww.swiss.com.

Turkish Airlines US ☎1-800/874-8875, Canada ☎1-866/435-9849, UK ☎020/7766 9300, Ireland ☎01/844 7920, Australia ☎02/9299 8400, South Africa ☎011/447 3444, Israel ☎03/517 0108; ⓦwww.thy.com.

Thai Airways US ☎1-212/949-8424, UK ☎0870/606 0911, Australia ☎1300/651 960, New Zealand ☎09/377 3886; ⓦwww.thaiair.com.

Thomsonfly UK ☎0871/231 4691, ⓦwww .thomsonfly.com.

Agents and operators

ISSTA UK ☎020/8202 0800, ⓦwww.issta.com. British branch of Israel's main youth and student travel firm (but not only for youths or students).

Longwood Holidays UK ☎020/8418 2500, ⓦwww.longwoodholidays.co.uk. Middle East specialists offering Jerusalem city breaks.

North South Travel UK ☎01245/608 291, ⓦwww.northsouthtravel.co.uk. Friendly,

competitive travel agency, offering discounted fares worldwide. Profits are used to support projects in the developing world, especially the promotion of sustainable tourism.

STA Travel UK ☎0871/230 0040, ⓦwww .statravel.co.uk, US ☎1-800/781-4040, ⓦwww .statravel.com, Australia ☎134 STA, ⓦwww .statravel.com.au, New Zealand ☎0800/474400, ⓦwww.statravel.co.nz, South Africa ☎0861/781 781, ⓦwww.statravel.co.za. Specialists in independent travel; also student IDs, travel insurance, and more. Good discounts for students and under-26s.

Superstar Holidays UK ☎020/7121 1500, ⓦwww.superstar.co.uk. El Al agents whose package deals include Jerusalem city breaks.

Trailfinders UK ☎0845/058 5858, Ireland ☎01/677 7888, Australia ☎1300/780 212; ⓦwww.trailfinders.com. One of the best-informed and most efficient agents for independent travellers.

Travelink UK ☎020/8931 8000, ⓦwww .travelinkuk.com. Israel travel specialists.

Travel Cuts Canada ☎1-866/246-9762, US ☎1-800/592-2887; ⓦwww.travelcuts.com. Canadian youth and student travel firm.

Arrival

Jerusalem is in some ways quite easy to get your bearings in, with the Old City at the heart of things, downtown West Jerusalem immediately to its northwest, and East Jerusalem immediately to its north. Coming from Tel Aviv by bus or train, you'll arrive in West Jerusalem, some distance from the centre, and need to take a bus or cab into town. From Ben Gurion airport, on the other hand, a service taxi (*sherut*) will take you to your hotel door, or at the very least, to the nearest Old City gate. Coming from the east (Jordan and the West Bank), you'll probably arrive in East Jerusalem.

By air

Israel's main international airport, **Ben Gurion** (Tel Aviv), is located 50km west of Jerusalem near the town of Lydda (Lod). All international flights arrive at terminal 3, domestic flights at terminal 1 (terminal 2 is currently out of use, but may be used in the future for low-cost airlines). Banks, ATMs and car rental facilities are available in the arrivals hall. For further information about the airport, visit the Israel Airports Authority website at Ⓦwww.iaa.gov.il/rashat.

A cab from Ben Gurion into Jerusalem will cost around 250NIS (£42/US$60) and take around 45 minutes. Alternatively Nesher Taxis (see p.27), run a 24-hour **sherut** (minibus) service from outside the terminal buildings, leaving when full, or an hour after the first passenger arrives, and currently costing 50NIS (£8.50/US$12). Nesher will usually drop you anywhere in town, though they do not currently drop off at the Damascus Gate, so you may have to make do with the New Gate or the Jaffa Gate if you are staying in the Old City, or with the *Jerusalem Hotel* (not far from Damascus Gate; see p.169) for East Jerusalem. It is also possible to reach Jerusalem **by bus** from the main gate of the airpoirt (#5 to "Airport City" and then #947 to Jerusalem's Egged Central Bus Station), with a typical total journey time of 1hr 20min at a cost of 26.40NIS (£4.40/US$6.25), just over half the price of a Nesher *sherut*, but a lot less convenient.

The airport terminal also has a rail station, so you could feasibly get a **train**, though this would mean going to Tel Aviv and catching a Jerusalem-bound train there – a very long way round indeed.

By bus

Arriving from within Israel by **bus** you'll find yourself at the Egged Central Bus Station on the Jaffa Road in West Jerusalem, about 2km from the city centre and the New Gate (the nearest entrance to the Old City). Numerous city buses run east along the Jaffa Road into town: #6, #13, #18 and #20 for downtown West Jerusalem (Mercaz Ha'Ir); #6 continues to a stop between the New Gate and the Damascus Gate. From around 2010, there will also be a tram service along the Jaffa Road to the city centre, New Gate and Damascus Gate. Should you decide to walk into town, exit onto the Jaffa Road, turn right and you'll be in central West Jerusalem after a kilometre and a half, and at the New Gate after two.

Buses from the West Bank drop you at one of the two bus stations in East Jerusalem (#18 from Ramallah at Nablus Road, #36 from Abu Dis at East Jerusalem Central Bus Station on Sultan Suleiman) both near the Damascus Gate. Bus #6 runs to West Jerusalem from near here, or it's a fifteen-minute walk – look for the walls of the Old City, turn right alongside them up Sultan Suleiman and Paratroopers Road until the wall ends, and then take a right up the Jaffa Road.

Mazda Tours **buses from Cairo or Amman** arrive at their office on the corner of Koresh and King Solomon at the northwest corner of the Old City, near the New Gate and the Jaffa Road.

By service taxi

Sheruts (service taxis) from Tel Aviv (55NIS) run 24 hours a day, and most will bring you to HaRav Kook Street, off Jaffa Road in the centre of downtown West Jerusalem. **Service taxis** from Allenby Bridge (35NIS) will leave you on Sultan Suleiman in East Jerusalem, near the Damascus Gate.

By train

Jerusalem's **train station** has temporarily been shifted out to the suburb of Malha, 4km southwest of the city centre. Because the location is so inconvenient, and because the train journey to Jerusalem is so much longer than the bus journey, only rail buffs are likely to be using the train.

There are ten **trains** a day to Malha from Tel Aviv via Lydda (Lod) and Ramla, except on Saturdays, when there is only one (at 10.30pm), and on Fridays the last train is at 2.45pm; journey time is an hour and forty minutes. Trains from other destinations, such as Haifa, connect at Tel Aviv (or, from Beer Sheba, at Lydda). For schedules see ⓦwww .rail.co.il/en. To **get into town** from Malha, take bus #4, #6 or #18 from outside the station. When buying your train ticket, ask about discounts for train passengers on city buses into town.

A new underground rail terminus is planned at Binyanei HaUma, on Jaffa Road near the bus station, and is expected to open around 2012.

By car

Jerusalem is on the West Bank's main artery, Route 60 (the Nablus–Hebron road), but most drivers will be approaching from Tel Aviv on the Ayalon Freeway (Route 1) via Latrun, a pretty straight run, taking about an hour. Coming into Jerusalem, steep gradients require you to switch down a gear (for more on driving see p.26).

Getting around

Walking is the best way to get around central Jerusalem, and certainly in the Old City, most of which is closed to traffic, though there are some steep slopes around town, and some of the Old City's "streets" are actually more like staircases. For longer distances, take a bus or a cab. A tram line is under construction.

Egged buses

Jerusalem's city **bus services**, run by Israel's national bus company Egged (☎02/530 4999; lines open Sun–Tues & Thurs 8.30am–4pm, Wed 8.30am–2pm), are regular and efficient, though few and far between east of the Green Line, and they **do not run on Shabbat** (ie, from before sunset on Friday and all day Saturday; see p.276). The flat fare of 5.70NIS also makes them expensive for short hops, but they come into their own for visits to places in the outer western suburbs, such as Yad VaShem and Ein Kerem. The most useful connections are shown in the box opposite. Egged do not currently publish information on Jerusalem city bus routes in English, largely because many routes have been diverted due to the construction of the new tramway (see opposite); a full list of routes can nonethless be found at ⓦen .wikipedia.org/wiki/list_of_egged_bus_lines, but note that these are subject to change.

Palestinian buses

One or two independent **Palestinian bus operators** run services to outer East Jerusalem, the most useful of which are: #36 from East Jerusalem Central Bus Station (also near the Damascus Gate) to Bethany and Abu Dis, via the Mount of Olives and Ras al-Amud; #75 from the Central Bus Station to Al-Tur; and #124 from the Central Bus Station

Egged bus connections

To	From Egged Central Bus Station	From King George Street/ Jaffa Road
King George Street/ Jaffa Road	#6, #13, #18, #20	–
Damascus Gate	#1, #6	#6
Dung Gate (for Wailing Wall)	#1, #2	#38
Mea Shearim	#1, #11, #15, #35	#4, #11, #35
Sanhedria	#10	#19
Mt Scopus	#23, #26, #28	#4a, #19
Israel Museum	#17	#17
Mt Herzl and Yad Vashem	#13, #17, #18, #20, #21, #23, #27, #39	#17, #18, #20, #21
Ein Kerem (village)	#17	#17
Ein Kerem (Hadassah Hospital)	#27	#19
Talpiot	#21, #102, #106	#21, #102, #103, #106
Malha (train station and mall)	#6, #18	#4, #6, #18
Biblical Zoo	#26	–

to the Rachel checkpoint (for Bethlehem). Note that some Arab buses have the same numbers as Egged buses – this does not mean that they run on the same routes.

Taxis

Tourists taking a **taxi** are often overcharged, but this is much less likely to happen if the driver uses the meter, which they are legally obliged to do on demand (though they may possibly then avoid taking the most direct route). If a driver does not want to use the meter, it will be because they want to overcharge you, so take another cab. A short hop in the city centre should cost around 20–30NIS; from the centre to the Israel Museum will cost around 30–40NIS, to Ein Karem around 60–80NIS. Note that fares are higher from 9pm to 5.30am and that many West Jerusalem taxi drivers will refuse to go to East Jerusalem. On the Arab side, a private taxi (as opposed to a service taxi – see below) is called a "special". It is not local practice to tip cabbies, but they always appreciate it of course.

Taxi firms

Note that a 4.10NIS booking fee applies if you call a taxi company rather than hailing a

cab in the street. All the firms listed here run seven days a week.

Abdo Sultan Suleiman (opposite Damascus Gate), East Jerusalem ☎02/628 3281.

Al-Aqsa 1 Ikhwan Esafa, East Jerusalem ☎02/627 3003.

Bar-Ilan 1 HaMarpeh, Har Hotzvim, West Jerusalem ☎02/586 6666.

HaPalmakh 20 Shai Agnon, West Jerusalem ☎02/679 3333.

Mount of Olives 24 Roba al-Adawiya, Al-Tur, East Jerusalem ☎02/627 2777.

Rehavia 3 Agron, West Jerusalem ☎02/625 4444.

Service taxis

On intercity runs, in addition to buses and private taxis, there are also **service taxis** (*servees* in Arabic, *sherut* in Hebrew), usually minibuses, which run a fixed route for a fixed charge and leave when full. Generally you won't find service taxis inside Jerusalem, but occasionally (for example between the Mount of Olives and the Damascus Gate) a special will function as a *servees* and charge a fixed fare for the run. This also sometimes applies in Bethlehem, from the checkpoint into town (see p.233).

Trams

A **tram** line (or light railway) is under construction and should be up and running

Palestinian bus routes

Palestinian buses serving East Jerusalem and other nearby West Bank destinations leave from Nablus Road Bus Station, or from East Jerusalem Central Bus Station on Sultan Suleiman. The most useful are:

#18 to Ramallah and Al-Bira (from Nablus Road Bus Station)

#21 to Bet Jala (from East Jerusalem Central Bus Station)

#36 to Bethany and Abu Dis (from East Jerusalem Central Bus Station)

#75 to Augusta Victoria Hospital, Al-Tur and the Mount of Olives (from East Jerusalem Central Bus Station)

#76 to Silwan (from East Jerusalem Central Bus Station)

#124 to Mar Elias and Rachel checkpoint (for Bethlehem) (from East Jerusalem Central Bus Station)

in 2010. The futuristic new tram bridge near the Egged Bus Station (see p.129) is already a Jerusalem landmark with its tall and elegant supporting column. The tram will run along Jaffa Road from the New Gate up to the Egged Central Bus Station, and then follow Sederot Herzl out as far as Mount Herzl and Yad Vashem. In the other direction from the New Gate, it will follow Paratroopers Road to the Damascus Gate and then head north up Hail HaHandassah (the Green Line, still in theory an international boundary) up towards Sheikh Jarrah, crossing into East Jerusalem to serve the Jewish settlements of Pisgat Zeev and Neve Yaakov.

Despite opposition from both the PLO (because it serves Israeli settlements in East Jerusalem) and local motorists and shopkeepers (whose business has been adversely affected during construction), the tram will eventually be a very welcome addition to the city's public transport system, and more lines are set to follow. Further information should eventually be posted online at ⓦwww.citypass.co.il. In the meantime, some information, and maps of the route (under "First System") can be found at ⓦwww.rakevetkala-jerusalem.org.il.

Driving

Israeli and Palestinian **driving** is notorious. Expect other motorists to drive aggressively, to tailgate dangerously on fast roads, to hog the overtaking lane on motorways (and overtake on the nearside) and not to bother indicating. At traffic lights (which change

directly from red to green, though some now count down with digital displays), you'll be honked immediately by drivers behind if you are not very quick off the mark when they change. That said, if you drive defensively and do not allow other motorists to intimidate you, you can drive as safely here as in any other Mediterranean country.

Around town, you'll find that Jerusalem's drivers are a little more relaxed than those in the rest of Israel, though you shouldn't expect them to ever give way. Most routes are well signposted. During **rush hours** (7–9am and 4–6pm), the city centre and major routes in and out of town are frequently gridlocked, and construction of the tramway (see above) has temporarily made this problem a lot worse. Note also that *Haredi* residents of Mea Shearim take a very dim view of driving on **Shabbat**, and may stone motorists who drive through their neighbourhood then.

Another problem lies in Jerusalem's position astride **the Green Line**. If you have an Israeli car, with yellow plates, it may attract hostility on the West Bank, while a Palestinian car can attract unwanted attention in Israel. In any case, most car rental agencies in Jerusalem will not allow you to drive their vehicles into "Area A" of the West Bank (under PA control), including Bethlehem, Bethany and Jericho.

Leaving town

The best way to get to most parts of Israel is by **Egged bus** from the Egged Central Bus Station, 2km from the city centre on Jaffa

Road. This can be reached on city bus #6 from Jaffa Road opposite the Post Office; #13, #18 or #20 from further up Jaffa Road, and will be served by the new tram. Direct **buses to Cairo** are operated by Mazada Tours (see p.20).

By air

For Tel Aviv (Ben Gurion) **airport**, Nesher Taxis at 23 Ben Yehuda (℡02/625 7227 or 1599/500 205, ⓦwww.neshertours.co.il) run a 24-hour shuttle service, and will pick up in most parts of town, but you need to book ahead, especially as their office is closed on Shabbat. Mike's Centre (see p.28) can also arrange transport to the airport, for 65NIS. Some Egged buses (#947 to Haifa, for example) stop at the airport gate on the Jerusalem–Tel Aviv freeway, but this leaves you with the problem of how to get to your terminal (a very long walk indeed), and for the small amount of money you save, it isn't worth the trouble.

Airline offices

El Al's office in Jerusalem is at 12 Hillel ℡02/677 0200. Other **airlines** mostly have their offices in Tel Aviv or at Ben Gurion airport (see pp.20–22 for phone numbers). The most useful **travel agent** is student travel specialist ISSTA, at 31 HaNeviim (at Jaffa Road) ℡02/535 8600, and 4 Herbert Samuel (off Zion Square) ℡02/621 1888, both offices open Monday to Thursday 9am to 7pm, Friday 8.30am to 1pm.

To Tel Aviv

Service taxis (*sherut*) to **Tel Aviv** are operated 24/7 by Habira (℡02/625 4545; usually from HaRav Kook, just off Jaffa Road, but on Saturdays from Heil HaHandassa, west side, just south of HaNeviim), with a less convenient six-day service run by HaUma on Jaffa

Road near the Egged Central Bus Station (℡02/538 9999), and the "*Haredi* express" to Tel Aviv's ultra-orthodox suburb of Bnei Brak by Geula at 20 Strauss near Mea Shearim (℡02/625 1222).

Until Binyanei HaUma station opens around 2012 (see p.24), taking a **train** to Tel Aviv involves trekking out to Malha, 4km south of the centre (buses #4 and #18 from King George St, #6 from Jaffa Rd), where there are ten daily departures (1hr 40min; no trains on Shabbat), connecting for destinations up and down the coast.

To West Bank destinations

There are few direct buses or service taxis to **West Bank** destinations except for those listed in the box opposite, plus Allenby Bridge, and of course Jewish settlements, including the Jewish side of Hebron (from which it is possible for foreigners to cross to the Palestinian side). Otherwise, you will need to take a bus to Ramallah for points north (including places just outside Jerusalem such as Al-Jib or Nabi Samwil), to Abu Dis for Jericho, and to Bethlehem for points south (including the Palestinian side of Hebron).

To Jordan via Allenby Bridge

Service taxis for **Allenby (King Hussein) Bridge** are operated by Abdo (1 Sultan Suleiman, opposite Damascus Gate ℡02/628 3281) and Alnijmeh (Sultan Suleiman, by *Golden Walls Hotel* ℡02/627 7466). The current fare is 35NIS. It's best to start off early for Amman; service taxis leave from 7am until around 11am Sunday through Thursday, but only until 9.30am on Fridays and Saturdays. After that, you will need to hire a "special" (private taxi), which will cost around 300NIS.

City tours

If you want to see the main sights quickly or perhaps want a more in-depth look at some aspect of the city, it can make sense to take a guided tour. Jerusalem has a large number available. A bus tour takes the weight off your feet, and can take you out of town too, but walking tours take you to places that buses cannot reach, most notably inside the Old City. Note that tour prices do not include site entry fees; if you are visiting a number of sights it may be worth investing in a combined ticket.

Bus tours

The easiest way to get a sense of the layout and size of Jerusalem is to take a panoramic tour on Egged's double-decker **bus #99** (see below). Several private firms also offer coach tours of Jerusalem and to places such as Masada and Nazareth. In addition to the firms listed here, hostels such as the *Palm* (see p.167) and *Citadel* (see p.166) offer Masada excursions.

Egged ☎1-700/707 577 or 03/920 3919, ☯www
.egged.co.il/eng. Runs the open-topped #99 tour taking in most areas of the city and many of the most important sights with commentary in eight languages including English. There are five daily departures (currently leaving the bus station at 9am, 11am, 1.30pm, 3.45pm and 6pm), except on Fridays, when only the first three run, and Saturdays, when there are none. You buy tickets on board. A day-ticket allowing you to change buses is 80NIS, a two-day ticket 110NIS. Egged also run a half-day Old City tour (US$42), a one-day Jerusalem tour (US$62), and day trips to, among other places, Masada (US$92), or Nazareth and the other main Christian sites in Galilee ($82).

Mike's Centre off Souk Khan al-Zeit by no. 162 (on the stairs leading to the Ninth Station of the Cross), Old City ☎02/628 2486, ☯www.
mikescentre.com. Tours to Masada (US$55), and to Nazareth and the Galilee holy sites (US$72).

United Tours ☎02/652 2187, ☯www.unitedtours
.co.il. Range of tours including "Jerusalem Old and New" (US$62) as well as Galilee and the Golan Heights (US$255).

Walking tours

In addition to the firms listed here, there are specialized walking tours run for groups by freelance tour guide Khalil Toufagji (☎02/234 4859), or by former Palestinian activist Ali Jiddah (☎052/283 1542). Israeli archeologists also run an occasional "Alternative Archeological Tour" in the area south of the Old City (see p.115).

Alternative Tours Jerusalem Hotel, Nablus Rd, East Jerusalem ☎052/286 4205, ☯www
.alternativetours.ps. A Palestinian take on the city and its politics, including a three-hour Old City tour (80NIS), a political tour of the city or outside it (100NIS), and trips to Bethlehem, Hebron, Jericho and other West Bank towns. Different tours run on different days depending on demand, and they usually require a minimum of five people.

Center for Jerusalem Studies Al-Quds University, Souq al-Qattanin, Old City ☎02/628 7517, ☯www
.jerusalem-studies.alquds.edu. Holds a number of interesting Old City walking tours; what's on offer changes from week to week, with details on the website.

Jerusalem City Council ☎02/531 4600, ☯tour
.jerusalem.muni.il. Free three-hour walking tour, leaving Saturday 10am from City Hall complex, 32 Jaffa Road. The section of the city covered changes from week to week.

Sandemans New Jerusalem Tours ☯www
.neweuropetours.eu. Free three-and-a-half-hour walking tours, departing from the tourist office inside the Jaffa Gate daily at 11pm.

Tours in English Jerusalem Hotel, Nablus Rd, East Jerusalem ☎09/777 0020, ☯www
.toursinenglish.com. Similar to Alternative Tours, with a Jerusalem tour every Monday (170NIS), Bethlehem on Tuesdays (265NIS), or Bethlehem and Hebron on Thursdays (265NIS).

Zion Walking Tours inside the Jaffa Gate, opposite the Citadel entrance, Old City ☎02/626 1561, ☯zionwt.dsites1.co.il. Old City tour three times daily (US$30), and other more specialized tours including the Western Wall Tunnel (see p.91), held less frequently but at similar prices. Also run a tour to Qumran and Ein Gedi.

Self-guided audio tours

As an alternative to joining a group or hiring a guide, the City Council offer a service allowing you to download your own audio guide from the internet. All you then need is an MP3 player and you can guide yourself at your own pace. A wide variety of routes are available for download – the site is at ⓦwww .jerusalemp3.com.

The settlers' organization Elad (see p.115) also offer a "Jerusalem Trail" audio tour on their website at ⓦwww.cityofdavid.org.il.

Combined tickets

For tourists visiting a lot of sights around Jerusalem, combined tickets are available giving a reduced rate for entry into a number of sights.

The **HolyPass**, available online (ⓦwww .holypass.co.il) for 99NIS, gives free entry to two "major" sights (and three "minor" ones (their classification, not ours), valid for a week, but not exceptionally good value (the most you can save is 13NIS). The "major" sights to choose from are the City of David, the Jerusalem Archaeological Park, the Tower of David, the Museum of Temple Treasures, the Burnt House, or the Generations Center: the "minor" sights are: the four Sepahrdi synagogues, the Jerusalem in the First Temple Period exhibition, the Ramparts Walk, the Roman Plaza beneath the Damascus Gate, the Wohl Museum, the Yishuv Court Museum, Zedekiah's Cave, the One Last Day Museum, or an archeological dig at Emek Tsurim. The pass also gives you a 5NIS discount on a bus #99 ticket, allows you to book the Western Wall tunnel tour (see p.91) just two days in advance, and gives discounts of between five and fifteen percent at certain shops and restaurants in the Old City's Jewish Quarter

There's also a **combined ticket** for the Jerusalem Archaeological Park, Ramparts Walk, Roman Plaza and Zedekiah's Cave (sold at the ticket offices of all three sites), which at 55NIS (valid for three days) saves you a whopping 33NIS on the price you'd pay for all of them separately. You'll also find combined tickets (sold at the ticket offices at the sites) for any two, or all three, of the Burnt House, Wohl Museum and One Last Day Museum – a ticket for all three, at 45NIS (valid for one day), saves you 12NIS.

Security and crime

Security is obviously a concern for visitors to Jerusalem and the other areas covered in this guide. In recent years there have been suicide bomb attacks on civilian targets in Jerusalem and Tel Aviv though at the time of writing violence had become more isolated (in the case of Jerusalem thanks in part to the construction of the Separation Wall, see p.234). There is also a slight risk of being caught up in political demonstrations which have the potential to turn violent. That said, tourists rarely encounter any problems. In fact, in terms of common crime, Jerusalem is a lot safer than most Western cities, though as anywhere you should always take precautions and stay as well informed as possible about the current situation.

Security

Because of the permanent state of tension, **security**, in the form of the police and army, is always present on the streets of Jerusalem. In public places, always keep your belongings with you since baggage left unattended may be reported to the police as suspicious, and either confiscated or detonated. Similarly, if you notice an **unguarded package**, you should report it to a bus driver, storeowner, hotel staff or whoever else seems relevant. Expect to have your **bags checked** frequently, especially at entrances to museums, large stores, supermarkets, cinemas and post offices. You are required by Israeli law to **carry ID** (which basically means your passport) at all times, but keep it well hidden from pickpockets. Going into sensitive sites, such as the Wailing Wall or Temple Mount, you'll have to pass through a metal detector and have your bag searched; it will save time for you and everybody else at such places if you carry the minimum of baggage and have your camera, keys, mobile and anything else that might go bleep ready to hand over before you go through the metal arch.

The Israeli **army** (IDF or *Tzahal*) are visible everywhere and the sight of fully armed khaki-clad soldiers walking around the streets is a common and, until you get used to it, slightly shocking one. Do remember, however, that pretty much everyone in Israel does military service. The army therefore consists of ordinary Israeli youths, and the soldiers you see out and about will often be off-duty and making their way home or to base.

Trouble spots

On the **West Bank** (including East Jerusalem and the Old City administered by Israel), there is a slight but real possibility of being caught up in **disturbances**. Any demonstration by Palestinians or Israeli settlers may turn violent. Always keep your ear to the ground and avoid troublespots. At the time of writing, the UK Foreign Office advised against all but essential travel to the West Bank other than to East Jerusalem, Bethlehem, Ramallah, Jericho and the Dead Sea area; note that this advice currently means avoiding Hebron, which is a notorious flashpoint (see p.241). The US State Department took a stronger line warning against all travel to the West Bank outside Jerusalem. Note also that **kidnapping** or attempted kidnapping of Western nationals in West Bank towns such as Nablus and Jenin is not unknown, so it is wise to follow travel advisories regarding which areas are safe to visit. Israeli **checkpoints** are ubiquitous all over the West Bank, but foreigners are usually fast-tracked unless they are (or look) Muslim or Arab. While you may find questioning and delays at these checkpoints annoying, remember that as a tourist you will not be subject to anything like the delays and indignities that local residents are – always answer questions politely and patiently, and whatever you do, don't lose your temper.

Government advisories

Australian Department of Foreign Affairs Ⓦ www.dfat.gov.au, www.smartraveller.gov.au.
British Foreign & Commonwealth Office Ⓦ www.fco.gov.uk/en.
Canadian Department of Foreign Affairs Ⓦ www.dfait-maeci.gc.ca.
Irish Department of Foreign Affairs Ⓦ www.foreignaffairs.gov.ie.
New Zealand Ministry of Foreign Affairs Ⓦ www.mft.govt.nz.
US State Department Ⓦ www.travel.state.gov.

Crime

The **crime rate** as such is not high in Jerusalem, though it's higher in poorer areas of East Jerusalem than it is on the more prosperous west side of town. Petty theft at cheap hostels (and also on Tel Aviv beaches) is unfortunately quite common, so never leave your valuables unattended in such places (most have safes or lockers available). Passports fetch high rates on the black market, and so are particular targets. In the Old City, especially in crowded areas, **pickpocketing** is also quite common. If you do need to report a crime, the police stations by the Citadel, in the Russian Compound, and at 107 Jaffa Rd are used to dealing with tourists. There's also a dedicated **tourist police** post at the entrance to the Church of the Holy Sepulchre. **Police** on the street in West Jerusalem are part of the ordinary civilian police force (Ⓦ www.police.gov.il/english); most of those in East Jerusalem (including the Old City) belong to the Border Police, who are part of the IDF.

Drugs are strictly illegal in Israel, even cannabis (though it is quite widely used), and you will at the very least be deported if you are caught with any. If you look the type, or if you look Palestinian, especially if walking around late at night, and often at entrances to the Old City, the police may stop you to check your ID, and if they do that, they may also go through your pockets. Note, too, that **jay-walking** is illegal, so stick to official crossings and wait for the green man, or you could incur a fine.

Sexual harassment

Generally speaking, **sexual harassment** of women is no more an issue in Jerusalem than it would be at home, and Israeli and Palestinian women alike are pretty tough and take no nonsense. As a tourist, especially if you are young, and especially if you are blonde, you will attract a certain amount of male attention. This may be more noticeable in East Jerusalem and the Old City than in West Jerusalem, and it's a good idea to avoid deserted Old City streets at night. Following the rules on **modest dress** (see below) will help avoid unwanted attention. Of more concern are the reported incidents of sexual assault of female tourists on the Mount of Olives, and though none of these are recent, it's an area worth avoiding on your own, and especially at night. It's also a good idea, if taking a cab with a male driver, to sit at the back rather than in the front passenger seat. Note that under Israeli law sexual harassment is a criminal offence. If the very worst should happen, the Rape Crisis Centre has an emergency hotline for victims of rape and sexual harassment at ☎1202 or 02/625 5558.

Culture and etiquette

In Jerusalem, religion and politics are never far away, and people's views on both can be fervent if not fanatical. You are unlikely to avoid political discussions, but it is always best to be tactful if you disagree with people, and remember that views which may be considered extreme in the West are quite commonplace among Israelis and Palestinians.

As far as **religion** is concerned, you would be unlikely (and indeed unwise) to enter into any debate on the subject, but you should bear in mind that religious people can seriously object to what they consider "immodest" clothing, particularly on women, and particularly in religious buildings, on Temple Mount, or in the ultra-orthodox Jewish district of Mea Shearim. **Modest attire** – loose-fitting dresses, or long skirts and long-sleeved baggy tops – is therefore advisable at all times and a must at religious sites and in orthodox areas – keep yourself well covered, with no shorts or bare shoulders (at Muslim sites in particular, men should be covered to below the shoulder and below the knee, women to the wrist and the ankle). T-shirts are usually permissable for men if they cover the shoulder, though some people in Mea Shearim frown on even short sleeves, and also on women wearing trousers. Ignoring these dress codes may make you the target of hostility from religious Jews and Arabs alike – usually in the form of verbal abuse, but violence such as stone-throwing is not unknown.

Public displays of affection are frowned on by religious Jews and Muslims alike, and people who drive through ultra-orthodox areas on **Shabbat** may find their car being stoned by residents. During religious fasts such as **Ramadan** and **Yom Kippur**, people will also object to you eating or smoking in public, and you may feel it would be inconsiderate anyway; in any case, you should always be able to find a part of town where people are not fasting.

Photography can be contentious. Always ask before you start snapping away at people (especially *Haredi* Jews, who object to taking photographs on the basis that it constitutes "making a graven image"), or inside synagogues, churches or mosques. It is likewise best to avoid taking photographs in places that could be regarded as security installations (airports or checkpoints for example); at the very least, ask permission first. Also be wary of photographing outbreaks of trouble: it is not unknown for Israeli soldiers to break or confiscate cameras.

Gay and lesbian travellers

Israel is the most gay-friendly country in the Middle East. Palestine, on the other hand, is extremely hostile to gay people, some hundreds of whom, from the West Bank and Gaza, live illegally in hiding in Israel as a result. Israel's gay scene however centres on Tel Aviv; in Jerusalem it is extremely low-key.

Israel legalized sex between men in 1988 (thanks to the Mandate-era British law on the subject, it was never illegal between women – the preferred wisdom being that lesbianism didn't exist). In 1992, Israel banned discrimination on grounds of sexuality. Lesbian couples can adopt children born to one of them by artificial insemination, and though gay marriage isn't possible in Israel (where only religious weddings are allowed), single-sex marriages from abroad are recognized, which gives them the same status as inter-denominational heterosexual marriages.

In **PA-controlled areas**, by contrast, sodomy remains a crime, attracting a six- to ten-year sentence, and the law is enforced by police entrapment squads, with beatings meted out to those arrested for it. Persecution of gay men and lesbians by family and neighbours is no less severe.

Despite Israel's laudably tolerant official attitude, Jerusalem's gay life has lately been in retreat. The city used to host an annual Gay Pride Parade, but opposition from the religious right forced it in 2008 to relocate to Tel Aviv. On top of this, Jerusalem's only **gay bar**, *Shushan*, closed in 2007, leaving its unusually assorted clientele of *Haredi*, Palestinan and secular Jewish gays without a hangout. The bohemian café *Tmol Shilshom* (see p.164) is gay-friendly, but mostly heterosexual. For gay men, the traditional cruising ground is **Independence Park** (see p.136), as it is in Tel Aviv, and the two synonymous parks gave their name to Amir Sumaka'i Fink and Jacob Press's book, *Independence Park: The Lives of Gay Men in Israel* (Stanford University Press, 1999), a collection of twelve first-hand accounts of gay life for Israeli men.

Contacts

Jerusalem Open House ☎02/625 0502, ✆www .worldpride.net. Jerusalem's main gay organization runs a community centre on the first floor at 2 Hasoreg, Sundays through Thursdays 10am–5pm, and has a group specially for English speakers (Ⓔenglish.joh@gmail.com).

Pride Tours ☎04/810 0999, ✆www.pridetours .co.il. Gay-friendly Haifa-based Israeli tour company specializing in tailor-made tours for individuals, couples or small groups.

Travelling with children

Jerusalem is not an especially difficult place to visit with children, and aside from the security situation (see p.29), presents no special problems.

Essential **supplies**, such as disposable nappies (diapers) and baby food, are easily available in supermarkets, including Supersol (see p.222), and larger pharmacies, such as Superpharm (see p.39). Shilav, in the Jerusalem Mall (*kanyon*) at Malha (see p.222), is the local branch of Israel's main children's clothing and equipment chain (🌐 www.shilav .co.il), which should be able to sort you out if you've forgotten anything.

Breastfeeding in public is fine in downtown West Jerusalem, so long as you are a little bit discreet about it. In Mea Shearim, however, it is a definite no-no, and in East Jerusalem it should be very discreet.

Children (especially young ones) are more susceptible than adults to **heatstroke** and **dehydration**, and should always wear a sunhat, and have high-factor sunscreen applied to exposed skin if spending time in the sun. The other thing that children are very susceptible to is an upset tummy. Note that most antidiarrhoeal drugs are not suitable for young children; always read the dosage instructions or consult a doctor for guidance. Israeli and Palestinian **food** is not especially spicy, and should not be a particular challenge, but branches of American fast food chains exist in downtown West Jerusalem should you need them (see p.177).

There are plenty of **things for kids to do** in Jerusalem. The most obvious attractions are the Biblical Zoo (p.156) and the Train Puppet Theater (p.203). The Bloomfield Science Museum (p.148) should also appeal to most young people, and the Mifletzet (see p.155) certainly will, though it's quite a way from the centre just for a slide. The youth wing in the Israel Museum (p.146) – when it reopens – may be of interest to older children, who may also enjoy the Time Elevator (p.125) and Hezekiah's Tunnel (p.114).

What younger children may not like, especially if you are visiting West Bank towns such as Bethlehem (p.231), let alone Hebron (p.241) – where you should definitely not be taking children – are the **checkpoints** and their undercurrent of tension, though it should not be too different from passing through an airport, and foreigners, especially with children, will in any case be fast-tracked.

Mark Podwal's book, *Jerusalem Sky: Stars, Crosses and Crescents* (reviewed on p.289), introduces children to Jerusalem as a city holy to three faiths, while avoiding its troubles and controversies.

Travellers with disabilities

Israel has advanced in leaps and bounds in increasing accessibility, but it is not yet up to Western standards. Modern public buildings are usually accessible, so you should have no trouble getting around places such as museums, shopping malls or cinemas if they are not too old. Large, expensive hotels are also likely to be fully accessible, especially if new; little Old City private hostels on the other hand are not, but modern official youth hostels are.

Modern museums, such as the Israel Museum (see p.144), Bible Lands Museum (see p.147), Bloomfield Science Museum (see p.148) and Ticho House (see p.128), are all wheelchair-accessible, as is Yad VaShem (see p.151), and some of these also have aids for people with impaired vision or hearing. The Wailing Wall is accessible (with even a disabled toilet on site), and the Holy Sepulchre is partly accessible (there are a few small steps at ground level, and Calvary is up a steep staircase), but Temple Mount is not accessible unless you can arrange to enter via Bab al-Asbat, in the northeastern corner, off the Via Dolorosa, which is normally open only to Muslims. The Jerusalem Centre for the Performing Arts (see p.202) and Teddy Stadium (see p.205) are also wheelchair-accessible.

Getting around the Old City in a wheelchair is difficult but not impossible. It would certainly help to have an assistant, as there are a lot of steep slopes and single steps. The Via Dolorosa is like a staircase in some parts, but the section from the Lions' Gate to Al-Wad road is negotiable (though you'd need to get up to Lions' Gate), as is Al-Wad from there to the Wailing Wall. In West Jerusalem, things are easier, but even there, don't expect kerb ramps at road junctions for example.

The best source of **information** for visitors with disabilities is the excellent *Access in Israel* by Gordon Couch. Published in 2000, it's a little bit dated now, but it has a wealth of information on accessible accommodation, and a wonderful step-free map of the Old City for wheelchair users, which unfortunately is not available in the online version of the book at ⓦ www.accessinisrael.org.

Hostels and **hotels** which have rooms adapted for wheelchair users include: *Agron Youth Hostel* (see p.167), *Yitzhak Rabin Youth Hostel* (p.173), *Christ Church Guest House* (see p.168), *Eldan* (p.171), *Inbal* (p.175), *King David* (p.175), *King Solomon* (p.175), *Prima Kings* (p.175), *Mount Zion* (see p.175), *Sheraton* (p.175) and *Ramat Rahel Kibbutz* (p.176), but some of these have only one adapted room, and it's a good idea to book as far in advance as possible, and always check of course that they can meet your specific needs.

Hotels which claim to be wheelchair-accessible but do not have specially adapted rooms include *Beit Shmuel Hostel* (p.171) and the *Ambassador Hotel* (p.169). The *Gloria* (p.168) can accommodate wheelchairs up to 70cm wide only.

Contacts for people with disabilities

Access 4 You ☎ 03/967 7796, ⓦ www.access4you
.co.il. Firm renting electric scooters for people with limited mobility. You have the scooter delivered to your hotel, and picked up there when you leave.

Access Israel ☎ 057/723 9239, ⓦ www.aisrael
.org. Israeli organization promoting accessibility. Their website is full of information on accessibility issues, but a lot of the links are out of date.

Yad Sarah ⓦ www.yadsarah.org. Can arrange airport pick-ups for foreign visitors arriving in wheelchairs (☎ 700/501 800, ⓔ transportation @yadsarah.org.il), and also lends out (free of charge but for a deposit) some 300 sorts of equipment including sixteen different types of wheelchair (☎ 02/644 4444, ⓔ equipment@yadsarah.org.il).

The media

The media in Hebrew is extremely diverse, but that in Arabic is much more limited. English-language publications are even thinner on the ground, with only one daily newspaper in English, though there are a few magazines. On television, however, many programmes are in English with Hebrew and/or Arabic subtitles.

English language press

The main English-language **newspaper** is the conservative Israeli daily (except Sat) *Jerusalem Post* (ⓦwww.jpost.com). Most of its news is Israeli but it does have some international coverage, plus a rundown of TV and radio programmes, cinema listings, night pharmacies, exchange rates, weather and handy phone numbers. The Friday edition is particularly helpful, with a supplement giving more detailed "what's on" information.

The other Israeli newspaper available in English is the liberal daily *Haaretz* (ⓦwww.haaretz.com), which is somewhat more heavyweight than the *Jerusalem Post*, and gives a rather more considered Israeli view of the news. The English edition is not sold separately but comes as a supplement with the *International Herald Tribune*. Like the *Jerusalem Post*, it has a weekend section on Friday with entertainment listings.

Other English-language publications covering news and politics include: the *Jerusalem Report*, a glossy news magazine similar in style to *Time* or *Newsweek*.

There are no longer any Palestinian newspapers or magazines in English, so if you want a Palestinian angle on the news, you will have to look **online**. Websites worth checking include the Jerusalem Media and Communication Centre (ⓦwww.jmcc.org), the Alternative Information Centre (ⓦwww.alternativenews.org) and the Palestine News Network (ⓦenglish.pnn.ps).

The World News Network's Jerusalem page at ⓦwww.wn.com/jerusalem is a good source of local news from an organization with no Israeli or Palestinian axe to grind; its stories come from a variety of international sources.

TV

Israel has two terrestrial **television channels**, but a large number of stations on digital, cable or satellite, of which pretty much all hotels and local households have one or the other. More time is devoted to politics in comparison to British or American TV, with lots of political discussion shows, but there's also the usual diet of quiz shows, dramas, soaps and sitcoms, plus English-language films and programmes from the UK and US, subtitled in Hebrew and sometimes Arabic, or even Russian. Channel 1 is financed by TV licence fees and carries no advertising (though it has programme sponsorship), Channel 2 is financed by commercials and caters more to popular taste. Channel 10 is very similar. Middle East TV, a Christian-run station that broadcast from South Lebanon under Israeli occupation, now broadcasts from Cyprus and is available on most Israeli sets. A number of channels are also provided by satellite broadcaster Yes and by cable provider HOT.

Radio

Israeli **radio stations** include Radio 1 (Reshet Aleph, mostly talk shows in Hebrew) on 531 and 1458 MW and 98.4 FM, HaDerekh (music and traffic news for motorists; 88 FM), and the Voice of Music (Kol HaMusiqa; 91.3 FM) playing classical music. Radio 3 (Reshet Gimel; 97.8 FM) plays commercial (and usually old) pop music. The Voice of Israel (101.3 FM) broadcasts news in English at 6.30am, 12.30pm and 8.30pm. The Israeli Broadcasting Authority maintains a full list of frequencies online at ⓦwww.iba.org.il /reception. The independent Palestinian station, Radio Bethlehem 2000 (ⓦradio bethlehem2000.net), broadcasts mainly Arabic talk shows but also some music on

89.6 and 106.4 FM. Radio Ajyal (www.radio ajyal.com; 103.4 FM) has a similar mix but with more music on.

The BBC World Service (www.bbc .co.uk/worldservice) can be picked up on 1323 MW. The Voice of America (www .voa.gov) can be received at certain times on 1593 MW, and on 9480, 9685, 11,765 and 15,205 SW.

Travel essentials

Costs

Jerusalem, especially West Jerusalem, can be expensive, but it is possible to live cheaply if you are careful. Your biggest single cost will probably be **accommodation**, with the cheaper hostels charging 30–50NIS (£5–8.50/US$7.50–13.25/€5.60–9.35) a night for a dorm, 120–200NIS for a double room (£20–35/US$32–55/€22.50–37.50). In a mid-range hotel, you can expect to be paying US$120–180 (£78–120/€95–145) a night, and for a four-star place upwards of US$200 (£130/€160). A single room may cost you the same as a double, though you would usually expect to pay a quarter to a third less.

Eating out can also hit your wallet, but the quality of food matches the price. You can fill up at a hummus joint for as little as 15NIS (£2.50/US$4/€2.80). A typical meal will cost you 50–80NIS (£8.50–13.50/US$13–21 /€9.50–15) at a cheap place including a drink, 100–150NIS (£17–26/US$26–40 /€18–28) in a mid-range restaurant, and 200–250NIS (£35–45/US$50–65/€35–50) in a relatively pricey establishment. Service is not generally included in bills, and you are generally expected to leave a **tip** of around 12 to 15 percent (in fact many waiting staff get no pay other than tips).

That being the case, you can survive in Jerusalem on a **daily budget** of £40/US$65/€50 if you stay in a hostel dorm, eat simply, don't go out drinking, and don't buy too many souvenirs. Staying in mid range hotel and eating in moderately priced restaurants, with the odd splurge, you can expect to spend around £140/US$200/€160 a day. On the other hand, if you stay in a five-star hotel, eat in the best restaurants and take taxis everywhere, you'll easily be getting through some £350/US$500/€400 a day.

VAT (sales tax)

Value Added Tax (17 percent) for items (other than tobacco and electrical or photographic goods) bought at stores recommended by the Tourism Ministry is refundable at the airport when you leave Israel (or when leaving the West Bank at Allenby), provided the goods are in a sealed transparent bag, and that you have an invoice stating the amount of VAT paid. You are also exempt from VAT on hotel bills, car rental or air tickets, so long as you pay in local currency.

Student discounts

If you are a full-time student, it's worth getting an **International Student ID Card** (ISIC, www.isiccard.com), especially if you plan to do a lot of sightseeing, as it can usually save you a few bucks – generally in the order of around 25 percent – on entry charges at museums and archeological sites.

Electricity

The electricity supply is 220v 50Hz. Israel has its own three-pin plugs and sockets, but they will take two-pin European plugs. British, Irish, North American and Australasian plugs will need an adapter (which you should bring from home), and double-round-pin electric shavers, if they have fatter pins than

European plugs, will probably also need one (easily available locally). American and Canadian appliances will need a transformer, too, unless multi-voltage.

Entry requirements

Citizens of the US, Canada, the UK, Ireland, Australia, New Zealand, South Africa and most EU countries, do not need a **visa** to travel to Israel for up to three months (though you may only be given one month if arriving by land), but foreign passports must be **valid for at least six months** beyond your date of entry. Anyone with Israeli dual nationality is required to use their Israeli passport; the same applies for anyone with Palestinian dual nationality – Palestinian passport holders also require proof of Jerusalem residence or a permit to enter Israel or Jerusalem (but not to enter the West Bank via Allenby Bridge).

You may be **screened on entry** into Israel. This involves a series of questions about who you are, where you are going, and the purpose of your visit. If you have a Muslim-sounding name, or have visited Arab countries, you may get extra attention from the security services. If you are Jewish, and particularly if you have family in Israel, you are unlikely to be submitted to much questioning. Note also that Israeli stamps in your passport can cause problems when travelling on to Arab countries (see p.21).

Visa extensions and work permits

Visa extensions can be obtained by appointment only from the Ministry of Interior Office at 1 Shlomzion HaMalka, by the junction of Koresh (to make an appointment call ☏02/629 0239 – they say to call Sun–Thurs 10am–2pm, but in practice it is extremely difficult to get through, and best to start calling around 8am). When you do get an appointment you will need to show proof of your ability to support yourself. The fee is 145NIS, and you'll need a passport photo. It always helps to dress well and give an air of affluence and respectability. The usual extension is three months, but they may only give you a month. You are unlikely to get a **work permit** without a contract from an employer, and a reason why they need to employ a foreigner (one law firm gives details

of the process at ⊛www.ktalegal.com – click on "work visas" under "relocation to Israel"), but visas for study or for kibbutz volunteer work should be no problem.

Duty free

Duty-free allowances include a litre of spirits, plus two litres of wine, plus 200 cigarettes or 250g of tobacco, and jewellery or electronic goods for your personal use.

Israeli embassies and consulates abroad

A comprehensive, up-to-date list of Israeli diplomatic missions abroad can be found at ⊛www.mfa.gov.il/mfa/sherut/israeliabroad /continents.

Australia 6 Turrana St, Yarralumla, Canberra, ACT 2600 ☏02/6215 4500, ⊛canberra.mfa.gov.il.
Canada 50 O'Connor St, Suite 1005, Ottawa, ON K1P 6L2 ☏613/567-6450, ⊛ottawa.mfa.gov.il; 180 Bloor St West, Suite 700, Toronto, ON M5S 2V6 ☏416/640-8500, ⊛toronto.mfa.gov.il; 1155 Rene Levesque W, Suite 2620, Montreal, PQ H3B 4S5 ☏514/940-8500, ⊛montreal.mfa.gov.il.
Cyprus 4 Ioanni Gripari St, PO Box 25159, Nicosia ☏022/369 500, ⊛nicosia.mfa.gov.il.
Egypt 6 Sharia Ibn al-Malek, Cairo ☏02/3332 1500, ⊜info@cairo.mfa.gov.il; 15 Sharia Mina, Kafar-Abdou, Roushdy, Alexandria ☏03/544 9501, ⊜info@alexandria.mfa.gov.il.
Ireland 122 Pembroke Rd, Dublin 4 ☏01/230 9400, ⊛dublin.mfa.gov.il.
Jordan 47 Maysaloun St, Rabiya, PO Box 950866, Amman 11195 ☏06/550 3500, ⊜info@amman .mfa.gov.il.
New Zealand is covered by the Israeli embassy in Australia.
South Africa 428 Kings Highway, Lynnwood, Pretoria ☏012/470 3500, ⊛pretoria.mfa.gov.il.
UK 2 Palace Green, London W8 4QB ☏020/7957 9500, ⊛london.mfa.gov.il.
US 3514 International Drive, NW, Washington, DC 20008 ☏202/364-5500, ⊛www.israelemb.org; 1100 Spring St, Suite 440, Atlanta, GA 30309-2823 ☏404/487-6500, ⊛atlanta.mfa.gov.il; 20 Park Plaza, Suite 1020, Boston, MA 02116 ☏617/535-0200, ⊛boston.mfa.gov.il; 111 E Wacker Drive, Suite 1308, Chicago, IL 60601 ☏312/297-4800, ⊛chicago.mfa.gov.il; 24 Greenway Plaza, Suite 1500, Houston, TX 77046 ☏713/627-3780, ⊛houston.mfa.gov.il; 6380 Wilshire Blvd, Suite 1700, Los Angeles, CA 90048 ☏323/852-5500, ⊛www.israeliconsulatela.org; 100 N Biscayne Blvd, Suite 1800, Miami, FL 33132 ☏305/925-9400,

ⓦmiami.mfa.gov.il; 800 2nd Ave, New York, NY 10017 ☎212/499-5400, ⓦwww.israelfm.org; 1880 John F. Kennedy Blvd, Suite 1818, Philadelphia, PA 19103 ☎215/546-5556, ⓦphiladelphia.mfa.gov.il; 456 Montgomery St, Suite 2100, San Francisco, CA 94104 ☎415/844-7500, ⓦwww.israelemb .org/sanfran.

Foreign embassies and consulates

Although West Jerusalem is the seat of Israel's government, most foreign countries do not recognize it as the country's capital, and have their embassies in Tel Aviv. However, many have **consulates** in East Jerusalem to cover the West Bank, and some have them in West Jerusalem too. The Israeli Foreign Affairs Ministry maintains a full list of embassies (but not consulates) online at ⓦwww.mfa.gov.il /mfa/sherut/foreigninisrael/continents.

Embassies in Tel Aviv

Australia Level 28, Discount Bank Tower, 23 Rehov Yehuda Halevi (corner of Herzl) ☎03/693 5000, ⓦwww.australianembassy.org.il
Canada 3/5 Rehov Nirim ☎03/636 3300
Ireland 17th Floor, The Tower, 3 Rehov Daniel Frisch ☎03/696 4166
South Africa Top Tower, 50 Rehov Dizengoff ☎03/525 2566, ⓦwww.safis.co.il
UK 1 Rehov Ben Yehuda ☎03/510 0166, ⓦukinisrael.fco.gov.uk/en
US 71 Rehov Hayarkon ☎03/519 7575, ⓦusembassy-israel.org.il

Jerusalem consulates

UK 19 Nashashibi, Sheikh Jarrah ☎02/541 4100, ⓦukinjerusalem.fco.gov.uk.
US 18 Agron, West Jerusalem ☎02/622 6909; 27 Nablus Rd, East Jerusalem ☎02/622 7230, ⓦjerusalem.usconsulate.gov.

Health

Health care in Israel is excellent, with **hospitals** well above the standards of many Western countries. In fact, some travellers, particularly from the US, are visiting Israel specifically to have medical work carried out given its comparative cost at home. Israelis join a compulsory health insurance scheme but foreigners require their own health or travel insurance.

No **vaccinations** are required, but it's always worth being up to date with your

> If you are taken seriously ill or involved in an accident, dial ☎101 for an **ambulance**

vaccinations before travelling. **Mosquitoes** can be a problem during the summer but they do not carry malaria.

Stomach upsets

The only illness you're especially likely to encounter is an attack of **diarrhoea** (shilshul in Hebrew, is-haal in Arabic). This may simply be due to a change in diet, but could also be caused by eating street food that's been left out uncovered for too long. Be choosy and wash all fruit and vegetables and you should avoid an outbreak. If symptoms persist, and especially in the case of children, ensure that fluid levels are kept up: dissolving rehydration salts (available at any pharmacy) in water helps your body absorb it. Failing that, half a teaspoon of table salt with four of sugar in a litre of water a day should see you all right. For the duration of the bout avoid greasy or spicy food, caffeine and most fruit and dairy products. Drugs such as Lomotil or Immodium are only really only advisable as a stopgap if you need to travel.

Jerusalem **tap water** is fine to drink, and bottled water is widely available anyway.

Heat and dehydration

Never underestimate the heat: it's surprisingly easy to get **sunstroke** while sightseeing during the summer months. A hat is an essential precaution – the classic kibbutznik hat is ideal, and can be soaked in water for an extra cooling effect. Even a hazy Middle Eastern sun can burn fiercely so a high-factor sunscreen (available in Israel, but much more expensive than at home), is another essential item. Remember also to drink plenty of fluids to avoid **dehydration**. A potentially fatal hazard to be aware of is **heatstroke**. Signs are a very high body temperature without a feeling of fever, accompanied by headaches and disorientation/irrational behaviour. Lowering body temperature, with a tepid shower or bath for example, is the first step in treatment, but you should always seek further medical advice.

Watch your step!

One thing to be aware of is that the **stone streets** of the Old City have in many places been worn smooth. They can be treacherously slippery when wet, and very hard when fallen on.

Pharmacies and dentists

Minor complaints can be dealt with at a **pharmacy** (*mirkahat* in Hebrew, *saydalia* in Arabic). Pharmacists are well trained and usually helpful, and you will almost certainly find someone who speaks English. For more serious complaints, go to a **doctor** (*rofei* in Hebrew, *tabeeb* or *doktur* in Arabic); they almost all speak English. For emergency **dental treatment** call ℡02/563 2303 8am–8pm (29a Keren HaYesod, but call first), with a doctor on call after hours. English-speaking dentists include Dr Samuel Abramson (12 Keren HaYesod ℡02/623 4679) and Dr Elisha Reichenberg (2 Hillel ℡02/645 2033). **Opticians** in the city centre include Optica Halperin (49 Jaffa Rd ℡02/622 2228).

There is always a duty **pharmacy** open at night and over Shabbat; a list is posted in all West Jerusalem pharmacy windows, but only in Hebrew; the *Jerusalem Post* prints a list in English. Centrally located pharmacies include:
Alba 42 Jaffa Rd, on the corner of HaHavatzelet, West Jerusalem (see map, p.127). Sun–Thurs 7am–7pm, Fri 7am–2pm.
Dr Bella 6 King David St, West Jerusalem (see map, p.127). Sun, Mon, Wed & Thurs 7.30am–7pm, Tues 7.30am–3pm, Fri 7.30am–2.30pm.
Habash Pharmacy 104 Al-Wad Rd, Old City (see map, p.73). Daily 8am–7pm.
Superpharm 5 HaHistadrut, West Jerusalem (see map, p.127). Sun–Thurs 8am–midnight, Fri 8am–3pm, Sat 7pm–midnight.

Hospitals

Augusta Victoria ℡02/627 9911, ⊛www.avh .org/english.html. East Jerusalem's largest hospital, founded in 1910 for Palestine's German community.
Bikur Holim ℡02/646 4111, ⊛www.bikurholim .org.il. Centrally located at the junction of Strauss and Haneviim in downtown West Jerusalem, with an emergency department.

Hadassah University Hospital ℡02/677 8555, ⊛www.hadassah.org.il/English. The Hadassah organization's hospitals at Ein Kerem and Mount Scopus have such a reputation that rich foreigners even come here from abroad for their private operations. The hospitals also pride themselves on serving all local residents, regardless of race, religion or ethnic origin.
Herzog Hospital ℡02/531 6875, ⊛www .herzoghospital.org. Located in Givat Shaul, specializes in geriatric, pediatric and psychiatric health care.
Shaare Zedek Medical Center ℡02/666-6666, ⊛www.szmc.org.il/eng. Located at 12 Bayit near Mount Herzl, with a well-equipped emergency department.

Insurance

As anywhere else, **travel insurance** is vital in case of accident or serious illness in Jerusalem, and handy in case of theft or loss of belongings. The only exception is if you are covered by a private health insurance scheme from home, but always check before travelling.

Also bear in mind that you will not usually be covered if you go to places your government advises against visiting; this may include much of the West Bank – notably Hebron – and depending on the political situation, it may apply to Bethlehem and Jericho, and even to East Jerusalem and parts of Israel itself. Always therefore take a look at your government's travel advisory information (see p.30) before travelling, and if in doubt, check with your insurance company.

Internet

It's easy to access the internet in Jerusalem. On top of the numerous **internet cafés** (see the list on p.40 for the most convenient ones), where you'll typically pay 6–15NIS per hour, there are lots of **wi-fi hotspots** where you can get online for free if you have an internet-enabled laptop, though of course your connection will not be secure (so don't type in credit card numbers, for example). Wi-fi hotspots include the Ben Yehuda Street *midrahov* (pedestrianized area) in downtown West Jerusalem, as well as Safra Square by City Hall, and the whole of the German Colony, plus a hundred or so more in malls, museums and university campus sites. In addition, a fair few bars and cafés provide free wi-fi for their customers.

Internet cafés

Ali Baba 6 Via Dolorosa (between the Sixth and Seventh Stations of the Cross), Muslim Quarter, Old City. Daily 10am–10pm. 6NIS per hr.
Café internet 31 Jaffa Rd, West Jerusalem. Sun–Thurs 9am–11pm, Fri 9am–2pm. 12NIS per hr.
Cafe Net In the Egged Central Bus Station, West Jerusalem. Sun–Thurs 5.30am–midnight, Fri 5.30am–Shabbat, Sat Shabbat–midnight. 12NIS per hr.
Freeline 51 Aqabat al-Khanqah, Christian Quarter, Old City, opposite the Eighth Station of the Cross. Daily 10am–midnight. 8NIS per hr.
Mike's Centre on the stairs leading to the Ninth Station of the Cross, by 172 Souq Khan al-Zeit, Old City. Daily 9am–11pm. 10NIS per hr.
Pelephone 2 Lunz, West Jerusalem (in the Ben Yehuda Street *midrahov*). Sun–Thurs 10am–10pm, Fri 10am–2pm. 10NIS per hr.

Laundry

Laundry Place at 12 Shamai in downtown West Jerusalem is the cheapest (Sun–Thurs 8.30am–8pm, Fri 8.30am–3pm; around 30NIS a load), though many hotels and hostels have an in-house laundry service, either officially, or run by members of staff. In the Old City, Mike's Centre (see "Internet cafés" above) also offers a laundry service.

Libraries and cultural centres

American Center 19 Keren HaYesod, West Jerusalem ℡02/625 5755, ᐃusembassy-israel .org.il/ac. Has a library (Sun–Thurs 10am–4pm, Fri 9am–noon), but mostly for the benefit of Israelis and Palestinians seeking information about the US.
British Council 31 Nablus Rd, East Jerusalem ℡02/626 7111, ᐃwww.britishcouncil.org/ps (Mon–Thurs 7.30am–3.30pm, Fri 7.30am–1.30pm, closing an hour earlier during Ramadan). The West Jerusalem branch was closed at the time of writing pending a change of location – for the latest information, see ᐃwww.britishcouncil.org/israel.
Central Municipal Library Bet Ha'Am Central Municipal Library, 11 Betzalel, West Jerusalem ℡02/623 4168 (Sun–Thurs 10am–6.45pm). For more casual reading; holds mainly Hebrew books, but has some English titles..
National Library of Israel Edmond Safra Campus, Givat Ram, West Jerusalem ℡02/658 5027, ᐃjnul .huji.ac.il/eng (Sun, Tues & Thurs 9am–7pm, Mon & Wed 9am–9pm, Fri 9am–1pm). Both Israel's National Library, and also the Hebrew Univerity's main library,

mainly used for academic research, with a catalogue that can be accessed via the website.

Mail

The main **post office** is on Jaffa Road in West Jerusalem (Sun–Thurs 7am–7pm, Fri and eve of Jewish festivals 7am–noon) with poste restante and exchange facilities plus a Western Union counter for money transfers. East Jerusalem's main office is at the corner of Salah al-Din and Sultan Suleiman (Sun–Thurs 8am–6pm, Fri 8am–noon). Branch offices include one inside the Jaffa Gate opposite the Citadel entrance (Sun–Thurs 8am–6pm, Fri 8am–noon). Stamps can also be bought from stationers, souvenir shops, bookshops and large hotels. Unless otherwise specified, mail addressed to Poste Restante (general delivery) will be delivered to the Jaffa Road post office.

Mail delivery from Jerusalem is pretty reliable, an air mail letter or postcard typically taking five to seven days to reach Britain or Ireland, a week to ten days to North America, Australasia or South Africa. Note, however, that Bethlehem, Jericho, Bethany and Abu Dis are under the control of the **Palestinian Authority**, which has its own post office and issues its own stamps; postal services from PA-controlled areas take a lot longer than those run by the Israeli post office. You cannot use Israeli stamps to send mail from PA-controlled areas, nor vice versa.

Maps

You can get a free, but not very detailed **map** from the tourist office at the Jaffa Gate. The Arab Hotel Association put out a better free map, sometimes available at hotels in East Jerusalem, which also covers Bethlehem. For more detail, *Mapa's* (1:13,500; 37NIS) is the best. Its closest rival is *Carta's* (1:15,000; 37NIS), which is also available as a street atlas in book form. Both can be purchased from bookshops such as Steimatsky (see p.218). There's also a cheaper map put out in several languages by Drive Productions, which covers the city centre on a scale of 1:10,000, and is available from souvenir shops in the Old City (anything from 6NIS to 20NIS); it has a map of the Old City on the back which is cluttered with pictures and not very easy to read. You may still find a rather better Old City map put out by a firm of Jewish Quarter residents called the "Jewish Quarter Tourism Administration Ltd", and based on an aerial photograph, though it shows the Jewish Quarter as extending most of the way up to the Damascus Gate.

Money

The local **currency** is the New Israeli Shekel (NIS), made up of 100 agorot. Banknotes come in denominations of 200NIS, 100NIS, 50NIS and 20NIS, with coins of 10NIS, 5NIS, 2NIS, 1NIS, 50 agorot and 10 agorot. At time of writing, there were approximately 3.50NIS to the US dollar, 6.35NIS to the pound sterling, and 5NIS to the euro.

Visa, Mastercard and American Express are accepted in many shops, restaurants and hotels, but not in the very cheapest places. Occasionally mid-range or upscale restaurants won't take plastic, so it's always worth asking before sitting down to a meal.

Banks and ATMs

Banks are ubiquitous in West Jerusalem, and you should have no trouble finding one. Most have **ATMs** – Zion Square has several. In East Jerusalem and the Old City, banks with ATMs are much thinner on the ground; the only one in the Old City is in the Jewish Quarter on Tiferet Yisra'el, just by Hurva Square, and it frequently doesn't work. In East Jerusalem, there's a Bank Leumi with an ATM on Salah al-Din; the Mercantile Bank on the corner of Salah al-Din and Abu Taleb (by the *Christmas Hotel*) also has an ATM, but it is known for charging very high rates for withdrawals. Some shops and restaurants also have ATMs, but the same story of high withdrawal charges applies. In general, if possible, it is best to go to West Jerusalem and use one of the main banks there such as Bank Leumi. It's also worth checking what your card issuer at home will charge you for making withdrawals abroad – some, such as the UK mutual building society Nationwide, make no charge at all, but the more rapacious banks can charge well over five percent. Israeli ATMs usually allow you to withdraw up to 2500NIS per day.

Currency exchange

If you're changing cash, and especially if it's Jordanian dinars, **moneychangers** are far better than banks and keep longer hours, but its always a good idea to shop around and compare exchange and commission rates before choosing. You'll find money-changers along Ben Yehuda Street in West Jerusalem, especially by Zion Square, and also on Salah al-Din in East Jerusalem, with a couple actually in the Damascus Gate. **Post offices** will also change cash at good rates with no commission charges.

Opening hours and public holidays

Most ordinary **shops** in West Jerusalem open Sunday to Thursday 9am to 7pm, but close around 2 or 3pm on Fridays and the eves of Jewish festivals. Shops selling art, jewellery or judaica (Jewish religious items) may open a little bit later, typically round 10am. In East Jerusalem, shops tend to open Saturday to Thursday 9am to 7pm, and may open Friday mornings; Christian-owned shops, on the other hand, will open Monday to Saturday 9am to 7pm, and close on Sundays.

Banking hours are not completely standard, but typically Sunday to Thursday 8.30am to 2.30pm. Some branches may open Friday mornings (8.30am–noon or so), some may close on Sundays, and some may open in the evening (Bank Leumi at 22 King George St and on Zion Square, for example, open Mondays and Thursdays 4–6.15pm).

Israeli **public holidays** are almost all Jewish religious holidays (the first and last days of Passover, Shavuot, Rosh HaShannah, Yom Kippur, first and last days of Sukkot). The only other Israeli public holiday is Independence Day (Yom Ha'Atzma'ut). All are set according to the Jewish calendar (see pp.212–213). Muslim establishments will close (usually for 2/3 days) for the two Eid festivals, whose dates are set according to the Islamic calendar (see pp.212–213). Christian establishments will close on Christmas Day, Good Friday and Easter Monday, but not all

Christian denominations celebrate these on the same day (see pp.212–213).

Phones

Mobile (cell) phones can be rented at Ben Gurion airport, or through many hotels, but it is cheaper to take your own phone and get an Israeli SIM-card from local providers such as Orange or Simcom. Expect to pay around 100NIS for a pay-as-you-go SIM-card including 40–50NIS of credit, but make sure the card is valid for international calls, as not all of them are. Also make sure that your phone will work in Israel and the Palestinian Territories (British, European, Australasian and South African phones will; North American ones may not). Note that, because of the narrow streets and stone buildings, phone **reception** is very bad at ground level in the Old City.

To **call Jerusalem from abroad**, dial your country's international access code (00 from most countries, 011 from North America, 0011 from Australia), then 972 for Israel and Palestine, 2 for Jerusalem if calling a landline, and the seven-digit subscriber number. To call a mobile, you'll have a two-figure code (such as 52 or 54) instead of the 2 for Jerusalem. To call abroad, from Jerusalem, dial the international access code (00), then your country code (see box below), the area code (omitting the initial zero if there is one; this does not apply to North America) and the subscriber number.

Calling abroad is easy. You can do it from a hotel (pricey), with a mobile (slightly cheaper), with a phonecard from a public call box (cheaper still), or at Mike's Centre (see p.40), which offers very economic rates. If you've got a laptop with access to a **VOIP network** such as Skype, then you get the best rates of all.

Many phone companies issue calling cards that you can use abroad and charge to your home bill, but these will be much more expensive than paying locally. You can also call home collect, using a "home country direct" number, but again this will cost you much more than paying locally.

Time

Jerusalem is on GMT+2, which means that in principle it is two hours ahead of the British Isles, seven hours ahead of the US East Coast (EST), eleven hours ahead of the North American West Coast (PST), six hours behind West Australia, eight hours behind eastern Australia, ten hours behind New Zealand, and one hour ahead of South Africa, but daylight saving time in those places or locally may vary that difference by one or two hours. Israel puts clocks forward for daylight saving in March, and back again before the Jewish New Year (usually in Sept or early Oct).

Tourist information

The **Israeli Government Tourist Office** is on Omar Katab Square, just inside the Jaffa Gate, on the left, (Sun–Thurs 8.30am–5pm, Fri 8am–1.30pm; ☎02/628 0403, ✉orenm @tourism.gov.il). The staff are friendly and informative, offering free leaflets, maps and publications, but they can be less enthusiastic

---

Useful numbers and codes

International dialling codes

	To Israel	From Israel
UK	☎00 972	☎00 44
Ireland	☎00 972	☎00 353
US & Canada	☎011 972	☎001
Australia	☎0011 972	☎00 61
New Zealand	☎00 972	☎00 64
South Africa	☎09 972	☎00 216

Useful numbers

Ambulance ☎911, 101 or 02/652 3133
Fire ☎102
Police ☎100

Directory enquiries ☎144
International operator ☎188

or informed about the Palestinian side of things. For information about East Jerusalem and the rest of the West Bank, therefore, you're often better off going to the **Christian Information Centre**, across Omar Ibn al-Khattab Square (Mon, Wed & Fri 8.30am–5.30pm, Tues & Thurs 8.30am–4pm, Sat 8.30am–12.30pm; ☏02/627 2692, ☻www .cicts.org); the staff are extremely patient and helpful, and have lists of pilgrim accommodation, as well as various maps and other publications, mostly highlighting things of Christian interest. The **Palestinian Authority's tourism ministry** has information offices in Bethlehem (see p.233), Jericho (see p.245) and other West Bank towns, but not in Jerusalem itself, nor abroad. The free pamphlet *This Week in Palestine*, available at East Jerusalem hotels, lists events, accommodation, cultural centres and restaurants in East Jerusalem (and the rest of the West Bank and Gaza), but without much commentary.

Israeli tourist offices abroad

UK 180 Oxford St, London W1D 1NN ☏020/7299 1100, ☻info@igto.co.uk.
US Toll-free ☏1-888/77-ISRAEL; 1349 West Peachtree St, NE, Suite 1799, Atlanta, GA 30309 ☏1-404/541-2770, ☻infoatlanta@imot.org; 205 North Michigan Ave, Suite 2520, Chicago, IL 60601 ☏1-312/803-7080 ☻shirlya@imot.org; 6380 Wilshire Blvd, Suite 1718, Los Angeles, CA 90048 ☏1-323/658-7463, ☻danma@imot.org; 800 2nd Ave, New York, NY 10017 ☏1-212/499-5660, ☻igtonewyork@imot.org.
Canada 180 Bloor Street West, Suite 700, Toronto, ON M5S 2V6 ☏1-888/77-ISRAEL or 1-416/964-3784, ☻info@igto.ca.

Tourist information websites

Christian Information Centre ☻www.cicts.org. Has listings for all kinds of things of Christian interest, including church services in town, but also items of more general interest such as transport.
Go Jerusalem ☻www.gojerusalem.com. Excellent and extensive listings of events, restaurants, cafés, bars, accommodation, and all sorts of other things; not always completely up to date, but near as dammit.
Israeli Tourism Ministry ☻www.goisrael.com. Has a useful section on Jerusalem, including features on 88 different tourist sights.
Jerusalem.com ☻www.jerusalem.com. An excellent site for listings and reviews of hotels,

restaurants, museums and other places of interest, plus latest news of what's on in town.
Jerusalem Municipality Tourist Information ☻www.visit-jerusalem.com. The best feature here by far is Jerusalem *Mosaic*, a monthly online news-sheet for visitors to the city.
Palestinian Tourism Ministry ☻www .visit-palestine.com. Limited information, but does maintain listings of accommodation and tour operators in Jerusalem and Bethlehem.
Virtual Jerusalem Tour ☻www.md.huji.ac.il/vjt. A photo-led virtual tour of the city, maintained by the Hebrew University's medical faculty.

General websites

B'tselem ☻www.btselem.org/english/jerusalem. Israel's main human rights organization maintain a section on their website covering the situation in Jerusalem, particularly East Jerusalem.
Israeli Foreign Affairs Ministry ☻www.mfa .gov.il. Click on "Jerusalem" in the bar on the left for the official Israeli view on Jerusalem's status and the city's latest news.
Jewish Virtual Library ☻www.jewishvirtuallibrary .org/jsource/Peace/jerutoc.html. A strongly Zionist take on Jerusalem from the American-Israeli Cooperative Enterprise.

Work or study in Jerusalem

Jerusalem is not the best place to find work: less is available and wages are lower than in Tel Aviv or Eilat. Hostels often need casual staff who'll work for board and lodging. Remember, however, that it is illegal to work on a tourist visa; you will certainly be deported if caught, and you could face a fine or even prison. For more on work permits, see p.37.

Staying on as a **student** is a more viable option. The Hebrew University's Rothberg International School (see list on p.44) for example, offers summer courses in Hebrew, Arabic or a number of academic disciplines, typically costing around US$1300 plus US$600 for accommodation. There are Hebrew language courses (*ulpanim*) available all over town, offering Hebrew tuition at all levels, but usually geared to Jewish immigrants rather than tourists. Practising Jews, and sometimes others with a special interest, can alternatively opt for a theology course at a *yeshiva* (seminary), but note that some *yeshivas* may not accept you if you are not ethnically Jewish through your maternal line. Many *yeshivas* also offer Hebrew language courses(*ulpan*) .

Study contacts

Al-Quds University ☏02/628 7517, ⊛www.jerusalem-studies.alquds.edu. Jerusalem's main Palestinian University offers Arabic language courses at Khan Tankaz, in the heart of the Old City, or a degree course in Jerusalem Studies.

Bet Ha'Am 11 Betzalel ☏02/625 4156. In the same building as the Gereard Behar Center and city library, offering morning *ulpan* classes to all comers.

Hebrew Union College ☏02/620 3333, ⊛www.huc.edu. Hebrew language *ulpan* run by the Reform Judaism movement's main academic institute (see p.136), with courses for all levels including beginners.

Jerusalem University College (American Institute of Holy Land Studies) ☏02/671 8628, US ☏1-800/891-9408. Christian university specializing in biblical history and geography, Middle Eastern studies, and biblical languages, with long-term and short-term courses available.

Rothberg International School (Hebrew Univeristy) ☏02/588 2600, ⊛overseas.huji.ac.il. Year-long or single-semester courses in a variety of disciplines, taught in English. Courses on offer include Hebrew and Arabic language.

Yeshivas

Conservative Yeshiva 10a Agron ☏02/622 3116, ⊛www.conservativeyeshiva.org. Despite its name, one of the more liberal *yeshivas*, also offering a summer *ulpan* (Hebrew language course).

Darche Noam ☏02/651 1178, US ☏1-888/233-6678, Canada ☏1-416/638-2419, UK ☏020/8203 7658; ⊛www.darchenoam.org. A variety of Jewish studies programmes for men, women and (married) couples.

Ohr Somayach ☏02/581 0315, ⊛ohr.edu. Non-Hasidic *yeshiva* catering for Jewish people with scant religious background who wish to return to orthodoxy. Offers three-week, six-week and semester-long courses.

Pardes Institute ☏02/673 5210, US ☏1-212/447-4333; ⊛www.pardes.org.il. College for Jewish studies in Talpiot with a variety of courses in religion or Hebrew language.

Yeshivat Dvar Yerusahalayim (Jerusalem Academy of Jewish Studies) ☏02/652 2817, ⊛www.dvar.org.il. *Yeshiva* in Har Nof offering Jewish studies courses to absolute beginners; its main aim is to bring non-practising Jews back into the orthodox fold.

The City

The City

1. The Jaffa Gate and the Armenian Quarter......................47

2. The Via Dolorsa and the Christian Quarter......................55

3. The Muslim Quarter...72

4. The Jewish Quarter...84

5. The Temple Mount..99

6. East Jerusalem..108

7. West Jerusalem..124

8. Outlying areas..144

The Jaffa Gate and the Armenian Quarter

With seven entrance gates and four distinct quarters, deciding where to begin a tour of the Old City can be tricky. The **Jaffa Gate** is as good a starting point as any. This is the main western entrance to the Old City and the most convenient starting point for the **Ramparts Walk**, a stroll around Jerusalem's sixteenth-century walls, the very best way to make your first acquaintance with the Old City.

The Jaffa Gate opens up into the busy **Omar Ibn al-Khattab Square** full of cafés and souvenir sellers. Running east from here, David Street splits the **Armenian Quarter** to the south from the Christian Quarter to the north. Smaller and quieter than the Old City's other three quarters, the Armenian Quarter is a city in miniature, home to a dwindling two-thousand-member community which maintains a separate language, alphabet and culture. Its **attractions** include the imposing **Citadel** (also known as the Tower of David), one of the city's most interesting sights – a historical and strategic stronghold where you can explore archeological remains dating back through the ages, and then come back in the evening to enjoy a state-of-the-art sound and light show. The heart of the quarter is **St James's Cathedral**, one of Jerusalem's loveliest churches, whose services follow the beautiful Armenian liturgy. Also here is the world's very **first Christian church**, St Mark's in the Syrian Convent, where mass is still celebrated in the ancient Syriac tongue. At the quarter's southern end, the **Zion Gate**, pockmarked with bullet holes from the fighting in 1948, provides access to neighbouring Mount Zion (see p.141).

The Jaffa Gate

The turreted **Jaffa Gate** (Sha'ar Yafo in Hebrew, Bab al-Khalil in Arabic) is one of the most imposing in Jerusalem and dates from the early sixteenth century. As with so many places in the city, the gate's names reflect the differing viewpoints of its varied population: the English and Hebrew names both refer to the ancient port of Jaffa on the Mediterranean coast, embarkation point for immigrants, pilgrims and early tourists, while the Arabic comes from the holy town of Hebron (Al-Khalil; see p.241). Cars can enter the Old City here, thanks

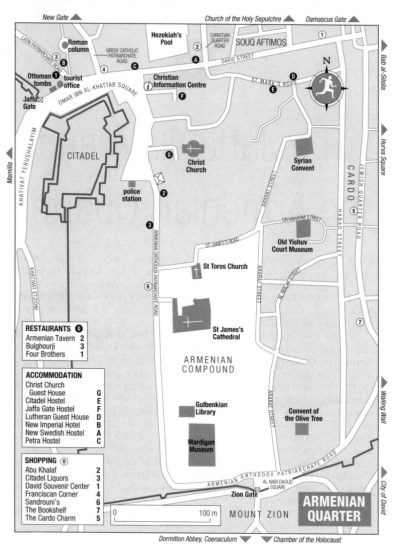

New Gate ▲   Church of the Holy Sepulchre ▲   Damascus Gate ▲

Bab al-Silsila ▶

Hurva Square ▶

Waling Wall ▶

City of David ▶

Mamilla ◀

RESTAURANTS ⓞ
Armenian Tavern	2
Bulghourji	3
Four Brothers	1

ACCOMMODATION
Christ Church Guest House	G
Citadel Hostel	E
Jaffa Gate Hostel	F
Lutheran Guest House	D
New Imperial Hotel	B
New Swedish Hostel	A
Petra Hostel	C

SHOPPING ⓞ
Abu Khalaf	2
Citadel Liquors	3
David Souvenir Center	1
Franciscan Corner	4
Sandrouni's	6
The Bookshelf	7
The Cardo Charm	5

0   100 m

Dormition Abbey, Coenaculum ▼   ▼ Chamber of the Holocaust

to the touring kaiser, Wilhelm II. The story goes that, when he made his visit in 1898, the Ottoman authorities, mindful of a legend that every conqueror of the city will enter through the gate, had a **breach** made in the wall between the gate and the Citadel so that the kaiser and his entourage would enter through that instead. The gate itself is on the north side of the breach. When he took Jerusalem for the British in 1917, General Edmund Allenby famously refused to enter through the kaiser's breach and insisted on dismounting, along with his entourage, and entering on foot through the gate itself as a mark of respect to the city.

If you're coming from West Jerusalem, you'll approach along the southern end of the Jaffa Road, which passes alongside the city wall. A concrete **plaza** now bridges the road, connecting the Jaffa Gate to the new Mamilla development (see p.136).

Omar Ibn al-Khattab Square

Once through the L-shaped gateway, **Omar Ibn al-Khattab Square** meets you with a tourist office (see p.42), shops, cafés, hostels and hustlers all aimed at capturing the tourist trade. Just inside the gate, beside the tourist office, two trees in a small, fenced-off compound indicate the positions of two **Ottoman tombs**, belonging to the architects who designed the walls for Suleiman the Magnificent. The sultan had both of them executed, according to one story because they mistakenly left Mount Zion outside the walls, or, according to another tale, because Suleiman didn't want them to build anything else which might surpass their walls. The right-hand grave still bears, in the Ottoman style, a stone turban at its head.

Just across Latin Patriarchate Road (in the Christian Quarter, strictly speaking), the *New Imperial Hotel* (see p.168) sits atop a covered arcade. In the middle of the arcade, a truncated **Roman column** dating from around 200 AD honours one Marcus Junius Maximus of the Tenth Legion, who may have been the governor of Judea at the time. The building containing the *New Imperial Hotel*, along with the neighbouring one housing the *Petra Hostel*, became the centre of a **controversy** in 2005 when it emerged that Jewish investors had bought the land they stand on in a secret deal with the Greek Orthodox Church. Palestinian members of the church were outraged given the sensitive location of the land. In response, an extraordinary Pan-Orthodox Synod was convened in Istanbul, which not only deposed the Greek Patriarch, Irineos I, but also had his name struck off all the official lists; the Israelis were furious, and initially refused to recognize or deal with the new patriarch Theophilos III.

Across the square, opposite the Citadel, the **Christ Church** was built in 1842 under the supervision of the first Anglican bishop of Jerusalem, Michael Solomon Alexander, a rabbi who converted to Christianity. The cool, airy interior reflects this Jewish influence, with a wooden screen inscribed with the Lord's Prayer in Hebrew as a centrepiece.

Suleiman the Magnificent and the walls of Jerusalem

In days of old, a city needed walls to defend it from attack and to allow rulers to use it as a military base. When the Roman Emperor **Hadrian** had the Jewish city of Jerusalem razed in 135 AD and founded Aelia Capitolina in its place, he didn't endow it with walls, possibly fearing that it might be used as a stronghold by rebels, but walls were eventually added, probably when the Tenth Legion left in 289 AD, and they followed roughly the course of today's city ramparts. The Roman walls were augmented or altered over the centuries (Caliph **Al-Zahir** had them rebuilt in the mid-eleventh century after a series of earthquakes had severely damaged them), but essentially they remained in place until 1218, when the Ayyubid sultan **Al-Mu'azzam**, fearful that the city might be taken and used as a base by the Crusaders, had them pulled down, with only the Citadel (see p.50) left standing. This rendered Jerusalem defenceless, effectively transforming it from a city into little more than a large village. So it remained until 1536, when the Ottoman sultan **Suleiman the Magnificent** had a dream in which the Prophet Mohammed appeared and told him to see to the city's defence. Suleiman immediately put his finest architects on the case, and in 1541 the walls were completed, looking pretty much as they are today, Jerusalem's greatest architectural legacy from the Ottoman period.

Straight ahead from the gate, the main Tariq Suweiqet Alloun, now called **David Street** (Khutt Da'ud) runs east through the main market area into the heart of the Old City, separating the Armenian and Christian quarters (to the right and left respectively). The route is often used by Israelis and Israeli-led tour groups en route to the main sights. To the right of the square, Armenian Orthodox Patriarchate Road leads into the heart of the Armenian Quarter.

Hidden away behind the buildings on the north side of David Street, and inaccessible to the public – though you can see it from the roof of the *Petra Hotel* (see p.167) – **Hezekiah's Pool** was originally a reservoir which used to be fed by aqueducts from the Mamilla Pool (see p.136), and is indeed thought to date from the reign of Judah's King Hezekiah (715–687 BC). A nineteenth-century travel guidebook notes that the pool's water was generally used only for washing purposes, but that poor people sometimes resorted to drinking it, with the result that many of them became seriously ill. Today the pool is empty, and used as a rubbish tip, but plans are afoot to do it up and open it as a public space.

The Ramparts Walk

The Jaffa Gate is the best place to begin the **Ramparts Walk** (Sat–Thurs 9am–4pm, Fri & eve of holidays 9am–2pm; 16NIS, student 8NIS) around the walls of the Old City. Built between 1537 and 1540 AD, the ramparts were commissioned by the Ottoman sultan Suleiman the Magnificent (see box, p.49). They run for 4km and you can walk along two sections: the northern section between the Jaffa Gate and the Lions' Gate, and the southern section between the Citadel and the Dung Gate. The section of the wall alongside Temple Mount is not accessible to the public.

Although you can exit from the walk at any of the seven gates (an eighth – the Golden Gate on the eastern wall of Temple Mount – is closed until the appearance, or Second Coming, of the Messiah), you can **enter** only from the Jaffa Gate, where there is an entrance at the northern side of the gate (by Stern's jeweller's) for the northern section, and one at the moat by the Citadel on the southern side for the southern section, or the Damascus Gate (the entrance is inside the Roman Plaza below the gateway, see p.74).

You can buy **tickets** for the Ramparts Walk (16NIS) at any of the three entrance points; alternatively, you can purchase a combined ticket (55NIS valid three days) which includes one visit to the Jerusalem Archaeological Park (see p.86), the Roman Plaza at Damascus Gate (see p.74), and Zedekiah's Cave (King Solomon's Quarries) just to the east of Damascus Gate (see p.108). Note that although the Ramparts are open on Saturdays, you cannot buy tickets then – they can be bought in advance; in theory they can be bought online at ⓦ www .pami.co.il, but the site is in Hebrew only.

The Citadel (Tower of David)

Carefully excavated, with all the periods of its development clearly marked, the imposing **Citadel** next to the Jaffa Gate, commonly (but incorrectly) known as the **Tower of David** (April–Nov Sat–Thurs 10am–5pm, Fri 10am–2pm; Nov–March Sun–Thurs 10am–4pm, Fri 10am–2pm; 30NIS; combined museum entry with sound and light show ticket 65NIS; free guided tours in

▲ The steep outer walls of the Citadel

English Sun–Fri 11am; Ⓦwww.towerofdavid.org.il) is well worth taking time to explore. The site will take a good couple of hours to see properly.

Surrounded by a dry **moat**, the Citadel occupies a strategic position on the western hill of the Old City fortified by every ruler of Jerusalem since the second century BC, when it was at the city's northwestern corner and highest point. Herod strengthened the old Hasmonean walls by adding three new towers, and the historian Josephus tells us there was an adjoining **palace** "baffling all description", remains of which have been excavated in the Armenian garden to the south. This palace were the Jerusalem residence of the Roman Procurator (whose headquarters was in Caesarea) until the Romans burned it down during the Jewish Revolt of 66–70 AD. When the city was razed by the Romans in 70 AD, only one of Herod's three towers – the Phasael, named after his brother – remained standing. During the Byzantine period the tower, and by extension the Citadel as a whole, acquired its alternative name, the Tower of David, after the **Byzantines**, mistakenly identifying the hill as Mount Zion, presumed it to be David's Palace. The Citadel was gradually built up under Muslim and Crusader rule, acquiring the basis of its present shape in 1310 under the Mamluk sultan Al-Nasir Muhammad. Suleiman the Magnificent later constructed a square with a monumental gateway in the east. The **minaret** (no public access to the top), a prominent Jerusalem landmark, was added between 1635 and 1655, and took over the title of "Tower of David" in the nineteenth century, so that the term sometimes refers to the Citadel as a whole, and sometimes specifically to the minaret.

From the **Phasael tower** in the northeast corner of the Citadel, there are good views over the excavations inside and the Old City outside, as well as into the distance south and west. On the way up, a terrace overlooking the excavations has plaques identifying the different periods of all the remains you can see. These include part of the **Hasmonean city wall**, a **Roman cistern**, and the ramparts of the **Ummayad Citadel** which held out against the Crusaders in 1099.

The Jerusalem History Museum

The rooms around the "archeological garden" containing the excavations have been turned into a **Museum of the History of Jerusalem**, a fascinating exhibition illustrating the history of Jerusalem from Jebusite times until the present. For each period there is a model of the city as it was, culminating with a magnificent zinc model made by Hungarian artist Stefan Illes in 1872. Every half-hour, a beautifully animated film is shown in the Phasael Tower, summarizing the city's history in fourteen minutes. There's also a spectacular evening **Sound and Light Show** (in English Mon, Tues & Wed, April–Oct 8pm & 10pm, Nov–March 7pm & 9pm; 50NIS; combined ticket for the museum and the show 65NIS; running time 45min), billed as "the most sophisticated in the world" and featuring state-of-the-art special effects projected onto the walls of the Citadel. Themes include King David, of course, the city's fall to the Babylonians and then the Romans, the rise of Christianity, Mohammed's night journey to heaven, the Crusades, and the British Mandate. It ends with a prayer for peace in the city. If you're going in winter, remember that it can get quite chilly sitting outdoors in the evening, so bring a sweater or jacket.

The Armenian Compound

Running south from the Citadel, Armenian Orthodox Patriarchate Road narrows into a short tunnel, at the end of which a door on the left leads into the walled **Armenian Compound** (Deir al-Arman). Home to a religious community of five hundred and containing a number of buildings that provide

Jerusalem's Armenian Community

There have been **Armenians** in Jerusalem since before the Byzantine period – immigrants from ancient Armenia (corresponding now to eastern Turkey, modern Armenia, Azerbijan and Georgia), which, in 301 AD, became the first state to accept Christianity as its religion. As early as 638 AD, Caliph Omar Ibn al-Khattab guaranteed the religious rights of Jerusalem's Armenian community, a guarantee respected by subsequent Muslim rulers. Under Crusader rule too, the Armenians fared better than the other eastern churches due to links between the Crusader kingdoms and the Armenian kingdom of Cilicia. Armenia itself fell to the Mamluks in 1375, and later came under the rule of the Seljuks and Ottomans, who actively suppressed Armenian culture and political aspirations. As the Ottoman Empire crumbled, Armenians became pawns in Europe-wide power struggles, and were victims of several **massacres** at the hands of the Turks, whose policy escalated from pogroms to **genocide** during World War I (when Armenians were suspected of having enemy sympathies), culminating in 1915 with the incarceration in concentration camps of most of the population and their subsequent murder. At the start of the war, there were two million ethnic Armenians living in Turkey; after the war, the figure was barely 100,000, with around half a million came to Jerusalem to join the already established religious community. Today, the former Soviet Republic of Armenia is again an independent state but the 1915 holocaust casts a shadow over the community almost as great as that of the Nazi Holocaust over the Jews, and you'll see posters detailing the massacre all over the quarter.

an interesting snapshot of Armenian culture and history, it's a pleasant, tranquil place to wander around.

St James's Cathedral

St James's Cathedral (open for services only: Mon–Fri 6–7.30am, 3–3.30pm, Sat & Sun 2.30–3pm) dedicated to Jesus's brother James the Righteous (the first Bishop of Jerusalem), is one of the loveliest churches in Jerusalem – its rich carpets, carvings, paintings and countless golden lamps make it positively glow with light and colour. There has been a church on the site since the fifth century, but the cathedral which stands today was built in the middle of the twelfth century. It was substantially renovated in the eighteenth century under an Armenian Patriarch known as Gregory the Chainbearer, and most of the interior decoration dates from that time. At the entrance are pieces of wood and bronze – *nakus* – which were hit with a wooden mallet to announce prayer times from the ninth century when the ringing of church bells was prohibited by Palestine's Muslim rulers. In 1948, with bombs and mortars whizzing overhead, the Old City's Armenian community sought refuge within the cathedral's sturdy walls; over a thousand shells fell on or around it but nobody inside was touched. Some say that St James himself was seen on the roof, dressed in white, warding off the missiles with his own hands. The cathedral's daily service features some lovely hymns and chants that are unique to the Armenian liturgy, and anyone with an interest in sacred music will find it fascinating.

The Mardigian Museum

In addition to the Gulbenkian Library and the Church of St Toros, repositories respectively of priceless collections of Armenian books and manuscripts, the peaceful, open courtyard of the Armenia Compound also houses the **Mardigian Museum of Armenian Art and History** (formerly Mon–Sat 10am–4.30pm; 5NIS; but closed for renovations on our last check). The rich collection is arranged in some of the 38 rooms that were formerly the living quarters of Armenian seminary students, set around an ochre stone courtyard dotted with cypress trees, and illustrates the culture and history of Jerusalem's Armenian community, as well as the 1915 genocide of Armenians in Turkey. The collection features Roman and Byzantine **mosaics** believed to have been made by Armenian artists, but the most important and attractive exhibits are the jewel-encrusted, brilliantly coloured, **illuminated manuscripts**, some dating from the tenth century. Other highlights include the collection of eighteenth-century yellow, white and sky-blue **tiles** from northwest Turkey (together with the more familiar blue tiles which predominate in Jerusalem), intricate seventeenth-century filigree artefacts, and ritual objects such as jewelled crosses, mitres and embroidery.

Outside the main compound, and not usually open to the public, is the delightful **Convent of the Olive Tree** (Deir al-Zeitouna), where Jesus is said to have been tied to be scourged before his crucifixion (Mark 15:15; John 19:1). Armenian Orthodox Patriarchate Road continues from here south towards the Zion Gate and Mount Zion (see p.141).

The Syrian Orthodox Convent and Church

North of the Armenian Cathedral, St James's Road leads into the quarter's main residential area. On the left, down Ararat Street, is the **Syrian Convent** (Mon–Sat April–Sept 8am–5pm, Oct–March 8am–6pm) belonging to the Syrian Orthodox Church, who are also known as Jacobites after their founder Jacob Baradai. The Jacobites use the ancient language of Classical Syriac (which you can see in the form of an inscription in the mosaic above the door), and are one of the smallest Christian sects in Jerusalem, established here since the end of the sixth century. They claim that **St Mark's Church**, inside the convent, stands on the site of St Peter's first church – the first in Christendom – where the Virgin Mary was baptized and the Last Supper eaten (a claim to rival the Coenaculum on Mount Zion, see p.142).

If you continue north up Ararat Street, it brings you onto St Mark's Road – turn left for the Jaffa Gate (see p.47), right for the central souqs (see p.76). If, on the other hand, you head south down Ararat to the junction with St James's Road, you can either turn right along that to go back to Armenian Orthodox Patriarchate Road, or take a left instead towards the Jewish Quarter, passing the Old Yishuv Court Museum (see p.93).

2

The Via Dolorosa and the Christian Quarter

For most of those who come to Jerusalem as Christian pilgrims, the most important thing they will do is to walk the **Via Dolorosa**, an approximation of the path along which Jesus dragged his cross. Starting in the Muslim Quarter near the **Lions' Gate**, the Via Dolorosa ends at the **Church of the Holy Sepulchre**, site of the crucifixion, and heart of the Old City's Christian Quarter. Aside from the church, the quarter is relatively thin (by Jerusalem's standards) on sights, though it does have a number of good places to stay, eat and shop. The language here is Arabic and the people very definitely Palestinian, but the fact that it is largely Christian gives it a slightly more European feel. Most local residents are Greek Orthodox, and Greek influence is strong – you'll notice it in the way people dress, and in the style of the buildings, many of which bear Greek inscriptions. The Christian influence is apparent in other ways too: shops in the quarter stock alcohol for instance, while others sell crosses and icons of the Virgin Mary, and on the streets you'll encounter all manner of clergy, wearing habits and robes of a myriad different styles to go with the many different churches they represent.

If you are approaching the quarter along the **Via Dolorosa**, you'll need to get to the Lions' Gate, which can be reached via the Muslim Quarter, or from East Jerusalem via Herod's Gate. From West Jerusalem, it is served by Egged buses #1 and #2. Otherwise, the quickest way into the Christian Quarter from West Jerusalem is via the **New Gate** (see p.71), though many tourists enter the quarter through the **Jaffa Gate** at its southwest corner (see p.47).

The Lions' Gate and around

In a city where everything seems to have at least two names, the **Lions' Gate**, on the eastern ramparts, actually boasts four. It is commonly known as Lions' Gate, after the pair of lions flanking the entrance (see p.4). Actually, they are panthers, symbols of the Mamluk sultan Baybars I (Baybars the Great), an important hero in Islamic history, who halted the Mongols' relentless westward advance, and all but drove the Crusaders from Palestine (less heroically, he also banned beer and hashish, though it is said that he himself was partial to an

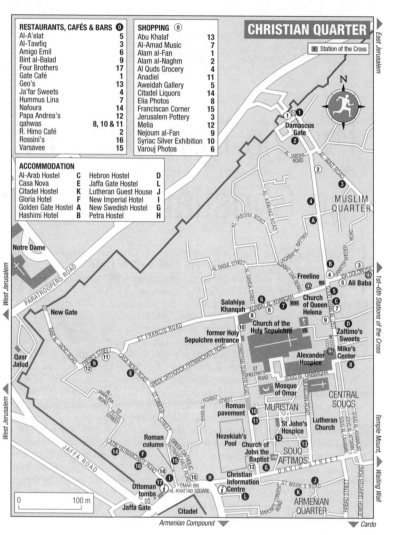

CHRISTIAN QUARTER

▮ Station of the Cross

RESTAURANTS, CAFÉS & BARS ●

Al-A'elat	5
Al-Tawfiq	3
Amigo Emil	6
Bint al-Balad	9
Four Brothers	17
Gate Café	1
Geo's	13
Ja'far Sweets	4
Hummus Lina	7
Nafoura	14
Papa Andrea's	12
qahwas	8, 10 & 11
R. Himo Café	2
Rossini's	16
Varsavee	15

SHOPPING ●

Abu Khalaf	13
Al-Amad Music	7
Alam al-Fan	1
Alam al-Naghm	2
Al Quds Grocery	4
Anadiel	11
Aweidah Gallery	5
Citadel Liquors	14
Elia Photos	8
Franciscan Corner	15
Jerusalem Pottery	3
Melia	12
Nejoum al-Fan	9
Syriac Silver Exhibition	10
Varouj Photos	6

ACCOMMODATION

Al-Arab Hostel	C	Hebron Hostel	D
Casa Nova	E	Jaffa Gate Hostel	L
Citadel Hostel	K	Lutheran Guest House	J
Gloria Hotel	F	New Imperial Hotel	I
Golden Gate Hostel	A	New Swedish Hostel	G
Hashimi Hotel	B	Petra Hostel	H

alcoholic drink made from fermented mare's milk). The "lions", which must previously have adorned a building from Baybars's time, were put here on the orders of Suleiman the Magnificent, apparently because he (or his father, Selim the Grim) had dreamed that he would be eaten by lions if he didn't rebuild Jerusalem's ramparts. A more mundane explanation is that he had them put here to celebrate Selim's defeat of the Mamluks.

The gate is also called **St Stephen's Gate** after the very first Christian martyr, who was cast out of the city and stoned to death on a false charge of blasphemy (Acts 7:58). Stephen's tomb was "discovered" in 415 outside the Damascus Gate, but the location of his martyrdom was moved to the Lions' Gate for the convenience of Christian pilgrims, who were not allowed to enter via the northern (Damascus) gate after Saladin reconquered the city from the Crusaders in 1187. In Arabic the Lions' Gate is **Bab al-Ghor** (Jordan Valley Gate) or alternatively **Bab Sittna Maryam** (Gate of Our Lady Mary), since the Virgin Mary was born just inside (see below). The gate is the way into the Old City if you're coming from the direction of the Mount of Olives, across the Kidron Valley (see p.117), and it leads to the Via Dolorosa.

The Churches of St Anne

Inside the Lions' Gate, in a large walled compound to the right of **Al-Mujahideen Road**, stand two **Churches of St Anne**, named after the mother of the Virgin Mary. Nearest to the Lions' Gate is the **Greek Orthodox church** (ring on the bell 10am–5pm; donation expected). Inside is a small cave-like chapel where you can see the spot held by Greek Orthodox tradition to be the location of Mary's birth, and downstairs the tombs of her parents, St Anne and St Joachim. The next doorway to the west leads to the **Greek Catholic church** (Mon–Sat: April–Sept 8am–noon & 2–6pm; Oct–March 8am–noon & 2–5pm; 7NIS), one of the simplest and most beautiful Crusader buildings in the country. Though the style is Romanesque, it incorporates a number of Middle Eastern features, including the pointed arches, and the fluted fringe around the top of the uppermost window (the Crusaders later introduced these features to Europe). Inside, the columns and vaulting are almost unadorned, but their proportions give the interior a lightness that is very pleasing to the eye. A less obvious but no less important design feature is the church's absolutely perfect acoustics for choral singing – many pilgrim groups come here to sing hymns for that very reason, and it's well worth staying to listen if you should be lucky enough to coincide with such a group. Stairs inside lead down into the ancient crypt, where there are mosaics and columns dating from Byzantine times, and where Catholic tradition places Mary's birth, though the priests here today decline to be dogmatic on the subject of where Mary was actually born.

The Pools of Bethesda

In the same compound as the Catholic St Anne's church (same hours and ticket) lie the ruins of the two great **Pools of Bethesda**, constructed around 200 BC to supply water to the Temple. The waters, believed to have medicinal qualities, were used by Jesus to cure a man who "had an infirmity thirty and eight years", according to the Gospel of St John (5:1–13). Excavations show the remains of five porches referred to by the Gospel, with the small natural caves nearby adapted as baths for the thousands of sufferers who came here during Roman times to seek a cure for their various afflictions. In the third century, the Romans built a temple to Serapis on the site, which the Byzantines knocked down and replaced with a basilica. Remains of all these can be seen as you follow the walkway around the pools. At one point you can even descend into the depths of a Roman cistern. A detailed plan on the site explains what's what. Objects found during excavations are held in a small **museum**, which is usually open only by appointment (☎02/628 3285, ✉mafrpoc@jrol.com).

South of Al-Mujahideen Road

A turn left off Al-Mujahideen Road after St Anne's and through a small arch brings you to one of the entrances to the Temple Mount, **Bab Hitta** (Absolution Gate, closed to non-Muslims). The street leading to the gate contains a fourteenth-century pilgrim's hospice called Ribat al-Maridini (the first door on the right), and (at the end on the right) the 1299 tomb of an Ayyubid prince, Al-Awhad, with reused Crusader columns embedded on each side of the doorway. Next left after Bab Hitta Road, King Faisal Road leads into the Temple Mount compound at **Bab al-'Atm** (Gate of Darkness; closed to non-Muslims), and also contains two fine Mamluk doorways, both built in the alternating red and white stone (*ablaq*) so typical of the Mamluks, with stalac-tite-like decorations (*murqanas*) above. The venerable, iron-clad door of the **Madrasa al-Sallamiya** is surmounted by black and white medallions – the one on the right says, "There is no god but Allah"; the one on the left says "Mohammed is God's messenger". A little beyond, the doorway of the **Madrasa al-Dawadariya** has one large *murqana* hanging threateningly down above it, almost like a stone sword of Damocles.

A little way further along Al-Mujahideen Road, on the right, Aqabat al-Darwish leads up to **Herod's Gate**, and thence to East Jerusalem, while straight on, Al-Mujahideen becomes the Via Dolorosa.

The Via Dolorosa

In Christian tradition, the **Via Dolorosa** ("Way of Sorrow" or "Way of the Cross") is the route taken by Jesus from Pilate's judgement hall to Golgotha, the site of the crucifixion – a path since followed by countless millions of pilgrims, from the Madrasa al-Omariya, 300m west of the Lions' Gate in the Muslim Quarter, to its end at the Church of the Holy Sepulchre. Along its five-hundred-metre length are the **fourteen Stations of the Cross**, each commemorating an event in the Gospel narrative, but actually a relatively recent innovation, with some stations located only in the nineteenth century. All the stations are marked by black iron **plaques** bearing the number of the station in Roman numerals, but they can be difficult to spot, particularly when the route enters the souq proper.

One way to be sure of locating all fourteen stations, and to experience the devotional flavour, is to join the **Franciscans' procession**. Led by Franciscan friars (appointed guardians of Jerusalem's holy sites by the Pope in 1342), this begins at the Umariya School (the First Station of the Cross; see opposite) on Fridays at 3pm in winter, or 4pm during daylight saving, which is, as near as possible, the time and day of Jesus's original ordeal. The procession stops at each of the Stations of the Cross for a prayer and Bible reading, usually in English and Italian, and hymns are sung in between. The participants are accompanied by a ceremonial guard called a *kawas*, originally appointed by the Ottomans, who still wears a fez and Ottoman uniform, and carries a whip. During Lent, the procession is joined by some thousands of people, culminating of course on Good Friday, when it is absolutely huge. For information about alternative tours, ask at the Christian Information Centre (see p.43) or at tour agencies.

History of the Via Dolorosa

The **route** of the Via Dolorosa has changed several times over the centuries. In Byzantine times, Christian pilgrims followed a similar path to the one today but didn't stop along the way. By the eighth century, the route had moved: beginning at the Garden of Gethsemane on the Mount of Olives, it headed south to Mount Zion and then doubled back around the Temple Mount to the Holy Sepulchre. A split in the Latin Church in the Middle Ages meant that for a period there were two rival routes: the group with churches to the west went westwards, those with property to the east, eastwards, while from the fourteenth to the sixteenth century, the route followed that of the Franciscans, starting at the Holy Sepulchre and comprising eight stations. However, in the meantime, a tradition of fourteen stations, marking the order of events in the Gospels, was developing in Europe and, so as not to disappoint European pilgrims, the difference was made up.

Whether the Via Dolorosa as now followed corresponds to historical reality still remains a matter of controversy. Some Protestants believe Jesus would have been led north, towards the Garden Tomb, while Dominican Catholics set out from Herod's Palace at Jaffa Gate where Pontius Pilate usually stayed when he came from Caesarea to police the crowds on Jewish feasts. If he did condemn Jesus here, the path to the crucifixion would most likely have gone eastwards along what is now David Street, north at the central souqs, and then west to the Holy Sepulchre. All this seems to matter little, however, to the crowds of pilgrims who walk the path, particularly during Easter Week.

The First Station

The **First Station**, at the **Umariya School**, 300m west of the Lions' Gate, is held to be the site where Pontius Pilate condemned Jesus to death (Matthew 27:11–24; Mark 15:1–15; Luke 23:1–25; John 18:28–19:16). Steps on the left (opposite the second station) lead up to the courtyard of the school. It stands on the site of a Roman fortress named "Antonia" by Herod after his friend Mark Anthony. The fortress was razed after Titus captured it from the rebels during the Jewish War, but part of its wall remains in the foundations of what is now the school. The caretaker may possibly be kind enough to allow you to enter the school if you ask (and would no doubt appreciate a tip for his trouble), but the only time it is officially open is when the Franciscans gather here to begin their procession on Friday afternoon (see opposite). From the top of the steps in the south of the schoolyard you can view the whole of the Temple Mount compound. Beneath the school, at street level, is the exit of the controversial Western Wall tunnel (see p.91).

The Second Station

Jesus took up the cross at the **Second Station**, across the road, next to the Franciscan monastery known as the **Sanctuary of the Flagellation and the Condemnation** (daily: April–Sept 7.30am–6pm; Oct–March 7.30am–5pm).

The **Church of the Condemnation** (or Chapel of Judgement) on the left, is where Jesus was sentenced to crucifixion, and where Pontius Pilate famously washed his hands of the decision (Matthew 27:15–26; Mark 15:6–15). The five-domed building, originally Byzantine, was rebuilt in 1904. The floor on the right-hand side of the church, made of huge stone blocks cut with grooves, was once the pavement of the city's eastern forum.

On the right of the courtyard, the **Church of the Flagellation** marks the spot where Jesus was given a crown of thorns and beaten and mocked by Roman soldiers (Matthew 27:27–30; Mark 15:16–19; John 19:1–3). It was the Crusaders who first built a chapel here, but it was abandoned, along with the rest of the site, when the city fell to the Khwarizmians in 1254. In 1838, the Egyptian ruler Ibrahim Pasha gave the site to the Franciscans, who rebuilt the church, and it was restored again in 1929 by Antonio Barluzzi (see p.121), who had the beautiful stained-glass windows put in. The one behind the altar depicts the flagellation itself, while those on the side show Barabbas (the thief pardoned in place of Jesus) celebrating his release, and Pilate washing his hands. The crown of thorns is commemorated in the ceiling, where a representation of it decorates the inside of the dome.

The Lithostratos

The next turning to the south, Tariq Bab al-Ghawanima, leads to the north-western gate of Temple Mount. Just beyond, on the north side of the Via Dolorosa, is the **Convent of the Sisters of Zion**, under which are preserved large pieces of the **Lithostratos** (Pavement of Justice) where Jesus was tried (daily 8am–5pm; 8NIS), though actually, like the floor in the Church of the Condemnation, it was part of the pavement of the eastern forum. The grooves carved in its stone surface are variously explained as channels for rainwater (see the huge subterranean cistern below) or as a device to prevent horses slipping. What is agreed, however, is that the squares, triangles and other scratch marks on the slabs were made by game-playing Roman soldiers.

The Ecce Homo Arch

Spanning the street just west of the entrance to the Lithostratos, the **Ecce Homo Arch** is where Pontius Pilate identified Jesus to the crowd, saying "*Ecce homo*" ("Behold the man"– John 19:5). The arch is in fact part of the central span of a triple archway dating from the reign of Hadrian, a century after Pilate's time, and was a monumental arch installed in the lesser of the Roman city's two forums, which stood on this site. It was given the name Ecce Homo Arch in the sixteenth century.

You can see more of the gate by entering the **viewing chamber** of the Ecce Homo Church, on the north side of the road just beyond, and looking through

▲ The Ecce Homo Arch, Via Dolorosa

a glass window into the church (which is otherwise not open). The rest of the central arch and one of the two smaller arches flanking it can clearly be seen in their original Roman form. The plaque explaining what you are seeing seems to have been removed, but there is a plan of the gateway and the Lithostratos on the wall behind you as you look into the church.

Between the arch and the third station, also on the north side of the street, a building belonging to the Greek Orthodox Patriarchate (not open to the public) bears a plaque to the left of the door identifying it as the **Prison of Christ**. The plaque refers to a cave in the basement which is supposed to have been the prison where Jesus and Barabbas were held, but in fact the tradition that it was the prison of Christ was only established in 1911, and it is far more likely to have been a stable associated with the Antonia Fortress which once stood here.

The Third and Fourth Stations

Lying at the junction with Al-Wad Road, the **Third Station**, marked by a relief sculpture above the door of a small Polish chapel (Mon–Sat 9am–5pm), is where Jesus fell for the first time under the weight of the cross. Next door, the Armenian **Church of Our Lady of the Spasm** (daily 9am–5pm) commemorates the **Fourth Station**, where Mary stood and watched her son go by. Down in the crypt (entered via the souvenir shop attached to the third station) is a remarkable fifth-century mosaic floor, where you can see the outline of a pair of sandals, said to be Mary's footprints.

The Fifth Station

The **Fifth Station** is on the corner where the Via Dolorosa turns right off Al-Wad Road and becomes a narrow stepped street as it wends its way uphill. A "handprint" on the wall to the right of the doorway is attributed to Jesus as he leant against it and it was here that Simon the Cyrenian, from Libya, was forced by Roman soldiers to help Jesus carry the cross (Matthew 27:32; Mark 15:21; Luke 23:26).

The Sixth Station

From Al-Wad Road, the Via Dolorosa climbs steeply up steps to the **Sixth Station** (80m up, on the left) where, according to accounts dating from the fourteenth century, **St Veronica** wiped Jesus's face, the image of which became imprinted on her handkerchief. The same cloth, known as the *Sudarium*, or Veil of Veronica (the name Veronica may be a corruption of the Latin *vera icon* – true picture), is also said to have cured Emperor Tiberius of an illness; held for many years in the Vatican, it disappeared in the sixteenth century and its current whereabouts is unknown, though it may still be in some Vatican vault somewhere. A column embedded in the wall, and inscribed with the words "6 St/ pia Veronica faciem Christi linteo deterci" (6th station: pious Veronica wiped the face of Christ with a cloth) marks the spot. The Syrian Catholic **chapel** here, built in 1882, was renovated in 1953 by Italian architect Antonio Barluzzi.

The Seventh Station

At the Via Dolorosa's junction with Souq Khan al-Zeit, a Franciscan chapel (Mon–Sat 9am–5pm) marks the **Seventh Station**, where Jesus fell for the

The **Tenth to Fourteenth Stations** of the Cross are inside the Church of the Holy Sepulchre (see p.75). To get to them, you have to go round to the main entrance of the church: head south down Souq Khan al-Zeit to the end, turn right into Souq al-Dabbagha and go straight on to the doorway at the end of the street.

second time. Inside the door of the chapel is a column from the Cardo Maximus of Hadrian's city, which ran along what is now Souq Khan al-Zeit (see p.75). The site is also sometimes called the Gate of Judgement because it was thought that Jesus, on his way to Gologotha, exited here through a gate (possibly the Old Gate mentioned in Nehemiah 12:39) in what were, before Hadrian's time, the city walls; apparently, notices announcing death sentences were affixed to this gate, hence the name.

The Eighth Station

Taking a right up the steps of Aqabat al-Khanqah, you come to the **Eighth Station**, 50m up on the left, where a stone in the wall, with a hole in the middle, is inscribed with a cross, the initials "IC" and "XC" for "Jesus Christ" in Latin and Greek above, and the Greek word "NIKA", meaning "victor" below (the inscription thus means, "Jesus Christ is victorious"). This station marks the spot where Jesus consoled the lamenting women of Jerusalem (Luke 23:27–31).

The Ninth Station

To find the **Ninth Station**, go back to Souq Khan al-Zeit and turn right (south). After 100m, shortly before the end of the street, a stairway on the right leads up to Mike's Centre (see p.40), before turning and continuing up another flight. At the top, follow the path round to the Coptic Patriarchate, where a plaque on a buttress on the right indicates the ninth station, where Jesus fell a third time. The actual spot is believed to be marked by the **Roman column** to the left of the Coptic Patriarchate's doorway. To the left of the column, a doorway leads into the **Ethiopian Compound** (see below). Opposite that doorway, to the right of the Coptic Patriarchate is the **Church of Queen Helena** (see opposite).

At the bottom of the stairs, set back from the street is **Zaltimo's Sweets** (daily 10am–8pm), a small shop notable mainly for the fact that its back room contains the doorway from the original Roman Church of the Holy Sepulchre. The shopkeeper will usually allow tourists in to see it for 10NIS.

The Ethiopian Compound

Situated on a rooftop next to the ninth station of the cross (to the right of the entrance to the Coptic Patriarchate) and directly above the Church of the Holy Sepulchre's Chapel of St Helena, the **Ethiopian Compound** or **Deir al-Sultan** (Monastery of the Sultan) is home to a community of Ethiopian monks, who managed to wrest it from Egypt's Coptic Church after centuries of wrangling.

The Ethiopians formerly controlled a number of chapels inside the Church of the Holy Sepulchre but lost their rights in the seventeenth century when they were unable to pay taxes they owed to the Ottoman authorities. They were then consigned to the roof, but in the nineteenth century, documents

Ethiopians in Jerusalem

The **Ethiopians** of Jeruslaem whose presence here dates back to the fourth century, are one of the oldest expatriate Christian communities anywhere. Traditionally, they have been associated with five holy sites, including the Church of the Nativity in Bethlehem and the Grotto of David on Mount Zion. David, whose tribe was Judah, is the father of the Ethiopian Orthodox Church, which claims to have been founded by his grandson King Menelik, son of Solomon and the Queen of Sheba; both the Lion of Judah and the Star of David are embroidered in gold and silver on the monks' ceremonial robes.

specifying their rights were burned, and the Ottomans gave the roof to the Copts, who changed the locks to exclude their Ethiopian rivals. In 1961, a Jordanian Court gave the Ethiopians back their roof, but then reversed the decision, so in 1970, while the Copts were away praying, Ethiopian monks changed the locks and reoccupied the area.

Twenty-six monks now live in the "village" – basically a cluster of huts on the roof of the church. The Coptic Church has ruled that its members cannot visit Jerusalem as pilgrims until the conflict is settled. Meanwhile, a Coptic monk is allowed to sit in an agreed spot to maintain his church's claim; when he tried to move his seat into the shade on one hot day in June 2002, a fist-fight ensued between Copts and Ethiopians, which left eleven monks injured. More recently, Israeli engineers have warned that the roof is in imminent danger of collapse and needs to be repaired as a matter of extreme urgency. Israel has offered to pay for the repairs, but no agreement on carrying them out has so far been forthcoming from the Ethiopians and the Copts.

The Church of Queen Helena

Opposite the door to the Ethiopian compound is the rather poky Coptic **Church of Queen Helena** (daily 10am–5pm). Inside, you can descend via a small stairway into a rather dank (but in summer pleasantly cool) ancient cistern of unknown antiquity discovered by Constantine's mother, St Helena (see p.65), while checking out the locations of Christian sites here, but you will need to bring a light.

The Church of the Holy Sepulchre

The holiest site in Christendom it may be, but the **Church of the Holy Sepulchre** (daily: April–Sept 5am–9pm; Oct–March 4am–8pm) lacks the immediate dramatic impact of the Dome of the Rock or the Wailing Wall. Largely obscured from view in most parts of the city, its multiple domes are more easily spotted from the rooftops – from the Lutheran Church, for example (see p.70), or the rooftop walk (see p.93), or *Papa Andrea's* restaurant (see p.187), or from somewhere outside the Old City altogether, such as the Mount of Olives (see p.118).

Traditionally ascribed as the site of **Christ's crucifixion**, **burial and resurrection**, it is the centre of Christian worship in Jerusalem and the most venerated Christian shrine in the world. Here, within the church, are the last five **Stations of the Cross** (see p.67): the tenth station, where Jesus was stripped of his clothes; the eleventh, where he was nailed to the cross; the

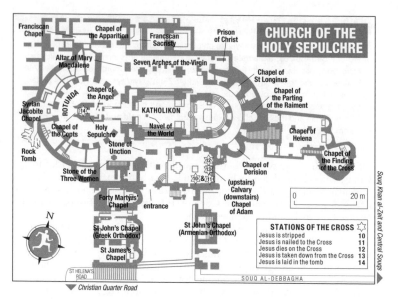

Map: Church of the Holy Sepulchre, with Stations of the Cross and chapel locations.

Labels on map: Franciscan Chapel · Chapel of the Apparition · Franciscan Sacristy · Prison of Christ · **CHURCH OF THE HOLY SEPULCHRE** · Altar of Mary Magdalene · Seven Arches of the Virgin · Chapel of St Longinus · Chapel of the Angel · Chapel of the Parting of the Raiment · Syrian Jacobite Chapel · ROTUNDA · KATHOLIKON · Chapel of the Copts · Holy Sepulchre · Navel of the World · Chapel of Helena · Rock Tomb · Stone of Unction · Chapel of the Finding of the Cross · Stone of the Three Women · Chapel of Derision · Forty Martyrs' Chapel · entrance · (upstairs) Calvary (downstairs) Chapel of Adam · St John's Chapel (Greek Orthodox) · St John's Chapel (Armenian Orthodox) · St James's Chapel · ST HELENA'S ROAD · SOUQ AL-DEBBAGHA · Souq Khan al-Zeit and Central Souqs

0   20 m

STATIONS OF THE CROSS
Jesus is stripped — 10
Jesus is nailed to the Cross — 11
Jesus dies on the Cross — 12
Jesus is taken down from the Cross — 13
Jesus is laid in the tomb — 14

Christian Quarter Road

twelfth, where he died on the cross; the thirteenth where his body was removed from the cross; and the fourteenth, his tomb. The first four are all on the **Hill of Calvary** enclosed inside the church and the fifth, the tomb – the Holy Sepulchre itself, from which the church gets its name – forms the centrepiece at the heart of the building.

The **interior** of the church is a vast and rambling arena of ponderous stone architecture and gloomy, smoke-blackened recesses. It's also very noisy, constantly permeated with the din of repairs and the hum of tourists and pilgrims, and filled at prayer times with a cacophony of rival chants from the various religious communities who none too happily share it as a place of worship (see box opposite) – if you're expecting an atmosphere of harmony and meditation then forget it; you're about as likely to find it here as in the market outside.

Getting to the Holy Sepulchre

The entrance to the church is located just north of the Muristan (see p.69). If you are following the Via Dolorosa or coming from the Damascus Gate, head south down Souq Khan al-Zeit to the end (where it reaches the central souqs and becomes Souq al-Attarin), and turn right into Souq al-Dabbagha, passing the Alexander Hospice on your right and the Lutheran Church on your left. Continue straight on to the small doorway at the end, which leads to the Holy Sepulchre's forecourt.

Coming from the Jaffa Gate, go straight ahead down David Street and either take a left up Christian Quarter Road and then the third right down St Helena's Road, or else continue down David Street to Muristan Road, taking a left there and another (along Souq al-Dabbagha) at the end.

History of the Holy Sepulchre

The earliest known Christian church on this site dates from before 66 AD, but the area was levelled by the Roman Emperor Hadrian, who then raised a temple to Aphrodite here in 135 AD, following the Second Jewish Revolt.

Following his conversion to Christianity, the Emperor Constantine dispatched his mother, **St Helena**, to the Holy Land in 326 AD to establish the true locations of Christian holy sites. Since it was standard practice to build temples on sites held sacred to other religions, especially subversive ones, Hadrian's construction of the temple to Aphrodite here led Helena to identify the site as the location of the crucifixion and burial. She also claimed to have found the **True Cross** in an underground cave nearby. **Constantine** had a church built here which was completed in 348 AD. The authenticity of the claim that this is indeed Calvary, where Jesus was buried, depends on the assumption that in Roman times the site lay outside the city walls (challenged by some but probably correct, as confirmed by excavations under the Alexander Hospice, see p.71). Jewish burial grounds were traditionally located outside the walls, and St John's Gospel (19:20) states that Golgotha, the site of the crucifixion, was

---

Unholy rows at the Holy Sepulchre

The Church of the Holy Sepulchre has long been the subject of interdenominational **disputes** that leave its everyday operations and upkeep in something approaching a state of chaos. It is shared by six Christian communities – the Latins (Roman Catholics), Greek Orthodox, Armenian Orthodox, Syrian Orthodox (Jacobites), Ethiopians and Copts – who cohabit on an uneasy "cold war" footing. Their rights are defined by a **Status Quo** on holy sites, fixed by decree of the Ottoman sultan in 1757, reaffirmed in 1852, and codified in more detail by a British government Commission in 1922, regulating among other things who can do what and when in the church. The authorities may alter the regulations, but only if there is no objection from any religious group.

Under the Status Quo, each denomination controls certain areas of the building and exercises the liturgy at different times of the day or night, while others are permitted only certain ceremonies on special occasions. **Repairs** are especially problematic under these circumstances. Restoration work following the 1927 earthquake wasn't completed until 1988, after thirty years of argument (finally resolved in a 1958 works agreement) and a further thirty years of construction. Even the smallest repairs can be a major source of contention, as those carrying them out can then lay claim to the area, while larger renovations require a degree of collaboration rarely forthcoming. Thus, in the restoration of three pillars in the Rotunda, the square pillar owned by the Greek Orthodox was renovated by them, while the other two Corinthian pillars were restored by their owners, the Armenians. The recess in the wall behind is another disputed zone, owned by the Armenians but used by the Copts. Numerous disputes over rights in the church exist, some frozen by the Status Quo, but not forgotten by their protagonists.

Nor are disagreements between the churches resolved in a becomingly religious manner. On the contrary, they quite often degenerate into **punch-ups** of a most unholy nature. An English pilgrim, visiting in 1697, told how Greeks and Catholics, even then, "sometimes proceeded to blows" during their disputes, as evidence of which a Franciscan father showed him a large scar on his arm, apparently bestowed by a Greek priest in one such set-to. 2002 saw a fist-fight between Ethiopians and Copts over the positioning of a chair on the roof (see p.63), and in 2004, Greeks and Catholics came to blows because the Franciscan friars had left open the door of their chapel during a Greek Orthodox ceremony. The most recent flare-up occurred on Palm Sunday in 2008 when the Armenians tried to (literally) kick out a Greek priest who was present at one of their ceremonies in apparent violation of the Status Quo; this sparked off a violent brawl in which two Armenian worshippers were arrested. Since no sect will trust the others with the **key**, the church is opened and closed daily by a local Muslim family who have been its custodians since the twelfth century.

"nigh to the city". The site's authenticity is not accepted by everyone, however: some believe that Jesus was buried in the Garden Tomb on Nablus Road outside the present-day city walls (see p.111).

Constantine's church was destroyed by the Persians in 614 AD and restored two years later by the Greeks. When he accepted the surrender of Jerusalem in 638 AD, the Muslim caliph **Omar Ibn al-Khattab** declined to pray in the church on the grounds that his doing so would encourage his Muslim followers to convert the building into a mosque. "Such generosity," notes Jerome Murphy-O'Connor, author of the *Archaeological Guide to the Holy Land* (see p.285), "had unfortunate consequences; had the church become a mosque it would not have been destroyed by the Fatimid caliph Hakim in 1009". Al-Hakim – known for his excesses as Egypt's Caligula but revered as divine by the Druze religion – had the church razed, but the Byzantines rebuilt it in 1048, with the permission of his son and successor, Al-Zahir. Fifty-one years later it was the target of the invading European **Crusader** armies, who built the structure you see today. The church was again damaged by a fire in 1808, allegedly started by a drunken monk who then tried to douse it with aquavit. The main doorway of Constantine's 384 AD church still survives at the back of Zaltimo's Sweets at 172 Souq Khan al-Zeit (see p.62).

The entrance

The **entrance** in use today dates from 1048. Its two doorways – of which the right-hand one has long since been blocked up – are classic Crusader constructions, their arches almost round in the Romanesque style, but just slightly pointed, and decorated with the same fluted border seen on the upper window of the Church of St Anne (see p.57). The two large windows immediately above exactly echo the form of the doorways. At one time, there was also a **side entrance**, now blocked off, which can be seen in Christian Quarter Road, opposite the end of Greek Orthodox Patriarchate Road. The right-hand archway of the main entrance has likewise been blocked up, leaving only the left-hand one. The steps to the right of the entrance originally led up to Calvary, but that route is also now blocked, and Calvary can now only be reached from inside the church (see opposite).

Hanging from the window above the blocked-up right-hand doorway of the main entrance, you'll see a ladder. Known as the "**immovable ladder**", it has been there since before the reaffirmation of the Status Quo in 1852. According to one story, the Armenians placed it there to climb out of the window onto the ledge for a spot of fresh air in the days when the Ottomans taxed Christian clergy every time they entered or left the church. Though the Armenians claim ownership of the windows and ledge, the Greeks claim that the ledge is theirs. They therefore disputed the Armenians' right to use the ladder, and it cannot be removed until the dispute is settled. Indeed, if it goes rotten, it must be replaced.

The Stone of Unction

Immediately inside the church's main entrance, the **Stone of Unction** (or Stone of Anointing) is a limestone slab which, according to Greek tradition, marks the spot where Christ was removed from the cross, while Roman Catholics believe that Jesus was anointed here before burial. You'll see many worshippers prostrating themselves to kiss the stone, but in fact the slab itself is not even supposed to be the one on which Jesus was laid – it was placed here to mark the location in 1810, replacing the twelfth-century original which was smashed when the rotunda collapsed in the 1808 fire. Behind it, on a wall built by the Greek Orthodox Church over the graves of four Crusader kings, is a recent but very impressive mosaic depicting the crucifixion and burial of Christ.

Calvary (Golgotha)

The site of the crucifixion – **Calvary** or **Golgotha**, the place of the skull – is to the right of the Stone of Unction as you enter the church, up a steep flight of stairs. At the top of the stairs is a room containing three altars. On the right is the Roman Catholic **Altar of the Crucifixion** containing the tenth and eleventh stations of the cross (each marked on the altar table), where Jesus was stripped and then nailed to the wood. On the left, the glittery **Greek Orthodox Altar** covers a silver-inlaid hole marking the twelfth station of the cross – the spot where **Christ's cross** stood. In the middle is the **Stabat Mater**, the thirteenth station of the cross, marked by a statue of Mary, her heart pierced with a sword representing grief. This is where Jesus's body was taken down from the cross and given to his mother and also where, according to the Catholics, Mary stood at the foot of the cross. The statue was given to the church by the queen of Portugal in 1778.

The Chapel of Adam

Underneath Calvary, the Greek Orthodox **Chapel of Adam** is supposed to be where the biblical character Adam, the first man (Genesis 2:7), was buried. Christians have believed since at least the second century that Adam was buried here, although Jewish tradition has it that he was buried on Temple Mount.

At the back of the chapel are two stone benches. These previously housed the tombs of the (Catholic) Crusader kings Godfrey of Bouillon and Baldwin I, but the Greeks removed them in 1809.

▲ Priest at the Chapel of Copts, Holy Sepulchre

The Rotunda

On the other side of the Stone of Unction, under a marble canopy, is the **Stone of the Three Women**, marking the spot where the Armenians believe Jesus's mother Mary, her sister and Mary Magdalene stood by the cross (as opposed to the Catholics, who believe Mary stood at Stabat Mater; see p.67).

Past the Stone of the Three Women is the **Rotunda**, the only part of the church (apart from some of its foundations) that survives from Constantine's original structure, an eleven-metre-high dome supported by eighteen massive columns. Above them, concentric rows of round arches reach up towards the centre of the dome, a window surrounded by golden sun-rays and stars, all of which are modern, dating from 1997.

Beneath the dome is the fourteenth and final station of the cross – the **Holy Sepulchre** or **Tomb of Christ** itself – inside a kiosk-like marble tomb monument called the **Edicule**, which was built over the original rock burial chamber. Rebuilt in the eleventh century (after the original was destroyed by Al-Hakim), again in 1555, and again after the 1808 fire, the current structure seems to incorporate all of the earlier ones, plus the original rock tomb, all wrapped inside it like the layers of an onion. The tomb is set amidst a glittering jumble of 43 lamps provided by the various denominations. Entrance to the chamber is through an anteroom, the **Chapel of the Angel**, which contains the stone on which the angel sat to tell of Christ's resurrection (Matthew 28:1). The tomb chamber room itself is tiny, and able to hold only four people at a time, so be prepared to wait in line. A fragment of the original tomb can be seen in the **Chapel of the Copts**, at the back of the Edicule.

Opposite the Chapel of the Copts, in the fourth-century Constantinian walls, is the **Syrian Jacobite Chapel**, which looks abandoned; this is because it was damaged by fire and, owing to Greek objections, the Syrians have not yet been able to obtain the consent of the other sects to restore it. A low door behind the chapel leads into a Jewish **rock tomb** dating from the first century, and said by some (on no particular evidence) to be the final resting place of Joseph of Arimathea, who provided the tomb, according to two of the Gospels his own, for Jesus (Matthew 27:57–60; Mark 15:42-47; Luke 24:50–53; John 19:38–42). Whether or not, however, this tomb really is Joseph's, its presence here is further evidence that the site was at that time outside the walls of the city, since burials would not have taken place within them.

The Katholikon and Eastern Chapels

Opposite the Rotunda, the main Crusader church or **Katholikon** now belongs to the Greek Orthodox Church – its principal feature is its domed ceiling, faced with golden mosaic tiles. The marble basin under the dome, the *omphalos* or "Navel of the World". The name comes from a time in the Middle Ages when the world was thought (in Europe) to have three parts – Europe, Asia and Africa – joined by the Holy Land and in particular Jerusalem: this spot was held by Christians to be the very centre of the world, where the three parts met (Muslims, on the other hand, reckoned it to be the rock in the Dome, and Jews the Temple's Holy of Holies).

Beyond the Katholikon, at the eastern end of the church, the domed twelfth-century Armenian **Chapel of St Helena** is one of the most attractive places in the church, with its chandelier, floor mosaic and Crusader vaulted ceiling. On the stairs going down to it, the walls are covered with crosses scratched by medieval pilgrims. In the right-hand corner, another flight of steps leads down

The Miracle of the Holy Fire

Every year, at 2pm on Holy Saturday (the day before the Orthodox Easter Sunday), a **miracle** occurs in the Holy Sepulchre. After a grand procession around the church, all the lights inside are put out, and the Greek Orthodox Patriarch enters alone into the Holy Sepulchre itself carrying a bundle of candles. When he emerges, lo and behold, the candles have been miraculously lit with a clear white or blue flame which is used to light the candles of the congregation.

This miracle of the Holy Fire has been performed since at least the early ninth century. In 947 the Abbasid Caliphs, calling the ceremony a "magic ritual", tried to put a stop to it, but were unable to keep the crowds of pilgrims away, and in 1101 the Crusaders gave the ritual to the Catholics, who failed to get the Holy Fire to work. When the Armenians tried to take over in 1579, it is said, the fire sprang out of the tomb and split asunder one of the pillars of the church.

Today the ritual attracts thousands of pilgrims, and the church is already jam-packed by around 7am on the day. Lack of sufficient crowd control led to some 400 people being crushed or suffocated to death in 1834, a scene the Israeli police are not keen to have repeated, and they therefore block off the surrounding streets as soon as the church is full. The event is broadcast live on TV in Orthodox countries such as Russia and Greece, and flames lit with the holy fire are flown out to Orthodox countries within hours of the event.

Obviously, not everybody believes that the holy fire really is a pukka miracle, but if it's a trick, nobody has so far been able to demonstrate how it works, though one suggestion is that the candles are previously dipped in self-igniting phosphorous. In his book *Miracle or Deception? – the "Holy Light" of Jerusalem* (available only in Greek), sceptic Michael Kalopoulos claims to have replicated the Holy Fire, but the faithful continue to believe anyway. A website at ⓦ www.holyfire.org is dedicated to the miracle.

into the **Chapel of the Finding of the Cross**. This is supposed to be the cistern where, with the assistance of a Jew named Judas, St Helena found the True Cross (nails and all), but actually it's part of a seventh-century BC quarry where high-quality building stone was hewn from underneath the inferior rock which now forms the ceiling. Behind the Catholic altar (the one on the left, the other one being Greek Orthodox), the life-size statue of Helena with the Cross was donated in 1855 by an Austrian aristocrat, Archduke Ferdinand Maximilian Joseph (later, emperor of Mexico).

The Muristan

Immediately south of the Holy Sepulchre is the area known as the **Muristan** – a group of unnamed little streets set around a square with several cafés and restaurants, and an ornate (but dry) fountain built in 1903 to mark the silver jubilee of the Ottoman sultan Abd al-Hamid II. The area was once crowded with lodging houses for pilgrims and travellers which is how it gets its name – "Muristan" is Persian for hospital or hospice. Today you'll find a number of churches and other religious institutions here, and in the Greek bazaar known as **Souq Aftimos** to its south, shops crammed with tourist paraphernalia – leather goods in particular.

The Muristan was originally the main forum of Hadrian's city, Aelia Capitolina. Charlemagne founded the pilgrims' enclave here in the early ninth century, and although it was damaged in 1009 when the Fatimid caliph Al-Hakim had the Church of the Holy Sepulchre demolished (see p.66), many of the buildings were restored in the eleventh century by a group of merchants from Amalfi in Italy (then an independent republic).

On the west side of the Muristan, overlooking the fountain, **St John's Hospice**, has been occupied since April 1990 by Jewish settlers from a group called Ateret Cohanim, and is identifiable by the Israeli flags hanging from its upper windows.

The Church of St John the Baptist

In the southwest corner of the square, but entered from Christian Quarter Road, the **Church of St John the Baptist** (no regular hours: ring the bell during daytime to request entry) is the oldest church in Jerusalem. Dating originally from the fifth century, it is one of the buildings renovated by the Amalfi merchants, though the two small bell towers framing a striking blue-domed roof are later additions. The Crusader order of the Knights of St John of Jerusalem (also known as the Knights Hospitallers) was founded here, and will be familiar to many visitors in their modern form as the St John Ambulance charity. The church, which is Greek Orthodox, has a gilded altar screen, and its interior is decorated with icons of John the Baptist; one of them (on the right just inside the entrance) incorporates what is said to be a fragment of his skull.

The Mosque of Omar

In the northwest corner of the square, facing onto Souq al-Dabbagha, the true **Mosque of Omar** (not to be confused with the Dome of the Rock, which is sometimes mistakenly referred to by the same name) was built in 1193 to commemorate Caliph Omar's prayers in the courtyard of the Holy Sepulchre in 638 (see p.66). Entered via St Helena Street off Christian Quarter Road, it is closed to non-Muslims. Its distinctive square minaret, dating from the mid-fifteenth century, incorporates Crusader masonry in its base. The top of the minaret is in the same style and (despite the difference in ground level) at exactly the same altitude as a minaret added in 1417 to the twelfth-century **Salahiya Khanqah** (a hostel for Sufi mystics) on the corner of Aqabat al-Khanqah with Christian Quarter Road; the mid-point of a line drawn between the two minarets is directly over the entrance to the Tomb of Christ in the Holy Sepulchre, an alignment that must be deliberate. Muslims revere Jesus as a prophet, though they do not believe that he was crucified (Koran 4:157).

The Lutheran Church

The imposing and rather austere-looking **Lutheran Church of the Redeemer** (Mon–Fri 9am–12.30pm & 1–3pm, Sat 9am–12.30pm; ⓦwww .evangelisch-in-jerusalem.org) in the northeast corner of the Muristan, was commissioned by German Crown Prince Friedrich Wilhelm, who bought the site during a visit in 1869. It was built over St Mary of the Latins, a church erected by the Amalfi merchants that had fallen into a state of disrepair, and traces of the original church remain in the medieval northern gate, decorated with the signs of the zodiac and the symbols of the months. It's well worth climbing to the top of the tower (5NIS) for wonderful **views** over the Old City – you can make out the shape of the Holy Sepulchre and see as far as the Mount of Olives and Mount Zion. The church is sometimes used for concerts of classical or liturgical music (see p.202).

The Alexander Hospice

Opposite the Lutheran Church's northern entrance on Souq al-Dabbagha, the **Alexander Hospice** (daily 9am–6pm; 5NIS) is not really a hospice at all, but a centre for the Russian Orthodox mission in Jerusalem, built in 1881 to accommodate pilgrims. Inside it is the church of Jerusalem's Russian Orthodox community – St Alexander's Russian Chapel, which is open only for prayers, on Thursday mornings at 7am. Steps to the right of the entrance as you go in lead down to the **excavations** beneath the chapel, which have revealed sections of the Herodian city's second northern wall, indicating that Calvary was indeed outside the city walls in Jesus's time, a fact disputed by those who doubt the authenticity of the Holy Sepulchre as the site of the crucifixion (see p.65). There are also remnants of an arch from the time of Hadrian which may have led into the Forum of Aelia Capitolina. This vies with the Seventh Station of the Cross (see p.62) as the site of the Gate of Judgement.

The New Gate

The **New Gate** (Bab al-Jadid), in the Old City's northwestern corner, was added in 1887 to provide access between the Christian Quarter within the city walls and new Christian properties outside them. It leads into one of the quietest parts of the Old City, and few tourists use it, as it's off the main routes and away from most of the sights, but there are one or two interesting shops along the way, including Melia arts and crafts (see p.221) and Elia Photos (see p.227), and it is by far the quickest route on foot between West Jerusalem and most parts of the Old City.

Outside the gate, and just to the west, a little garden takes up a bay in the wall's northwest corner. In it are the remains of an eleventh-century tower called **Qasr Jalud** (Goliath Fort), apparently because of a tradition that the biblical King David felled the Philistine giant Goliath with a stone from his sling at this spot, even though the Bible (I Samuel 17:1) says it happened at a place called Sokoh, which is near Hebron.

The Muslim Quarter

T he **Muslim Quarter** is the largest of the Old City's four quarters, and the most classically Middle Eastern in feel with winding market streets, headscarf-clad residents and wonderful Islamic architecture, especially from the Mamluk period (1260–1516). While many of the most beautiful features of these buildings are hidden inside and around internal courtyards, few of them open to the public, their facades are often splendid enough sights in themselves. Aside from the architecture, the quarter's most prominent highlights include the teeming plazas either side of the **Damascus Gate**, and the Roman excavations beneath it, as well as **Souk Khan al-Zeit**, the Old City's liveliest shopping street, where you can buy anything from Middle Eastern sweets to clothes, gold jewellery or music CDs. The quarter's main thoroughfare is **Al-Wad Road** which eventually leads down to the Wailing Wall. Some of the finest examples of Mamluk architecture are found in the little streets leading east from Al-Wad Road to the gates of the Temple Mount compound (Haram al-Sharif). The **Little Wailing Wall** hidden away down the back alleys here, gives a taste of what the larger one must have been like back in Ottoman and Mandate times. At the southern boundary of the quarter, **Bab al-Silsila Street** is full of more interesting Islamic buildings. The Muslim Quarter is also traversed by the **Via Dolorosa**, believed to be the route taken by Jesus to his place of execution (though this is covered in chapter two; see pp.58–62).

The most direct approach to the Muslim Quarter is from the north via the bustling **Damascus Gate**, itself one of the sights of the quarter. Buses #1 and #2 from West Jerusalem run past the Damascus Gate, **Herod's Gate** and the **Lions' Gate**, all points of access to the Muslim Quarter.

The Damascus Gate

Always busy, with bustling market areas on either side, the **Damascus Gate** is the largest, most elaborate and heavily fortified of the Old City's seven gates, topped by battlements, with loopholes for firing from, and turrets on either side. The large opening directly above the entrance was used to rain down boiling oil or heavy missiles on invaders trying to enter. Within, the gate is chicaned with a double right-angle turn, again to impede hostile invaders. Nowadays the main conduit between East Jerusalem and the Muslim Quarter, the top of the gate (which you can visit on the Ramparts Walk; see p.50) gives a **view** over the comings and goings on either side, and is a favoured vantage point for Israeli

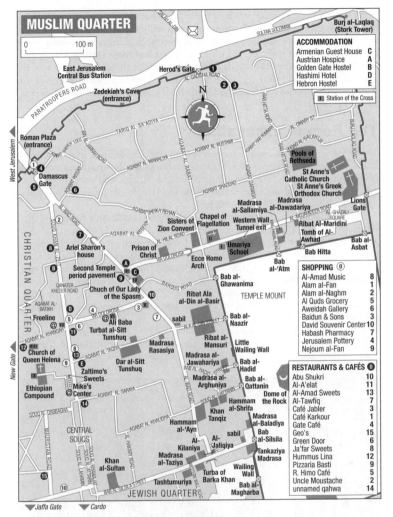

troops in times of trouble. The gate is said to have been designed by Suleiman the Magnificent's famous chief architect, Koca Sinan (see box, p.49) and is the only city gate to have been excavated, revealing a Roman gate and plaza beneath. The Damascus Gate is one of the points at which you can begin the **Ramparts Walk** around the walls of Jerusalem (see p.50), heading east towards the Lions' Gate, or west towards the Jaffa Gate.

Outside the gate

One of the best places to absorb the atmosphere of Jerusalem is on the steps outside the city walls leading down from Sultan Suleiman Street to the Damascus Gate. Here the whole of the city's eastern half seems to converge in a melee of pilgrims, shoppers and tourists streaming in and out of the Old City past assorted beggars, street traders, *tamar hindi* (tamarind cordial) vendors in their wine-red costumes, and country women selling fruit and veg. From stalls around the gate you can get snacks, local sweets, clothing, food, even phone chargers. The place really buzzes on Fridays and Saturdays and on Jewish and Muslim holidays, when thousands of worshippers pass through on their way to pray at the Wailing Wall or Al-Aqsa Mosque, while towards the end of Ramadan the gateway is festooned with bright lights and the whole area is awake till late at night.

The Roman excavations

To the right of the gate, as you look at it from the outside, steps lead down and under the footway (where there's a small café) to the **Roman excavations** (Sat–Thurs 9am–4pm, Fri 9am–1pm; 10NIS, no tickets sold on Saturday but can be bought in advance, or, if you can read Hebrew, online at Ⓦwww.pami .co.il; combined ticket 55NIS – see p.50).

Underneath the gate and predating it by 1400 years, **Hadrian's Arch** is all that survives of a triumphal gateway commissioned by Emperor Hadrian in 135 AD as part of his new town, Aelia Capitolina. Down at what was, in Roman times, street level, it was the eastern flanking arch of a triple gateway much like the Ecce Homo arch (see p.60), the main, central span being directly underneath the modern gate entrance. The arch leads through to the **Roman Plaza** – a pavement of huge irregular stones that formed the start of the Cardo (see opposite). At the centre of the plaza, Hadrian had a column erected, which originally bore a statue of him and later, in Byzantine times, a cross. Both the gateway and column are clearly depicted on the Madaba Map (see p.8) and it was this column (*'amud* in Arabic) that gave the gate its Arabic name – **Bab al-'Amud** (Gate of the Column); the English name, and also the Hebrew, **Sha'ar Shekhem**

▲ Traders outside the Damascus Gate

(Nablus Gate), reflect the fact that it stands at the start of the ancient road (still called the Nablus Road) which heads north to Nablus and Damascus. Hadrian's arch was apparently built on the site of an older gate installed in what was then an outer wall of the city under Herod Agrippa in 41 AD.

In a recess at the side of the exposed section of the Roman Plaza, you can see where bored Roman soldiers carved a **gaming board** into one of the paving stones to help them while away the time. The old Roman guard tower (the area to your left as you enter through Hadrian's arch) was evidently put to use in Byzantine or Ummayad times as an olive oil factory; you can still see the **oil press** with its large millstone, which was probably turned by a donkey or an ox. The oil factory gave its name to the shopping street Souq Khan al-Zeit (see below). The millstone was evidently made from an old column, and it has even been speculated that this could have been Hadrian's original column, which has never been found. The wooden parts of the oil press are of course modern reconstructions.

Inside the gate

Within the gate itself, you'll find moneychangers and a music shop (see p.226), and through it on the inner side, you emerge onto a busy **plaza**, on several levels with steps and ramps to help it down a steep slope. The plaza is flanked by cafés (see p.182) where you can sit and watch the varied assortment of people passing through the gate. Shops and stalls along the stepped plaza sell *ka'ak* (bread rings), falafel, sweets, juices and assorted snacks, while itinerant vendors proffer an array of goods you never knew you wanted. Just to the west of the gate entrance, a small passage leads through to a busy little square where clothes are sold. At the bottom of the plaza, the road forks into two main thoroughfares through the Old City, both of which follow the course of streets built under Hadrian: to the right, Souq Khan al-Zeit, the main north–south artery (the Roman Cardo Maximus), and to the left Al-Wad Road (the lesser Roman Cardo), which leads through the heart of the Muslim Quarter to the Wailing Wall.

Souq Khan al-Zeit and around

The western fork leading south from the Damascus Gate is **Souq Khan al-Zeit** (the Market of Inn of the Oil), a chaotic, tunnel-like market street full of shops and shoppers, not to mention the smells, sounds and colours of the spices, music, clothing and household goods it sells. Traversed by the Via Dolorosa, the street is named after the oil factory whose press can still be seen beneath the Damascus gate (see above). Originally Hadrian's Cardo Maximus, the main thoroughfare of Roman and Byzantine Jerusalem, this street is nearly two thousand years old, and divides the Muslim and Christian Quarters. As the busiest shopping street in the Old City, it can often get jam-packed – fine if you're simply browsing, frustrating if you want to get somewhere. The main bottleneck is at the Seventh Station of the Cross (see p.61), where the Via Dolorosa crosses it, and which invariably seems to have a large group of pilgrims standing outside it. To get through, boys pushing heavily loaded barrows (the main form of transport in the souq) give due warning of their approach: if you hear a voice yelling "Alo, Alo", hit the wall. Everything from nuts and designer clothes to electrical goods, CDs, tapes and

DVDs, shoes, and pots and pans can be found here, and if the shop you're in doesn't have it, the owner's brother a few doors down probably will. Of all the streets in the Old City, this is the most atmospheric, loud, crowded and exciting by day, but pretty much dead, and actually quite eerie after 8pm when all the shops are closed and the crowds gone home.

The central souqs

Souq Khan al-Zeit continues down to the **central souqs** – a covered area of three parallel streets, which has been the centre of the Old City and its market since Byzantine times. **Souq al-Attarin**, straight ahead, originally a market for spices and perfumes, now sells mainly clothes, as does its offshoot **Souq al-Khawajat**, originally a market for gold. Both are narrower than Souq Khal al-Zeit, but less frenetic, and actually less of a squash. **Souq al-Lahamin**, to their west, is the meat market, and definitely not for the squeamish – delights on offer include numerous varieties of offal, and whole sheep's heads complete with eyes. The wire mesh covering the gaps in the market's roof was installed by the city council after Jewish extremists dropped a grenade from above in 1992, killing one of the shopkeepers and injuring several others.

The central souqs form a junction at the centre of the Old City where all four quarters meet. From their northern end, Souq al-Dabbagha leads west to the Muristan and Holy Sepulchre (see p.64). From their southern end, the Cardo (or, if that is closed, Jewish Quarter Road) will take you south along the western edge of the Jewish Quarter, David Street leads west and uphill to the Jaffa Gate, and Bab al-Silsila Street (see pp.81–82) descends east towards the Wailing Wall and the Temple Mount compound.

Al-Wad Road

Al-Wad Road (Tariq al-Wad), the eastern fork which splits off from Souq Khan al-Zeit at the bottom of the stairs inside the Damascus Gate, is the chief route from East Jerusalem to the Temple Mount compound and the Wailing Wall, cutting across the Via Dolorosa on the way and marking the course of the **Tyropoeon Valley** (*Al-Wad* means "the valley"), which runs southeast right through the city. Like Souq Khan al-Zeit it has been one of the main roads through the Old City since Roman times, and is clearly shown on the Madaba Map (see box, p.8), but unlike Souq Khan al-Zeit, it is more a thoroughfare than a shopping street, a lot less crowded, and generally free-flowing. It also tends to have a more religious flavour, as it's used both by Muslims heading to the Temple Mount compound, and by Jews heading to the Wailing Wall. North of the Via Dolorosa, the streets off to the east (the left if coming from the Damascus Gate) lead into the Muslim Quarter's main residential area, and to Herod's Gate (see p.82). South of the Via Dolorosa, they lead to various gates of the Temple Mount compound. Along these streets, **Ala al-Din Street**, **Bab al-Hadid Street** and **Souq al-Qattanin** you'll find several ornate *madrasas* and other Islamic buildings although note that these streets can often be off-limits to non-Muslims (see box opposite).

Because it adjoins Temple Mount and leads to the Wailing Wall, this area of the Old City, as well as Bab al-Silsila Street (see p.81), is a major target for **Jewish settlers** (see also box, p.273) This further south you go along Al-Wad Rad towards

3

No entry!

Note that **non-Muslims** may be barred from entering streets leading to the gates of the Temple Mount compound from Al-Wad Road, the assumption being that you intend to enter the Temple Mount through one of the Muslim-only gates (non-Muslims may enter through the Bab al-Magharba alongside the Wailing Wall, see p.99). You should be able to explain to the Israeli police who cordon off the entrances (or local residents who may also object) that you do not intend to go onto the Mount itself and should therefore be allowed to look around, but this cannot be guaranteed.

the Wailing Wall the more noticeable this becomes with several buildings taken over as homes, *yeshivas* or religious bookshops. Predictably, there is a certain amount of friction with the quarter's majority Palestinian population. Although the tension is not as raw now as it sometimes has been, the undercurrent is always there and sometimes quite noticeable.

Ariel Sharon's house

One of the most visible settler homes in the quarter is that of **Ariel Sharon**, Israel's Prime Minister from 2001 to 2006, a man particularly loathed by Palestinians, who hold him responsible, as defence minister in 1982, for massacres by Lebanese Phalangists at the Beirut Palestinian refugee camps of Sabra and Shatila. It was Sharon's provocative excursion onto Temple Mount in September 2000 (see p.101) that sparked off the second Intifada and finally scuppered the Oslo Peace Accord. His house, above an archway spanning the street about 50m down from the junction with Souq Khan al-Zeit, is easily recognizable: while most settlers fly Israeli flags from their houses, Sharon's has two hanging all the way down its south side, and a large menorah (Jewish candelabra) on top. This gesture, aimed at the local Palestinian population, is just that, however: Sharon occasionally spent the night, but he never actually lived here.

The Austrian Hospice

About 100m further down on the left, the Via Dolorosa (see p.58) leads eastwards to the Lions' Gate (see p.55). At its junction with Al-Wad Road, the **Austrian Hospice** (see p.165 for accommodation details) opened in 1857 as the first national pilgrims' hospice in the Holy Land. It was seized by the British as German property in 1939 and given by them to Jordan as a hospital in 1948. Taken by the Israelis in 1967, part of it was used by them as a police post before it was finally returned to the Austrian Catholic church, who reopened it as a guesthouse in 1988.

Beyond the hospice (if you are heading south), **streets off Al-Wad** to the east – Ala al-Din Street (see below), Bab al-Hadid Street (see p.78) and Souq al-Qattanin (see p.80) – lead to the gates of the Temple Mount compound (only Muslims may enter through these gates) and contain some particularly fine Islamic buildings. Al-Wad itself ends up at the entrance tunnel leading to the Wailing Wall esplanade.

Ala al-Din Street (the "African Quarter")

A hundred metres south of the Austrian Hospice, Al-Wad Road reaches a junction where an Ottoman fountain on the east side (one of six installed under

Suleiman the Magnificent; see p.80) indicates the beginning of **Ala al-Din Street**. Also known variously as Bab al-Naazir Street, Inspector's Gate Street, Bab al-Habs Street or Prison Gate Street, it leads to Bab al-Naazir (Inspector's Gate), one of the entrances to the Temple Mount compound. The street has been dubbed **"the African Quarter"**, as it is home to a close-knit black community of "Afro-Palestinians", a term used by members of the community themselves. They are descended from African Muslims who came to Jerusalem on pilgrimage when it was under British and Jordanian rule. Many of them live in the building on the right, **Ribat al-Mansuri**, whose two finely decorated windows belong to a large and impressively restored main hall. The monumental entrance arch of distinctive red and cream stone opens into a large and impressive vaulted porch – the inscription states that it was built in 1282 by Sultan Al-Mansur. Opposite, **Ribat Ala al-Din al-Basir** is one of the earliest Mamluk buildings in Jerusalem. Founded in 1267 as a pilgrims' hospice, it has an arched gateway with stone benches (*mastabas*) on either side. The cells around the inner courtyard were put to less religious use when the *ribats* were used as prisons by the Turks (Al-Mansuri for those condemned to a sentence, Al-Basir for those condemned to death) – a function they served until 1914, giving the street one of its alternative names, Bab al-Habs Street (Prison Gate Street). On the right of the courtyard is al-Basir's burial chamber.

Aqabat al-Taqiya

Across Al-Wad, directly opposite Ala al-Din Street, **Aqabat al-Taqiya** leads up to meet Souq Khan al-Zeit. The third building on the left as you go up Aqabat al-Taqiya is noticeably Mamluk, with lots of *ablaq* but an unusual scalloped arch over the doorway; this is the **Madrasa Rasasiya**, dating from the early sixteenth century and one of Jerusalem's last Mamluk buildings. The name *Rasasiya*, meaning "of lead", comes from the lead which was used instead of mortar to join its stones.

Further up Aqabat al-Taqiya, no. 30, on its southern side, is one of the finest Mamluk facades in the Old City. It belongs to **Dar al-Sitt Tunshuq**, the palace of Lady Tunshuq, whose story appears to be one of rags to riches, as she seems to have been a slave of Central Asian origin, but she must have been very rich in later life to have had this grand mansion built. Of its three doorways, the easternmost is surmounted by *murqanas* (see box opposite), though the beautiful inlay around the window has deteriorated badly, and most has fallen out over the years. Uphill slightly, the middle doorway, which leads to a carpentry workshop, is less lofty than the other two, topped by an *ablaq* in red, white and black stone, with jigsaw-like *ablaq* work in black and white above the lintel and around the small round window over the door. The westernmost doorway, though also rather deteriorated, still preserves much of the fine, multicoloured inlay around the window above the door, around which snakes a frieze of Arabic calligraphy. Lady Tunshuq died in 1398. Her last resting place is a tomb inside the **Turbat al-Sitt Tunshuq** opposite the eastern doorway of her mansion at no. 33, again decorated with *ablaq*, including some particularly well-executed jigsaw-like *ablaq* above the windows.

Bab al-Hadid Street

The next street off Al-Wad Road, heading south from Ala al-Din Street, is the winding **Bab al-Hadid Street**, peeling east off Al-Wad to another of the Temple Mount's entrances, Bab al-Hadid (the Iron Gate). Along here are some

Mamluk architecure in the Old City

The **Mamluks** were a series of army chiefs who took over the Egyptian empire, including Palestine, from Saladin's Ayyubid successors in 1250, and ran it until they were ousted by the Ottomans in 1516 (see p.271). At the start of the Mamluk period, Jerusalem was part of the Syrian province whose capital was Damascus, but in 1376 its status was raised and its governor appointed directly from the Mamluk capital, Cairo. This increased importance was reflected in the construction of many beautiful buildings – colleges, hospices and mausoleums – all over the city and the restoration of existing ones. Mamluk buildings are noted for the lightness of their design, the distinctive arched entrances and the use of red, white and black striped masonry, known as **ablaq**, possibly derived from the Roman technique of *opus mixtum* in which stone and brick were alternated. Another typical feature of Mamluk architecture are the stalactite-like decorations, called **murqanas**, which adorn the inside of domes or the tops of doorways and recesses. The Mamluks also developed kufic lettering – the oldest form of Arabic script, superseded by the joined-up *naskhi* script used in modern Arabic inscriptions – to its most ornate form, and the geometric arabesques which are now familiar features of Muslim decoration were also developed by the Mamluks; other common artistic flourishes include elaborate bronze work on doors, carved wooden pulpits, beautiful mosaics and stained glass. Calligraphy and geometrical designs are especially important in Islamic art, which avoids "graven images" of people or animals. During the Mamluks' 250-year reign, there were over fifty rulers, and prominent members of previous regimes were often exiled to Jerusalem when power changed hands, adding further to the number of fine Mamluk buildings in the city.

A detailed study of Jerusalem's Mamluk architecture can be found in the excellent (but expensive and hard-to-find) *Mamluk Jerusalem* by Michael Burgoyne (see p.287).

madrasas (schools of Islamic learning) that are among the finest Mamluk buildings in the city. Opposite the junction, on Al-Wad Road, a white **marble plaque** inscribed in Hebrew marks the spot where a Jewish settler was murdered in 1991 by two Palestinian youths.

Down towards the other end of Bab al-Hadid Street, on the north side as you approach Bab al-Hadid, is the plain red and white *ablaq* doorway of the **Madrasa al-Jawhariya**. The Jawhariya (closed to the public) was also a hospice and traditionally housed important visitors to Jerusalem – one of the two *qadis* (judges) sent from Cairo in 1475 to mediate in the dispute over the Ramban Synagogue (see p.95) received a delegation of the Jewish community at his lodgings here.

Opposite, the cruciform 1358 **Madrasa al-Arghuniya** (now residential and not open to the public) stands behind another red and white stone arch. Around its inner vaulted courtyard are the tombs of Argun al-Kamili (the *madrasa's* founder) and **Sharif Hussein bin Ali**, Sharif of Mecca and leader of the Arab Revolt against the Turks in World War I. The Sharif joined the Allies after being given assurances of support for the foundation of an independent Arab state – at much the same time as Britain and France were plotting to carve up the area between them.

A simple, cream-coloured arch, originally part of the Madrasa al-Arghuniya, now leads into its contemporary, the **Madrasa al-Khatuniya**, just to the east. The long vaulted passage opens into a courtyard enclosed by cells, an assembly hall and a domed chamber. On the other side of the archway is **Madrasa al-Muzhariya**, commissioned in 1480 by Abu Bakr Ibn Muzhir – one-time head of the Chancery Bureau in Cairo – who left his mark all over the Arab world, financing two public fountains in Mecca, a *ribat* and *madrasa* in Medina and another in Cairo. Here, the tall entrance arch is decorated with black and white mosaics and, to the left of the doorway, a pair of identical iron-grilled windows are finely embellished with red and cream stone on grey marble. The inner courtyard is surrounded by rooms once used by students, but which are now family homes.

The Little Wailing Wall

If you want an idea of what the Wailing Wall looked like before the Western Wall Esplanade was opened up in 1967, head down the passage leading off to the left at the very end of Bab al-Hadid Street. This will take you to the **Little Wailing Wall** (HaKotel HaQatan), a short length of the western supporting wall of the Temple Mount compound, surrounded by houses, as the Wailing Wall itself was before the demolition of the Magharba Quarter (see p.88). Because it has not been excavated, only the two bottom rows of stones are original, as you can clearly see from their size (lower layers can be seen in the Western Wall Tunnel, which passes underneath you here; see p.91). Some religious Jews actually prefer this location for prayer to the proper Wailing Wall, partly because it is quieter, but mainly because it is closer to the actual location of the Jewish temples of Solomon and Herod.

Souq al-Qattanin

East off Al-Wad at the junction with Aqabat al-Khalidiya, and linking it with Bab al-Qattanin in the western wall of the Temple Mount, the tunnel-like **Souq al-Qattanin** (Cotton Merchants' Market) was one of several new markets added to Jerusalem during the Mamluk period. Built in 1336–37, the covered souq was designed as a commercial centre for Sultan Al-Nazir Mohammed and Emir Tanqiz al-Nasiri, a celebrated Mamluk governor of Damascus (1312–40). Monumental entrances graced each end, shops, with living quarters above, ran all the way along its length, and there were also two public bathhouses and a caravanserai. By the nineteenth century, the Souq al-Qattanin had fallen into decay; it was restored by the Waqf and re-opened in 1974. Now once again a fully functioning souq, its wide vaulted roof gives it a rather cavernous, almost subterranean feel. It's at its busiest around prayer times, when Muslim worshippers pass through on their way to or from the Temple Mount. While the souq is usually off-limits to non-Muslims, you should be allowed to look around if you explain that you do not want to go onto the Mount. On Friday evenings, Jewish groups hold a prayer meeting here in protest at the fact they are not allowed to pray on the Temple Mount itself.

On the corner where Souq al-Qattanin meets Al-Wad, a traditional bathhouse, **Hammam al-'Ayn**, has long been closed, though restoration is promised from time to time. Another old bathhouse, the Hammam al-Shrifa, further along the street on the right, has also long since seen its last bather. Next to it, the **Khan Tanqiz**, an old caravanserai like the Khan al-Sultan (see p.82) is now Al-Quds University's Centre of Jerusalem Studies, not officially open to the public, but they'll almost certainly let you in for a look if you ask.

On Al-Wad Road, just south of the junction with Souq al-Qattanin, you'll notice a decorated **Ottoman sabil** (drinking fountain) dating from 1536. It was part of the same building plan, ordered by Suleiman the Magnificent, which included the reconstruction of the ramparts (see p.271). Suleiman had six of these *sabils* installed in the Old City.

The Holy City
Religious buildings in Jerusalem

Jerusalem's skyline has been dominated by places of worship ever since King David installed the Ark of the Covenant and Solomon built his Temple around it. Today you are unlikely to leave the city without visiting a synagogue, mosque or church, and understanding how these buildings work can help give you an insight into the city's major religions, and the different ways in which their members gather to pray together

Synagogues

Synagogues always face Temple Mount, a direction indicated by a cupboard called the ark (*aron kodesh*). This contains the handwritten Torah scrolls (*sefer torah*). The scrolls are taken out and read to the congregation in weekly instalments from a platform in the middle of the synagogue called the *bima*. A perpetual light called the *ner tamid* hangs in front of the ark, and next to the ark is the pulpit (usually just a seat) from which the rabbi preaches his sermon. In an Orthodox synagogue, men and women pray apart, sometimes separated by a screen. In larger synagogues, women sit upstairs in the ladies' gallery, like the circle of a theatre, while men sit downstairs in the stalls.

The most impressive synagogue in Jerusalem is the rebuilt Hurva (see p.94), but there's no shortage of fascinating smaller examples around the Jewish Quarter (see p.84) and modern ones such as the Yeshurun and the Great Synagogue in West Jerusalem (see p.128).

Torah scrolls held aloft at the Wailing Wall ▲

Inside the Yohanan ben Zakkai Synagogue ▼

Look out for...

Ablaq Alternating stone blocks of different colours – sometimes black and white, other times red and white – almost a dead giveaway that a building dates from the Mamluk period.

Domes A very common feature in churches (the Holy Sepulchre, for example), synagogues (such as the Hurva) and Mosques (Al-Aqsa), and also, of course, the Dome of the Rock.

Pointed arches We think of them as Gothic, but they were originally Islamic – the very first ones were built in Ramla, a town between Jerusalem and Tel Aviv.

Vaulted ceilings An extension on the idea of a pointed arch, and very typical of Crusader churches.

Mosques

Mosques all face Mecca, the birthplace of Islam and direction of prayer, shown by the *mihrab*, a shallow alcove in the Mecca-facing *qibla* wall. Large mosques usually have a courtyard, sometimes with a fountain for washing before prayer. At the *qibla* end of the courtyard, nearest Mecca, is the prayer hall, ritually pure, and usually separated from the rest of the mosque by a step or balustrade (worshippers remove their shoes before entering).

In a large, congregational mosque (called a *jema'a*, and used for Friday prayer, as opposed to a small, everyday mosque called a *masjid*), the imam (minister) leads prayers and gives his sermon from a *minbar* – a pulpit, usually just a flight of steps in ornately carved wood. Otherwise the prayer hall is bare – the congregation sit on a floor covered with carpets.

Most congregational mosques have a minaret from where the *muezzin* calls the faithful to prayer. Once upon a time the *muezzin* climbed the minaret and called the faithful with lung-power alone; nowadays speakers are used and the call to prayer is usually recorded.

Although not strictly speaking a mosque, Jerusalem's most famous – and beautiful – piece of Islamic religious architecture is, of course, the Dome of the Rock (see p.102). Actual mosques include the nearby Al-Aqsa (see p.104), the Sidi Umar in the Jewish Quarter (see p.95) and the Mosque of Omar (see p.70) in the Christian Quarter – all are closed to non-Muslims. Other Islamic buildings found in Jerusalem include *madrasas* (koranic schools), *sabils* (public fountains for drinking or ablutions), *khans* (merchants' hostels), *ribats* (pilgrims' hostels) and *khanqahs* (hostels for Sufi mendicants).

▲ The Al-Aqsa Mosque, Temple Mount

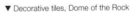
▼ Decorative tiles, Dome of the Rock

All Nations Church, East Jerusalem ▲

Worshipper at the Church of the Holy Sepulchre ▼

Churches

In a Catholic or Orthodox church, the service is directed towards the altar, a table at the front, usually on a raised platform, from which the priest gives communion. The area behind the altar is called the chancel, and it may be where the choir sit. In some Catholic churches, a screen behind the altar separates the chancel from the rest of the church. In an Eastern Orthodox church, a larger screen called the iconostasis, which is covered in icons (images of saints), separates the altar and chancel from the nave, the body of the church in which the congregation sit.

Some churches are built in the form of a cross, created with two wings called transepts on either side of the nave. In a large church, there may also be recessed chapels around the walls, each dedicated to a specific saint, as well as a crypt in the basement, originally used to house holy relics. Many churches will also have a font, a basin of water used for baptism.

In addition to the vast Holy Sepulchre (see p.63), Jerusalem is full of fascinating smaller churches including the Catholic Churches of St Anne near the Lions' Gate (see p.57) and Antonio Barluzzi's Dominus Flevit (see p.119) and All Nations Church (see p.119) on the Mount of Olives.

Jerusalem stone

One of the things that unites Jerusalem's secular and religious buildings is the use of Jerusalem stone, a local pale limestone quarried since ancient times. The stone gives the city its distinctive golden hue, especially in the sunlight of early morning or late afternoon. In 1918 British governor Ronald Storrs made its use compulsory and the rule continues to be observed to this day.

Bab al-Silsila Street

South of Souq al-Qattanin, Al-Wad goes into a tunnel under **Bab al-Silsila Street**, which runs from the centre of the Old City eastwards to the principal gate of the Temple Mount – Bab al-Silsila (Chain Gate). The street crosses Al-Wad on a wide bridge which dates from Herod's time but was rebuilt in the early Islamic period; the eastern part of the bridge is also known as Wilson's Arch (see p.91). Heading south through the tunnel, you pass through a security check and enter the Western Wall Esplanade (see p.89). Otherwise, a stairway on the left leads up onto Bab al-Silsila Street.

Given its location close to the Temple Mount and the presence of militant Jewish settlers (see also p.76), security is tight. The section that leads to Bab al-Silsila itself is now usually guarded by Israeli police who will allow access to Muslims only (see also box, p.77). For non-Muslims therefore, the only way to look at the buildings on that end of the street is to visit Temple Mount via Bab al-Magharba and exit through Bab al-Silsila. For that reason, the eastern end of the street is covered in chapter five (see p.106).

Al-Jaliqiya and Madrasa al-Taziya

The building on the north side of Bab al-Silsila Street immediately west of the stairway down to Al-Wad is **Al-Jaliqiya**, the tomb chamber of Baybars al-Jaliq, a general in the Mamluk army which emerged victorious against the Mongols at the Battle of Homs in 1281. The building is closed to the public, and for some reason hardboard has been placed against the window to prevent you looking in to see Al-Jaliq's tomb through the iron grille. The graceful calligraphy above it is a funerary inscription.

Continuing west on Bab al-Silsila Street, you enter the market area. The buildings now become increasingly difficult to identify, with their facades more often than not draped by clothes and hangings to attract tourists. However, look up and, jutting out at first-floor level over the north side of the street at no. 113, you'll see a carved wooden *mashrabiya* (a screen allowing women to see the street while themselves remaining unobserved), part of the **Madrasa al-Taziya**, which was built in 1362 for the Mamluk emir Sayf al-Din Taz. The emir rose from the position of cup-bearer to Sultan Al-Malik Mohammed to become governor of Aleppo, but was arrested and imprisoned in Alexandria after a palace plot in 1358 – a fall from grace that left him with a relatively plain memorial, its only elaborate decoration a large grilled window with a dedicatory inscription between two cups carved on the lintel. The upper-storey window is typical of nineteenth-century Ottoman construction and is believed to have replaced an earlier Mamluk *mashrabiya*. The building is now a private home.

Al-Kilaniya

Next door to the Al-Taziya, to its west, the three-domed **Al-Kilaniya** is notable for its splendid high arched doorway, decorated with *murqana* stalactites. The building has been described as both a *turba* (tomb) and a *madrasa* (school), and is thought to have been erected in 1352. You can usually get a better view of the doorway and roof by stepping back into Western Wall Road opposite (which leads down into the Western Wall Esplanade), but scaffolding was preventing this on our last check. The central and eastern domes of Al-Kilaniya rest on octagonal drums, while the western one has a sixteen-sided one. On either side of the domed and carved entrance are decorative grilled windows.

The Turba of Barka Khan

Opposite Al-Kilaniya, on the corner of Western Wall Road, the **Turba of Barka Khan** was built between 1265 and 1280 for Emir Barka Khan, commander of the Khwarizmians, a Tartar tribe that reached Gaza in 1244 but whose power was broken two years later in a battle at Homs (Syria), during which Barka Khan was killed. Also buried here are his two sons, Badr al-Din and Husam al-Din; both fought against the Crusaders in the army of Baybars the Great (see p.55), who married their sister. In 1900, the *turba* was converted into the **Khalidi Library**, containing some 12,000 books and manuscripts collected by Sheikh Raghib al-Khalidi.

The Tashtumuriya

On the western corner of the same junction, the **Tashtumuriya** (covered by scaffolding at our last check) is a particularly magnificent example of Mamluk architecture. Built in 1382, it houses the domed tomb of Emir Tashtumur and his son Ibrahim. Tashtumur was a noted Islamic scholar, First Secretary of State to Sultan Sha'ban until the latter's assassination, and governor of Safed from 1380 to 1382. The facade illustrates two features typical of Mamluk architecture: its high arched entrance, up a flight of stairs, is decorated with *murqana* (plaster stalactites), while to the right, the square decorative windows of the mausoleum boast sills embellished with fine examples of *ablaq* (see box, p.79).

Khan al-Sultan

At the western end of Bab al-Silsila Street, you approach the heart of the central market, where Jewish Quarter Road leads southwards, and Souq al-Khawajat lies to the north. Just east of this junction, an elegant vaulted passageway on the northern side of the street leads into a former caravanserai known as **Khan al-Sultan**. It appears to date originally from Crusader times, but was rebuilt and enlarged in 1386 under Sultan Barquq, it's a typical medieval urban *khan* where merchants stayed while they sold their goods to local retailers: the chambers on either side of the vaulted market hall were used to store merchandise, while the rooms on the upper floor were the merchants' lodgings. The large courtyard at its northern end was used to stable animals.

Just beyond Khan al-Sultan, at its western end, Bab al-Silsila Street meets the central souqs (see p.76). A right turn here and then a quick left will take you up David Street to the Jaffa Gate; alternatively, a right turn and then straight on takes you through the central souqs and then up Souk Khan al-Zeit to the Damascus Gate.

Herod's Gate and around

Herod's Gate, about 400m east of the Damascus Gate and north of the Via Dolorosa, is not much used by tourists, unless popping through to get a falafel or *kubbe* at *Uncle Moustache* (see p.185). The quiet residential neighbourhood inside does however give a feeling of what the Old City must have been like under Jordanian rule and is almost a world apart from the mad throng which seems at times to engulf the rest of the Old City.

The English name "Herod's Gate" is based on the mistaken belief of sixteenth-century pilgrims that the monastery of Deir Abu Adas, to which it led, had formerly been the palace of King Herod Antipas. In Arabic it was called Bab al-Sahira (Gate of the Unsleeping), and referred to a cemetery opposite that was reserved for those who had done *haj* to Mecca – the first to be resurrected on Judgement Day, so it is believed. This later became corrupted to Bab al-Zahra (Flower Gate, translated to give the gate its Hebrew name, Sha'ar HaPrahim), and the new name was then rationalized as being derived from the floral rosettes above the outer doorway. In the mid-eleventh century, this corner of the city was its Jewish quarter, but when the Crusaders, using a siege tower managed to breach the city walls in 1099, about 100m east of where Herod's Gate now stands, they proceeded to slaughter the Jewish inhabitants within, replacing them with a contingent of Syrian Christians.

The gate was originally chicaned with a ninety-degree turn to delay hostile invaders – you entered from the east side (where the original archway is still visible on the outside) – but a straight-through entrance was installed in 1875 to give easier access.

The tower at the very northeastern corner of the Old City, called **Burj al-Laqlaq** (the Stork Tower), dates from the construction of the walls in 1537. You'll be lucky to see any storks on it today. Since the nineteenth century, this corner of the city, adjoining Burj al-Laqlaq, has been home to a small community of **Gypsies**, from a people called the Dom or Domari, originally of Rajasthani origin like the Romanies of Europe. A tiny minority of just a thousand people, the Domari face discrimination from Jews and Palestinians alike: "To the Arabs, we are *Nawari*, which means 'dirty Gypsies'; to the Jews and the authorities, we are Arabs. We lose on all sides," a spokesman told the *Jerusalem Post*. The Domari have a community centre and craft shop in Shuafat, East Jerusalem (see p.228), and a website at ⓦdomarisociety.googlepages.com.

The Jewish Quarter

The revitalized **Jewish Quarter** is a world apart from the rest of the Old City. Badly damaged during the battles of 1948 and left largely derelict under Jordanian rule, it was entirely rebuilt in the 1980s. Today it is a weathy neighbourhood with upmarket apartments, boutiques and art galleries alongside its ancient sites. While the other three quarters feel somehow closed in and at times claustrophobic, the Jewish Quarter is spacious and open, though it does rather lack the hustle and bustle of the rest of the Old City and can feel a little soulless.

The quarter's main attraction and Judaism's holiest site is the **Wailing Wall**, the ancient retaining wall of the Temple Mount where Jews worldwide have aspired for centuries to pray. Aside from the Wall, the main highlights include the **Jerusalem Archaeological Park**, a huge and impressive maze of excavations spanning two and half millennia, the controversial **Western Wall Tunnels**, which offer a subterranean voyage along the foundations of Temple Mount's Western Wall, and a number of well-restored old **synagogues**, most notably the rebuilt **Hurva**. On its western edge, you can stroll along the **Cardo**, the main street of Byzantine Jerusalem, and imagine yourself back in the days of Rome and Byzantium, while to its north, the **rooftop promenade** offers an altogether different view of Jerusalem, from the roofs of the Old City's central souqs.

The quarter is bounded by Bab al-Silsila Street to the north and Habad Street (Souq al-Husur) to the west, though it has always encroached to some extent on the Armenian Quarter beyond. You can reach it **from the Jaffa Gate** (see p.47), straight ahead down David Street, or **from the Damascus Gate** (see p.72) via Al-Wad Road, or else **through the Dung Gate** (see p.86), the latter two options leading to the Wailing Wall. The quarter is clearly signposted and most sites have explanatory notes and diagrams. Note that it closes down on Friday afternoon, Shabbat and Jewish holidays, but these are good times for a quiet stroll. Useful **websites** on the quarter include the Jewish Quarter Development Company's (Ⓦ www.rova-yehudi.org.il/en) and one by a couple of local residents (Ⓦ www.myrova.com).

History

In the time of King Hezekiah (c.715–687 BC), this area was a new extension westward from the original City of David (see p.113), and one of the richest parts of town. The Jews, expelled from Jerusalem by the Romans and then the Crusaders, were eventually allowed back in 1187 by Saladin, but it wasn't until 1267, with the arrival from Spain of the great **Rabbi Nahmanides** (Ramban – see p.95), that this quarter became established as the centre of the city's small Jewish community. Nahmanides established learning centres, and had a

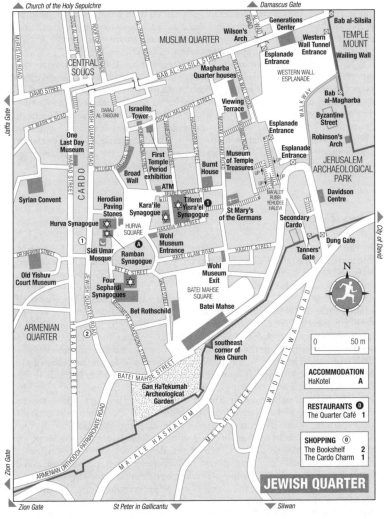

▲ Church of the Holy Sepulchre   ▲ Damascus Gate

JEWISH QUARTER

ACCOMMODATION	
HaKotel	**A**

RESTAURANTS ①	
The Quarter Café	**1**

SHOPPING ⓪	
The Bookshelf	**2**
The Cardo Charm	**1**

synagogue erected here (see p.95). The population received a further boost three centuries later with the arrival of more Spanish Jews, this time refugees from the Inquisition, and then again in 1700 with the arrival of the Ashkenazi Jews from Poland, though the latter were expelled twenty years later (see p.94), and banned from the city until 1820.

Despite the ban on the Ashkenazim, there was a continual Jewish presence of some sort in the quarter from Saladin's time onwards. This ended in the **1948 war**, when the quarter finally capitulated to Jordanian forces after fierce fighting, during which much of it was destroyed. After tense negotiations with a delegation of rabbis, the Jordanians gave the civilian Jewish population of 1300 a two-hour ceasefire to evacuate, after which Jordanian troops ransacked Jewish homes and sites in the area. Under Jordanian rule, the quarter was used to house refugees from inside the Green Line, and remained run-down and neglected, but its fortunes improved considerably after Israel took it over in 1967. Massive private and government funding saw the area extensively excavated, rebuilt and expanded in a sixteen-year reconstruction project carried out by the Jewish Quarter Development Company (Wwww.rova-yehudi.org.il/en).

With completion of the redevelopment project in 1983, the quarter was repopulated with Jewish residents. Apartments here are very expensive, and those who can afford them are mainly Jewish Americans (you'll hear more English spoken around the quarter than Hebrew) who are strongly religious and Zionist. The area is also dotted with *yeshivas*, whose students are predominantly American "born-again" Jews. Palestinians are prevented by Israeli law from acquiring houses in the Jewish Quarter following a 1981 **Supreme Court decision** which prohibits non-Jews from buying property here, but a few Palestinian families do still remain in what is left of the old Magharba Quarter (see p.90).

The Dung Gate

As the only city gate leading directly into the Jewish Quarter and the most direct approach to the Wailing Wall and Temple Mount, the **Dung Gate** (served by buses #1 and #2 from the Damascus Gate, and #38 from King George Street and Jaffa Road) is the point at which most Israeli tours enter the Old City, with the result that the approach road can be clogged with tour buses. The gate itself looks a little odd when seen from outside the walls, a wide rectangle topped with a narrow pointed archway; the reason for this is that it was originally a small pedestrian gate, widened to take traffic in 1952, and remodelled in 1985 with rounded corners on the lintel to make a more stylish entry for the Wailing Wall esplanade. The gate's Arabic name, **Bab Harat al-Magharba** (Gate of the Moorish Quarter), derives from the fact that the area immediately inside it was traditionally inhabited by people of North African descent (see p.90). In Hebrew the gate is known as **Sha'ar HaKotel** – (Wailing) Wall Gate. Its English name is said to come from the time when the area inside it was a rubbish dump – the Byzantines started this by throwing rubbish from Temple Mount onto the street in front of the Wailing Wall to show their contempt for the Jews' most holy shrine. In fact, however, there was a gate of that name in this area in biblical times (mentioned in Nehemiah 2:13), probably so called because rubbish from the Temple was taken out through it for disposal.

On your left as you enter the Dung Gate are excavations of the "**Secondary Cardo**", a Byzantine continuation of the Roman street that is now Al-Wad Road (see p.75). The Secondary Cardo leads out of the city through a small gate in the wall, known as the **Tanners' Gate**, probably because it once led to the city tanneries. It's actually part of an old medieval wall and is older than the Dung Gate, the latter being part of Suleiman the Magnificent's ramparts, which were built over the remains of the medieval wall.

Jerusalem Archaeological Park

On the right just inside the Dung Gate and on the southern side of Mount Moriah the **Jerusalem Archaeological Park** (Sun–Thurs 8am–5pm, Fri 8am–2pm; 30NIS; see p.50 for the 55NIS combined ticket; ☎02/627 7550, Wwww.archpark.org.il) is one of the city's best archeological sites, encompassing the whole of Jerusalem's history in one area. Here, you can see the remains of structures ranging from the tenth century BC, the time of Solomon, to the sixteenth-century reign of Sultan Suleiman the Magnificent – above all, the majestic hundred-metre-wide **flight of steps** that led pilgrims up to the **Hulda Gates** (a double gate and a triple gate), original entrances to the Temple precincts. Other finds include the ruins of a vast public building from the First Temple period, sections of **Robinson's Arch**, formerly a footbridge into Herod's Temple (see p.90), beneath it a section of paved **Byzantine street** complete with shops along the west side, and to the east a Byzantine residential quarter, including a two-storey house with mosaic floors.

Muslim buildings have been excavated here, too: an administrative complex from the Ummayad period (661–749 AD) including the **caliph's palace**, and a tower built by the Fatimids (969–1071 AD) and repaired by the Crusaders, the Ayyubids and the Mamluks.

Next to the park, the **Davidson Center** (same ticket as the Archaeological Park) features a virtual reconstruction of the area as it was in Herod's day, but is open by appointment and to groups only, though they may allow you to join one if you call to arrange it.

The Wailing Wall

Along with the Dome of the Rock, Jerusalem's most resonant image is the **Wailing Wall**, the most sacred Jewish site in the world. Officially, it's called the **Western Wall** (HaKotel HaMa'aravi in Hebrew or simply the **Kotel**), though strictly speaking this term refers to the whole length of the Temple Mount's western containing wall. The area used for praying is invariably referred to in English as the Wailing Wall, a term coined by British troops in 1917; previously it was known to travellers as "the wailing place of the Jews", because Jewish people traditionally came here to mourn the destruction of their ancient Temple. Since 1967, there has been an attempt to insist on "Western Wall" as a more politically correct term, but the popular name still persists, and indeed is far more evocative.

The part of the Wall that we see today is only a small section of what survives. More can be seen inside the synagogues to its left, and along the Western Wall Tunnel (see p.91), but even in the small section ordinarily visible, there are in fact another nineteen courses of stones beneath the modern-day ground level.

Notes to God

Close up, the Wailing Wall resembles an enormous message board to the Almighty; every nook and cranny in its massive ancient stones is stuffed with slips of paper bearing the personal **prayers** of the devout and the needy. Twice a year the prayer notes are taken away and buried in a Jewish cemetery to make way for more. In 2008 a note written by Barack Obama when he visited the Wall was published by Hebrew tabloid paper *Maariv*. The newspaper was strongly criticized in Israel as the notes are considered entirely private.

Ancient it may be, but the Wall is bang up to date with modern communications: its official website Ⓦenglish.thekotel.org allows you type out a prayer online and have it placed in the wall on your behalf. Alternatively, at Ⓦwww.westernwallprayers .org, you can have an Orthodox Jew pray for you at the Wall for forty days – the price varies between US$90 and US$1800, depending on whether you want a standard, exclusive or premier prayer.

For the best **view** of the Wall go to one of the vantage points overlooking the esplanade from the other side (see pp.89–90), from where you will also see the Dome of the Rock rising above it. Don't forget to come back in the evening when it is illuminated. The best **time to visit** is on a Friday evening when Shabbat comes in, or the eves of festivals, and on a Saturday or festival morning, when the main service is held.

Note that the Wall is subject to the same rules of **behaviour** as an Orthodox synagogue: modest dress is required, smoking and photography are forbidden on Shabbat or Jewish holidays, and men and married women must cover their heads when approaching. All approaches to the Wall are subject to airport-style **security** – bags are searched and you have to pass through a metal detector, removing cameras, phones and metal objects from your pockets to do so. At busy times this means that you may have to queue to get in. To save time, it is wise to come as unencumbered as possible.

History of the Wall

Though considered by Jews to be the only surviving remnant of the **Second Temple**, the Wall was never actually part of the Temple as such, but rather the western wall of a retaining structure built under **Herod** to support the plaza above – the massive stones of the lower section are typical of Herod's building style and date from 20 BC, while the upper part of smaller stones was rebuilt during the Muslim period.

When the **Romans** destroyed Herod's Temple after the Jewish War in 70 AD, only the western wall of the Temple's inner sanctum was left standing, but over the centuries that followed, Jewish **pilgrims** in Jerusalem gathered for prayer on Temple Mount when possible, or on the Mount of Olives when not. In the **fifteenth century**, as the idea spread that Jewish people should not enter the Temple sanctuary itself because they were no longer able to attain the necessary degree of ritual purity (see p.101), Jews began instead to gather in front of this wall to pray, and gradually traditions which had been associated with the western wall of the Temple's inner sanctum transferred themselves to this wall.

In the late 1530s, during the construction of the city ramparts, Ottoman sultan **Suleiman the Magnificent** issued an edict giving Jews the right to pray in front of the Wall, and had his official architect design a small area between the Wall and the neighbouring Magharba Quarter where they could do so. Since then, the Wall has always been considered the Jews' single most sacred site, and their exclusion from it between 1948 and 1967 was a cruel deprivation that was very deeply felt. In fact, the armistice agreement guaranteed Israeli Jews access to the Wall, but the Jordanians refused to honour this. Israel's recapture of the Wall in 1967 was thus one of the state's most joyous moments, and the exclusion of Jews from this their holiest site under Jordanian rule (the Jordanians even installed a urinal against it) goes a long way to explain Israel's subsequent attitude towards East Jerusalem. Within a month of taking the Old City, the Israelis bulldozed the twelfth-century Magharba Quarter in front of the Wall (giving residents only three hours to evacuate their homes) so as to make way for the massive esplanade you see today.

As part of the Haram al-Sharif (Temple Mount compound), the Wall is also sacred to Muslims who, in an effort to lay claim to it, identified it as the place where Mohammed tethered his winged mount, Al-Burak, before ascending to heaven on his night journey, despite the fact that the Al-Aqsa Mosque was the traditional site of that holy event. In fact under the terms of the Status Quo (see p.65) the Wall is technically Muslim property, belonging to the Waqf, who also own the synagogue area in front of it.

▲ Orthodox Jews praying at the Wailing Wall

The prayer area and esplanade

The large plaza in front of the Wall is divided into a **prayer area** adjoining the Wall, and a large **esplanade** behind that. The prayer area is treated as a synagogue. The congregation, mainly Orthodox Jewish men clad in black and white prayer shawls (*tallit*), sway back and forth with vigour as they pray. Congregations are largest on Friday evenings, Shabbat mornings (when scrolls of the Torah are read here), Jewish holidays, and for the fast of Tisha beAv (the ninth day of the Hebrew month of Av) commemorating the destruction of both Temples. The praying area is divided into two sections: the smaller part on the right reserved for women, the larger one for men. *Haredi* Jews have long opposed women conducting prayer services at the Wall, claiming that only men may lead prayer – a situation that has led to clashes, with *Haredi yeshiva* students even throwing excrement and other projectiles on occasion at Reform Jewish women trying to conduct a service.

The prayer area is separated by a metal railing from the vast, unshaded **esplanade** behind, which replaced the former Magharba Quarter (see opposite) in 1967. Prior to that, only a narrow alley separated the Wall from the nearest houses; pre-1948 paintings, prints and photographs capture the intimacy of the devout at prayer, while around them non-Jews go about their daily business. The Little Wailing Wall (see p.80), gives some idea of what that must have been like. Nowadays, Jewish people come from all over the world to hold Bar or Bat Mitzvah services for their children in the esplanade, and it presents an especially impressive sight in the run-up to the New Year when packed with hundreds of young people who come here to sing hymns of praise throughout the night.

Viewpoints over the Wall

The best **views** of the Wailing Wall are from the terraces overlooking it in the Jewish Quarter. The views from these also take in the Dome of the Rock and Al-Aqsa Mosque. Many of the terraces belong to *yeshivas* or even private homes,

The right to pray: changing the Status Quo

Historically, the **right of Jews to pray** at the Wall was guaranteed by the 1757 **Status Quo** (see p.65), under which, Muslims owned the Wall, but Jews had the right to stand on the pavement in front of it and pray. With the rise of Zionism, however, the religious significance of the Wall acquired a more political bent. When Jewish worshippers attempted to introduce a partition screen at the Wall in 1928, to divide male from female worshippers, Muslims objected that this breached the Status Quo. The Mandatory authorities agreed and ordered its removal. The Jews then complained that their freedom of worship had been violated, and the issue became an increasingly acrimonious bone of contention. Acting under directions from the Grand Mufti, Haj Amin al-Husseini (see p.107), Arab builders started construction work in the area around the Wall to disrupt Jewish prayers; an action which the British ordered to stop, though that didn't prevent both sides from holding rival demonstrations at the Wall. Matters came to a head on August 23, 1929, after the death of a Jewish boy stabbed during a row with a group of Arab boys in a football field. Rival mobs gathered in the city, and the ensuing clashes left 29 Jews and 38 Arabs dead and scores wounded. The **rioting** lasted a week and spread throughout the country, forcing the British to bring in troops from Egypt to quell it, by which time 220 people had been killed. The worst incident in the rioting was the massacre of the Jewish community in Hebron (see p.241).

but one or two are accessible to the public, and are most easily reached from Bab al-Silsila Street.

The main viewpoint can be found by turning south off Bab al-Silsila Street onto Misgav Ladakh (the gate here into the Jewish Quarter is sometimes locked at night). After thirty metres you emerge onto a plaza. The old building to the right, a former *madrasa*, is now a Jewish religious school. Beyond it, Misgav Ladakh continues up stairs towards the Museum of Temple Treasures (see p.98). The last remaining Palestinian families from the old **Magharba Quarter** also live in houses adjoining this plaza – they are descended from Moroccans and Tunisians who originally came to Jerusalem in the twelfth century, hence the quarter's name, Magharba, which means "of the Moors". At the far left-hand end of the plaza, stairs lead up and then down to **HaTamid Road**, where a terrace on the left, by no. 6, gives a fine view over the Wall, with the Dome of the Rock and Al-Aqsa Mosque behind it.

You can alternatively reach HaTamid Road by climbing the staircase behind the Western Wall Esplanade: exit via the southern gate, head directly to the west side of the esplanade, climb up the stairs to Ma'alot Rabbi Yehuda HaLevi, and continue up the next flight ahead, beneath the Aish HaTorah World Center, turning right at the top onto HaTamid Road.

The Wall can also be viewed from **Western Wall Road**, directly below HaTamid. You can access this directly from Bab al-Silsila Street, or you can head 50m south from the viewing terrace along HaTamid, where, under an arch, a right turn takes you onto a staircase leading down to Western Wall Road.

Robinson's Arch and Wilson's Arch

High on the southern end of the Western Wall (above the Jerusalem Archaeological Park, see p.86) are the remains of the fifteen-metre-high **Robinson's Arch**, the first of two bridges over the town's central Tyropoeon Valley that allowed access from the western part of the city into Herod's Temple. To its right, a ramp leads up to the **Bab al-Magharba** (Moors' Gate), the only entry onto Temple Mount open to non-Muslims.

To the north of the Wall, **Wilson's Arch**, named after the archeologist Charles Wilson who discovered it in 1868, formed part of a two-storey ancient bridge carrying Bab al-Silsila Street (see p.81) from west to east, across the Tyropoeon Valley, to the Temple Mount. Below the arch, a series of **vaulted chambers** used as a synagogue (open round the clock but access to men only) connect to the Western Wall tunnel (see below) and feature sections dating from the Second Temple period, the Ummayad period (seventh to eighth century) and from the fifteenth to sixteenth century. Two deep shafts in the floor of the prayer hall extend to the base of the Western Wall, so you can actually see how far down it goes.

The Generations Center

On the northern side of the esplanade is the **Generations Center,** an exhibition illustrating the history of the Jewish people which may be visited by appointment only (20NIS; ☎02/627 1333). Using huge glass sculptures by British artist Jeremy Langford, with a play of light through the glass, it incorporates archeological finds unearthed during its construction – including a ritual bath from the Second Temple period, and walls from First Temple and Crusader times. The exhibition's stated aim is to make Jewish visitors feel that "Each one of us is a link in a long chain of generations." Starting with glass pillars representing the biblical patriarchs, you progress through rooms depicting the time of the prophets, the destruction of the Temple, Jewish people's yearning over the ages for Jerusalem, the Holocaust, and the foundation of the State of Israel. The last part of the exhibition, the **Hall of Light**, tells the story of Rabbi Yisra'el Halevi, who longed all his life to see Jerusalem, but was murdered by the Nazis and never lived to see it; an Israeli paratrooper then hears his story from one of the rabbi's students, and is thus inspired to fight for the city in 1967 and regain the Wailing Wall for Jewish people of future generations.

The Western Wall Tunnel

More of the Western Wall that runs along a south–north axis at the edge of the Muslim Quarter, together with other structures beneath it, have been excavated in the **Western Wall Tunnel**, the opening of whose exit on Al-Mujahideen Street/Via Dolorosa caused widespread protest in September 1996 (see box, p.59). Given the (still) politically sensitive nature of the excavations, it is not possible to enter them on your own but you can arrange to visit as part of a group on a ninety-minute guided tour either with the Western Wall Heritage Foundation (☎02/627 1333, ⓦwww.thekotel.org; 25NIS) or with the Jewish Student Information Centre (3 Bet-El on Hurva Square ☎02/628 2634; 35NIS). It's worth booking as far ahead as possible (the Western Wall Heritage Foundation recommend two months, but certainly at least a week) as the number of people per tour is limited and they fill up fast.

The tour

The tunnel starts under Wilson's Arch and reveals fourteenth-century "**secret passages**" from the Mamluk period where, inside the vault under the Herodian double-decker bridge (see above), food and water were held in reserve. Next door is an auditorium where you can see what Jerusalem looked like in Second Temple days, by means of a wonderfully detailed 3-D **model** complete with lights and moving parts. From here, you descend two storeys back in time to remains dating from the Hasmonean period, before proceeding alongside the

The Tunnel War

The **protests** (known as the "tunnel war") which followed the opening of the tunnel in 1996 left 62 Palestinians and 14 Israeli soldiers dead, with over 1200 wounded. The trouble arose because Palestinians believed that the tunnel threatened the foundations of the Al-Aqsa Mosque and the Dome of the Rock. In fact, the tunnel lies to the west of Temple Mount and never actually goes under it. Moreover, the tunnels are ancient, and the only newly excavated part was the exit by the Via Dolorosa. Nonetheless, the Muslims' fears were not entirely unfounded, since Jewish archeologists working unofficially had in fact already tried to dig inward under Temple Mount via Warren's Gate (see below). The opening of the tunnel by Binyamin Netanyahu's Likud administration without prior consultation with the Islamic Waqf or the Palestinian Authority was also an assertion of **sovereignty** over East Jerusalem that Palestinians considered confrontational, and contrary to the spirit of the Oslo Accords then in effect, and the more so because Yitzhak Rabin's previous Labour administration had deliberately declined to open the tunnel specifically for that reason.

Western Wall, starting at a spot where a single **massive stone**, nearly 14m long and weighing 128 tonnes was placed as a solid support in case of earthquakes. Just north of here is Warren's Gate and beyond it a **synagogue**, apparently dating from Ummayad times. It was located here because the site was thought to be close to the Foundation Stone (*Even HaShivta*), from which, according to the Babylonian Talmud, the world was created, and to the Holy of Holies, or inner sanctum of Solomon's Temple, on the other side of the gate. Israeli archeologists exploring the tunnels in 1987 tried to dig through Warren's Gate and reach the Holy of Holies where, among all sorts of other treasures, the biblical Ark of the Covenant is thought to be buried. The project was unofficial and highly secret since both Orthodox Jews (worried about profaning the site) and Muslims (worried about the foundations of the Dome of the Rock above) would have screamed blue murder had they known of it. Perhaps it was lucky then that these would-be Indiana Joneses were halted by the discovery of a massive cistern full of water behind the gate, which prevented them from digging any further.

The tunnel continues rather claustrophobically until the **bedrock**, whose level rises as you proceed northward, meets the level of the floor. Beyond it is a Hasmonean water cistern. The last part of the walk is perhaps the most impressive: a glass walkway leads over the narrow **Hasmonean Aqueduct**, bordered by towering slabs of green algae-stained rock, and on to a treacherous-looking staircase that descends from street level to the **Struthion Pool** – used as a cistern in Roman times. The tour exits by the First Station of the Cross on the Via Dolorosa in the Muslim Quarter (see p.59).

The Cardo and around

One of the most atmospheric of the Jewish Quarter's archeological sites is the **Cardo Maximus**, the wide, colonnaded main street of Hadrian's Aelia Capitolina (see p.75). This part of it is in fact a Byzantine extension of the original Roman Cardo, which began at what is now the Damascus Gate and continued down what is now Souq Khan al-Zeit. The Cardo was the city's principal thoroughfare and later the Crusaders' main market. Lying at a lower level between the two modern roads that form the traditional western limit of the quarter – Habad Street, leading north from the Zion Gate to David Street, and Jewish Quarter Road, running parallel to the east – this part of the Cardo has been restored in a tasteful and manner; as you walk along the Byzantine pavement between Byzantine colonnades, it isn't hard to imagine yourself back in its heyday.

The vaulted **northern end** of the excavated section (open and lit up at night) now contains upmarket gift shops and art galleries, plus part of the Hasmonean city wall and remains of buildings from the First Temple period. Also in this section, you'll find the **One Last Day Museum** (Sun–Thurs 9am–5pm, Fri 9am–1pm; 12NIS; combined ticket with the Wohl Museum 25NIS, with the Burnt House 32NIS, with both 45NIS; ☏02/627 3916), a small collection of photos by *Life* magazine photographer John Philips recording the Jewish Quarter's 1948 fall to Transjordan's Arab Legion.

The rooftop promenade

At the northern end of Habad Street, you can get a different perspective on the Old City by climbing the metal stairway that leads up onto the **rooftops**, and lets you peer down through the skylights. Roughly ahead from the top of the stairs is a route to the Wailing Wall, while to the left the promenade passes over the central souqs (see p.76). There's also a children's playground up here, and good views of the Lutheran Church and the roof of the Holy Sepulchre. This route is used by Jewish settlers in the Muslim Quarter to get to the Jewish Quarter without passing through the Arab streets below.

The Old Yishuv Court Museum

West of the Cardo, off Habad Street at 6 Or HaHayim St (strictly speaking in the Armenian Quarter), the **Old Yishuv Court Museum** (Sun–Thurs 10am–3pm, Fri 10am–1pm; 18NIS) is a building that formerly housed two synagogues. One of the two, the HaAri Synagogue, was named after the great kabbalist Isaac Luria, known as HaAri – which means "the lion", but is also an acronym of Adonainu Rabbi Yitzhaq (our master Rabbi Isaac) – who was born here in 1534 and went on to create his own brand of kabbalism (Jewish mysticism) in the Galilean town of Safed. The other synagogue formerly housed here, the Or HaHayim, was Jerusalem's main Ashkenazi synagogue from 1812 until its evacuation in 1948. The restored complex, set around an inner courtyard, has its rooms decked out in period decor and shows aspects of everyday life in the Jewish Quarter from the mid-nineteenth century to the end of Ottoman rule after World War I.

Pelugat HaKotel Street

East of the Cardo's northern end, **Pelugat HaKotel Street** contains a couple of archeological remains, though you'd need to be an enthusiast of ancient walls to go out of your way to see them. Open to the street, the **Broad Wall** is an unusually thick section of the fortification erected under Hezekiah to enclose the city's western suburbs and protect them from the invading Assyrians. It is known as the Broad Wall after a wall referred to as such in Nehemiah 3:8 and 12:38 which may be the same one.

At the northern end of the street, on Shonei Halakhot, a flight of stairs leads down to the misleadingly named **Israelite Tower**, which is in fact part of a gate dating from the seventh century BC. Babylonian arrowheads found here testify to the fact that it saw action in the Babylonian siege of Jerusalem in 586 BC. Unfortunately, the Israelite Tower has been closed for some time, and there is no news of a reopening date. Opposite the tower on Shonei Halakhot, a **Jerusalem in the First Temple Period** exhibition (Sun–Thurs 9am–4pm; 18NIS) contains a few artefacts, including a Canaanite god described as "testimony to the phenomenon of idolatry", and a rather irritating audio-visual presentation on the history of Jerusalem in First Temple Times which seems aimed at children rather than adults. On the positive side, the staff give an English explanation of the artefacts, and there is an interesting model of the city as it was in First Temple times, which they also explain.

Hurva Square and around

The Jewish Quarter's hub is **Hurva Square**, named after what was once the Old City's most important synagogue, now being rebuilt on the square's western side. A number of other historical synagogues and other sights are all within easy walking distance. On the square itself, remnants of the past include some very large and rough ancient paving stones – probably Herodian, and probably originally covered by smoother stones – and a (functioning) British postbox from Mandate times.

The Hurva Synagogue

On the square's west side, the **Hurva Synagogue**, formerly the centre of Jerusalem's Ashkenazi community and the quarter's pride, ruined, rebuilt, then totally destroyed, has now risen, phoenix-like, from its ashes.

Jerusalem's small Ashkenazi community had had a synagogue on the site since the thirteenth century, but construction of the Hurva didn't begin until 1700, with the arrival of a group of Ashkenazi immigrants from Poland, led by Rabbi Judah the Hassid. On his death, construction stopped, and failure by the Ashkenazim to pay the debts incurred in its building led to riots and resulted in their expulsion from the city in 1720. The synagogue, half-built and derelict, then picked up its nickname, *HaHurva*, meaning "the ruin". In the 1830s, a group of Lithuanian Ashkenazi Jews started lobbying the Ottomans for permission to rebuild it, and construction restarted in 1856, with the new synagogue opening eight years later.

In May 1948, the synagogue became the last holdout in the quarter for the **Haganah** (Jewish militia). The Jordanian Arab Legion, fighting house by house to take the quarter, issued an ultimatum: surrender or we bomb the Hurva. The Jews decided to fight on, and the Jordanians carried out their threat, blowing a hole in the wall, driving out the Haganah, and then systematically destroying the building. In 1977, the Israelis erected a rather incongruous-looking arch to span what used to be the central hall, a sad monument to the synagogue's past glory, but also a reminder of the Jordanians' act of destruction.

In 2005, the Jewish Quarter Development Company announced a 28-million-shekel (US$6.6 million) **reconstruction project** to restore the Hurva to its former state. True, building techniques are not what they were (the original certainly wasn't made largely of concrete as the new one is), but superficially at least, the new Hurva will be as far as possible like a replica of the old, a beautiful third dome on the Old City skyline alongside the Dome of the Rock and the Holy Sepulchre. It should be completed in time for Rosh HaShannah 2009.

The Ramban Synagogue and Sidi Umar Mosque

Adjoining the Hurva on its south side, **the Ramban Synagogue** (open only for morning and evening prayers) is the oldest synagogue in Jerusalem. It was founded by the famous medieval scholar Nahmanides (aka Rabbi Moshe Ben Nahman – "Ramban" is an acronym of his name), who came to Jerusalem as a refugee from Christian Spain in 1267. Horrified to find but two Jewish families in the whole city, Nahmanides set about building a synagogue, originally on Mount Zion, and turned it into a centre for Talmudic learning that brought Jewish scholars from far and wide into the city. After his death, in 1270, the synagogue was rebuilt at this new location – sunk below ground level because no synagogue or church at that time was allowed to be taller than a mosque – and it quickly became the centre of Jewish life in Mamluk Jerusalem.

In 1417, as Muslims and Christians vied to have the tallest and the most prestigious religious buildings in the Holy City, Muslims rebuilt the minaret of the then disused twelfth-century **Sidi Umar Mosque** next door to the Ramban, and started using it again, but to reach it they had to cross the Ramban Synagogue's forecourt, and this they began to resent. When heavy rain brought down the synagogue roof in 1473, mosque officials objected to its repair. The sultan ruled for the Jews, and the roof was rebuilt, but raiders broke in and smashed up the synagogue. The sultan ordered it to be rebuilt again, and the congregation grew, but so did resentment from the neighbours, who lobbied Mamluk and Ottoman authorities alike to close it. Finally, in 1587, the Ottomans agreed, and the synagogue was shut down. The building was later used as a warehouse and a flour mill, and suffered serious damage in 1948, but the Israelis renovated it after retaking the Old City in 1967, and reopened it as a synagogue.

Four Sephardi synagogues

Southeast of Jewish Quarter Road, in Mishmeret HaKehuna Street, the **Four Sephardi Synagogues** (Sun, Mon, Wed, Thurs 9.30am–4pm, Tues & Fri 9.30am–1pm; 7NIS) were built in the seventeenth century, deep below ground level in accordance with an Ottoman regulation that forbade synagogue roofs from being higher than those of surrounding buildings. Once the centre of Jewish life in the city, the four houses of prayer remain at the religious heart of Jerusalem's Sephardic community. Ransacked and gutted when the Jordanians took the Jewish Quarter in 1948, they were restored after 1967. Much of the furniture in them now was taken from old Italian synagogues whose congregations had emigrated to Israel.

The most important of the four is the **Rabbi Yohanan Ben Zakkai Synagogue**, built around 1610. It is named after a first-century sage who is said to have taught his pupils on the site and who, according to legend, was smuggled out of Jerusalem during the siege of 70 AD to meet the then general Vespasian and plead with him to spare the city of Yavne as a home for Jewish scholars. Note the twin Arks, surmounted with a bright blue and gold mural. On a high shelf, the synagogue keeps a *shofar* (ram's horn) and a pot of oil, whose purpose is to herald and anoint the Messiah, when he eventually turns up. The Zakkai, known in Ladino (a Spanish dialect spoken by Sephardi Jews) as the **Kal Grande** ("Great Congregation") was the centre of Jewish life in Jerusalem throughout the seventeenth and eighteenth centuries, and remained the quarter's most important synagogue until 1948.

Of the adjoining synagogues, the **Stambouli (Istanbul) Synagogue**, with its gilded seventeenth-century Italian Ark and a four-columned *bima* (platform), was built in 1764 by immigrants from Turkey, hence its name. The **Emtza'i (Central) Synagogue**, the smallest of the four, was originally the courtyard of the Zakkai, roofed over and turned into a small synagogue in the eighteenth century.

The **Eliyahu HaNavi** (Elijah the Prophet) is probably the oldest of the four synagogues, and may have been established by worshippers from the Ramban Synagogue (see p.95) after that was closed down. According to legend, the congregation here were unable one Yom Kippur to gather together a *minyan*, the quorum of ten men required to say certain prayers. A mysterious old man then appeared and took a seat by the door, allowing the congregation to hold their service. Then, when it was over, he entered a room with no other exit, and promptly vanished. The congregation, realizing that the mysterious stranger was none other than the prophet Elijah, named their synagogue after him. The chair at the entrance replaces the one on which Elijah is said to have sat. Tradition has it that if you sit in the chair, you will then meet your future spouse. The synagogue's Torah scrolls are kept in a magnificent sixteenth-century hand-carved wooden ark with golden pillars and a dome, salvaged from a synagogue in Livorno that was destroyed during World War II.

The Kara'ite and Tiferet Yisra'el synagogues

To the east of Hurva Square, on HaKarai'm Street, the **Kara'ite Synagogue** once served the city's community of Kara'ites, a sect that broke away from Judaism in the seventh century AD and almost split the faith asunder. Rejecting the Talmud and the teachings of the rabbis in favour of a literal interpretation of the Torah, Kara'ism spread through Jewish communities from Spain to Iraq but fell prey to internal divisions and is now a tiny sect with just some 7000 followers in Israel. The synagogue, originally built in the tenth century, was destroyed by the Jordanians in the 1960s, and rebuilt after the Six Day War. In theory it is open to the public, with a small exhibition about the Kara'ite community inside; in practice, you'll be lucky to find it open.

East off Jewish Quarter Road, Tiferet Yisra'el Street leads past the ruins, topped by grey cement, of the nineteenth-century **Tiferet Yisra'el** or Nissan Bek Hassidic Synagogue, which was destroyed in 1948. The ruins have been left as they were, apart from adding the cement to keep them from crumbling. When the Jewish Quarter was first restored, the site was maintained and you could walk through it, but it has now been closed up and seems to be used mainly for dumping litter.

The Wohl Archeological Museum

Near the Kara'ite and Tiferet Yisra'el synagogues, with its entrance on HaKara'im Street is the entrance to the fascinating **Wohl Archeological Museum** (Sun–Thurs 9am–4.30pm, Fri 9am–12.30pm; 15NIS; combined ticket with the Burnt House 35NIS, with the One Last Day Museum 25NIS, with both 45NIS; ☎02/628 8141). Here you can explore the remains, some very well preserved and all well presented, of six priests' mansions dating from Herodian times. At a time when Jerusalem as a whole was enjoying increased prosperity, this area, known as the Upper City, became one of the most sought-after locations in which to live. The remains alone give you a good idea of the opulence of the buildings in their heyday, and a general feel for the art, culture and everyday life of some of Jerusalem's wealthier citizens. Descending from street level, you enter the basement bathroom of the **Western Building**, complete with *mikve* (ritual bath; plural *mikvaot*), cisterns and mosaic floor. From here, a corridor leads past a display of finds from the site to the **Middle Complex**, containing the remains of two houses, stone furniture and another fine mosaic. Beyond it is the most important house on the site, the **Mansion**, a large house on two levels: the (formerly) ground floor built around a patio, and the basement containing a whole series of *mikvaot*, more mosaics, and the remains of an ancient fresco. A scale model of the building shows what it would have looked like in its prime. Adjoining the Mansion are, to its north, a colonnaded court known as the **Peristyle Building** and, to its southeast, the large and unrestored **Southern Building**, its rooms also built around a central patio. The exit from the Wohl Museum brings you out onto Misgav Ladakh Road, which leads north to Bab al-Silsila Street.

The Burnt House

On the north side of Tiferet Yisra'el Street, not far from the Tiferet Yisra'el Synagogue, the **Burnt House** (Sun–Thurs 9am–4.30pm, Fri 9am–12.30pm; 25NIS; combined ticket with the Wohl Museum 35NIS, with the One Last Day Museum 32NIS, with both 45NIS) is one of the most intriguing sites in the Jewish Quarter. The house, which would have been luxurious in its time, belonged to the priestly Kathros family and was torched during Titus's destruction of the city in 70 AD, as described by Josephus in *The Jewish War* (6:403); the charred remains provide an eerie snapshot of domestic life at the moment the fire swept through. An entrance corridor, four rooms, kitchen and *mikva* (ritual bath) can all be easily made out from the excavations. Among the more gruesome finds were the charred remains of a woman's arm – its owner presumed to have died struggling to escape the fire, the circumstances of which are vividly recreated in a half-hourly fifteen-minute **audiovisual show** (language depending on audience). In addition to the house itself, there are some less interesting excavations of the Herodian city.

The eastern edge of the quarter

Just east of the Burnt House, on Misgav Ladakh Street, stands a twelfth-century complex consisting of a hospital, hospice and the church of **St Mary's of the Germans** – a Crusader church built as a pilgrim centre and run by German members of the Order of St John. These have survived despite objections from some ultra-Orthodox Jews to the presence of a church on their doorstep. Roofless as it now is, though with most of its walls intact, the church is a peaceful spot to take a break from sightseeing. The broad stone steps next to the church lead past the newly rebuilt **Porat Yosef**

Yeshiva (designed by Israeli architect Moshe Safdie and the largest in the quarter), down to the Wailing Wall piazza.

North of St Mary's, at 19 Misgav Ladakh, one of the most extreme of the born-again Jewish sects active in the quarter have set up a "**Museum of Temple Treasures**" (Sun–Thurs 9am–5pm, Fri 9am–noon; 20NIS; ☎02/626 4545, ⓦwww.templeinstitute.org) to entice visitors to contribute to their cause by paying to see ritual items for use in the Temple, reconstructed to specifications given in the Bible and the Talmud. These vessels, trumpets and other items are not just of historical interest: the aim of the group is to reclaim Temple Mount from the Muslims, knock down the Dome of the Rock and build in its place a Third Temple in which the vessels they display will actually be used.

The southern edge of the quarter

Batei Mahse Square, on the Jewish Quarter's southern edge, is the place where Israeli forces defending the quarter finally surrendered to the Transjordanian army after 14 days of heavy fighting; 290 defenders were taken prisoner, and 1300 residents evacuated. A monument to the fallen can be found just off the square's northwestern corner. The houses on the south side are the original **Batei Mahse**, almshouses built in 1862 for destitute Jewish immigrants from Europe. The tenants were chosen by lot, a third from the Netherlands, a third from Hungary and a third from other countries. The impressive building on the square's west side is **Bet Rothschild**, built in 1871 as tenements for the quarter's poor. In front of it, two **Hasmonean-period columns** have been reconstructed from pieces found during excavations.

More impressive excavations can be found to the south in the **Gan HaTekumah Archeological Garden**. Though not identified, most of the remains that you can see are Crusader buildings, but those in the northeastern corner were once part of the **Nea Church**, a huge basilica built under Justinian in 543 AD and clearly marked on the Madaba Map (see p.8). Once the city's largest church, it extended nearly all the way to what is now Jewish Quarter Road, and was destroyed by an earthquake on a date that may resonate: 11 September 747. It was never rebuilt.

Temple Mount

The vast paved esplanade of **Al-Haram al-Sharif** (the Noble Sanctuary), usually known in English as **Temple Mount**, covers almost a fifth of the Old City, and is a magnificent pedestal for Jerusalem's greatest triumph of Islamic art – the spectacular **Dome of the Rock**. The complex also contains the smaller, silver-domed **Al-Aqsa Mosque**, and scores of lesser Islamic monuments – *mastabas* (raised platforms), *mihrabs* (prayer niches) and *sabils* (fountains) – as well as the library of Al-Aqsa and the Islamic museum.

The compound has ten open **gates** and four closed ones – worth exploring in themselves, from both outside and inside the walls of the enclosure, but non-Muslims may enter through only one gate, the **Bab al-Magharba** (Moors' Gate), located alongside the Wailing Wall (entry by the southern gate of the Western Wall Esplanade; Sun–Thurs 7.30–10.30am & 12.20–1.30pm, but these times are often subject to change). Visitors are subject to security checks with metal detectors and bag searches, as a result of which there are often long queues; it's a good idea to come as early and as unencumbered as possible.

Since Ariel Sharon's walkabout of September 2000, the interior of the Dome and the Al-Aqsa Mosque have been open only to Muslims. As at all religious sites, dress must be modest; eating, drinking and smoking are not allowed (though local Muslim families bring picnics and nobody seems to mind). Certain parts of the complex, mostly along the eastern wall, are **off-limits to visitors**. No signs advise you of this however, so the only way to know that you've strayed into such an area is that site officials will start shouting at you.

History

Mount Moriah, on which the complex stands, is traditionally held to be the site where **Abraham** prepared to sacrifice his son (Isaac according to Judaism and Christianity; his older brother Ishmael according to Islam). Here, in 960 BC, David's son Solomon is believed to have erected the **First Temple** to house the Ark of the Covenant which David had brought to Jerusalem. Solomon's Temple was burned to the ground by the Babylonians in 586 BC.

The **Second Temple** was consecrated in 515 BC, rebuilt under Herod in 20 BC, and systematically destroyed by Titus in 70 AD following the First Jewish Revolt, although the western wall of the Holy of Holies (inner sanctum) was left standing for some years. After the Second Jewish Revolt in 135 AD, with Jerusalem again razed to the ground, **Hadrian** had a temple to Jupiter erected on the Mount, but when the empire adopted Christianity as its official religion, the site was all but abandoned, and the Byzantines used it as a rubbish dump. That was how **Caliph Omar** found it when he

TEMPLE MOUNT

accepted the surrender of Jerusalem in 638 AD. Omar ordered it to be cleaned up, and had a small mosque built at the southern end of the sanctuary, where Al-Aqsa now stands. In 688, Caliph Abd al-Malik Ibn Marawan commissioned the Dome of the Rock and ordered the construction of a permanent Al-Aqsa Mosque.

The **Crusaders** converted the Dome into a church, and Christian pilgrims came to pray in it, believing it to be the site of the Temple. After Saladin's reconquest of Jerusalem, Jews began again to pray on the Mount, but gradually the idea arose that, as they were not able to perform the necessary ritual purification rites, they should not enter the Temple precincts (see box below). Meanwhile, rulers from Saladin's **Ayyubid** dynasty (1193–1260) and their successors the **Mamluks** (1260–1516) began to endow the Mount with domes, fountains and *madrasas*, shaping the site into much the form it retains today.

Since Saladin's time, the Haram (Temple Mount compound) has been the responsibility of an Islamic **Waqf** (religious trust). Israel continued to respect this arrangement after 1967, though the site's Islamic sites have been the target of several attacks by extremist groups and individuals. The most extensive damage to property was caused in 1969 by a deranged Australian Christian, who **set fire to Al-Aqsa Mosque**. Since then there have been a number of attempts by Jewish nationalists to either destroy the Dome and Al-Aqsa or conduct clandestine archeological digs beneath the Mount. In October 1990, members of the militant settler group Ateret Cohanim attempted to place a Foundation Stone for a new Temple; in the **riots** that ensued, nineteen people died and three hundred were wounded. In response, Israel enacted a law forbidding Jews and Christians to pray on the site, even individually and in silence.

The closure of Al-Aqsa and the Dome to non-Muslims dates from September 2000, when, with the Oslo Accords between Israel and the Palestinian Authority on their last legs, opposition leader (as he then was) **Ariel Sharon**, accompanied by hundreds of Israeli riot police, went for a walkabout on the Mount, intending to assert "the right of every Jew to visit Jerusalem's holy places" but

Can observant Jews visit Temple Mount?

Temple Mount is also, of course, the world's most sacred Jewish site – so sacred in fact, that many observant Jews regard it as forbidden, and veneration of its holiness is nowadays expressed at the Wailing Wall rather than on the Mount itself. This situation has its origins in the restrictions placed on worshippers at the Second Temple. In those times Jews were obliged to undergo **purification rites in** order to enter the main part of the compound, the Court of the Israelites. Among these rites was the obligation to be sprinkled with the ashes of a **red heifer** conforming to stringent biblical specifications (Numbers 19:1–10). Within the Court of the Israelites, certain areas were restricted to the tribe of Levi or the priesthood, and the **Holy of Holies** (inner sanctum) could be entered only by the High Priest himself, and that only once a year on Yom Kippur.

After the destruction of the Temple, Jews continued, whenever they were able, to pray on the Mount. However, by the fifteenth century, the idea had developed that, because nobody knew where the Holy of Holies had stood, and because it was impossible to find a red heifer to confer the necessary state of ritual purity, Jews could not enter the Temple Mount precincts for fear of trespassing on a forbidden area. When Israel took the Old City in 1967, the country's Ashkenazi and Sephardi **chief rabbis** issued a statement confirming this prohibition, and in 2005 a large group of rabbis from all shades of orthodoxy issued a further statement supporting this. Nonetheless, a few rabbis affiliated to right-wing political groups argue that Jews may visit some or all of the site, and the **Temple Institute**, a fringe group who run the Museum of Temple Treasures (see p.98), have been trying to find a red heifer which conforms to biblical specifications so that they can build a third temple in place of the Dome and Al-Aqsa.

Meanwhile, less observant Jewish people continue to visit the site, despite notices at the entrance which point out that Jewish religious law forbids them to do so, while right-wing groups hold a prayer meeting every Friday night in the Souq al-Qattanin (see p.80) to protest the Israeli prohibition against them praying on the Mount itself.

also "to show that, under a Likud government, it [Temple Mount] will remain under Israeli sovereignty". Though the Israeli government, the Waqf and the Palestinian Authority all tried to prevent trouble, and Sharon did nothing overtly provocative, his visit sparked off riots on the Mount that spread nation-wide and initiated the Second Intifada.

The Dome of the Rock

With its landmark golden dome, dazzling blue mosaics and exquisite, mathe-matically perfect proportions, the octagonal **Dome of the Rock** (Qubbat al-Sakhra) is one of the greatest masterpieces of Islamic architecture and an enduring symbol of Jerusalem. **Caliph Abd al-Malik Ibn Marawan** had the Dome constructed to put Islam on an equal footing with its predecessors, Judaism and Christianity, and to compete with the Church of the Holy Sepulchre – "lest that should dazzle the minds of the Muslims," as Al-Muqaddasi puts it. Such was his devotion to his creation, that Ibn Marawan is said to have employed 52 official cleaners to wash the building with a mixture of saffron, musk and ambergris in rose water before prayer times.

Though it is sometimes mistakenly called the "Mosque of Omar", the Dome is not actually a mosque at all. It has no *qibla* wall, and no prayer hall, and a *mihrab* only in the cave underneath. Rather, it is a shrine built to house the **rock** inside it, held to be the very one where Abraham intended to sacrifice his son (Genesis 22:1–14; Koran 37:100–109). The rock itself was left protruding from the pavement of Herod's Temple site after its destruction by the Romans, but it is not known why Abd al-Malik decided it was the one in the story of Abraham's intended sacrifice. A pilgrim from Bordeaux reports that Jewish people venerated a "perforated stone" on the Mount in 333 AD, but it is not clear whether it was the same rock, nor why the Jews were vener-ating it. In the Old Testament story (Genesis 22:2), God tells Abraham to take his son to a mountain in "the land of Moriah", and by the fourth century BC, Jewish tradition had identified Temple Mount as the same place, but the story does not appear to have been associated with this specific rock until Abd al-Malik decided to commemorate it by having the Dome built over it.

The exterior

On the Dome's **exterior**, the walls are faced with marble slabs topped with glazed green and blue tiles; the outer face of the drum is similarly tiled. The present designs – a combination of Koranic inscription, geometrical shapes and vines and flowers – were originally commissioned by Suleiman the Magnificent in the sixteenth century and have been repeatedly renovated and repaired since. In the 1960s, the **dome** was covered with anodized aluminium, lighter than the lead covering that had been causing structural damage to the building, and cheaper than the gold which supposedly once kept out the elements before being melted down to pay off the debts of a profligate caliph.

Inside the Dome

If you are Muslim, you can enter to see the **interior** of the Dome, which is open from just before *fajr* (the first of the five daily prayers, performed at dawn) until just after *isha'a* (the last prayer, performed at nightfall). At prayer times on Fridays, the Dome is reserved for women, while men pray in Al-Aqsa. The floor is covered with rich, deep carpets, the walls decorated with bands of predominantly gold and green glass, mother-of-pearl and gold sheet mosaics, dating from the original construction. The eponymous **rock** in the centre seems incongruous amid all the splendour. Vague impressions on the rock are attributed to the **Prophet's footprint** and the imprint of the hand of the archangel Gabriel, who restrained the rock as it tried to follow the Prophet up to heaven. Hairs from Mohammed's beard are kept in a shrine next to it which is opened once a year, on the 27th of Ramadan. Around the rock, **the inner circle** is formed by twelve marble columns and four piers supporting the patterned golden dome, a soft greenish-gold light permeating through its sixteen stained-glass windows. The inner circle is surrounded by two octagons, the first formed by sixteen columns and eight piers, the second by the outer walls. A **cave** beneath the rock contains two small shrines to Ibrahim (Abraham) and Al-Khader (a supernatural spirit of whom, according to Islamic tradition, St George and the biblical prophet Elijah were both incarnations). At one time pilgrims were shown places where assorted biblical characters, including Abraham, David, Solomon, Elijah and even Enoch, were supposed to have prayed. Underneath the cave, in the Bir al-Arwah (Well of Souls), spirits are said to await Judgement Day.

Mohammed's Night Journey

Glory be to Him, who carried His servant by night
from the Holy Mosque to the Further Mosque
the precincts of which we have blessed.

(Koran 17:1)

Though the koranic sura (chapter) in which this verse occurs is called "The Night Journey", only this opening passage describes the journey itself. "The Holy Mosque" is evidently the Kaaba in Mecca, and Muslim tradition has always held that "the Further Mosque" (Al-Masjid al-Aqsa) is Jerusalem's Temple Mount. A mosque in this context simply means a place set aside for prayer to God. Some Christian and Jewish scholars have challenged the tradition, but Islam holds that Solomon's Temple was the second place in the world set aside to worship Allah (after the Kaaba), so it is pretty clear from the context that "Al-Masjid al-Aqsa" means Temple Mount, especially since the Koran adds the words, "which we have blessed." As for the actual journey which God's servant (Mohammed) is said to have made, no details are given, and it probably referred originally to a dream or a vision. Indeed, many Muslims accept that Mohammed came to Jerusalem in spirit rather than physically, but a *hadith* (reported saying of the Prophet) describes how the archangel Gabriel led Mohammed to an animal called Buraq, which was like a donkey or a mule with wings on its thighs. On this winged mount, Mohammed flew to Jerusalem where he met Abraham, Moses, Jesus and other biblical prophets. In some traditions, he then ascended through the seven levels of heaven, reaching paradise itself, where he spoke personally to God, before returning to his home in Mecca.

It is said – perhaps unsurprisingly – that many did not believe Mohammed had been to Jerusalem and back in a single night, but Mohammed's comrade Abu Bakr, who had seen Jerusalem when he came here as a merchant, asked the Prophet to describe it, which he did accurately, thus proving that he had indeed visited the holy ciy.

Al-Aqsa Mosque and around

Simpler and less grandiose than the Dome of the Rock, the silver-domed **Masjid al-Aqsa** – the Farthest Mosque – is darker, cooler and less richly decorated within, its atmosphere more conducive to quiet meditation. Throughout its history the mosque has been constantly damaged by earthquakes and continually rebuilt; its relatively modern interior is a result of substantal restoration between 1938 and 1942. It was Caliph Omar who originally had a simple wooden mosque erected here to commemorate Mohammed's "night journey" (see box, p.103), and in 690 AD, Caliph Abd al-Malik ordered the construction of a permanent mosque on the site, which, after being damaged by tremors in 713–14, was restored under Abd al-Malik's son, Caliph Al-Walid I. The mosque was destroyed by an earthquake in 747, and rebuilt again in 780 under Caliph Mohammed al-Mahdi. It then had twenty aisles instead of the seven that exist today. The present structure is essentially that of Caliph Al-Zaher who rebuilt it after yet another earthquake in 1033.

In 1099, the **Crusader** leader Godfrey de Bouillon set up his headquarters here. On its west side he built his armoury – the beautiful arched buildings now used as the Women's Mosque and the Islamic Museum (see opposite) – and the mosque became a church, its dome topped with a cross. The underground vaults, living up to their traditional name of Solomon's Stables, housed Crusader horses. The military order of the Knights Templar, founded in 1118, was named after the complex, known by the Crusaders simply as the Templum. **Saladin** removed the Templar constructions from the west side of the mosque, decorated the beautiful *mihrab*, and brought from Damascus a fabulous cedarwood *minbar*

▲ Al-Aqsa Mosque, Temple Mount

(pulpit), inlaid with ivory and mother-of-pearl, commissioned in preparation for the city's liberation from the Crusaders; sadly the *minbar* was later destroyed in the fire of 1969 (see p.101).

The interior

Today, only Muslims may enter the mosque, passing through the impressive arched main doorway into the **central aisle**, the widest of the seven, which has a beautiful carved and painted roof supported by massive columns of pale marble. To the west of the *minbar* are two small prayer niches dedicated to Moses and Jesus. The exquisite green, gold and blue mosaic work of the **dome** was commissioned by Saladin in 1189, and the similarity of the motifs to those in the Dome of the Rock have led some to believe that the original artists were ordered to make copies. The dome is supported by four arches and inset with seven of the mosque's 121 stained-glass windows.

Solomon's Stables

Outside the main northern entrance of the Al-Aqsa Mosque, a flight of steps leads down into **Solomon's Stables**, a labyrinth of massive pillars and arches (usually closed to the public) where sacrificial animals in the days of the Second Temple may have been housed. Certainly, animals were at one time tethered in it. A long vaulted passage leads from here to the closed Double Gate on the southern wall of the compound.

The Islamic Museum

To the west of Al-Aqsa Mosque, the **Islamic Museum**, established in 1923, is the oldest museum in Jerusalem. Unfortunately it is currently closed, and no information is forthcoming about when it will reopen. The museum, housed in two historic buildings – one Ayyubid, the other Crusader – is so much in harmony with the rest of the Noble Sanctuary that you barely realize that it's a secular building. Its collection ranges from tiny flasks for kohl eye make-up to giant architectural elements from mosques. Top exhibits include the nineteenth-century **cannon** that was fired to mark the start of the fast during Ramadan and the burnt remains of the great cedarwood **minbar** given to the Al-Aqsa Mosque by Saladin in 1187 (see opposite).

The Golden Gate

The **Golden Gate** in the east wall of Temple Mount was originally Herodian, but replaced with a double gate under the Ummayads, and blocked off in the eighth century. This is the gate through which the Jewish Messiah is expected to enter the city, as Jesus is believed to have done, though the Bible (Matthew 21:10; Mark 11:11) does not make it clear through which gate he entered. To the north of the Golden Gate is **Kursi Suleiman** (Solomon's Throne), a small double-domed structure where the wise king is said to have died. The **arcades** in the north wall, originally built by the Crusaders, were restored in 1213; those along the west wall date from the fourteenth century, as does the minaret here.

Smaller domes and fountains

Apart from the Dome of the Rock, a further nine domes can be seen within the complex, of which three deserve to be highlighted. Northwest of the Dome of the Rock, the **Dome of the Ascension** (Qubbat al-Miraj) was restored in 1200 AD, though its original date of construction is unknown. Between here and the Dome of the Rock, the **Dome of the Prophet** (Qubbat al-Nabi) was built on eight marble columns around 1845, while just east of the Dome of the Rock, at the exact centre of the compound, the **Dome of the Chain** (Qubbat al-Silsila) is variously explained as a scale model for the Dome of the Rock or as the Treasury of Temple Mount; its name derives from a legend that, during Solomon's time, those who told a lie while holding onto a chain hung from the roof were struck dead. The inside of the dome is beautifully decorated with blue and while tiles, the *mihrab* (in the structure's single wall) is typically Mamluk, with lots of stripey *ablaq*, including the almost flame-like triple-coloured arch which surmounts it.

Seven **fountains** can also be found in the compound, the most impressive of which is the **Sabil of Sultan Qaitbey**, west of the Dome of the Rock, in front of the Al-Aqsa Library. Classically Mamluk (especially the dome), it is named after the sultan who had it restored in 1482. Directly south of the Dome of the Rock and in line with Al-Aqsa Mosque, the fountain known as **Al-Kas** (The Cup) is used for washing before prayer; it originally drew its water supply from springs near Hebron. At the top of the stairway leading from Al-Kas to the Dome of the Rock – one of eight stairways leading up to the platform – is the *minbar* of Judge Burhan al-Din, built in 1388.

Bab al-Silsila and around

Bab al-Silsila (the Chain Gate, so called for the same reason as the Dome of the Chain; see above) leads onto a section of street (Bab al-Silsila Street) that non-Muslims may not be able to enter except from Temple Mount (see p.81), and which contains a number of points of interest.

The gate itself, directly above Robinson's Arch (see p.90) may well stand on the site of the Kiponos Gate, one of the five gateways to Herod's Temple. The gate in place today was built by the Crusaders, as you'll see if you exit Temple Mount through it and then turn around to look at it – the decorative columns on either side of the double gate are clearly Crusader in origin. The **minaret** above the gate dates from 1329, and replaced an structure erected six centuries earlier in Ummayad times. In the sixteenth century, the Bab al-Silsila minaret was the first to issue the five-times-daily call to prayer, giving the cue for muezzins across the city to make the call too.

Outside the gate

In the middle of the small square immediately outside the gate is a green metal-domed structure that was once a well. Immediately opposite the gates is one of Sultan Suleiman's *sabils* (drinking fountains; see p.80). The rosette at the top of the recess must originally have come from a Crusader building before being incorporated in the *sabil*.

On the north side of the little square, the small arched doorway is the entrance to the **Madrasa al-Baladiya**, built in 1380 as a mausoleum for Sayf al-Din al-Ahmadi, governor of Aleppo, which now houses the Al-Aqsa Library. To the west of Al-Baladiya, a simple but distinctive arched recess leads to the main entrance of the women's hospice, the **Ribat al-Nisa'**, one of the many institutions founded by Emir Tankiz al-Nasiri (see p.80).

The Tankaziya Madrasa

One of Emir Tankiz's most impressive legacies, the three-storeyed **Tankaziya Madrasa**, lies opposite the women's hospice, on the south side of Bab al-Silsila Street. Its striking portal is decorated with black and white stone and an inscription dating it to 729 AH (1329 AD). The *madrasa*, traditionally held to stand on the site of the council of the Jews where St Paul was brought by Romans in the book of Acts (22:30–23:10), itself served as a law court in the mid-fifteenth century. By 1483 it had become the seat of the town *qadi* (judge), while from the nineteenth century until the British Mandate it was Jerusalem's main court of justice. In the late 1920s it became the residence of the Grand Mufti, Haj Amin al-Husseini, a scion of one of Palestine's two leading political families. He was appointed by the British governor Herbert Samuel, probably with the intention of getting his family on side, but his appointment proved a big mistake. Outwardly charming but actually deeply unpleasant, Haj Amin used his position to stir up trouble, and was largely responsible for instigating the anti-Semitic riots of 1929. During World War II he went to Germany to work with the Nazis, of whom he was an enthusiastic supporter. After 1948, the Jordanians used the *madrasa* as a secondary school, but since 1967 it has been taken over by Israel's "Border Police", a military force used to keep order in East Jerusalem, with their own entrance from the *madrasa* onto Temple Mount.

Two medieval tombs

Beyond the little square, on the north side of Bab al-Silsila Street at no.151, the 1311 **Turba al-Sa'adiya** (also called Dar al-Khalidi) is the tomb of Sa'ad al-Din Mas'ud, a Mamluk official who had been chamberlain in Damascus. The building is now a private residence, not open to the public.

Just to the west at no.149, the **Turba of Turkan Khatun** is, so the story goes, the grave of a Mongol princess who died in Jerusalem while on a pilgrimage to Mecca around 1352. Again, you can't go inside, but the beautifully composed square facade is a masterpiece of design, with carvings that border on the psychedelic in their intricacy. Above the two windows, each bordered by red and cream stone, are two panels of elaborate geometric designs, topped in turn by two square stone panels, decorated with a more fluid, swirling pattern and separated by an inscription. A large square-patterned border surrounds the whole facade, while an intricate twelve-pointed star is its centrepiece.

A hundred metres further west on the north side of the street is the stairway leading down to Al-Wad Road and the Wailing Wall (see p.81). The rest of Bab al-Silsila Street, continuing up towards the Central Souqs, is covered on pp.81–82.

6

East Jerusalem

East Jerusalem, the Palestinian side of town, is quite distinct from West Jerusalem, less glitzy and more Middle Eastern in feel. Though not as ancient as the Old City, its centre seems caught in more of a time warp, little changed since the days of Jordanian rule when most of it was built. Since 1967 the Israeli authorities have been reluctant to invest here and normal life has been severely hampered by the walls and checkpoints which now cut the district off from its West Bank hinterland. The area is also a prime target for Jewish settlements which has lead to friction with the local population (see Contexts, p.273). Nonetheless there is plenty to see and do the tourist. The main downtown area along the **Nablus Road** offers excellent shopping, particularly on Sultan Suleiman where traders lay out their wares on the ground and you can stop for a glass of almond milk and snack on Middle Eastern treats. Among the nearby sights worth exploring are the **Garden Tomb**, thought by some to be the true tomb of Christ, and, further west, the excellent (and free) **Rockefeller Museum** of archeology. South of the Old City walls, the **City of David** is Jerusalem's original site, now a slick tourist attraction. Here you can walk knee-deep in water along **Hezekiah's Tunnel** whose construction is detailed in the Bible. Nearby, the **Kidron Valley** is home to some impressive ancient tombs, many of them attributed to characters from the Bible, while looming above it is the **Mount of Olives**, loaded with biblical significance and offering spectacular views across Jerusalem. Another historic hill, **Mount Scopus** dominates the northwest of the area and offers more wonderful views as well as the refreshing botanical gardens of the Hebrew University.

The downtown area and Nablus Road

The main built-up area of East Jerusalem is located north of the Old City walls. Most of the other places of interest are spread along the **Nablus Road**, which proceeds from the Damascus Gate (the Nablus Gate, as it is in Arabic) out to the suburb of Sheikh Jarrah and on towards – naturally – Nablus.

Zedekiah's Cave (King Solomon's Quarries)

Entered from Sultan Suleiman Street, outside the city wall between the Damascus and Herod's gates, **Zedekiah's Cave** (Sat–Thurs 9am–4pm, Fri 9am–1pm; 16NIS, no tickets sold on Saturday but can be bought online or in advance; combined ticket 55NIS – see p.50), named after Judah's last king, is a

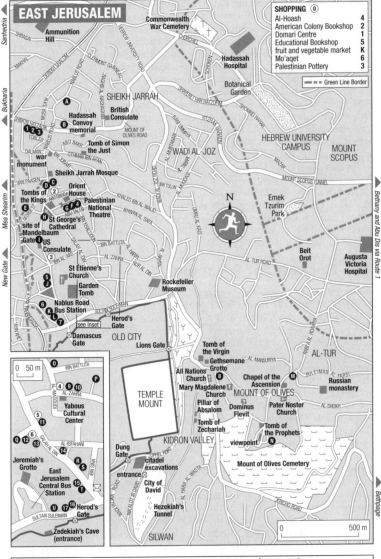

EAST JERUSALEM

① & Shuafat

Sanhedria

Bukharia

Mea Shearim

New Gate

Ammunition Hill

Commonwealth War Cemetery

Hadassah Hospital

SHOPPING ⓞ

Al-Hoash	4
American Colony Bookshop	2
Domari Centre	1
Educational Bookshop	5
fruit and vegetable market	K
Mo'aqet	6
Palestinian Pottery	3

----- Green Line Border

SHEIKH JARRAH

Hadassah Convoy memorial

British Consulate

Botanical Garden

war monument

Tomb of Simon the Just

Sheikh Jarrah Mosque

WADI AL-JOZ

HEBREW UNIVERSITY CAMPUS

MOUNT SCOPUS

Orient House

Tombs of the Kings

Palestinian National Theatre

Emek Tzurim Park

St George's Cathedral

site of Mandelbaum Gate

US Consulate

Beit Orot

Augusta Victoria Hospital

St Étienne's Church

Garden Tomb

Rockefeller Museum

AL-TUR ROAD

Nablus Road Bus Station

Herod's Gate

Damascus Gate

OLD CITY

see inset

Lions Gate

Tomb of the Virgin

Gethsemane Grotto

AL-TUR

All Nations Church

Mary Magdalene Church

Chapel of the Ascension

Russian monastery

Pillar of Absalom

Dominus Flevit

MOUNT OF OLIVES

Pater Noster Church

TEMPLE MOUNT

Tomb of Zechariah

Tomb of the Prophets

Dung Gate

KIDRON VALLEY

viewpoint

citadel excavations

entrance

City of David

Mount of Olives Cemetery

Hezekiah's Tunnel

SILWAN

Inset:

0   50 m

IBN BATTUTA

AL-ZAHRA

Yabous Cultural Center

AL-ISFAHANI

Jeremiah's Grotto

East Jerusalem Central Bus Station

Herod's Gate

SULTAN SULEIMAN

Zedekiah's Cave (entrance)

0   500 m

Bethany and Abu Dis via Route 1

Bethpage

6

EAST JERUSALEM

ACCOMMODATION

Addar Suite	D	Metropole	S	
Ambassador	A	Mount of Olives	M	
American Colony	C	Mount Scopus	B	
Azzahra	P	New Metropole	R	
Capitol	Q	Olive Tree	E	
Christmas Hotel	G	Palm Hostel	K	
Faisal Hostel	L	Ritz	O	
Golden Walls	U	Rivoli	T	
Jerusalem Hotel	J	St George's Guest		
Legacy	I	House	H	
Meridian	F	Seven Arches	N	

RESTAURANTS, CAFÉS & BARS ⓞ

Abo Ali	14	Café Europe	10
Alarz	16	Cellar Bar	C
Al-Ayed	7	Eiffel Sweets	17
All Nations Café	8	El Dorado	13
all-night bakeries	6	Falafel al-Bakri	15
Al-Mehbash	5	Gossip	3
Al-Shuleh Grill	11	Kan Zaman	J
Arabesque	C	Lotus and Olive Garden	4
Askadinya	2	Pasha's	1
Azzahra	O	Patisserie Suisse	12
Borderline	1	Philadelphia	9

small natural cave that became a quarry during the Second Temple period. The well-lit, stepped descent plunges into a grotto 200m deep under the Old City, and even if there isn't much to see in the cavernous stone interior, it's still an awesome experience, albeit not one for the claustrophobic. The cave is also known as **King Solomon's Quarries**, and although it's unlikely that King Solomon had stones quarried from here, material was being removed and used for important public buildings in Jerusalem right up to the beginning of the twentieth century. Jewish tradition holds that this was a tunnel used by King Zedekiah (597–587 BC) as an escape route to Jericho when he fled from the Babylonians after their capture of Jerusalem. Even if the legend is true, Zedekiah didn't get far: the Bible relates (II Kings 25:5–7) how Nebuchadnezzar's forces captured him, killed his sons in front of him, then put out his eyes and carried him in chains to Babylon.

Opposite Zedekiah's Cave is East Jerusalem Central Bus Station, and behind it, the rocky knoll known as Gordon's Calvary on which the Garden Tomb is located (see opposite). In the rockface, two "eye sockets" give it the appearance of a skull. Through them is a cave called **Jeremiah's Grotto** (not open to the public) traditionally held to be the place where the biblical prophet was imprisoned in 605 BC, and wrote his book of Lamentations over the city's impending fall to the forces of Babylon.

The Rockefeller Museum

About 250m east of the Herod's Gate, on the hill opposite the northeast corner of the Old City is the **Rockefeller Museum**, formerly the Palestine Archeological Museum (Sun, Mon, Wed & Thurs 10am–3pm, Sat 10am–2pm; free). The museum, housed in a massive Neo-Gothic structure with a distinctive octagonal turret, is named after American oil magnate John D. Rockefeller, who financed its construction in 1927. Nationalized by the Jordanians in 1966 the museum was taken over by the Israelis in 1967 after which its main exhibit the Dead Sea Scrolls were moved to the Israel Museum. However, even without the scrolls its collection is still one of the finest in the Middle East.

The museum is best toured in a clockwise direction. Turning left as you enter is the **South Octagon**, which displays a statue of Ramses III (1186–55 BC), the only piece of Egyptian monumental sculpture so far found in Israel and Palestine. The **South Gallery** has some of the museum's most impressive finds, including the **Galilee Skull**, belonging to a pre-modern human from the Lower Paleolithic period, around 200,000 BC. Also on display are assorted Stone Age implements, and some rather grotesque **skulls** covered with plaster and with shell eyes with painted-on pupils. Progressing up the gallery, you come into the Bronze Age, and indeed the biblical period, represented in the form of figurines, alabaster and ceramic jars, cutlery and jewellery.

The **South Room** holds wooden panels from Al-Aqsa Mosque intricately carved in Byzantine style, probably by Coptic Christian artists, and beyond it, the **West Hall** is dedicated to items from Hisham's Palace in Jericho (see p.247). Most have been reconstructed from pieces of stucco detached by the 747 AD earthquake which destroyed the palace. They include various human heads and figures, dating from a time before Islam eschewed such representation.

The **North Room**'s Crusader pieces include two twelfth-century lintels from the entrance to the Church of the Holy Sepulchre, one representing the forces of good, the other evil. Beyond, in the **North Gallery**, in the first bay on the left (the Iron Age section) the Phoenician-style **Megiddo Ivories** (nos. 44–82) include one (no. 69) thought by popular Egyptologist David Rohl (see p.246) to depict King Solomon. Other exhibits include (no. 374, further down on the right) a gruesome trepanned skull from the seventh century BC. The **North Octagon** houses finds from ancient synagogues, including a mosaic inscription in Aramaic from the synagogue at Ein Gedi (see p.249). The last room is the **Tower Hall**, where you'll find Greco-Roman statuary and some Canaanite gods.

The Garden Tomb

6

Two hundred metres up Nablus Road from the Damascus Gate, along a short alleyway to the east, is the **Garden Tomb** (Mon–Sat 9am–noon & 2–5.30pm; free; ☎02/627 2745, Ⓦwww.gardentomb.com), regarded by some Protestants as the true site of Christ's burial. It was first noted by Charles George Gordon, the British general and sometime governor of Sudan ("Gordon of Khartoum"), on a visit to Jerusalem in 1883. Picturing the city as a skeleton, with the Dome of the Rock as the pelvis and Solomon's Quarries as the ribs, Gordon suggested that the hill to the north of the Damascus Gate was the Golgotha or "place of the skull" referred to in the Gospels, and it was therefore also known as **Gordon's Calvary**. The two "eye sockets" of Jeremiah's Grotto (see opposite) also make the hill look strikingly like a skull. The tangible result of Gordon's hypothesis today is a beautiful **garden** of flowers and shrubs, pools and streams: a refreshingly tranquil spot. First laid out by a group of Anglicans in 1892, and now run by the Garden Tomb Association from London, it contains an unspectacular two-chambered **tomb** carved out of the stone and thought to date from the first to fifth centuries AD. It is now generally admitted that the site is unlikely to be that of Christ's tomb, but its quiet surroundings are more conducive to prayer and meditation than that of the Holy Sepulchre.

St Étienne's Church

Beyond the Garden Tomb, **St Étienne's Church** (daily 6.30am–7.30pm, ring bell; free) was built in 1900 for the French Dominicans. It stands on the site of a Byzantine church destroyed by the Persians in 614 AD (see p.270) and a Crusader chapel, which the Franks themselves destroyed in 1187 to prevent Saladin using it when he lay siege to the city. It was originally built to house bones discovered outside what is now the Damascus Gate and interpreted as those of St Stephen (St Étienne in French) – at the time he was believed to have been stoned to death outside that gate rather than the Lions' Gate (see p.56). The Byzantine Empress Eudokia, wife of Theodosius II and a great lover of Jerusalem, had the church built in 460 AD to house the bones, and was herself buried there when she died four months later. The rugs on the floor protect surviving fragments of the mosaic floor of Eudokia's original church – you can roll back the rugs to see the mosaics.

St George's Cathedral

Further up Nablus Road, **St George's Anglican Cathedral**, which dates from 1889, was an attempt to build a piece of England's green and pleasant land in Jerusalem; all it lacks is the adjoining village green and game of cricket. Inside, to the left of the entrance, the font was donated by Queen Victoria in 1898. In the north transept (down towards the altar on the left), the coat of arms which stood above the entrance to the British governor's residence during the Mandate period now hangs on the wall, having been brought here in 1948 when British rule ended. The church is nowadays used by Jerusalem's

Palestinian Anglican community as well as by English-speaking visitors, and the adjoining compound, set around a beautiful courtyard garden, contains a hostel (see p.170) and café.

The Tombs of the Kings

Just beyond St George's Cathedral, at the corner where Nablus Road meets Salah al-Din is the **Tombs of the Kings** (closed for renovation at last check, but the caretaker may let you in for a tip if you knock). Once thought to be the burial site of the kings of Judah, it is now believed to belong to Queen Helena of Adiabene, an independent state within the Parthian Empire. A wide flight of time-worn steps descends into a large open courtyard (used as the venue for the East Jerusalem Music Festival; see p.214) in which a covered porch is carved into the rock. To the right of the porch, a tiny entrance, once closed and hidden by a rolling stone, leads into an underground labyrinth of chambers and passages – bring a light if you want to explore.

Orient House

Behind the Tombs of the Kings, at 8 Abu Obeida, **Orient House** was formerly the Jerusalem office of the PLO. Built in 1897, the house belonged to the Al-Husseinis, one of the two main Palestinian political families. During the time of the Oslo Peace Accords (1993–2001), it was almost like a Palestinian embassy, though not officially recognized by Israel, whose government would protest whenever any foreign dignitary paid court there. During the Second Intifada, following a particularly nasty suicide bomb attack in West Jerusalem in which fifteen people died, the Israelis closed it up, and today Orient House stands empty and forlorn. Its website, however, is still online at Ⓦ www.orienthouse.org.

The American Colony

At the end of the nineteenth century, as Ottoman power declined, various Christian foreigners began founding suburbs outside the city walls. The Russian Compound (see p.135) was one such, the German Colony (see p.139) another, and in 1880, Anna and Horatio Spafford, Presbyterians from Chicago, founded the **American Colony**, originally a missionary centre, which became a small suburb, later joined by a group of like-minded Swedes. All that remains of the colony today is the hotel of the same name (see p.173), previously the home of an Ottoman merchant, which the Spaffords used as their HQ.

Tomb of Simon the Just

Just beyond the hotel, the small **Sheikh Jarrah Mosque**, housing the tomb of a twelfth-century saint, gives its name to the district that lies beyond it. As you ascend into Sheikh Jarrah, a **monument** on the right, on the corner of Ibn Jubair, commemorates Israeli paratroopers who died fighting for control of the neighbourhood in the 1967 Six Day War. If you turn right here, and then immediately left, Othman Ibn Afan brings you to (on the left) the **Tomb of Simon the Just** (Shimon HaTzadik), venerated by ultra-orthodox *Haredi* Jews, who believe it to be the tomb of a fourth-century BC high priest revered for his piety and devotion. The fact that archeologists have found an inscription showing it to be the tomb of one Julia Sabina, probably a Roman military officer's wife, does not deter the *Haredim*, who worship in a small synagogue next to the tomb, and look decidedly out of place in this Arab neighbourhood, though some of them have moved into houses overlooking the tomb. The tomb is host to a pilgrimage every year on Lag beOmer (the 33rd day after Passover).

Before 1948, a number of Jewish families lived in this area, and the Israeli courts have lately been evicting Palestinian families from homes which had then belonged to Jews; these are then given to Jewish settlers (not to the Jewish families which formerly occupied them).

The Hadassah convoy monument

Above the Tomb of Simon the Just, on Mount of Olives Road, not far from the *Mount Scopus Hotel*, a black stone monument commemorates the **Hadassah convoy massacre**, which occurred in April 1948, during Israel's War of Independence. A ten-vehicle Haganah convoy, including two ambulances bringing medical personnel and wounded to the Hadassah Hospital, in the Jewish-held enclave on Mount Scopus, was ambushed by local Arab irregulars, after the convoy's schedule was leaked to the Arabs by a British officer. Two days after Deir Yassin (see p.153), Arab fighters were not inclined to be merciful to the mostly unarmed Jewish medical officers and wounded militiamen on the convoy (including a single wounded Irgun fighter who'd been at Deir Yassin), and killed them indiscriminately. The British dragged their feet for hours before intervening, by which time 77 people had been killed; indeed, some Zionist sources imply that the British deliberately colluded. Despite the massacre, Israeli convoys continued to ply the same route to supply Mount Scopus, even after 1948 (see pp.122–123).

Ammunition Hill

Above Sheikh Jarrah, just to the south of Sederot Levi Eshkol, and served by bus #4 from King George Street, **Ammunition Hill** (Givat HaTahamoshet; Sun–Thurs 9am–6pm, closing an hour earlier in winter, Fri 9am–1pm; 15NIS; ℡02/582 8442, Ⓦwww.givathatachmosht.org.il), was the Jordanians' main defensive position in 1967. The successful assault on this position by Israeli forces in the **Six Day War** gave them control of East Jerusalem. The **trenches** from the battle are faithfully preserved, and there's a **museum** in the former Jordanian command post bunker. Its display of military insignia and names and photos of dead soldiers will really only be of interest to war buffs and Israeli patriots, though the films about the victory which are shown in the auditorium are more exciting, and the trenches themselves, set in a grassy park with views over East Jerusalem, are a good place to get away from the bustle and fumes of the city below.

From Ammunition Hill it's 1km west to the tombs of the Sanhedrin (see p.131). Bus #26 runs to Sanhedria and the Egged Central Bus Station, and the other way to Mount Scopus.

The City of David and around

South of the Old City walls, the ridge on which it stands splits into two spurs. The western spur is Mount Zion (see p.141), the eastern spur, Mount Ophel, is the **City of David**, the original site of Jerusalem, actually predating David and inhabited since at least 1800BC. Excavations in the 1960s provided the earliest evidence of human habitation in the area with the discovery of early Canaanite graves and since then no fewer than twenty-five strata of settlement have been dug up here.

The entrance and **visitors' centre** for the City of David Archeological Park (Sun–Thurs 8am–7pm, Fri 8am–3pm; ⓦwww.cityofdavid.org.il), now run by the settlers' organization Elad (see opposite), is on Ma'alot Ir David, just off Ophel Road south of the Dung Gate, and can be reached on bus #1 or #2 from the Egged Central Bus Station or near the Damascus Gate. Entry to the site is free, but to visit Hezekiah's Tunnel and Warren's Shaft (both of which close two hours before the rest of the site), you need to buy a 23NIS ticket (and have appropriate clothing; see below); it is in any case worth picking up a map from the entrance, which explains each of the numbered places on the site. There are guided tours at 10am and 4pm (50NIS), and you can borrow a flashlight (3NIS) for the tunnels. The entrance is at the top of a very steep slope, with long stairs down into the excavations, but for those who can't make the climb back, there is transport back to the top (5NIS).

The excavations across the street are on the site of the **citadel** of the Jebusite and Davidic city (in fact, the term "Zion" may originally have referred specifically to this citadel). The site will eventually be open to the public.

The Royal Quarter

Along the western side, in the **Royal Quarter** ("Area G"), is a wall dating from the Second Temple period. There are remains, too, of the eighteen-metre-high stepped-stone **citadel foundations**, and of buildings destroyed in the Babylonian conquest of 586 BC, including the **burnt room**, and another which seems to have been a **public archive** – 53 clay seals (*bullae*) were found in it, most notably one belonging to Gemariah the son of Shaphan, who is mentioned in the Bible (Jeremiah 36:10). At the very bottom of the stairs down through the Royal Quarter is the **Canaanite Channel**, a water conduit which appears to date from the time of the city's original Bronze Age fortifications.

Hezekiah's Tunnel

The most interesting thing in the City of David, and one of Jerusalem's highlights, is a walk through **Hezekiah's Tunnel** a 512-metre-long under-ground passage mentioned in the Bible. As the tunnel is 70cm deep in water (about knee height), you will need to come with clothes and footwear that you don't mind getting wet. You will also need a light (flashlights can be rented at the visitors' centre; they ask you not to use candles).

The tunnel was commissioned by King Hezekiah, who, under siege from the Assyrians in 701 BC took elaborate measures to protect the city's water supply. He blocked off the **Spring of Gihon**, the ancient lifeblood of the city, and diverted its waters down to the west side of the City of David (II Chronicles 32:30), thus denying his enemies access to it and allowing the citizens to outlast the siege. The tunnel – amazingly, especially considering its twists and turns – was carved out by two teams of men working simultaneously from either end; they recorded their eventual meeting in the middle with the **Siloam Inscription** which tells how, "While there were still three cubits to go, the voice of a man [on the other side] calling to his workmates could be heard through a cleft in the rock...and on the day the tunnel was driven through, the miners were working towards each other, pick against

In Jerusalem the whiff of politics is never far from its archeological sites. A prime example is the City of David Archeological Park. Today one of the city's most popular tourist attractions, it has been run for the past decade by Jewish settler group **Elad** (also known as the Ir David Foundation). While Elad argues that it is not itself involved in the excavation work, subcontracting to the Israel's Antiquities Authority, its control of the park has far-reaching implications, not least the establishment of new Jewish settlements in the nearby village of Silwan. Excavation work along tunnels running under the village has also angered local residents who claim that it is damaging the foundations of their homes. Recently, Israeli archeologists opposed to the placing of such authority into the hands of a group like Elad have started their own free two-hour **Alternative Archeological Tour**, which is held on an occasional basis and can be booked online at ⓦ www.alt-arch.org.

pick". The inscription was removed in Ottoman times, and is now in the Museum of the Ancient Orient in Istanbul, but you can still see where the two teams met from the difference in levels of the roof and floor.

At the end of the tunnel, you emerge blinking into daylight at the **Pool of Siloam**, where, as the Bible story goes, a blind man was cured after washing there on the instructions of Jesus (John 9:8). The steps and pillars here date from the Byzantine period, but the pool dates way back, certainly to Hezekiah's time, and quite possibly to Jebusite times. Nowadays it's rather smelly, and definitely not medicinal.

Warren's Shaft

Above Hezekiah's Tunnel is the entrance to the vertical shaft known as **Warren's Shaft**. Named after its nineteenth-century discoverer Charles Warren, it is thought to have been driven through the rock by the Jebusites to gain access to the spring a good millennium earlier than Hezekiah's Tunnel, and may also have been used by David's emissary Joab to penetrate the city's defences (II Samuel 5:8). You enter this feat of aquatic engineering through a renovated **Ottoman building** which also houses a small **museum** with a small exhibit of pottery found at the site, a model of the Warren's Shaft water system, and colour photos of Captain Warren's expedition and the present excavations. A spiral stairway from the exhibition room leads to a stupendous rock-hewn tunnel descending to the mouth of the shaft – an incredibly deep well from where, if it's quiet enough, you can hear the distant gurgle of the running spring water.

The Kidron Valley

West of the City of David and at the foot of the Mount of Olives is the **Kidron Valley**. A number of ancient tombs stand adjacent to each other beside the modern road that runs along the valley. Near to its junction with the Jericho Road the elaborate but curious bottle-shaped **Pillar of Absalom** dates from the first century AD, but is held to be the tomb of King David's rebellious son who, according to II Samuel 18:17, was cast into "a very great pit in the wood" and buried under "a very great heap of stones". Indeed, Jewish and Christian pilgrims used to throw stones at the tomb in abhorrence of Absalom's disloyalty to his father. Behind it are a group of rock tombs known as the **Tomb of Jehosaphat** after one of Judah's more illustrious monarchs (870–848BC);

▲ Absalom's Pillar in the Kidron Valley

Absalom's Pillar may simply have been a memorial for those buried in this tomb, almost certainly members of a single family.

Just south of Absalom's Pillar is a tomb identified from its Hebrew inscription as that of the priestly **family of Hezir**, referred to in I Chronicles 24:15. Next to that, with its pointed roof standing away from the rock, the **Tomb of Zechariah**, in fact probably a cenotaph marking the Hezir family's tombs, is supposed to be the resting place of the biblical prophet whose image of the Day of the Lord inspired the Mount of Olives cemetery (see p.119). The rock tomb just south of Zechariah's Tomb is unidentified.

Excellent views over the Kidron Valley tombs are to be had from **Ophel Road** above, from which steps lead down to the unpaved road along the valley. The valley (originally a stream) actually begins near the Tomb of Simon the Just in Sheikh Jarrah (see p.112).

Silwan

South of the City of David is the Palestinian village of **Silwan**, whose name comes from biblical Siloam (Shiloah in Hebrew). The village is built on a hillside containing around fifty seventh- and eighth-century BC rock tombs, squatted in medieval times by monks, and from the sixteenth century by poor local families, who formed the basis of the modern village. The most impressive of the tombs is the **Tomb of Pharaoh's Daughter** (*kubr bint faraon*), a five-metre-high cubic monolith believed to date from the ninth to the seventh century BC, which originally had a pyramid-shaped roof. It stands at the eastern end of the village about halfway up, but is not easy to find – local residents don't tend to be very helpful, and may in any case assume that you are looking for the Hezir family's necropolis (see above), which is known as Pharaoh's Tomb in Arabic. Another burial structure from First Temple period, known as the **Tomb of the Royal Steward**, is now part of a house on Silwan's main street. It once belonged to an important official in ancient Judah, possibly King Hezekiah's steward Shebna, who was lampooned by the biblical prophet Isaiah (22:15–16) for hewing out "a sepulchre on high".

Since the 1990s, Silwan has been the target of Jewish **settlers** backed by an organization called Elad (see box, p.115) which aims to move in Jewish families to create what it calls "an irreversible situation in the holy basin around the Old City." In support of the settlers' claims on Silwan, Elad points out that the neighbourhood was home to a Yemeni Jewish community established in 1884, which at its height numbered up to 150 families, all driven out by the Arabs during their 1936–39 Palestinian Revolt against the British.

Silwan can be reached on bus #76 from East Jerusalem Central Bus Station on Sultan Suleiman.

The Mount of Olives

The **Mount Of Olives**, nowadays dotted more with churches, shrines and cemeteries than olive trees, affords a magnificent view over the whole of Jerusalem. It is cited in the Old Testament as the place where David mourned the death of his recalcitrant son Absalom (II Samuel 15:30), and is closely associated with Jesus who used to walk over it from Bethany to Jerusalem – it was from its slopes that "He beheld the city and wept over it" (Luke 19:41) and it was here, in the Garden of Gethsemane, that he was arrested (Matthew 26:36–56, Mark 14:32–51).

The best way to see the Mount of Olives is to start at the top and walk down – a distance of around 1km. Wear sensible footwear as the path is sometimes steep and time-worn, get here early – morning is the best time for photographs of the view – and allow the best part of a day for the visit (avoid Sunday when many of the sites are closed). **Bus #75** from East Jerusalem Central Bus Station runs to the village of **Al-Tur**, from where it's around 400m to the summit. If you're fit, you could walk up from the Rockefeller Museum in East Jerusalem or from the Old City's Lions' Gate. Note that there have been reports of pickpockets in the area and, following incidents of harassment and even sexual assault on female tourists in the area, it is not advisable for women to wander round the Mount of Olives on foot alone.

The Chapel of the Ascension

In Al-Tur, just south of the *Mount of Olives Hotel* (see p.170), the minuscule **mosque** known as the **Chapel of the Ascension** (daily: summer 8am–5.30pm, winter 8am–4.30pm; 5NIS) is where, as stated in some versions of St Luke's Gospel (24:51), Jesus was "carried up into heaven" forty days after the Resurrection – the rock inside the octagonal shrine is said to be marked with the footprint Jesus left as he ascended. There has been a church on the site since 390 AD but this small and rather disappointing building was erected by the Crusaders, and converted into a mosque by Saladin in 1198, with a *mihrab* added in 1200. The presence of a mosque on the site is not as strange as it might seem, given that Islam recognizes Jesus as a prophet.

The small **burial crypt** next to the mosque has something for all three local religions: Jews believe it contains the grave of the seventh-century BC prophet

Huldah, one of only seven women prophets mentioned in the Old Testament (II Kings 22:14–20); Christians hold it to be the tomb of the fifth-century saint **Pelagia**; and Muslims maintain that **Rabi'a al-Adawiya**, an eighth-century holy woman, is buried here.

East of the Chapel of the Ascension, the White (Tsarist) **Russian monastery and church** (closed to the public) is where the head of John the Baptist is said to have been found. Its six-storey bell tower crowning just about the highest point in Jerusalem has lent its name to the village, Al-Tur meaning "the tower" in Arabic.

Pater Noster Church

South of the Chapel of the Ascension, past a grove of ancient olive trees, **Pater Noster Church** (Mon–Sat 8.30am–noon & 3–5pm) is set in an enclosed garden and built over the cave in which Jesus preached on the ultimate conflict of good and evil leading to the end of the world (Matthew 24:1–25). The original **Eleona Basilica** (Basilica of Olives), built under the direction of St Helena, was destroyed by the Persians in 614 AD. It was the Crusaders, believing this to be the place where Jesus taught his disciples the Lord's Prayer, who gave the church its present name – Pater Noster being Latin for "Our Father". However, the building that stands here today dates from 1894, when the site was under the care of Carmelite nuns. Inside, a short flight of stairs from the south side of the open courtyard leads to the **tomb of the Princesse de la Tour d'Auvergne** who bought the property in 1868 and had the Lord's Prayer inscribed in 62 languages on tiled panels in the entrance and cloister.

The viewpoint

The road south from Pater Noster Church along the crest of the hill brings you to the **Seven Arches hotel** (see p.170) which offers an unbeatable view of the city – especially Temple Mount – that adorns many postcards. You can snap it for yourself if you're able to elbow yourself some lens room among the busloads of tourists and their retinue of hustling young "tourist guides" at the "Rehav'am Lookout", as the Israelis have christened it. Morning is the best time to come if you want to take a picture, as the sun will then be in the right direction. Postcards, prayer beads and wooden camels are on offer here, or you could have your photo taken on a camel (agree the price before getting on).

The Tomb of the Prophets

Going down some steps across the road just north of the hotel, you come to the **Tomb of the Prophets** on the left (Mon–Thurs 9am–3pm; free), the traditionally ascribed resting place of the last three Old Testament prophets: Haggai, Zechariah and Malachi. The 100-metre-long semicircular outer corridor contains fifty tombs belonging to first-century BC Jews and fourth- and fifth-century AD Christians, whilst the inner tunnel was used for prayers. The keys to this three-thousand-year-old catacomb have been held for generations by the Othman family who live next door, who are usually happy to light your way (though you could also bring a light) and give you a detailed guided tour of the tombs, for a small consideration. Tea, coffee and other refreshments are available.

Mount of Olives Jewish Cemetery

Just below the Tomb of the Prophets, to the right, lies the **common grave** of 48 soldiers who died in the 1948 war, and who were reinterred here shortly after the occupation. It is part of the vast **Jewish cemetery**, the biggest and oldest in the world, and a symbol of the belief that when the "day of the Lord" comes, as foretold by the prophet Zechariah (14:1–9), "His feet will stand on the Mount of Olives", which "will be split in two from east to west", and everyone buried here will be resurrected. Later Jewish tradition associates the prophesied event with the arrival of a Christian-style Messiah, entering Jerusalem as did Jesus, through the **Golden Gate** opposite. Under Jordanian rule, many Jewish graves here were desecrated, some by simple vandalism, others by construction projects including the *Seven Arches* hotel (see p.170) and the widening of the Jericho Road in 1966.

Famous people buried in the cemetery include former Irgun leader and Israeli Prime Minister Menahem Begin (see p.138), author S.Y. (Shai) Agnon (see p.156), and former UK chief rabbi Immanuel Jakobovits. Also among those awaiting Judgement Day here is crooked British press mogul Robert Maxwell.

Dominus Flevit

The path downhill from the Mount of Olives summit leads to the Franciscan Church of **Dominus Flevit**, on the right (daily 8–11.45am & 2.30–5pm), inside whose grounds, to the right as you enter, are the excavations of four burial chambers with ossuaries, dating from 100 BC to 300 AD. The church itself, built over the remains of a fifth-century monastic chapel whose mosaic floors it preserves, was designed in 1955 by the Italian architect Antonio Barluzzi in the shape of the tear shed by Jesus (Dominus Flevit means "The Lord Wept") as he foresaw the fate of Jerusalem (Luke 19:41). Its exquisitely simple outer form hides a more elaborate interior: above the altar, the arched wrought-iron grille window framing the golden Dome of the Rock in the distance is a popular postcard image.

The Church of St Mary Magdalene

Halfway down the steep path from the summit of the Mount of Olives, on your right if descending, is the White Russian **Church of St Mary Magdalene** (Tues & Thurs 10am–noon) whose seven golden cupolas make it one of Jerusalem's most distinctive landmarks, though it's equally worth a visit for the delightful icons and wall paintings inside. Erected in 1885 by Tsar Alexander III in the old Russian style, the crypt holds the remains of his mother, the Grand Duchess Elizabeth, killed in the Russian Revolution of 1917. Also buried here is Princess Alice of Greece, Queen Elizabeth's mother-in-law, whose philanthropic actions included harbouring Jews during the Nazi occupation of Greece. A museum in the convent preserves a beautiful fifth-century mosaic dedicated to "Susannah mother of Artavan".

The All Nations Church

Where the path down from the Mount of Olives meets the Jericho Road, the **Church of All Nations** (daily 8am–noon & 2–5pm; free) was so named because its construction in 1924 was financed by twelve different countries. Its other name – the **Gethsemane Basilica of the Agony** – derives from it being the place where Jesus came to pray with his disciples while awaiting Judas's kiss of betrayal (Matthew 26:36–49, Mark 14:32–45, Luke 22:39–48); Jesus, unsurprisingly, being in a state of depression or "being in an agony", according to Luke.

Designed by Antonio Barluzzi (see box opposite), the church is built over the ruins of two others: the Egeria dating from around 380 AD, and a Crusader basilica of around 1170. Above the entrance is a striking modern Byzantine-style mosaic arch while the rock in the nave is where Jesus is said to have prayed before being arrested. This, as well as parts of a mosaic floor, belongs to the fourth-century church. The basilica stands in the beautiful **Garden of Gethsemane** (the Church of St Mary Magdalene also claims that distinction), said to be two thousand years old, and full of flowers and ancient gnarled olive trees, one of which Judas may have hanged himself from.

Before pressing on, you can take a break at the **All Nations Café**, to the right a little up the hill, and enjoy a cold drink at its outside tables.

The Tomb of the Virgin

At the bottom of the Mount of Olives, across Al-Mansuriya Street from the Garden of Gethsemane, the **Tomb of the Virgin** (daily 6am–12.30pm & 2.30–5.30pm; free) is the supposed burial place of Mary, the mother of Jesus. Writers of the late sixth century describe a church here but all the Crusaders found were ruins. The church was rebuilt in 1130 by Benedictines and taken over by Franciscans after the Crusaders left; since then Greek, Armenian, Syrian, Coptic and Ethiopian Christians have shared in the right to hold services here. The site is also venerated by Muslims since, on his night journey from Mecca to Jerusalem, the Prophet Mohammed is said to have spotted a light over Mary's tomb.

▲ All Nations Church by Antonio Balr

Antonio Barluzzi

A deeply pious Catholic, born within shouting distance of the Vatican in Rome, **Antonio Barluzzi** left a lasting impression on Jerusalem in the form of the churches he designed here. Barluzzi began drawing pictures of churches at the tender age of five, and with one brother a priest and another an architect, it seemed natural for him to study **architecture** in the service of the Church. Among the houses of worship he designed are Dominus Flevit on the Mount of Olives (see p.119), the Church of All Nations at its base (see p.119), the Church of the Visitation in Ein Karem (see p.154), the Franciscan Church in Bethany (see p.158), the Franciscan Church of the Angels at Bet Sahur (see p.239) and the Church of the Beatitudes at Tabgha in Galilee. Barluzzi also designed Jerusalem's Italian Hospital (see p.132), and helped restore a number of other buildings, including the churches at the Second and Sixth Stations of the Cross (see p.59 & p.61), and the chapel at Bethpage (see p.160). A biography, *Monuments to Glory* by Daniel Madden, has long been out of print but is sometimes available secondhand. Barluzzi spent his last days in a Franciscan monastery and died in Rome in December 1960, at the age of 76.

To the right of the twelfth-century flight of marble steps as you descend from the entrance is the **tomb of the Crusader Queen Melisande** who died in 1161 and opposite is the vault of members of her son King Baldwin II's family. At the bottom of the stairs is a Byzantine crypt, partly cut out of the rock, in which **Mary's stone tomb** (highly reminiscent of her son's Holy Sepulchre – see p.68) lies to the right. In the wall to the left is another rock tomb dating from the same period. The *mihrab* to the right of the tomb indicates the direction in which Mecca lies

The Grotto of Gethsemane

Just north of Mary's tomb, and entered from the same courtyard, the **Grotto of Gethsemane** (Mon, Tues, Wed, Fri & Sat 8.30am–noon & 2.30–5pm, Sun & Thurs 8.30am–noon & 2.30–3.40pm) is a rival to the Church of All Nations (see pp.119–120) as the spot where the disciples rested while Jesus prayed, and where Judas kissed him. The frequently restored cave contains traces of Byzantine mosaic floors, displayed under glass panels in the new stone floor. There's also a fresco and an ancient water cistern later used as a Byzantine burial vault.

Mount Scopus

East of Sheikh Jarrah, **Mount Scopus** offers excellent views, clean air and greenery, and houses Israel's leading university and a botanical garden. The mount has been of vital strategic importance since Roman times. Forces under Rome's governor of Syria, Cestius Gallus, set up camp here at the beginning of the Jewish War in 66 AD before an abortive attack on Jerusalem, as did forces under the future Roman Emperor Titus two years later when laying the siege that culminated in the final Roman victory over the city. The Crusaders camped here in 1099 before taking the city, as did the British after taking it in 1917. Although physically in East Jerusalem, Mount Scopus is spiritually – and in recent history – a part of the west. The northern part remained under Israeli control after the 1948 war, an isolated enclave maintained by fortnightly convoys under UN protection; the southern part was Jordanian, but the whole mount was a demilitarized zone, with a strip of no-man's-land between the two halves.

The Hebrew University

The **Hebrew University** on Mount Scopus gives the impression from afar that, like a SPECTRE complex in a James Bond movie, it could disappear underground at the touch of a button. It moved out after 1948, but returned to much expanded grounds after 1967, and have since been joined by vast new government buildings. On the eastern edge of the university grounds, an **amphitheatre** gives magnificent **views** as far as the Mountains of Moab as a backdrop. Sadly, even these pleasant heights are not above the troubles: in 2002 Hamas planted a bomb in one of the university's cafeterias which killed nine people and injured 85 others.

It's worth the extra climb to the top of the mount, to see the **botanical garden** (℡02/679 4012, ⊛www.botanic.co.il; Sat–Thurs 7am–nightfall, Fri 7am–3pm; 25NIS). Founded in the 1920s, it contains samples of flora mentioned in the Bible such as saffron, sesame, figs and almonds, and is tended today much as it would have been in biblical times, bar the unbiblical assistance of mechanical water sprinklers. On site is a reconstructed watchman's hut like those that once stood on every farm in the area, also some tombs dating back to the first century AD.

North of the university is **Hadassah Hospital** – a medical research and treatment centre of worldwide renown that also moved out after 1948 and back after 1967. Hadassah has a particular policy of treating all patients equally, regardless of religion or ethnicity. Just northwest of the hospital, a **Commonwealth War Cemetery** (Mon–Sat 10am–4pm) is the last resting place for 2472 Christian and Jewish soldiers who died serving in Allenby's army during World War One; many were from Australia or New Zealand, and Anzac Day is commemorated here on 25 April every year. A memorial wall lists the names of 3359 men who had to be buried in the field. Hindu and Muslim soldiers are buried in their own graveyard in Talpiot (see p.156).

Mount Scopus can be reached on bus #4a and #19 from King George Street, bus #26 from the Egged Central Bus Station via Sanhedria and Ammunition Hill.

Augusta Victoria Hospital

To the south, on what was Jordan's half of Mount Scopus, the **Augusta Victoria Hospital** was built in 1910, named after Kaiser Wilhelm's wife and used as the British governor general's residence after World War I. It now serves as the UNRWA hospital for the West Bank. In the grounds is the **Church of the Ascension**, whose distinctive square tower is a landmark visible citywide and gives, conversely, views over the whole city; should you wish to check this out, it is open to the public (Mon–Sat 8.30am–1pm; 5NIS), though the elevator has been out of commission for some years so you will have to walk up, which, at sixty metres high, is quite a climb if you don't like stairs. The hospital is served by bus #75 from East Jerusalem Central Bus Station on Sultan Suleiman.

Beit Orot

Just south of Augusta Victoria, at the junction of Rabi'a al-Adawiya and Al-Tur Road (aka Shmuel Ben Adaya), **Beit Orot** (Ⓦ www.beitorot.org) is a *yeshiva* (Jewish seminary) funded mainly by American money (notably from Miami gambling tycoon Irving Moskowitz) and keenly supported by Ehud Olmert (later Israel's Prime Minister) when he was mayor. A Jewish outpost in the heart of an almost exclusively Palestinian neighbourhood, the *yeshiva* is strongly associated with the settler movement and aims to be the nucleus of a new Jewish neighborhood on what it calls the "strategically crucial" north side of the Mount of Olives. A new Egged bus route (#48) now runs four times daily specifically to serve the *yeshiva*.

Beit Orot operates four-hour **tours** visiting settler outposts in areas such as Sheikh Jarrah (☎ 02/628 4155, extension 20), but its main interest to tourists lies in the fact that it has been chosen as the base for archeological visits to the neighbouring **Emek Tzurim National Park**, a former rubbish dump rehabilitated as a city park, where you can pay to help archeologists sift through earth and rubble looking for ancient finds (☎ 02/626 2341; Sun–Thurs 8am–4pm, Fri 8am–1pm; 15NIS; reservation required). The rubble being sifted was excavated illegally from the Stables of Solomon (see p.105) in 1999 by the Islamic Waqf, who surreptitiously dumped 13,000 tons of it in the Kidron Valley without any attempt to sift it for artefacts – an action described by Israel's Antiquities Authority as an "unprecedented archeological crime". In 2004 the rubble was brought to Emek Tzurim, and archeologists have been carefully going through it ever since.

7

West Jerusalem

Wegel
est Jerusalem, the Israeli "New City", is indeed relatively new by
Jerusalem standards, its first inhabitants having moved out from the
Old City barely a century and a half ago. In the ensuing years, and
especially since 1967, it has grown tremendously, but its centre is still
reasonably compact, and if you don't mind a longish walk, most of it can be
seen on foot, though there are also frequent and efficient buses. More
prosperous and cosmopolitan than East Jerusalem, the west is where you'll find
the greatest range of shops and most of the city's nightlife. In some of its neighbourhoods, with their leafy suburbs and buzzing cafés, you could imagine you
were in a modern European city whilst others bring you back to Israel with a
bump such as in the ultra-orthodox area of Mea Shearim.

The main thoroughfare is the **Jaffa Road** (sometimes referred to as "Yafo
Street"), which starts at the Old City's Jaffa Gate and heads northwest through
the heart of the downtown area, passing through **Zion Square** and crossing
King George Street before heading up toward the working-class Jewish
district of **Mahane Yehuda**. North of the Jaffa Road lies the *Haredi* community
of **Mea Shearim**, while to its south, King David Street leads down to Yemin
Moshe, the first Jewish neighbourhood to be built outside the city's walls, and
the Mandate-period district of **Talbiya**. East of here and adjoining the Old City
meanwhile, **Mount Zion**, contains West Jerusalem's most venerable sites,
including the Tomb of David and the reputed room of the Last Supper.

Note that the **Israel Museum**, **Knesset** and **Yad VaShem** are covered in the
following chapter, "Outlying areas".

Zion Square and around

West Jerusalem's hub is the small plaza of **Zion Square**, 600m up the Jaffa
Road from the northwest corner of the Old City and dominated by the rather
ugly *Kikar Zion* hotel. Running off it is a *midrahov* (pedestrianized area), packed
with cafés, restaurants and snack bars of every description. At night, the focus of
activity shifts to the streets just south in Nahalat Shiv'a. Running south from
here **King George Street** and **Jaffa Street** are two of West Jerusalem's main
thoroughfares both with a number of sights worth exploring.

Ben Yehuda Street

Ben Yehuda Street is the main street of the pedestrianized area off Zion
Square. Always abuzz with life it gets particularly crowded on Thursday and

Friday evenings. As the city's central shopping street, it's also quite lively during the rest of the week (though pretty much dead on Shabbat).

Sadly, Ben Yehuda has been a favourite target for terrorist attacks since members of a Palestinian Arab paramilitary group run by the Grand Mufti's cousin Abdel Khader al-Husseini planted a bomb here with the help of two British deserters in February 1948, which destroyed half the street and killed 54 people. The worst incident since then was in 1975, when a bomb planted in a refrigerator in Zion Square by Fatah left fifteen people dead and 77 wounded, but 2001 also saw a particularly nasty attack by Hamas in which two suicide bombers blew themselves up, and also left a car bomb fifty metres away, to go off twenty minutes later as paramedics were trying to ferry the wounded to hospital. It was a succession of attacks such as these which led Israeli public opinion to so strongly support construction of the Separation Wall (see p.234).

Nahalat Shiv'a

Between the pedestrianized Yoel Salomon, branching off Zion Square, and nearby Rivlin Street is **Nahalat Shiv'a**. Today, it's the epicentre of Jerusalem's bar scene but it's also one of West Jerusalem's oldest neighbourhoods, founded in 1869. Its small houses were each built around a patio with a cistern for water storage, and set the pattern for subsequent homes in West Jerusalem. The cisterns proved their worth during the siege of 1948, when the Arabs shut off West Jerusalem's water supply. Luckily, the local Haganah commander, David Shaltiel, had the foresight to order all the new city's cisterns filled before the British pulled out, enabling the district to hold out, albeit with strict water rationing. Since then, local residents have resisted all attempts by City Hall to knock down their quaint little houses and replace them with skyscrapers, and they finally won out in 1988, when the council decided to restore and conserve the neighbourhood. It is now full of bars, restaurants and arty shops.

The Museum of Italian Jewish Art

Near the southern end of Yoel Salomon, on its western side, a small side street, Bet HaKnesset, leads to the **Museum of Italian Jewish Art**, also accessible via 27 Hillel St (Mon 9am–2pm, Sun, Tues & Wed 9am–5pm, Thurs & Fri 9am–1pm; 15NIS; ☎02/624 1610, ⓦwww.jija.org). A sublime collection of Judaica (see box, p.224), its highlight is an ornate eighteenth-century synagogue transported lock, stock and barrel from Congliano in northern Italy's Veneto region in 1952, along with its community, who still follow the ancient Italian rite of worship. The museum's collection includes all kinds of religious objects, most of them rescued from Italian synagogues whose congregations had fled or been sent to concentration camps during World War II. The Congliano Synagogue is used for services on Shabbat and Jewish festivals, at which time the museum is closed.

The Time Elevator

Not far away at 32 Hillel St (Bet Agron), the **Time Elevator** (Sun–Thurs 10am–5pm, Fri 10am–2pm, Sat noon–6pm; 49NIS; ☎02/624 8381, ⓦwww .time-elevator-jerusalem.co.il) is a rollicking half-hour ride through Jerusalem's past with shaking seats and multimedia special effects to give the feel of a roller coaster. Housed in a former cinema, it's a little bit tacky, but in a fun kind of way, with Israeli actor Topol (of *Fiddler on the Roof* fame) providing the narration.

Map directory page

▲ Mount Scopus ▲ Mount of Olives

▲ Shufat & Ramallah ▲ Ammunition Hill

▲ Tomb of the Sanhedrin (150m)

RESTAURANTS, CAFÉS, BARS & NIGHTLIFE

24-hour bakery	53
Aldo	26, 35 & 44
Angelo's	28
Aroma	68
Artel	34
Babette	50
Barood	64
Bass	36
Besht Pundak	59
Birman	32
Blue Hole	58
Bohlinat	32
Café Hillel	27, 42 & 67
Caffit	32
Capricorn	11
Cielo	10
Colony Bar	20
Dama	31
Deutsch	56
El Gaucho	65
Focaccia	53
Gotham	72
HaLekhem shel Tomer	62
HaMarrakiya	17
HaSabiykh	73
HaTimani	39
Heimishe Essen	4
Hen	13
Hess	53
Holy Bagel	30
Izen	49
Jan's	20
La Guta	19
La Rôtisserie	66
Little Eucalyptus	E
Magic Fruit Juice	28
Mandarin	20
Masaryk	43
Megenanya	56
Mia	3
Mike's Place	76
Nadin	12
Nocturno	75
Notre Dame Coffee House	51
Off The Wall	22
Okhlim BaShuk	25
Pinnati	14
Rachela	57
Rehavia	6
Riff-Raff	47
Rimon	21
Rivlin	37
Sakura	63
Sea Dolphin	46
Shalom falafel	7 & 60
Shanty	33
Shegar	54
Shokolah	23
Sigmund	9
Sima	68
Sira	41
Sol	55
Spaghettim	8
Stardust	E
Tahanat HaCafé	40
Tal Bagels	2
Te'enim	38
Thai Sandwich	29
Ticho House	16
Tmol Shilshom	69
The Lab	X
The Record	70
Triple	61
Tutti-Frutti	71
Uganda	45
Village Green	5
Yankee's	15
Zabotinski	18
Zuni	

SHOPPING

Agfa Photo Schwarz	31
Ahava	13
Alba pharmacy	19
Archie Granot	Y
Arman Darian	52
Arts & Crafts Lane	25
Art Time	53
Avi Ben	41
Beit In	25
Ben Nayim	46
Bimot	43
Cadim	40
Camping Lematayel	3
Claire	35
Danny Azoulay	42
Danny Eliav	20
Defence	37
Dr Bella	15
Eden Fine Arts	16
GaiPaz	45
Gans	1
Gold	6
Gur Arieh	44
HaMashbir	34
Hatav Hashmini	41
Israeli Poster Center	25
Jerusalem Yarmulka	46
Jordan Books	47
Kippa Man	40
Klayim	20
Laundry Place	42
Leprechaun	36
Lucien Krief	22
Ludwig Meyer	10
Mashka'ot Agripas	1
Min Hastami	2
Moffet	23
Music House	51
Nahalat Shiv'a market	7
Nitzan Bike	25
Optica Halperin	8
Petit Musée	5
Rikma Yafa	17
Royal Collection	28
Sefer VaSefel	48
Shesh	
SPNI	A
Steinmatzky	38, 27 & 36
Stein	G
Steve's Packs	S
Sunbula	F
Super 24	J
Superpharm	W
Supersol	R
Third Ear	Z
The Book Gallery	bb
Tiferet	P
TishArt	U
Tower Records	V
Trionfo	cc
Yaakov Greenvurcel	Y
Yad Lakashish	aa
Zion Zakaim	M

ACCOMMODATION

Avital	T
Beit Shmuel	D
Dan Boutique	Q
David Citadel	C
Eldan	E
Habira	B
Harmony	K
Holiday 2000	R
Inbal	H
Jerusalem Hostel	I
Jerusalem Inn	O
Jerusalem Tower	L
Kaplan	X
Kikar Zion	
King David	
King Solomon	
Little House in the Colony	
Montefiore	
Mount Zion	
Noga	
Notre Dame Center	
Palatin	
Prima Kings	
St Andrew's Hospice	
Sheraton	
YHA Agron	
YHA Yitzhak Rabin	
YMCA Three Arches	
Zion	

Map features

MEA SHEARIM · site of Mandelbaum Gate · Museum on the Seam · St Paul's Church · Frutiger House · Italian Hospital · former Ethiopian consulate · Rothschild Hospital · Russian Cathedral · Underground Prisoners Museum · City Hall · Notre Dame · Ethiopian Church · Sergei House · Muscobiya police station · RUSSIAN COMPOUND · Zoology Building · Tabor House · Museum of Psalms · Ticho House · Mashiah Borochoff House · Mishkan Shmuel · site of Davidka monument · MAHANE YEHUDA · Pargod Theatre · Gerard Behar Center · Bet · Frumin House · NAHLA'OT · Kraft Family Stadium · Supreme Court · Egged Central Bus Station · David's Harp Bridge · International Conference Centre

▼ Abu Ghosh, Latrun & Tel Aviv ▼ Mount Herzl, Yad VaShem & Ein Karem

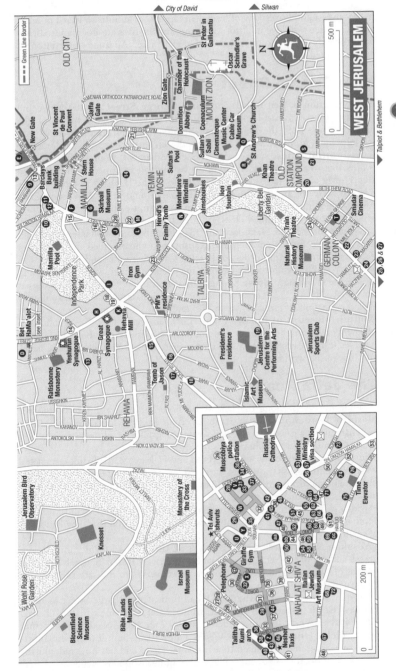

7

City of David   Silwan

--- Green Line Border

OLD CITY

New Gate

St Vincent de Paul Convent

ARMENIAN ORTHODOX PATRIARCHATE ROAD

Jaffa Gate

Zion Gate

Chamber of the Holocaust

St Peter in Gallicantu

Oscar Schindler's Grave

Dormition Abbey

Coenaculum

MOUNT ZION

Music Center

Cable Car Museum

St Andrew's Church

N

500 m

0

▶ Talpiot & Bethlehem

Barclays Bank building

Mamilla Stern House

Sultan's Pool

YEMIN MOSHE

Montefiore's Windmill

Sultan's Sabil

Cinematheque

Lion fountain

almshouses

Khan Theatre

OLD STATION COMPOUND

HEBRON ROAD

Skirball Museum

Herod's Family Tomb

Liberty Bell Garden

Train Theatre

Natural History Museum

Smadar Cinema

GERMAN COLONY

Mamilla Pool

Independence Park

Iron Gym

Iron fountain

TALBIYA

PM's residence

President's residence

Jerusalem Centre for the Performing Arts

Jerusalem Sports Club

Islamic Art Museum

Bet HaMa'alot

Yeshurun

Great Synagogue

Rehavia Mill

Ratisbonne Monastery

REHAVIA

Tomb of Jason

Jerusalem Bird Observatory

Monastery of the Cross

Wohl Rose Garden

Knesset

Israel Museum

Bloomfield Science Museum

Bible Lands Museum

WEST JERUSALEM

200 m

0

Muscobiya police station

Russian Cathedral

Interior Ministry visa section

Tel Aviv sheruts

Talitha Kumi arch

Nesher Taxis

Giraffe

Polephone

NAHALAT SHIV'A

Italian Jewish Art Museum

Time Elevator

It also gives a good overview of Jerusalem's history, told from an Israeli point of view. Children will love it, if not too young (under-fives are not admitted), but unfortunately they do not get a reduced rate. Advance reservation is recommended.

King George Street

At the junction of Ben Yehuda and **King George Street** is a distinctive and somewhat incongruous-looking clock arch and column northeast of the junction come from the Talitha Kumi Building, an orphanage and Arab girls' school which, from 1822 until 1901, stood 50m to the northwest. A little way south **Frumin House** housed the Knesset (parliament) from 1950–1966, and is now the tourist ministry. A few doors beyond, an apartment building called **Bet HaMa'alot**, is Jerusalem's best example of the Bauhaus-inspired "International Style" of architecture more commonly found in Tel Aviv (see p.257). Also in the Bauhaus style is the **Yeshurun Synagogue**, located at the junction of King George and Shmuel HaNagid streets. It was built in 1936 as the central synagogue for the area. Next door, the 1874 **Ratisbonne Monastery** was built in Italian style for Father Alphonse Ratisbonne, who founded the Fathers of Zion and Sisters of Zion orders of Roman Catholic monks and nuns.

Further south, by the junction of King George Street with Ramban and Agron, the rather ugly **Great Synagogue** (@jerusalemgreatsynagogue.com) at no. 56 dates from 1982. It boasts some fine stained-glass windows, and an unparalleled collection of *mezuzot* (see p.277), but its main feature of interest is the **Wolfson Museum of Judaica** (Sun–Thurs 9am–3pm; 15NIS) – a collection of Jewish religious items from communities worldwide (see box, p.224) that includes some beautiful pieces and rates as one of the best collections in Israel, and indeed the world.

The Jaffa Road

Heading northwest along the Jaffa Road from King George Street, you pass **Mashiah Borochoff House** at no. 64. Built in 1908 for a wealthy Uzbek merchant, it has a gateway topped by a pair of regal lions, and the portico is held up by Corinthian-style columns.

Further on, at the corner of Jaffa Road and HaNeviim, roadworks associated with the tram project (see p.25) have resulted in the temporary absence of a monument incorporating a **"Davidka"**, a home-made mortar that made up most of Israel's artillery at the beginning of the 1948 war. As there was only one Davidka in Jerusalem, the Israelis would fire off a few rounds, then move it to another location and fire a few more to give the impression that they had a few of them.

Mishkan Shmuel, a little way north at 92 Jaffa Rd, is a former immigrants' hostel and seminary set up in 1908 by American Rabbi Shmuel Levi; the sundial on the rather makeshift-looking facade serves to indicate the onset of Shabbat and religious festivals.

Heading southeast along the Jaffa Road from King George Street to reach **HaRav Kook Street**, on the left, named after Palestine's first Ashkenazi Chief Rabbi, who took up residence at no. 7 in 1902. Next to his former home, **Ticho House** (Sun, Mon, Wed & Thurs 10am–5pm, Tues 10am–10pm, Fri 10am–2pm; free) belonged to artist Anna Ticho and her husband, philanthropic eye-doctor Abraham Ticho. The house contains many of Anna's paintings – mostly quite abstract watercolours of Jerusalem scenery – some of

Abraham's correspondence, and his collection of lamps for the Jewish festival of lights, Hanukkah.

If you like bright colours and modern art, you might also care to pop into the **Museum of Psalms** at no. 5 (Sun–Thurs 10am–5pm, Fri 10am–2pm; 7NIS, voluntary donation; ☎02/623 0025, ⓦwww.museumofpsalms.com), to view works by Holocaust survivor, kabbalist and prolific painter Moshe Tzvi Berger, each canvas inspired by one of the psalms. His works hover somewhere between psychedelic and kitsch, but they're certainly worth seeing.

Mahane Yehuda market

Across the Jaffa Road, from Mishkan Shmuel (see opposite) the working-class district of **Mahane Yehuda** has a character of its own. Built to house Jewish immigrant workers, its chaotic maze of streets is crammed with minute houses of wildly differing character and little if any architectural integrity. The **market** here is famous for both the quality of its produce and the right-wing views of its stallholders (you'll see political stickers in Hebrew on many of the stalls). The busiest time to visit is on Friday, when it closes early for Shabbat, and locals are out in force to get in the food they need for the weekend. The market has unfortunately been a target for bomb attacks over the years, which explains the bag searches as you enter, and the heavy security presence here.

Just south of Mahane Yehuda, across Agrippas Street, **Nahla'ot** (also known as Mazkeret Moshe) is a predominantly Sephardi neighbourhood, increasingly populated by students and artists attracted by the cheap accommodation. Its narrow alleys are crowded and poor, but full of life and fascinating to wander around.

David's Harp Bridge

A kilometre beyond Mahane Yehuda, out past the **Egged Central Bus Station**, Jerusalem's newest landmark, visible all over town and as far afield as Bethlehem, is a quirky modern suspension bridge designed by Spanish architect Santiago Calatrava, and held up by 72 iron cables suspended from a single 118-metre-high kinked concrete mast. Called the **String Bridge**, or **David's Harp Bridge**, because it is supposed to represent the favoured instrument of ancient Israel's great monarch, it was constructed in 2008 to carry the new tram or light railway (see p.25) across the busy Shazar Boulevard. Jerusalemites love to moan about the bridge – over budget, over deadline, 250 million shekels to construct – but the fact is, it's a very elegant and impressive piece of engineering and already an important city landmark.

Mea Shearim

Founded in 1875 the quarter of **Mea Shearim**, northwest of the commercial centre, is home to the ultra-orthodox *Haredi* community. It retains a curiously East European feel with backstreets that could have been lifted straight out of a pre-Holocaust *shtetl* and residents dressed in black, some in the fashion of eighteenth-century Poland. The name Mea Shearim – literally "a hundred gates" – is actually the Hebrew for "a hundredfold" in Genesis 26:12 (in which the biblical patriarch Isaac moved into an area with a famine, sowed the land and reaped a hundredfold, becoming rich), but until 1915 the area was walled in, with six rather than a hundred iron gates, closed nightly (the base from the

▲ A street in Mea Shearim

Jerusalem Gate can still be seen on Ein Ya'akov at the junction with Salant).
Only strictly orthodox *Haredi* Jews were allowed to live here, and as it was then
on the edge of town, nobody tried to disturb their observant tranquillity,
though their attempts to retain this orthodox exclusivity today cause friction
with secular Jews wanting, for example, to drive through on Shabbat.

Visiting Mea Shearim

While plenty of tourists visit Mea Shearim it's best not to do so in a large
group as this may cause offence. Signs in English ask visitors to **dress
modestly** and this request should be taken seriously (even long trousers on
women are frowned on), as those who disregard it may be subject to abuse
or even stone throwing. *Haredim* also take serious objection to being photo-
graphed so it's probably best to leave your camera behind. Smoking on
Shabbat is also a no-no, and the whole area is closed to traffic on Shabbat.
Ostentatious Christianity (wearing a crucifix, for example) is regarded with
suspicion because people are afraid of Christians trying to convert them.
Buses #1 and #15 serve Mea Shearim from the Egged Central Bus Station
and near the Damascus Gate, #1 also from the Dung Gate. You'll see
synagogues and *yeshivot* everywhere in the quarter – each sect has its own
– and shops selling religious items abound. You'll also notice posters
(*pashkevilim*) on almost every spare bit of wall. These function as message
boards and feature fiery religious rhetoric.

Bukharia

North of Mea Shearim, the district of **Bukharia**, founded by Uzbek
immigrants at the end of the nineteenth century, is full of synagogues dating
from that period, some of them (such as the Masayef at 24 Joel) very tiny
indeed. Many have been taken over by *Haredim* spilling over from Mea
Shearim, but there are still some that practise the Uzbek rite. The colourful

little *shtetl*-style **market** at the southern end of Bukharim looks like something out of *Fiddler on the Roof*.

North of Yekhezkel Street you'll find **Bet Sefer Shafitsar** (the "Palace"), at 19 Ezra, built for two rich families at the beginning of the twentieth century, when it was the grandest house in Palestine. It is believed that the Messiah himself will be staying here when he eventually makes his appearance. Used in the 1940s by the Haganah to train new recruits and as a base for actions against the British, the building is now partly taken up by a school.

Sanhedria

Yekhezkel Street leads onto Shmuel HaNavi, where a left turn takes you after 200m to a major junction (with Hativat Hariel), beyond which, Sanhedrin Street on the right takes you past a public garden planted with fragrant pines and containing a number of first- and second-century **rock-cut tombs**. The last and most impressive of these is the **Tomb of the Sanhedrin**. The Sanhedrin was the council of rabbis who constituted the highest court of Jewish canon law. There is no particular reason for thinking that the people buried here really did belong to the Sanhedrin, but that's the tradition associated with the tomb, whose imposing square doorway is topped by a lintel carved with reliefs of fruit and foliage. It's supposed to be locked, but seems to have been broken open and left that way. If you do go inside, you'll need a light to see the catacombs in the main chamber and two side chambers. The tomb gave its name to the surrounding neighbourhood, **Sanhedria**.

You can reach the Tomb of the Sanhedrin on bus #10 from Mea Shearim, or #39 from the Egged Central Bus Station. From the main junction before you

Haredi Judaism

Haredi means "in awe" (of God), and **Haredism** is the strictest ("ultra-orthodox") strain of Judaism. It originated in Eastern Europe as a reaction against assimilation of Jews into the general population as laws segregating them into ghettos were abolished, and most particularly against attempts to "modernize" the religion by relaxing its strictures. Aside from scrupulous observance of all religious rules, *Haredi* Jews study the Torah every day, and are modest in the dress and habits – modest that is, not only in covering up, but also in not being ostentatious, which is why *Haredi* men usually wear black. *Haredi* women, not unlike their Muslim counterparts, cover themselves from wrist to ankle, and also hide their hair with a scarf, or sometimes a wig. *Haredi* rabbis have passed rulings against reading secular books or newspapers, against television, and inevitably, against the internet (though they eventually had to allow use of the web for business purposes). Other new technology is usually allowed – *Haredim* drive cars and use electrical appliances for example – but is always examined to see how it fits in with Jewish religious law.

Some *Haredim*, particularly members of the Neturei Karta movement, do not acknowledge the State of Israel which, until the Messiah arrives, they regard as profane, and have even negotiated with the PLO for acceptance as an anti-Zionist Palestinian Jewish community. Many of them forego employment and military service to study in *yeshivas* which are subsidized by the taxpayer. *Haredim* have campaigned to ban the sale of unkosher food, the showing of "indecent" films, and the opening of shops on Shabbat. All of this has caused much resentment and even hostility towards them on the part of secular Israelis but *Haredim* see themselves as defenders of the religion. Without their strictness, they believe, Judaism would eventually disappear.

get to Sanhedrin Street, Hativat Hariel leads eastward toward Ammunition Hill (see p.113), Sheikh Jarrah (see p.112) and Mount Scopus (see p.121).

The Street of the Prophets

From the site of the Davidka Monument at its junction with the Jaffa Road, **Rehov HaNeviim** – the **Street of the Prophets** – leads east across the Green Line to the Damascus Gate passing en route a number of impressive historic buildings whose history is recounted on blue plaques on their facades. One to look out for is the **Rothschild Hospital** at the corner of HaRav Kook; when it opened in 1888 with money donated by Baron Rothschild, it became the first Jewish hospital outside the Old City. No. 64 was the home of British Pre-Raphaelite painter **William Holman Hunt**, and **Tabor House**, three doors down at no. 58 (Mon–Fri 9am–1pm; free; ✆02/625 3822), was the home of **Conrad Schick**, a German-born architect who came to Jerusalem as a missionary in 1846 and was responsible for many of the new buildings constructed outside its walls during the rest of the nineteenth century, notably the Mea Shearim district (see p.129), which he helped plan out. His house, which of course he designed himself, includes some unusual architectural features – the upward-pointing corners of the roof, for example, are modelled on those of the sacrificial altars in the ancient Jewish Temples.

Ethiopia Street

North off HaNeviim, at 11 Ethiopia St, the former home of **Eliezar Ben Yehuda**, the inventor of Modern Hebrew, stands opposite the small, round, **Ethiopian Church** (daily March–Sept 7am–6pm, Oct–Feb 8am–5pm; free), which dates from 1874, and flies the red, green and gold banner of Ethiopia. Around it are the residences of monks and nuns of the church. It's worth a quick look inside the church to see the carpets, icons and Ethiopian-style furnishings and paintings.

Back on HaNeviim, the **former Ethiopian consulate** at no. 38 has mosaics on its facade quoting in Ghees (classical Ethiopian) the words of Revelation 5:5: "Behold the Lion of the tribe of Judah", and depicting said lion, symbol of the Ethiopian royal family, who claimed descent from King Solomon and the Queen of Sheba (hence the basis of Haile Selassie's Rastafarian status as Messiah).

Around the junction with Shivtei Israel

HaNeviim continues across **Shivtei Israel**, where there's a cluster of interesting buildings by the junction. The **Italian Hospital** at 27 Shivtei Israel, with its Florentine-style church tower, was designed by Antonio Barluzzi (see box, p.121) and used as a military hospital by Britain's Royal Air Force in World War II. It now belongs to the Israeli Ministry of Education.

On the other side of HaNeviim, at 32 Shivtei Israel, the neo-Romanesque stone chapel called **St Paul's Church** was put up in 1873 by the London-based Church Missionary Society. **Frutiger House**, next door, built in 1885 for a wealthy German banker, later housed **Menahem Ussishkin**, a Zionist leader of the late nineteenth and early twentieth centuries, who promoted the idea that a future Jewish state in Palestine should be based on agricultural settlements, which indeed it originally was. Subsequently the building became the residence of the British High Commissioner in Palestine. In September 1944, members of the Zionist paramilitary group known as the Stern Gang shot dead an Assistant Superintendent in the Palestine Police named Tom Wilkin right outside the house opposite (no. 27). The attack was a retaliation for Wilkin's part, two and a half years earlier, in the arrest and murder by British police in Tel Aviv of the gang's leader, Avraham Stern (see p.258).

The Green Line

At the eastern end of HaNeviim, Hail HaHandassa marks **the Green Line**, the 1949 armistice line between Israel and Jordan, and the change is quite startling as you cross it, passing from West into East Jerusalem (see p.7), and from Israel into the West Bank. Suddenly, it's Arabic being spoken around you instead of Hebrew, the shop signs are in Arabic and the people are wearing *keffiyas* instead of *kippas*; while ahead is the very Islamic Dome of the Rock. The Green Line is no longer a physical border, but it might be less of a jolt if you did have to stop at customs here and show your passport.

To the north, on the west side of Hail HaHandassa at its junction with Shivtei Israel, the **Museum On The Seam** (Sun–Thurs 9am–4pm, Fri 9am–2pm; 30NIS; ☎02/628 1278, ⊛www.mots.org.il), bills itself as "a socio-political contemporary art museum" and puts on avant-garde exhibitions of modern art. The "seam" in question is of course the Green Line. The distinctive pink stone building was a private home until 1948. It then became a frontier post for the IDF overlooking the former **Mandelbaum Gate** crosspoint just to its north (whose position is now marked by a concrete column with a sundial). From 1948 until 1967, the gate was used exclusively by UN personnel, diplomats and convoys to the Israeli Hebrew University enclave on Mount Scopus.

Musrara

During the Mandate, **Musrara** (or Morasha), the area bounded by Hail HaHandassa, HaNeviim and Shivtei Israel, was a well-off, largely Arab neighbourhood, but its Palestinian residents fled in 1948 and were not allowed back. Between then and 1967, the Green Line made it a dead-end, where the authorities housed poor Sephardi Jewish families, mainly refugees who'd been

---

Bevingrad

During the Mandate, the area bounded by Shivtei Israel, Heleni HaMalka and the Jaffa Road was a fortified administrative zone containing the vital installations of British rule and surrounded by barriers and barbed wire. It was nicknamed "**Bevingrad**" after British Foreign Secretary Ernest Bevin, who was hated by Palestine's Jews because he tried to placate the Arabs by putting a lid on postwar Jewish immigration. Indeed, the Immigration Department, at 9 Heleni HaMalka, was bombed in 1944 by the Irgun, who had repudiated their wartime truce with the British now that an Allied victory against Nazi Germany was assured.

Bevingrad finally fell when the British moved out in 1948. The Haganah (the mainstream Zionist militia), with the aid of sympathetic British and Jewish government employees managed to get hold of the exact timetable of withdrawal and moved in to take this strategic area immediately on its vacation and ahead of the Arabs.

driven out of Arab countries following Israel's declaration of independence. After the city's 1967 reunification, Musrara's now central location turned it into a sought-after neighbourhood, and more prosperous Ashkenazi residents started moving in. Local Sephardi youth set up a Black Panther movement, modelled on the American organization of the same name, to campaign for equal rights. Adina Hoffman tells the story of the area in *House of Windows* (see p.287), and Tours in English (see p.28) offer visits of the neighbourhood on the last Friday of the month accompanied by Reuven Aberjel, one of the founders of the Israeli Black Panthers.

Birdwatchers may care to note that Musrara is home to a colony of **lesser kestrels**. Local residents have been helping the Society for the Preservation of Nature in Israel (SPNI) to encourage these rare birds of prey, and nesting boxes have been installed on a number of roofs. The best time to see the kestrels is between February and June; the Jerusalem Bird Observatory (see p.149) can advise on where best to spot them.

The City Hall Complex and around

Just north of the Jaffa Gate, in the area between the Jaffa Road and Shivtei Israel Street, Jerusalem's new **City Hall** is part of a complex of much older buildings, some dating to the late nineteenth century, that now form part of the municipality offices. The complex, created between 1988 and 1993, incorporates the old British municipality building, a number of other historical buildings, and three new administrative buildings, all set around a public open space called **Safra Square**. The city council runs guided tours of the complex Mondays and Wednesdays at 10am (10NIS; book ahead on ☎02/629 5363), meeting at the entrance to the square from Jaffa Road.

Coming into the complex from Jaffa Road, the green area to your right is Daniel Garden, adorned with a sculpture from the Modern Head series by pop art pioneer Roy Lichtenstein, who gave it as a gift in memory of Israel's assassinated prime minister Yitzhak Rabin. Across the garden, the **Zoology Building** was previously used as a laboratory block by the Hebrew University.

At the southern end of the complex, the building at 2 Jaffa Rd, whose metal window grilles bear a "BB" monogram, was once the Jerusalem branch of **Barclays Bank**. The building's strategic location in 1948 ensured it a hefty spray of gunfire, whose marks it still bears. The building next door was known as the **Bagel Building** because it used to be a bagel bakery, and just along Shivtei Israel Street, 2 Safra Square (13 Shivtei Israel) formerly housed the Russian Consulate.

The Underground Prisoners Museum

Just to the north, behind City Hall, a turn west off Shivtei Israel Street leads to the former Central Prison, originally a hostel for female Russian pilgrims and now an **Underground Prisoners Museum** (Sun–Thurs 9am–5pm; 10NIS; bring ID and ring bell for entry), dedicated to members of the Jewish underground paramilitary groups, operating under the Mandate. Prisoners held here belonged mainly to the two right-wing Zionist groups, the Irgun and the Stern

Gang. Cell 17 now houses a small but interesting **exhibition** of prisoners' art, plus handcuffs, shackles and Mandate-era police truncheons from the days before the local constabulary came equipped with Uzis. Cell 31 has a more didactic exhibition on cooperation and resistance – the Zionists sided with the British during the Palestinian revolt of 1936–9, and the Irgun and the Haganah (but not the Stern Gang) called a truce with the British at the start of World War II; as soon as Allied victory was assured however, they went back to resisting, the Irgun and Stern Gang by methods rather more extreme than the Haganah, which is why it is they who filled the cells here. In cell 22, Stern Gang prisoners dug a **tunnel**, and escaped along with a number of Irgun inmates. Cells 32 and 34 have been reconstructed as they were at the time, but most interesting is cell 50, **death row**, where two prisoners managed to blow themselves up rather than face the **gallows** in the room next door, where eight of their fellow inmates took the drop.

The Russian Compound

North of City Hall is the **Russian Compound**. Legend has it the Assyrian army camped on this site when preparing to attack Jerusalem in 701 BC, as did Titus in 68 AD. Its modern name derives from its purchase in 1860 by Tsar Alexander II to provide services and accommodation for the twenty thousand or so Russian pilgrims who visited the city every year, virtually turning it into a walled city in its own right.

From the Underground Prisoners' Museum (see opposite), the road passes the 1863 **Duhovnia Russian Mission Building**, now a courthouse, on the way to the impressive green-domed **Russian Cathedral**, opened in 1872 (Tues–Fri 9am–1pm, Sat & Sun 9am–noon), and the notorious **"Muscobiya" police station**, where local Palestinian political detainees are usually held and questioned after their arrest. In front of it, a stone column dating from the Second Temple period lies abandoned on the ground, having been cracked during quarrying.

From here, past the compound's northern gate, you come onto Heleni HaMalka Street, on whose north side at no.13 stands the grandiose, turreted **Sergei House**, put up as a hostel for aristocratic Russian pilgrims in 1890 and now the HQ of the Society for the Preservation of Nature in Israel. In its grounds you can see some traditional olive presses and ancient water-drawing devices.

Notre Dame

On Paratroopers Road, high on the hill east of the City Hall Complex, the prominent landmark of the white stone **Notre Dame de France** (at its most impressive at night when floodlit) offers great views over the Old City and beyond from its terrace café (see p.183). Built in 1887 for the Assumptionist Fathers, and funded by public subscription in France, it found itself in the front line in 1948, when Israeli forces managed to hold it against a frontal assault by Transjordan's Arab Legion – take a look up the hill at it from the Damascus Gate and you'll see how strategic it was. Its south wing was bombed out in the battle and subsequently became an Israeli observation post facing Jordanian troops across the Green Line on the Old City ramparts from then until 1967. Notre Dame was taken over by the Vatican in 1973 and is now the Holy See's own pilgrim centre in Jerusalem.

Independence Park and around

Southwest of the City Hall Complex is **Independence Park**. At its eastern end, where the trees and undergrowth begin, lies a pre-1948 Muslim cemetery, **Mamilla**, a corruption of the Arabic *Ma'man Allah* (God's sanctuary). Among the graves, many of which have been desecrated or vandalized in the past (or buried under the car park lot in the southwest corner), is the domed cube of the **Zawiya Kubakiya**, the tomb of Mamluk Emir Aidughi Kubaki, governor of Safed and Aleppo before being exiled to Jerusalem and buried here on his death in 1289 AD.

In 2005, the Simon Wiesenthal Center, an American Jewish group which campaigns against anti-Semitism, announced that it would build a "**Museum of Tolerance and Human Dignity**" over areas of the disused cemetery, sparking off protests by both Palestinians and Israeli liberals. The Wiesenthal Center say that the museum will be built on what was previously a car park and will not involve further desecration of the graves. In 2008 Israel's Supreme Court over ruled objections to the project and building of the Frank Gehry -designed structure will now go ahead as planned.

In the centre of the cemetery, the now disused **Mamilla Pool** is typical of the cisterns excavated to supply water to the medieval city. Supposedly commissioned by Pontius Pilate, the pool once supplied water via an aqueduct to the Old City, but it now lies empty for much of the year, filled by rain only in the winter, when it becomes a magnet for birdlife. The park was the site of a terrible **massacre** in 614 AD, when Byzantine Jerusalem fell to the Persian Sassanids, supported by Babylonian and Palestinian Jews, who had suffered much under Byzantine rule. Persian forces rounded up the city's Christian population and, according to Christian sources, sold them to their Jewish allies, who slaughtered some thousands of them on this spot.

The Mamilla Development

The area between the park and the Jaffa Gate, along Rehov HaEmek (Mamilla Street), once a poor Jewish neighbourhood in Mandate Palestine, and scene of attacks by Arab mobs in 1947 following the publication of the UN's partition plan for Palestine, became a derelict no-man's-land between 1948 and 1967, but has now been reborn as the **Mamilla development**, a highly prestigious address containing an open-air shopping mall, and some of the most expensive homes in town (many of whose owners live abroad, visiting only on vacation). The 1868 **Convent of St Vincent de Paul** has been renovated as part of the development. The **Stern House**, where Zionist leader Theodor Herzl (see p.150) stayed in 1898, was among the buildings scheduled for demolition, but public opposition forced the city authorities to dismantle it brick by brick and reassemble it as part of the development. It now houses the Steimatsky bookshop.

King David Street

King David Street runs from Agron and Mamilla Street south toward Yemin Moshe, passing a number of sights worth checking out on the way, first of which is the Hebrew Union College, an academic institute run by the Reform Judaism movement (see p.44). Inside the college (at the far end of the courtyard, on the right), the **Skirball Museum** (Sun, Tues & Thurs 10am–4pm; free; ☎02/620 3333, ⓦwww.huc.edu/museums/jer) is a small exhibition of artefacts from three archeological sites (Tel Dan, Gezer and Aro'er). The museum is small but very well laid out, with photographs of the sites and finds including pots, figurines, an ancient dice and a ninth-century BC inscription from Tel Dan which refers to the rulers of Judah as "the House of David" – the earliest known reference to King David outside of the Bible.

A little further down the street, two of the most impressive buildings in West Jerusalem face each other. The **YMCA Three Arches Hotel** (see p.173) with its imposing tower and cupolas, was designed by the same architect as New York's Empire State Building, and its magnificent lobby, with vaulting reminiscent of Crusader constructions, is well worth popping in to see. You can also climb the ninety-metre bell tower (5NIS) for a great vantage point over the city, but only in groups of two or more since one visitor threw himself from the top. Opposite, the grandiose **King David Hotel**, Israel's most prestigious place to stay (see p.175), has hosted a huge assortment of celebs, VIPs and dignitaries. It was bombed by the Irgun in 1946, when it was the headquarters of the British Mandate authorities. The Irgun did in fact give warning of the attack by phone but this was not received in time to evacuate the building and 91 people died in the explosion. Even if you can't afford a room, you can still sample the hotel's grandeur by popping in to take tea or coffee in the lobby.

At the end of Abba Siqra Street, just south of the hotel, steps into a public garden lead down to what is supposed to be **King Herod's Family Tomb**. The beautifully constructed four-chambered tomb is empty, and it is not clear who was originally interred here, but it dates from the correct period. While it might possibly have housed his family, Herod himself is more widely believed to be buried at Herodion near Bethlehem (see p.239).

Yemin Moshe

Two hundred metres south of King Herod's Family Tomb, **Mishkenot Sha'ananim** (Dwellings of Tranquillity), was the first Jewish quarter to be built outside the Old City, starting with a row of **almshouses**. With battlements on the roof and a Star of David over the entrance, these were constructed in 1860 using money bequeathed by American Jewish philanthropist Judah Touro for the city's Jewish poor, and are now part of an upmarket guesthouse (see p.172). Moses Montefiore, the leader of Britain's Jewish community, was appointed executor of Touro's will and subsequently bought the adjoining land. The area thus became known as **Yemin Moshe**, (Moshe being Hebrew for Moses). Its red-roofed town houses and cottages built of Jerusalem stone are some of the loveliest houses in West Jerusalem but the area's most striking building is the narrow stone **windmill** that Montefiore – inspired by the mill in Rehavia (see p.141) – had built to provide flour for the settlement, although it was never actually used for that purpose. It served as an important Israeli observation post in 1948 and now houses a small **museum** (Sun–Thurs 9am–4pm, Fri 9am–1pm; free) dedicated to Montefiore's life and work. Outside it, his **carriage** is displayed, having been burnt in a fire in 1986, and restored in 1990. The terrace by the windmill offers excellent views of Mount Zion, and to the southeast, the Separation Wall snaking over the hills.

▲ Montefiore's windmill in Yemin Moshe, West Jerusalem

Along the Hebron Road

Down on the Hebron Road, between Yemin Moshe and the Old City, is the site of the **Sultan's Pool**, the sultan in question being Suleiman the Magnificent who had the 170m by 67m Herodian reservoir repaired in the sixteenth century while rebuilding the Old City walls. It's now the **Merrill Hassenfeld Amphitheatre** and one of the biggest venues for outdoor concerts in the country (see p.200). Suleiman also had a drinking fountain, called the **Sultan's Sabil**, installed just south of the pool on the Hebron Road.

The Begin Heritage Center and around

Heading south, the road passes the **Cinematheque**, Israel's premier film centre (see p.204). Just to its south, by the *Mount Zion Hotel*, a small **museum** (Sun–Thurs 9am–4pm, Fri 9am–1pm but often closed; free; ☏02/627 7550) tells the story of a secret **cable car** that supplied Israeli forces on Mount Zion during the 1948 war. There's also machinery from the cable car, which unfortunately no longer operates. The museum is often closed for no apparent reason so it's worth calling ahead if you plan to visit.

West of the Cinematheque, the **Menahem Begin Heritage Center** (Sun, Mon, Wed & Thurs 9am–4.30pm, Tues 9am–7pm, Fri 9am–noon; 20NIS; ☏02/565 2020, ⓦwww.begincenter.org.il) honours the former Irgun leader who graduated from bomb attacks on British officials and Arab civilians to become Israel's sixth Prime Minister, later winning the Nobel Peace Prize in 1978 for making peace with Egypt. Begin originally arrived in Palestine as a soldier in the Free Polish Army (see p.143) to fight the Nazis during World War II. The centre has a museum dedicated to his life but all visits are guided and must be booked in advance.

Across the street from the Begin Center, in **Liberty Bell Garden**, the impressive modern **lion fountain** features a fine pride of lions gushing water from their mouths. The park also houses a replica of Philadelphia's Liberty Bell, one of a number of such replicas around the world.

St Andrew's Church

Behind the Begin Center, a path leads up to **St Andrew's Church**, which belongs to the Church of Scotland and proudly flies the cross of Saint Andrew. The church was built to commemorate Britain's victory over the Ottoman Turks in World War I. On its floor, a brass plaque donated in 1929 by the people of Dunfermline and Melrose commemorates Robert the Bruce's "pious wish" that his heart be buried in Jerusalem. Though Robert's wish was never fulfilled (the knight entrusted with bringing it over was waylaid en route and the heart only just made it back to Scotland), the plaque does now in some way give him a presence in the holy city.

South of the church, the old **Khan Train Station**, now disused, has become the location for several bars and nightclubs (see p.198). The station was abandoned when the Tel Aviv–Jerusalem line was reopened as far as Malha (see p.24) in 2005 after being out of service for six years. In 1946 the station was targeted by Menahem Begin's Irgun, who left a bomb in a suitcase in the lobby which wrecked the station and killed a British soldier. Also nearby is the **Khan Theatre** (see p.203).

The German Colony

Behind the old railway station (see above), Emek Refaim Street leads into the **German Colony**. Reached by bus #4 or #21 from King George Street, or #18 from Jaffa Road and King David Street, the Colony was founded in 1873 by the Tempel Gemeinde or "Templars". Not to be confused with the Knights Templar of Crusader times, these "Templars" were a German Christian sect who saw themselves as the chosen people, with a mission to build the kingdom of God in the Holy Land, and the Colony's architecture still bears the stamp of their Teutonic influence. No. 16 Emek Refaim, built in 1877, is a classic example of this, down to the gothic inscription above the door (a quote from Isaiah 60:1). Around the corner, past the Smadar, Jerusalem's oldest movie theatre (see p.204), no. 12 Lloyd George St was a German hospice, and now houses the Konrad Adenauer institute. No. 25 Emek Refaim is more Middle Eastern, with its blue and white tiles, and no. 35 is notable for its Art Deco metal doors. The neighbourhood is now a trendy residential area full of popular cafés (see p.184). As for the "Templars", they were all rounded up and deported by the British in 1939, as the sect was rife with Nazi sympathizers.

The German Colony has a small **Natural History Museum** on Mohilever (Sun, Tues & Thurs 8.30am–1.30pm, Mon & Wed 8.30am–6pm, Sat 10am–2pm; 15NIS; ☏02/563 1116), but it's mostly for local schoolkids, contains little of interest (unless you're a fan of taxidermy), and most of the explanations are in Hebrew only. The model dinosaur is affectionately known to local residents as Zerubavel.

Talbiya

West of the Liberty Bell Garden, Jabotinsky Street heads into the **Talbiya** neighbourhood, with its beautiful houses and gardens dating from Mandate times, where Jews and Palestinians lived side by side until 1948. After 500m, Jabotinsky leads into HaNasi, with the **President's Residence** on the left, though you can't actually see the house from the street. Israel's president, a ceremonial head of state with no real political power, is elected by the Knesset (parliament) and is invariably a veteran politician.

Continuing round onto Chopin Street, you reach the **LA Mayer Memorial Museum for Islamic Art** at 2 HaPalmakh (Sun, Mon, Wed & Thurs 10am–3pm, Tues 10am–6pm, Fri & Sat 10am–2pm; 20NIS; ☎02/566 1291, ⓦwww.islamicart.co.il), which contains an attractive and well-laid-out collection of mainly seventeenth- and eighteenth-century pottery, glass, calligraphy, miniatures, woodwork, textiles, jewellery and ivory carving from as far afield as Egypt, Syria, Iraq, India and, above all, Iran (Palestinian artefacts are conspicuous by their absence). Look out also for the fascinating collection of antique clocks and watches, mainly from eighteenth- and nineteenth-century Europe.

The Monastery of the Cross

West of Talbiya, in the valley below Givat Ram (see p.144), the striking **Monastery of the Cross** (Mon–Sat: summer 10am–6.30pm, winter 10am–5pm; 15NIS) is a massive pink stone building topped by a dome and clock tower and founded in the eleventh century on the site where, according to legend, the tree grew from which Jesus's cross was made. The monastery has been Greek Orthodox since the seventeenth century, but the presence of Georgian inscriptions inside point to the nature of its earlier occupants. A massive metal-plated, wooden door leads into the church, which is shaped like a Greek cross; its walls are covered with frescoes. Behind the altar screen separating the sanctuary from the main body of the church (as in all Orthodox churches), a small shrine marks the site of the tree from which the cross was cut. The monastery can be reached on bus #9 or #17 from King George Street in central West Jerusalem.

Rehavia

To the north of Talbiya, the sedate neighbourhood of **Rehavia** was built in the 1920s as a "garden suburb" planned out by German Jewish architect Richard Kaufmann. Kaufmann personally designed 3 Balfour, now the Israeli **Prime Minister's Residence**, in the Bauhaus-inspired International Style of the time (see p.257). Israel's first prime minister, David Ben Gurion, did not live there but nearby on Ben Maimon (Rambam), and other Rehavia residents have included another former PM, Golda Meir, as well as pre-independence Zionist leaders Menahem Ussishkin (see p.132) and Arthur Ruppin, and Ethiopian Emperor Haile Selassie, who lived on Al-Harizi during World War II, when his country was occupied by Fascist Italy.

Hidden away between nos.10 and 12 Alfasi (also accessible between 23 and 25 Ben Maimon), the **Tomb of Jason** is a restored, pyramid-roofed, rock-cut tomb from the Hasmonean period. It belonged to the Sadducean high-priestly family of an Egyptian naval commander called Jason, who were expelled from Jerusalem by the Seleucids in 172 BC, but allowed back by the Hasmoneans under Alexander Jannaeus. The last burial here was in 30 AD. Unfortunately, you can't go inside, but you can take a breather in the small garden above the tomb.

Montefiore's mill at Yemin Moshe (see p.137) was inspired by the **Rehavia Mill** at 8 Ramban, near the corner of King George Street and Rambam (Ben Maimon), which was installed by the Greek Orthodox Patriarchate in the 1870s so that local residents could make their own flour. The wind proved an unreliable power source, and a motor had to be added to supplement it. Early in the twentieth century, the mill stopped making flour and was turned into apartments. In 1987 it was renovated and turned into a small shopping centre for a handful of upmarket stores and restaurants.

Mount Zion

Southwest of the Old City, **Mount Zion** is recognizable by the distinctive conical roof of Dormition Abbey. The Madaba Map (see p.8), shows the mount inside the city walls, but when Suleiman the Magnificent ordered the walls rebuilt in the mid-sixteenth century, his engineers left Mount Zion outside – a mistake for which, it is said, they paid with their lives (see p.49). This separation was reinforced from 1948 to 1967 by the Israel–Jordan armistice line, which cut Mount Zion off from the Old City. The Israelis were able to hold on to Mount Zion thanks to a secret night-time **cable car** supplying their positions from the Hebron Road next to what is now the *Mount Zion Hotel* (see p.175).

The name Zion became synonymous with Jerusalem, and by extension with the whole country. In Psalm 137, by the rivers of Babylon, the exiles wept "when we remembered Zion", and when they were allowed back in 538 BC, their homecoming was known as the Return to Zion, a term later used by Russian Jews seeking a new homeland in Palestine. This in turn led Nathan Birnbaum to coin the term "Zionism" for the Jewish nationalist movement in 1890; it was only two days before declaring independence that the Jewish state's founders finally settled on the name Israel rather than Zion. Yet despite all this, the name as applied to this hill is actually a mistake. The term originally referred to the neighbouring hill, Mount Ophel (see p.114), the hill where David built his capital (II Samuel 5:7 and I Chronicles 11:5), and it was a misunderstanding by Christian cartographers in the fourth century that transferred the name here.

Though strictly speaking part of West Jerusalem, Mount Zion is most logically explored at the same time as the City of David (see p.113), or the Old City's Armenian Quarter (see p.47). The easiest approach is through the **Zion Gate** in the Old City's southwest corner. Bus #38 will get you here from King George Street and the Jaffa Road, bus #1 or #2 from near the Damascus Gate.

Dormition Abbey

Mount Zion's most prominent landmark is the black, conical roof of the **Dormition Abbey** at the top of the hill (Mon, Tues, Wed & Fri 8.30am–noon & 12.40–6pm, Sat 8.30am–noon & 12.40–5.30pm, Thurs 9.30am–noon & 12.40–5.30pm, Sun & festivals 10.30–11.45am & 12.40–5.30pm). This attractive white stone building, erected in 1900, is traditionally believed to be on the site where Mary lived after her son's crucifixion, and also the site of her death, an event marked by a mausoleum in the bright modern **crypt**, decorated with twelve columns. The church itself is round and uncluttered, giving a strong feeling of lightness and space. Its six round chapels are decorated in gold, and it also features an impressive mosaic floor, and, above the main altar, a delightful golden mosaic of the Madonna and Child. Remains of a mosaic floor from the Byzantine basilica that previously stood here are kept under a glass cover in the courtyard, though the reflection off the glass makes them impossible to see. There's a **cafeteria** serving light refreshments, and a bookshop with a selection of maps and (mostly religious) literature.

The Coenaculum

Down the hill to the right and virtually in the shadow of the Abbey, the **Coenaculum** (from the Latin *Cenaca* meaning supper room; daily 9am–5pm), is reputedly the room in which the Last Supper took place. It is reached through a doorway on the left with an Ottoman inscription above it; inside, go up the stairs to the left. Somewhat smaller than the one depicted in Leonardo da Vinci's famous painting, the room also has pillars in the middle which might have made it difficult for Jesus and his disciples to have sat around a table. However, its authenticity is hardly an issue since, beautiful and peaceful as it is, and regardless of whether or not it stands on the site of the Last Supper, the room was actually built long after Jesus's time, under the Crusaders, with their characteristic pointed arches. Part of a Franciscan monastery until 1552, it was then made into a mosque by the Ottomans, who added a *mihrab* and some beautiful coloured-glass windows.

The Tomb of David

From the Coenaculum, turn right up the stairs by the minaret for the **roof**, from where there are views across the Kidron Valley to the Mount of Olives and beyond. Turn left and down the stairs for what is revered as the **Tomb of David**. Actually, according to the Old Testament (I Kings 2:10), David was buried in the City of David on Mount Ophel, so whoever might be buried here, it can't be the slingshot king – this room, a bare chamber containing a simple cenotaph draped with velvet, was declared his burial place in the tenth century AD based on the mix up with the name "Zion" (see p.141). The tomb's importance to Israelis increased between 1948 and 1967 when, with the Old City in Jordanian hands and the Western Wall out of bounds, the tomb became an alternative site of Jewish pilgrimage. Next to it and directly beneath the Coenaculum is the empty room where Jesus supposedly washed his disciples' feet after the last supper.

The Chamber of the Holocaust

East of David's Tomb, and also easily reached from the Zion Gate by going straight ahead and bearing left at the Franciscan monastery, the memorial **Chamber of the Holocaust** (Sun–Thurs 9am–3.45pm, Fri 9am–1.30pm; 12NIS; ☎02/671 5105, ⓦwww.holocaustchamber.org) is a dusty and sombre exhibition that served as Israel's tribute to the victims of the Holocaust before Yad VaShem (see p.151) was opened. Its main feature is a collection of Holocaust relics such as uniforms from Auschwitz, objects made from destroyed Torah scrolls, and bars of soap made from human fat. On a jacket that a Nazi official forced a Jewish tailor to make him from a Torah scroll, the tailor chose a passage from Leviticus 26 cursing the wicked. The chamber also contains an exhibition on contemporary neo-Naziism, featuring racist literature from around the world, but mostly the United States.

Schindler's grave

Across the main road to the south of David's Tomb and the Holocaust Memorial, the Protestant cemetery just below Mount Zion (of the three gates, it's the one on the right) houses the **tomb of Oskar Schindler**, the Holocaust's most famous "righteous gentile", an industrialist who managed to save an estimated 1200 Jews from Hitler's death camps, and whose efforts were made into a film by Steven Spielberg – *Schindler's List* – based on Thomas Keneally's 1982 Booker Prize-winning novel, *Schindler's Ark*. Reduced to poverty after the war, Schindler was brought to Israel for burial through the efforts of some of those he had rescued. His grave is in the lowest part of the cemetery, by a pathway over to the right; it's covered in stones left by Jewish visitors, the Jewish tradition being to leave a stone rather than flowers when visiting a grave.

Also in the lowest section of the cemetery is a monument to the troops of General Władysław Anders's **Free Polish Army** (one of whose soldiers was Menahem Begin; see p.138). The army was made of anti-Nazi Poles deported to Russia after Stalin's 1939 invasion of eastern Poland under the Nazi-Soviet Pact. Released by the Russians after Hitler turned on Stalin in 1941, they came to Palestine to help the British fight for the Suez Canal, then under threat from Rommel's Afrika Korps. In addition to those who fell during the war, many of Anders's troops perished while trying to get home afterwards.

St Peter in Gallicantu

On the eastern slope of Mount Zion stands the rather pretty white stone **Church of Saint Peter in Gallicantu** (Mon–Sat 8.30am–5pm), built in 1931 on the former site of Byzantine and Crusader structures. Jesus is believed to have been imprisoned here by the High Priest Caiaphas; this is where Peter three times denied knowing him, thus fulfilling the prophecy, "Before the cock crow, thou shalt deny me thrice" (Matthew 26:75). At the entrance, the view from the terrace out over the City of David and the valleys of Jerusalem is another unforgettable one. As you enter the church, check the Byzantine **mosaics** to your right, discovered during restoration work in 1992, one of which was damaged in the eighth century by iconoclasts, who smashed all the pictures. The modern church is decorated in blue, with lovely mosaics and a beautiful stained-glass cross in the roof depicting God enthroned on high. Further sections of the original fifth-century church are preserved in the crypt, which leads out to the garden, and further down to underground caves where some speculate that Peter and John were held (Acts 5:19–42) for preaching at the Temple following the Resurrection. Also here, the "Sacred Pit" is a dungeon excavated in 1889 where Jesus is said to have been held overnight while awaiting trial by Caiaphas and the Sanhedrin. Three Byzantine crosses are engraved on the walls of a hole from the ceiling of the pit to the floor of the crypt above.

Outlying areas

ascinating though the centre of Jerusalem may be, there are plenty of things to see in the suburbs and around the city too. Areas of interest include the hill of **Givat Ram**, home to the impressive **Israel Museum** – with its amazing collection of archeological finds, ancient and modern art, reconstructed synagogue and of course the Dead Sea Scrolls. Just opposite, the **Bible Lands Museum** is little known to tourists but well worth a visit for its excellent overview of the region's history. Also nearby is Israel's parliament, the **Knesset**, and the **Supreme Court**, both housed in striking buildings accessible to visitors. Further out on another hilltop location, **Yad VaShem** is Israel's moving tribute to the victims of the Holocaust and should not be missed. The outlying southwestern suburb of **Malha** is home of Jerusalem's biggest shopping mall, and its main football ground while further west, **Ein Karem**, an artists' colony in a former Palestinian village, is the site of John the Baptist's birth, and Marc Chagall's stained-glass windows celebrating the twelve tribes of Israel. South of the city, the monastery of **Mar Elias** is on the road to Bethlehem, while outside the city limits to the east is **Bethany**, where you can visit the very tomb in which Jesus raised Lazarus from the dead.

The Israel Museum and around

The prestigious **Israel Museum** (Sun, Mon, Wed, Thurs, Sat & holidays 10am–5pm, Tues 4–9 pm, Fri and holiday eve 10am–2pm; 36NIS; ☎02/670 8811, ⓦwww.english.imjnet.org.il) houses four extremely compelling exhibitions, and is an absolute must for anyone with any interest in the country's archeological heritage, or in modern or Jewish art. At the time of writing the museum was undergoing a **major refit** set to finish in May, 2010. While work is carried out only the Shrine of the Book, the model of Jerusalem, the youth wing and temporary exhibitions were open to the public.

A tour of the museum's highlights in English is at 11am every day except Tuesday, when it's at 4.30pm. Wheelchair-bound visitors can see almost all the museum, though you may have to use special entrances to some areas. The museum is served by buses #9 and #17 from King George Street.

On the way from the museum entrance to the main exhibitions, you pass an **archeology garden** of ancient mosaics and sculptures, and then the **Billy Rose Garden** of modern sculpture, where Rodin, Picasso and Henry Moore are among the sculptors represented, along with a giant apple core by Claes Oldenburg and Coosje van Bruggen.

The Shrine of the Book

The showpiece of the museum is the stylish, modern **Shrine of the Book** (free guided tours in English Sun, Mon, Wed & Thurs 1pm), which houses the famous **Dead Sea Scrolls** (see box below). Built in 1965, the Shrine is crowned by a distinctive white dome, shaped like the lids of the jars in which the scrolls were discovered. It was designed by American Jewish architects Armand P. Bartos and Frederic Kiesler to house the first seven scrolls to be discovered, which had been taken to the United States and acquired there by Israeli archeologists. When Israel occupied East Jerusalem in 1967, the authorities brought over the rest of the scrolls from the Rockefeller Museum to join the original seven.

As well as the scrolls themselves – which are displayed on the upper level of the building, and rotated every three months – other ancient manuscripts, including letters and documents dating from the Second Revolt of 135 AD, are housed on the lower level, together with some interesting domestic finds, such as house keys, utensils and glassware, which provide an insight into everyday life at the time of the revolt.

The Herodian Jerusalem Model

Located next to the Shrine of the Book, the **model of Jerusalem in the time of Herod** was originally commissioned by the owner of a hotel in Malha. When the hotel closed, the model came to the Israel Museum, and it's well worth seeing for the excellent impression it gives of what Jerusalem might have looked like in Herodian times with the Temple and Herod's Palace still standing. Made to a scale of 1:50 and measuring roughly 20m across, it was constructed

---

The Dead Sea Scrolls

Early in 1947, on an escarpment above the Dead Sea near Qumran, a Bedouin shepherd by the name of **Muhammed al-Dhib** climbed down into an underground cave and found some earthenware jars containing seven **ancient scrolls**, which he then sold to an antiquities dealer for the princely sum of £7. Since then over 800 fragments of scrolls have been discovered in the caves around Qumran leading them to be described as one of the greatest archeological finds of modern times. Dating from the second century BC to the first AD, the scrolls include **biblical texts** – of which they are the oldest known by over a thousand years – texts from the Apocrypha and Pseudepigrapha (non-canonical biblical works such as the Book of Enoch), and sectarian works apparently peculiar to the group which wrote them, including the *War of the Sons of Light against the Sons of Darkness*. Most enigmatic is the **Copper Scroll**, which appears to detail the location of hidden treasure.

It is generally believed that the scrolls were written by a monastic sect called the **Essenes**, who are described by the historian Josephus (*Jewish War* 2:119–61), and it is supposed that those were the people who lived at Qumran (see p.249), but none of this is certain, and these ideas have been challenged by a number of scholars, one of whom recently claimed that the Essenes were simply made up by Josephus. **Controversy** has also dogged the interpretation of the scrolls. The Jordanian authorities, and subsequently the Israelis, gave control over their study to a secretive clique of church-approved Catholic scholars who refused for years to publish most of them, resulting in a proliferation of conspiracy theories. Most notably, it was suggested that the scrolls referred to a split in the early church between St Paul and Jesus's brother James. It wasn't until the 1990s that most of the texts were eventually published.

with materials used at the time – marble, stone, copper, iron and wood – and to measurements derived from Josephus and the Talmud.

The youth wing

The museum's **Youth Wing** features exhibits on ecology and a selection of ancient artefacts of special interest to children. It also has a recycling room (☎02/670 8963), where, at workshops currently held on Tuesday evenings, children can make things from recycled materials. The wing always has plenty going on, and posts a schedule of its activities on the museum's website.

The Samuel Bronfman Archaeology Wing

The heart of the museum, closed until 2010 for renovations, is the **Samuel Bronfman Archaeology Wing**, displaying artefacts found in Israel and the Occupied Territories since 1948 (pre-1948 finds are in the Rockefeller Museum, see p.110).

The first room, dealing with **prehistory**, features stone masks from the seventh millennium BC and the Judean desert treasure of copper and ivory artefacts, some three thousand years younger. Next comes the **Canaanite** room, whose most striking exhibit is the series of fourteenth-century BC anthropoid sarcophagi, complete with podgy faces and little folded arms, from Deir al-Balah in the Gaza Strip – almost classic ancient Egyptian, but not quite. Likewise, in the **Israelite** room, ninth- to eighth-century BC ivory plaques from Samaria in the West Bank feature Egyptian motifs but are executed in a Phoenecian style.

Between the **Second Temple** and **Roman** rooms, the Pontius Pilate inscription from Caesarea reading "[PON]TIVS PILATVS [PRÆF]E-CTVS IVD[EÆ]" (Pontius Pilate, Prefect of Judea) was the first extrabiblical evidence for Pilate's existence, and the Roman room also has items belonging to rebels in the Second Revolt, and a magnificent bust of Emperor Hadrian who supressed it.

▲ The Shrine of the Book at the Israel Museum

The **Byzantine** room is most notable for its amazing mosaics including an ark flanked by *menorahs* from a synagogue at Bet She'an, one of David playing the harp from a synagogue in Gaza, and two wonderful mosaic pictures from a church at Kissufim next to the Gaza Strip of a lion taking a cow and a man fighting a bear. Finally, the "**neighbouring cultures**" room has artefacts from Egypt, Mesopotamia (Iraq) and other parts of the ancient Middle East.

The Jewish Art and Ethnography Wing

The museum's **Jewish Art and Ethnography** section features jewellery and costumes from Jewish communities worldwide, and a large collection of **Judaica** (see p.224) from all over the world, including Jewish costumes and a wealth of silver ornaments used to adorn scrolls of the Torah, but the most impressive highlights are the reconstructed **interiors of synagogues**. These include the beautiful eighteenth-century painted wooden ceiling of a synagogue from Horb (south Germany) by Eliezer Sussman, the magnificently ornate gold and blue interior of a baroque synagogue built in Vittorio Veneto (north Italy) in 1700, and the interior of the Kadavumbagan synagogue built and gradually added to between the fourteenth and seventeenth centuries in Cochin (south India). Also recreated here, thanks to Baron Edmund de Rothschild, is the **eighteenth-century Parisian salon** of his grandfather (also Baron Edmond), a French financier who strongly supported the early Zionist movement. Very elegant, in the rococo style of the period (it dates from the 1740s), the room contains furniture, paintings and objets d'art, with two enormous chandeliers and a huge mirror, originally part of a French aristocrat's Parisian *pied de terre*.

The Bezalel Art Wing

The **Bezalel Art Wing** is the museum's main permanent art exhibition, with a display of international and modern art that starts with **Asian** art, and moves on to **pre-Colombian** South American art including a brilliant spiky figure from Ecuador dated anywhere between 500BC and 500AD, as well as some marvellous Peruvian and Mayan ceramics Beyond is the **African** room, whose most striking exhibits include a group of awesome Dogon ritual masks from Mali, and a beaded headdress from Cameroon topped with an effigy of a dog.

From these you move into the **Impressionist and Post-Impressionist** rooms, where you'll find lesser-known but still impressive works by the likes of Renoir, Monet, Gaugin and Van Gough followed by even more big names in the **twentieth century** room, whose contributing artists include Braque, Kandinsky and of course the great Jewish artist Marc Chagall (see box, p.155) – who is nothing like as well represented as you might expect, though his painting *The Rabbi* is here – plus a good selection of surrealists including Dalí, de Chirico, Ernst and Magritte, as well as Francis Bacon.

The Bible Lands Museum

Across the street from the Israel Museum is one of Jerusalem's little-known gems, the **Bible Lands Museum** (Sun, Mon, Tues & Thurs 9.30am–5.30pm, Wed 9.30am–9.30pm; 32NIS; wheelchair accessible; free tours in English at 10.30am plus Wed 5.30pm; ⓦwww.blmj.org;). The museum presents a chronological overview of the ancient history of the Middle East and the Eastern Mediterranean helping to illustrate how the various cultures interconnected and influenced each other. Because it is not very well known, the Bible Lands Museum is usually free of tour groups, making it a quiet and relaxing place to wander around.

Highlights include, in room 4, a sixth-century magic incantation bowl bearing a spell against demons, curses, wicked spirits and evil-doers, and in room 9, an ancient Egyptian model of a slaughterhouse, with a figure slitting the throat of a steer. Between rooms 9 and 10, there's a wonderful anthropoid sarcophagus lid from Assyut in Egypt, and in room 10, a collection of small limestone canopic jars from an ancient Egyptian tomb, each designed to hold a different mummified organ, and topped with the head of a different Egyptian god. Room 11 is devoted to the Sea Peoples (including the biblical Philistines, who were a lot more cultured than is commonly believed) while room 16 displays finds from Persia including a magnificent gold lion's head dagger handle.

Among the museum's most enigmatic exhibits, displayed in room 14, are four **"kaf censers"** – wide, spoon-like bowls with a hollow stem, some decorated with a hand (*kaf*). These are interpreted as being the dishes, censers or "spoons" for incense referred to in the Old Testament (Exodus 25:29, I Kings 7:50, II Chronicles 4:22 and Jeremiah 52:18), but the hollow stem and *kaf* symbol is puzzling, leading some to suggest that they were used for smoking cannabis (*kif*); in fact it's much more likely that the stem was used to blow on the coals or incense in the bowl (indeed, a Syrian relief exists which depicts this).

The Bloomfield Science Museum

For a change from history and archeology, the **Bloomfield Science Museum** on Derekh Ruppin (Mon–Thurs 10am–6pm, Fri 10am–2pm, Sat 10am–4pm; 30NIS; wheelchair accessible; ☏02/654 4888, ⓦwww.mada.org.il/en) is dedicated to topics such as motion, electricity and human senses. In its airy, modern building you'll find lots of moving interactive exhibits – especially fun for kids with lots of levers to pull and buttons to press. As well as wave machines, light shows and electricity demonstrations other exhibits demonstrate how buildings stand up and even introduce the theory of relativity.

The Knesset and around

Across Derekh Ruppin from the museums **the Knesset**, Israel's one-chamber parliament (☏02/675 3416, ⓦwww.knesset.gov.il), occupies an understated cubic building whose simplicity and human scale avoid the pomposity or monolithic authoritarianism of so many seats of government. Just three storeys high and inaugurated in 1958, the building was designed by Joseph Klarwein, who won the commission in a competition among Israeli architects after Baron James de Rothschild left £1.25 million in his will for the purpose. In front of the entrance stands the symbol of the State, the seven-branched **menorah** (Jewish candelabra), this one donated by the British parliament, while the entrance hall features a **triple tapestry and mosaics** by Marc Chagall. The tapestries – depicting God's creation of the world, the Exodus from Egypt, and Jerusalem – are spectacularly colourful, as you'd expect from Chagall.

Guided tours in English leave from the foyer on Sunday and Thursday at 8.30am, noon and 1.45pm (arrive at least 15min early), or, if you want to see the Knesset at work, you could sit in on one of the sessions which take place

Knesset elections

The 120-seat Knesset is elected on the purest form of **proportional representation** – the party list – in which voters choose a political party but not a candidate, and parties get seats in more or less exactly the proportion of the vote that they receive. To run for election, a party must endorse "the Jewish and democratic nature" of the Israeli state, and parties considered to support racism or terrorism are also excluded, as are independent candidates. The electoral system has two main problems: first, it means that Israelis do not have their own representative or MP, with Knesset members responsible only to their parties; and second, no party ever has an overall majority, and **coalition-building** therefore involves handouts from the pork barrel (or kosher equivalent thereof), largely to Jewish religious fundamentalist parties, who usually seem to end up holding the balance of power To free the executive from some of the instability created by this system, the **Prime Minister** is now elected separately, while, on the positive side, PR does ensure representation to most Jewish political groups in the country, and to almost everyone who votes.

on Monday at 4pm, Tuesday at 4pm and Wednesday at 11am (in Hebrew of course); no fee, just join the queue. Note that for both the tours and sessions you will need to bring your passport. Also note that a dress code prohibits tank-tops, cropped tops, shorts, jeans, sandals, and even Crocs (2008's Israeli fashion craze) unless they are black or navy blue in colour.

The Bird Observatory

Just north of the Knesset, between it and the Supreme Court, is the **Jerusalem Bird Observatory** (24hr; free; ☏052/386 9488, ⓦwww.jbo.org.il) a one-acre conservation and bird monitoring centre with a hide. Tours (15NIS) in English are conducted on Tuesdays at 4pm, and visitors are welcome to visit for other activities such as catching and ringing birds, usually in the mornings (call for details). Over 140 different bird species have been spotted here including pelicans, eagles, vultures, cranes, owls, storks and kingfishers; the rarest local species is the Lesser Kestrel (see p.134). The best time to spot birdlife in Jerusalem is during the great migrations in March–May and August–November when birds stop here en route from Africa or Europe.

The Supreme Court

Israel's **Supreme Court** building (Sun–Thurs 8.30am–2.30pm; free; ☏02/675 9612), opened in 1992, is considered one of the country's finest pieces of modern architecture, and incorporates features that give a nod to architectural styles from different periods of Israel's history. The copper-clad **pyramid** in the library wing, for example, is supposed to recall the Tomb of Zechariah and the Pillar of Absalom in the Kidron Valley (see p.115), though the eye-like round window at the top makes it more resemble the masonic Great Seal on the back of a US one-dollar bill, much to the delight of conspiracy theorists. The **cloistered courtyard**, faced in stone from the Negev town of Mitzpe Ramon, recalls the central courtyard of the Rockefeller Museum (see p.110), while the **courtrooms** themselves, extending from the main hall like five fingers of a hand, are shaped like synagogues of the Talmudic period (200–600 AD). The **mosaic** in the entrance is from Al-Hamma (Hamat Gader), an enclave next to the Golan Heights, and the **stairway** leading up from the entrance is clearly designed to echo one of the steep streets of the Old City's Christian Quarter.

▲ The Menorah sculpture outside the Knesset

At the top, a **panoramic window** gives a vista over West Jerusalem. Turn up at noon (passport ID required), for a free **tour** of the court in English.

The legal system in Israel is something of a hybrid absorbing many of the features of the common-law system used during the Mandate, the Ottoman system which preceded it, and Jewish canon law. The Supreme Court is the country's final court of appeal, and also its constitutional court. In some ways it is quite different from Western systems such as those of England, Scotland or the United States, most notably in criminal trials, which are judge-only, with no jury.

Adjacent to the Supreme Court (with lanes leading to the court and to the Knesset), the nineteen-acre **Wohl Rose Park** is filled with some 400 different varieties of the flower (15,000-odd plants), worth stopping to admire even if you're not a connoisseur.

Mount Herzl

The **tomb of Theodor Herzl**, founder of Zionism, adorns a large pleasant park on **Mount Herzl**, 2km west of Givat Ram (Sat–Thurs 8am–4.45pm, Fri & holiday eves 8am–1pm, Sat and Jewish holidays 9am–4.45pm; free; ☎02/632 1515). Down some steps to the left of the entrance is a small **museum** (summer Sun–Thurs 9am–3.30pm, Fri 9am–12.30pm; 25NIS) devoted to Herzl's life and work and containing, in addition to the usual documents, books and photographs, the **study** – transported piece by piece from Vienna and reconstructed here – in which he wrote his famous Zionist treatise, *Alt-Neuland* (Old-New Land). As it happens, the idea of a Jewish state in Palestine predated Herzl, and was dubbed Zionism by Nathan Birnbaum in 1890, six years before Herzl published his seminal work *Der Judenstaat* (The Jewish State), but it was undoubtedly *Der Judenstaat* which gave Zionism its impetus; as the non-Jewish East European press panned it, Jews worldwide got in touch with Herzl, who organized a congress in Basel in 1897, thus founding the movement.

The park is also the last resting place of a number of other prominent Israeli and Zionist leaders, including three Israeli Prime Ministers: **Levi Eshkol** (PM 1963–9), **Golda Meir** (PM 1969–74), and **Yitzhak Rabin** (PM 1974–7 and 1992–5) as well as **Ze'ev Jabotinsky**, the originator of Zionism's right-wing "Revisionist" tendency. Jabotinsky died in 1940 in New York, and it was Levi Eshkol who had his body brought here in 1964, in fulfilment of the specification in Jabotinsky's will that his body should be brought to Palestine for burial, but only after the establishment of a Jewish state.

Mount Herzl can be reached on **bus** #13 or #18 from King David Street, bus #13, #18, #20 or #21 from the Jaffa Road, bus #17 or #21 from King George Street, or bus #17 from the Israel Museum. It will also be served by the new tram.

Yad VaShem

Adjacent to Mount Herzl, **Yad VaShem** (meaning "a memorial and a name" from Isaiah 56:5) is Israel's most important memorial to the victims of **the Holocaust**. A visit here is a deeply sorrowful, extremely moving and rather disturbing experience, but it is one that you may well feel duty-bound to make. Yad Vashem (Sun–Thurs 9am–5pm, Fri and holiday eves 9am–2pm; free; ☎02/644 3802, ⊛www.yadvashem.org) is linked to Mount Herzl by a direct pathway, and by regular free minibus shuttles. There are also free shuttles on site to bring you back from the far end to the entrance.

The Historical Museum

From the entrance, most visitors head straight to the **Historical Museum** (closed to children under 10), which attempts to convey the horrors of Nazi anti-Semitism with documents, photographs and a large number of film clips, including period newsreels and testimony from eyewitnesses. One of the most famous pictures, among the harrowing images of corpses and emaciated camp inmates, is that of a child in the Warsaw Ghetto, his hands raised in bewildered surrender. Only the incongruous addition of photos showing the British preventing Jewish immigrants from entering Palestine after World War Two dilutes the museum's powerful message.

Adjoining the museum, the **Hall of Names** records names and biographical details of as many victims as possible (searches can be made to try to find the fate of particular individuals), and there's also an **art museum** of works by

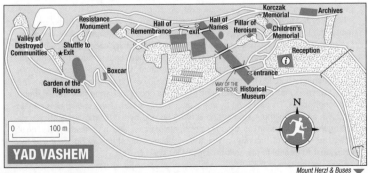

YAD VASHEM

0   100 m

N

Mount Herzl & Buses ▼▼

victims and survivors, many of them created in the near-impossible conditions of camps, ghettos and hideaways. The most moving are works by children.

The rest of the site

Beyond the Historical Museum, is the **Hall of Remembrance**, a sombre chamber whose stone floor is engraved with the names of 22 concentration camps, while an eternal flame burns above a casket of ashes from the cremation ovens. An area nearby is dedicated to the memory of those who perished fighting back in the 1943 Warsaw Ghetto uprising.

At the end of the site is a **boxcar** used to transport victims to the concentration camps by rail, and the **Valley of Destroyed Communities** commemorating communities wiped out whole by the Nazis.

On the way back to the exit, you pass the **Way of the Righteous**, honouring gentiles who helped the Jews despite the terrible danger to themselves in doing so. One of the boats used by Danish people to smuggle out the country's Jewish population ahead of the Nazi invasion is usually placed nearby, but was absent for restoration at last check. Nearby, a monument honours Janusz Korczak the

The Holocaust

"If all the trees in the world turned into pens, all the waters in the oceans turned into ink and the heavens turned into paper, it would still be insufficient material to describe the horrors these people suffered."
Leslie Hardman (Jewish chaplain assigned to Belsen after its liberation by the British army)

Of the approximately eleven million people murdered by the Nazis, some six million were Jewish. During the Holocaust (*HaShoah* in Hebrew) most of them were systematically exterminated in death camps as part of Hitler's "final solution to the Jewish problem". Of those not simply slaughtered, the rest were killed by forced labour, disease and malnutrition in conditions so appalling that Allied soldiers liberating the camps were literally sick on seeing them. Not all Hitler's victims were Jews (political activists, trade unionists, Romanies, gay people and people with physical and mental disabilities were rounded up and murdered), but Jews formed by far the biggest contingent. The "final solution" was the culmination of years of official anti-Semitism in Nazi-held territory, in which many non-Jews happily collaborated, though a few (the "righteous gentiles") risked their lives to prevent Jews falling into the hands of the Nazis. The Allies knew about the death camps by August 1942 but, despite pleas from Jewish organizations to bomb them, refused for military reasons to do so, or to allow free passage to Jews fleeing Nazi-occupied Europe. In the end, a third of the world's Jewish population, including ninety percent of all the Jews in Poland, perished in the worst act of genocide ever.

Many of those who survived the Holocaust eventually made it to Palestine, and many still live in Israel, though of course old age is now thinning their numbers. For many Jews, the Holocaust was the final proof that they needed a state of their own, a refuge from the anti-Semitism which has dogged them through the centuries. Indeed, it is often argued that, but for the Holocaust, the State of Israel would not have been founded. On the other hand, the passivity of the Holocaust's victims – the 1943 Warsaw Ghetto uprising was one of the few occasions when they turned round and fought back – is also seen by some as a lesson in how Jews should never again lie down and die without a fight, and is often quoted by those who advocate a hard line against Israel's enemies, though opponents of Israel, and in particular anti-Zionist Jews, are critical of the way in which they believe the state's supporters use the Holocaust to appeal to the guilt-feelings of Western liberals.

Jewish Polish author and teacher who set up an orphanage which he continued inside the Warsaw Ghetto, and who, in 1942, voluntarily went into the gas chamber at Treblinka with his orphans rather than desert them.

Deir Yassin

Five kilometres northwest of the city centre, on Katzanelbogen Street in the outer suburb of **Kfar Sha'ul**, and surrounded by forest, is the Kfar Sha'ul Mental Health Centre, where patients suffering from "Jerusalem Syndrome" (see p.6) and other psychoses come to recover. Its grounds contain the remains of an Arab village, **Deir Yassin**, whose fate in the 1948 war remains an emotive symbol for Palestinians and a source of shame for Israelis.

At 4.30am on 10 April 1948, the village of nine hundred inhabitants, which had co-existed in relative harmony with its Jewish neighbours, but was strategically located, was woken by a 132-man force of Irgun and Stern Gang irregulars. The mainstream Zionist militia, the Haganah, had allocated Deir Yassin to the right-wing irregulars in the belief that its capture would be difficult to mess up. However, the villagers put up a stronger defence than expected, though by afternoon they had run out of ammunition and those with arms had fled, leaving the Jewish irregulars to go from house to house killing the inhabitants, before driving the men to a nearby quarry, lining them up and shooting them. It was Jews from the neighbouring village of Givat Sha'ul who finally halted the slaughter.

A figure of 250 was originally given for the dead, but recent estimates suggest the number was around 120. However, propagandists on both sides sought to profit by exaggerating the atrocities. Arab sources spread false stories of rape and butchery to discredit the Zionists, who in turn used the incident to strike terror into other Arabs and hasten their flight. Meanwhile, safe within the boundaries of the psychiatric hospital, the houses of Deir Yassin remain as they were in 1948, making this, ironically, one of the best-preserved ex-Arab villages in Israel. It is not possible to enter the site, but you can see it very well through the wire fence that surrounds it. A **memorial procession** is held every year from Kanfey Nesharim Street in Givat Sha'ul to the gates of the Mental Health Centre and around the site in remembrance of the massacre.

Kfar Sha'ul can be reached by **bus** #2 from the Dung Gate, Damascus Gate and Shivtei Israel Street, #15 from Jaffa Road with Strauss, or #33 from Mount Herzl.

Ein Karem

Two kilometres southwest of Mount Herzl, and 7km west of the Old City, **Ein Karem** is traditionally held to be the birthplace of John the Baptist, the city of Judah mentioned by St Luke (1:39–40) in which the house of Zechariah, John's father stood. A quiet, leafy suburb surrounded by terraced hills dotted with olive and cypress trees, it was formerly a Palestinian Arab village, whose mixed Christian and Muslim population fled in 1948 and were not allowed to return. The village was then repopulated by Jewish refugees from Morocco and Romania, but today its beautiful old stone houses are mostly inhabited by artists and sculptors, with several art galleries and a variety of restaurants. Ein

Karem is served by **bus** #17 from King George Street, the Israel Museum and Mount Herzl.

The Church of Saint John the Baptist

North of the main road, the **Church of Saint John the Baptist** (Sun–Fri: April–Sept 8–11.45am & 2.30–5.45pm; Oct–March 8–11.45am & 2.30–4.45pm; free; ☎02/641 3639) was built in 1674 on the reputed site of the Baptist's birth, though the building combines remnants of many periods. A statue of Venus from the courtyard is exhibited in a Byzantine chapel under the modern church (not always open) along with fragments of a mosaic floor. In front of the church entrance, a grille in the floor allows you to see another Byzantine mosaic. Inside, the church is decorated with seventeenth-century paintings, and steps in the left-hand wall (inaccessible to the public) lead down to a trio of Byzantine rock tombs. To the right of the high altar is the altar of John's mother, Elizabeth, and on the left steps lead into a natural cave, held to be the **Grotto of the Nativity of Saint John**, in which a marble plaque under the altar marks the spot where the Baptist was born.

The Church of the Visitation

Across the main road and down the hill, a small mosque marks the site of **Mary's Spring** (also called the Spring of the Virgin) from which Ein Karem ("spring of the vineyard") took its name. Nowadays much of the water from the spring is put to practical use irrigating crops. Following the road round to the right, steps on the left after 100m lead up to the **Church of the Visitation** (Sun–Fri:April–Sept 8–11.45am & 2.30–6pm; Oct–March 8–11.45am & 2.30–5pm; free; ☎02/641-7291;), commemorating Mary's visit to John the Baptist's mother Elizabeth when she was pregnant. The Upper Church, built above ground level, was designed by Antonio Barluzzi and completed in 1955. Underneath it is the Lower Church, containing a natural grotto that once contained a small spring. In front of the church are the remnants of houses, some of them dating back to Roman times. During the Byzantine period the grotto became a place of worship, and later the Crusaders built a large, two-storeyed church over it, with a smaller one in front – both collapsed after the Crusaders left and in 1679 the area was bought by the Franciscans, who eventually – after nearly two centuries of trying – managed to get permission from the Ottoman authorities to restore it. The Lower Church, which they restored in 1862, is adorned with large frescoes; the Upper Church has a painted ceiling in fourteenth-century Tuscan style. The courtyard is decorated with ceramic tiles bearing the *Magnificat* (Mary's hymn of thanksgiving on meeting Elizabeth from Luke 1:46–55) in 42 languages.

The Chagall Windows

About 1km southwest of Ein Karem village, the **Hadassah Hospital**, founded in 1951 when the Mount Scopus site was abandoned, is famous for the twelve **Chagall windows** in its synagogue (Sun–Thurs 8am–1.15pm & 2–3.45pm, or 8am–1pm on the intermediate days of Passover and Sukkot; ☎02/677 6271, ⓦwww.hadassah.org.il). Free tours in English are given at 8am, 8.30am, 9.30am, 10.30am, noon, 12.30pm, 3pm and 3.30pm.

Each of the twelve windows, presented to the hospital by the artist in 1982, is dominated by one main colour and depicts one of the twelve sons of Jacob and tribes of Israel. The colours also match those of the gems worn on the breastplate

Marc Chagall

Although he never lived in Israel, **Marc Chagall** was a keen supporter of the Jewish State, and endowed it with many of his finest works of art. By far the most important Jewish artist to have put paintbrush to canvas, Chagall was born in Russia in 1887. His artistic talents led him to study in St Petersburg and in 1910 to Paris, where he became part of the Cubist movement, though he soon outgrew it. Chagall supported the Russian Revolution and became a Commissar for Fine Arts and was the director of the soviet Free Academy of Art, but his work proved too unorthodox for the Bolsheviks, and in 1922 he went back to France. In 1941, escaping the persecutions of the Vichy regime, he reached New York, returning after the war to the south of France, where he lived until his death in 1985. His paintings usually depict Jewish themes, especially scenes of early twentieth-century *shtetl* (East European Jewish village) life. The iconic figure of the fiddler on the roof is one of his motifs.

of the High Priest (Exodus 28:15–21), each of which represented one of the tribes and sons of Jacob (though actually, Joseph's two sons, Ephraim and Manasseh, were considered two separate tribes). The windows are also full of symbolism involving fish, birds, sheep and other animals. In the 1967 Six-Day War, four of the windows were damaged in the fighting, and Chagall had to fly over to restore them; in the end, he decided to leave three panes with bullet holes still in them in memory of the war.

There is no direct **transport** from Ein Karem village to the hospital. On foot you can continue along the path at the bottom of the steps to the Church of the Visitation, though travellers with walking difficulties may find the going difficult; otherwise, the hospital is served by bus #19 from King George Street, or #21 from Mount Herzl.

The Mifletzet

Everyone likes a good monster, and on the way to Ein Karem, you'll find a huge, three-tongued beast called the **Mifletzet**. Put up by French sculptor Niki de Saint Phalle, in a small park called Rabinovitch Garden in Kiryat Yovel (bus #20 from Jaffa Road), a kilometre southeast of Ein Karem, it's well known to anyone who was a kid in West Jerusalem since its 1971 installation. The seven-metre-high, black and white, pie-eyed fibreglass and concrete monster has three big red tongues hanging out of its slobbery mouth, each one a slide, so all you have to do is climb up inside, and choose which tongue to slide down. Of course, you're only going there for the kids' sake, but you might just have to test the slides out a few times yourself to be on the safe side.

Malha

Out on the southern edge of town, connected to central West Jerusalem by the Begin Expressway, as well as buses #4, #6 and #18, the suburb of **Malha** is most likely to be on your itinerary because it's where Jerusalem's **train station** is currently located, but Malha is also the location of **Teddy Stadium**, home to Jerusalem's three soccer teams (see p.205). Directly opposite the stadium, **Kanyon Yerushalayim** is the city's biggest shopping mall (see p.222).

The Biblical Zoo

A kilometre west of the station, stadium and mall, at the southern end of Derekh Gan HaHayot, the **Biblical Zoo**, or **Tisch Family Zoo** (Sun–Thurs 9am–6pm, Fri & eve of Jewish holidays 9am–4.30pm, Sat 10am–6pm; 42NIS; ℡02/675 0111, ⓦwww.jerusalemzoo.org.il) features animals mentioned in the Old Testament. As zoos go, it's pretty good, with reasonably spacious enclosures, and you can even take a tour of it on a toy train. As well as animals still indigenous to Israel and the Palestinian territories there are animals (such as Asian lions) which roamed the region in biblical times as well as endangered species here for conservation reasons. For kids there's a children's zoo with a petting corner. The zoo is wheelchair accessible, and chairs are available (on deposit of ID) for those who need them to tour the zoo. The zoo has its own train station, but is most easily accessed by bus #26 from Egged Central Bus Station or Mount Herzl, or #33 from the Kanyon Yerushalayim mall or Malha train station.

The Hill of Evil Counsel

Southeast of the city, the **Hill of Evil Counsel** (bus #8 from King George Street) is so called because, in Christian tradition, it was here that the Sanhedrin decided to turn Jesus over to the Romans. Its Arabic name, Jabal al-Muqabbar (Mount of Proclamation), derives from the tradition that it was from here that Caliph Omar Ibn al-Khattab first caught sight of the holy city and proclaimed the greatness of Allah in 638 AD. Many Jerusalemites found the hill's name appropriate when the British High Commissioner had his residence here during the Mandate – the palatial building, which stands on the top of the hill, surrounded by a garden complete with bandstand, is still known as **Government House** (Armon HaNatziv in Hebrew).

After 1948 the area was a demilitarized zone and served as the HQ of UN observers; it was taken by the Jordanians on the first day of the 1967 war but captured by Israeli forces later the same day. It is also the site of the **Haas Promenade**, whose view of the Old City rivals that from the Mount of Olives, and make it, together with the gardens below, a popular spot for courting couples.

Talpiot

You are most likely to come to the southern district of **Talpiot** if joining young Israelis out clubbing since it's home to the trendiest nightspots in town (see p.198). Originally built in the early 1920s as a Jewish "garden suburb", Talpiot was attacked by Arab mobs during the 1929 riots (see p.90), to the extent that women and children had to be evacuated to downtown West Jerusalem for safety. One early resident was Nobel Prize-winning author S.Y. (Shai) Agnon, best known for his novel *Only Yesterday* (see p.288); his home, **Beit Agnon**, at 16 Klauzner (Sun–Thurs 9am–1pm; 15NIS; ℡02/671 6498) is open to the public as a museum. Very nearby, on Kore HaDorot, a **Commonwealth War Cemetery** is the last resting place of Hindu and Muslim soldiers from Allenby's World War One army.

Neighbouring **East Talpiot** is a post-1967 settlement across the Green Line, and it was during expansion of this settlement in 1980 that building workers happened upon what is now known as the **Talpiot Tomb**, on Dov Gruner Street, off Olei Hagardom. The tomb, dating from the Second Temple period, contained ten ossuaries (receptacles for human bones), a form of burial most commonly used in the late first century BC and first century AD. The names on the ossuaries apparently included: Yeshua bar Yehosef (Jesus son of Joseph), Maria, Yose, Maramene e Mara and Yehuda bar Yeshua (Judah son of Jesus). This led to speculation that the deceased were in fact the biblical Jesus, his mother Mary, his brother Joses (mentioned in Mark 6:3), Mary Magdalene – held to be Jesus's wife (see p.159) – and, most controversially of all, a son of Jesus and Mary Magdalene named Judah. This would obviously conflict with the New Testament account of Jesus's life, burial and resurrection, and it would support some recent non-Christian speculation about Jesus's family life, but all the names were extremely common at the time, and there is really no special reason to think that the bones in the ossuaries must have belonged to the characters from the Bible. The tomb was subsequently resealed with a concrete slab and is not open to the public, the ossuaries are held in the vaults of the Rockefeller Museum and are not on public display, and the bones were reburied by the religious authorities in a modern Jewish cemetery.

Ramat Rahel

A kilometre or so south of Talpiot, **Kibbutz Ramat Rahel** (reached on bus #7 from Jaffa Road and King George Street; ☎02/670 2555, ⓦwww.ramatrachel .co.il;) was founded in 1916 on the site where the pregnant Virgin Mary is said to have paused on her way to Bethlehem, and boasts fruit and vegetable farms, a conference centre, swimming pool, and an elegant but expensive guesthouse (see p.176). There's also an **archeological garden** where you can see remains of a Roman bathhouse and a Byzantine church, and an observation point with views to Jerusalem and Bethlehem. Though surrounded by Jerusalem, Ramat Rahel is not officially part of the city and is independent of Jerusalem's municipal authorities.

Mar Elias

Five kilometres south of central Jerusalem and two kilometres short of the Bethlehem checkpoint, the white limestone building east of the road is the Greek Orthodox monastery of **Mar Elias**, founded in the sixth century and restored in 1160 with funds from the Holy Roman Emperor after being destroyed in an earthquake. According to one tradition, the prophet Elijah (Elias in Greek) slept here while fleeing Queen Jezebel (I Kings 19:3); others make it the burial place of St Elias, an Egyptian monk who became Patriarch of Jerusalem in 494, or Elias, Greek bishop of Bethlehem, who died in 1345, and the monastery did hold the tomb of a Bishop Elias up to the seventeenth century. Today, it is a popular pilgrimage site, believed to answer the prayers of barren women and ailing children. On the **Christmas Day procession** to Bethlehem, the Patriarchs traditionally pause here to be received by local dignitaries.

In front of the monastery, by the road, a **stone bench** honours the English pre-Raphaelite painter William Holman Hunt, who lived for many years in Jerusalem at 64 HaNeviim (see p.132) and painted some of his greatest works there. Inscribed in English, Greek, Arabic and Hebrew with the words "Thou shalt love the Lord thy God with all thy heart and with all thy soul, and thy neighbour as thyself" (both a Jewish and a Christian sentiment), the bench was commissioned by his widow, Edith after he died in 1910.

Just under a kilometre further south, on a hill to the west of the road, the **Tantur Ecumenical Institute** was established in 1964 to promote understanding between the Churches. The building, originally a hospice built in 1876, houses a large and impressive library. On the other side of the road, the **Field of Grey Peas**, covered with millions of small pebbles, gave rise to a parable in which a man sowing chickpeas (garbanzo beans) in the field was asked by the Virgin Mary (or, in some versions, Jesus) what it was he was sowing. "Stones," the man answered. "Very well," came the reply, "then you shall reap stones," and indeed, when the sower came to gather his crops, he found his chickpeas turned to stone. Thus for telling fibs he had to do without hummus for a year.

Mar Elias and Tantur can be reached on Egged bus #30 from Jaffa Road and Shlomzion HaMalka, or on bus #124 from East Jerusalem Central Bus Station on Sultan Suleiman.

Bethany (Al-Azariya)

Bethany is known in Arabic as **Al-Azariya**, a form of the Greek Lazarion or place of Lazarus, since this is where Lazarus was resurrected (John 11:1–44). Jesus also came here with his disciples after the events of Palm Sunday (Mark 11:11), and was anointed with precious ointment at the house of Simon the Leper before being betrayed by Judas (Mark 14:3–9; Matthew 26:6). Along with neighbouring Abu Dis, Bethany has now been cut off from direct access to Jerusalem by the Separation Wall (see p.234), but it is still possible to reach it by going around the wall via Route 1, which passes to the north of Mount Scopus (with great views). Bus #36 from East Jerusalem Central Bus Station on Sultan Suleiman runs this route, but note that some buses only go as far as the checkpoint at the edge of Jerusalem, so make sure you take one which goes all the way, and don't forget to bring your passport. The stop for Bethany is on a sharp curve in the road about 300m before the final stop; a lane, signposted "Bethany Souvenirs" and "St Lazarus Tomb", leads up the eastern slope of the Mount of Olives.

Bethany is under PA jurisdiction so, if you want to send a postcard from here you'll need to use a Palestinian stamp – you can buy them at the **post office** 300m beyond the Bethany bus stop in Abu Dis (Sat–Thurs 8am–3pm).

The Franciscan Church

Bethany's cruciform **Franciscan Church**, currently entered from the main road, but sometimes up the lane to its right (daily: April–Sept 8–11.45am & 2–6pm; Oct–March 8–11.45am & 2–5pm; free) was built in 1954, and designed, like many in Jerusalem, by the Italian architect Antonio Barluzzi (see p.121). The church may be modern but its grounds contain numerous earlier structures. On the left as you enter the courtyard under trapdoors (usually open) are remnants of mosaic floors from the earliest church at the site, built in the fourth century and destroyed by an earthquake. Adjacent to these are walls of a fifth-century church, razed by the Persians in 614 AD and later rebuilt and reinforced under Crusader rule – note the stone buttresses as you descend from the street into the courtyard. To this, Melisande the wife of Fulk of Anjou, Crusader king of Jerusalem, added a large Benedictine abbey in 1138, which, through its wheat and olive-oil production, became one of the wealthiest in the Crusader kingdom – a mill and oil press can be seen in one of the remaining rooms, accessible from the end of the church courtyard.

The Tomb of Lazarus

Up the lane, beyond the Franciscan Church, the 1187 **Al-Ozir Mosque** stands opposite a refreshment shop where "the **oldest well in Bethany**" is located "possibly inside the very house of Mary, Martha and Lazarus". Or possibly not.

The mosque had, by the end of the fourteenth century, supplanted the chapel erected by Melisande over the **Tomb of Lazarus**, whose entrance today lies just beyond it (daily 8am–5pm; "donation" expected). Descending into the tomb from street level, you go down 24 rough stone steps which lead into a dank cave with three rather uninspiring burial niches. If the door is closed, ask at the shop opposite.

The story of Lazarus, one of the most famous episodes in the New Testament (John 11:1–44), is also one of the most puzzling. Jesus, apparently a friend of the family, had been called here by Lazarus's sisters, Martha and Mary, because their brother was sick, but Jesus declared the sickness "for the glory of God, that the Son of God might be glorified thereby" (John 11:4), and Lazarus died. He had been entombed for four days when Jesus arrived in Bethany, pronounced, "I am the resurrection and the life: he that believeth in me, though he were dead, yet shall he live," (John 11:25), and ordered the stone covering the tomb to be rolled away, at which Lazarus, still in his shroud, emerged alive. The relationship between Jesus and Lazarus's family is never clearly explained, which has lately given rise to much speculation (see box below).

Mary and Martha

Though the story of Jesus's meeting with Lazarus's sisters, Mary and Martha itself seems unremarkable – Jesus and the disciples visit the house (Luke 10:38–42), and while Mary is "sat at Jesus's feet", Martha complains that she's been left with all the serving to do – it may have broader significance. St John tells us that this was the same Mary who elsewhere anoints Jesus (John 11:2), a story told slightly differently in all four Gospels (Matthew 26:6–13; Mark 14:3–9; Luke 7:36–50; John 12:1–9), but in St Luke's version she is identified as "a sinner", and traditionally with Mary Magdalene, though this is not explicit in the Gospels. Some modern writers (notably the authors of *The Holy Blood and the Holy Grail*, and *The Da Vinci Code*, essentially a conspiracy theory and a novel based upon it) have deduced from these sources, and from other references to Mary Magdalene, that she was Jesus's wife, later smeared in Christian tradition because of a rift between Jesus's family and the church under St Paul. Improbable though this may seem (and the evidence is highly circumstantial to say the least), it could, if true, explain Jesus's otherwise mysterious relationship with this Mary and her family.

Other sites in Bethany

Further up the lane, the attractive **Greek Orthodox Church**, with its silver dome, dates from 1883; you'll have to be content to look at the outside, however, as the gates are generally locked. Just up the alley beside it stands the ruined tower known as the **Castle of Lazarus**, once part of Melisande's Benedictine abbey, and thought to stand on the site of the House of Simon the Leper. To the west of the Greek Orthodox Church, excavations of ancient Bethany or **Bet Anania** have revealed evidence of habitation from the sixth century BC to the fourteenth century AD.

Bethphage

Now isolated from Bethany by the Separation Wall, **Bethphage** was where Jesus found a donkey to ride for his triumphal entry into Jerusalem on Palm Sunday (Matthew 21:1–11; Mark 11:1–10; Luke 19:29–38). It is also the place where the Franciscans' **Palm Sunday procession** begins; the procession seemed to be threatened by the construction of the Separation Wall, but the Israelis, bowing to protests, built a gate in the wall specifically to allow the procession to pass.

The Franciscan chapel, right next to the wall (daily 8–11.30am & 2–5pm) was built in 1883 on the remains of a medieval church commemorating Jesus's **meeting with Martha and Mary**, the sisters of Lazarus (see box, p.159). Inside the chapel – now cut off from its congregation, most of whom live in Bethany – a beautiful mural depicts Jesus's triumphant entry into Jerusalem. It seems to be based on a twelfth-century Crusader fresco that decorates the **Mounting Stone**, on which the Crusaders believed Jesus stepped to mount his donkey when he set out for Jerusalem – they were apparently oblivious of the fact that little help is needed to mount indigenous Palestinian donkeys, which were considerably smaller than their own massive war horses. A mirror allows you to see all the scenes painted on the stone. One scene, on the stone's north side, depicts the raising of Lazarus.

Although Bethphage cannot now be reached from Bethany, just half a kilometre down the road, it can be reached on foot from Jerusalem via Ras al-Amud and the Jericho Road over the Mount of Olives, but it's a hard, hour-long walk – if you do walk it, don't forget to take sun protection and water.

Listings

Listings

9 Accommodation 163

10 Eating 177

11 Drinking and nightlife 194

12 Entertainment 199

13 Sports and activities... 205

14 Festivals and holidays... 209

15 Shopping 216

9

Accommodation

There are plenty of hotels and hostels in Jerusalem and you shouldn't have any problem finding somewhere to stay during most of the year. On the other hand, the city does get well booked-up for the big **religious holidays**, so if you are coming at Christmas, Easter, Passover (usually around April) and the Jewish New Year or Sukkot (usually around Sept), it's best to book in advance, though you should at a pinch be able to find a bed in one of the less popular places anyway.

For atmosphere and proximity to the sights, the **Old City** is unbeatable as a place to stay, and it's here that you'll find most of the best budget options, usually in characterful old buildings. However, the labyrinthine lanes and poor street lighting mean that some parts can be unnerving after dark, so make sure you know your way home before you go exploring. **East Jerusalem**, within walking distance of the Old City gates, isn't quite as atmospheric but offers more in the way of amenities; its hotels are very good value, but Jewish Israeli taxi drivers may refuse to take you to them (if you use taxis and find a driver who's happy to take you between East and West Jerusalem, it might be an idea to get their phone number and call them when you need a cab). **West Jerusalem** has comparatively little inexpensive accommodation, and what it has can't touch the east side for character, but this is where you'll find most of the modern, mid-range to expensive hotels, and it's the place to stay if you want fitted carpets, international cuisine or kosher food. West Jerusalem also offers far more in the way of nightlife. If you are happy to stay out of town, it might also be worth considering a hotel in **Bethlehem** (see pp.233–235).

Hotel prices usually vary with the season, particularly in the more expensive establishments. **High season** is concentrated on the Jewish festival of Passover (usually around April), the Jewish New Year and Sukkot (usually around Sept), Christmas, and the summer months of July and August. **Low season** is from October to May, excluding the main Christian and Jewish holidays. At slack times a little bargaining over the price rarely goes amiss. Students may be entitled to a discount, so it's always worth asking, and some places, especially at the lower end of the market, may give discounts for guests staying more than a few days. In winter, it's worth testing the **hot water** when checking out a room in cheaper establishments, as supplies may be erratic.

Accommodation types

The cheapest places to stay, favoured by backpackers and budget travellers, are **private hostels**, most of which are located in the Christian and Muslim Quarters of the Old City. Generally speaking, those staying in hostels should

▲ The King David, Jerusalem's most famous hotel

expect to pay 30–50NIS (£5–8/US$8–13) for a bed in a dormitory, or 100–200NIS (£16.50–33/US$25–55) for a private room. Some hostels offer mattresses "under the stars", usually on the roof, from about 30NIS (£5/US$8), which can be more pleasant in summer. As well as cheap private hostels, there are also two **official hostels** run by Israel's YHA (ⓦwww.iyha.org.il/eng), which are more expensive (and one of them does not offer dorm beds); these are cleaner and more comfortable, and often full.

Proper **hotels** usually quote their rates in dollars or euros, and vary widely in price, from £50/US$75 for a double in a basic guesthouse in low season to well over £200/US$300 in a super-deluxe establishment. Low-cost and mid-range hotels are concentrated in the central parts of East and West Jerusalem, with most of the deluxe places scattered further afield, although the very best of the deluxe hotels tend to be reasonably central too. A fair few of the mid-range and even quite upmarket hotels in West Jerusalem have room decor reminiscent of the 1970s, while in East Jerusalem it can even be from the 1950s or 1960s. Generally speaking, you'll get more bang for your buck east of the Green Line than west (and still more if you stay in Bethlehem).

Christian hospices generally offer facilities much the same as those of the better hostels and at similar prices. They're geared primarily to Christian pilgrims (though usually open to non-Christians too), and may have quite austere regimes – early curfews, for example – but they can also be wonderfully peaceful and relaxing. Most places are impeccably clean and quiet and some offer dorm accommodation (sometimes women only) as well as rooms. The Christian Information Centre (see p.43 for details) has a list of Christian accommodation (also open to non-Christians) in Jerusalem, half of which is in the Old City or nearby.

Finally, private **bed and breakfast** accommodation and **self-catering apartments** are also available, often some way out of the city centre. For further details, check the website of the Home Accommodation Association of Jerusalem (ⓣ02/645 2198, ⓦwww.bnb.co.il/members.htm), which has details of 25 B&B options, some of them reasonably central. Prices are typically £50–125/US$80–200 per night for a double room with breakfast, and it's best if possible to give the place a once-over and be clear exactly what's included before taking the room.

Breakfast

Breakfast is usually included in low-priced and mid-range establishments. At its best, this is a massive buffet, and goes some way to offsetting the price of a room, but breakfasts can vary a lot in quality. Most hotels that serve breakfast in West Jerusalem offer the full **Israeli breakfast** (salad, fruit juice, eggs, and tea or coffee); many offer the choice of a **Continental breakfast** (coffee and croissant or cake) instead, while expensive establishments may even do an **American breakfast** (pancakes, eggs, hashbrowns, sausages, but not usually bacon of course). In East Jerusalem, breakfast is likely to be a Middle Eastern buffet, but upmarket establishments will offer the choice of American or Continental too

Cheap hostels and hotels

The lowest-priced and best-value hostels are found in the Old City and East Jerusalem. Most offer the choice of dorm beds, private rooms, or – the cheapest option and great in summer – a bed on the roof. Safe facilities are generally available (though you often have to pay), and curfews are the norm. They will probably have room if you just turn up, but it's advisable to book ahead if you want to stay in a particular hostel, especially at peak times of year such as Christmas or summer holidays.

Old City near Damascus Gate

All of these are shown on the map on p.73.
Armenian Guest House 36 Via Dolorosa
℡02/626 0880, Ⓔarmenianguesthouse
@hotmail.com. Sedate hostel in a modernized nineteenth-century stone building belonging to the Armenian Catholic Patriarchate and

attached to the Third Station of the Cross. There are single-sex dorms (mostly 6-bed), and private rooms with central heating, showers, TV and phones. Sun terrace but without a view. No curfew. Breakfast included; dorms €15, doubles ❸
Austrian Hospice of the Holy Family 37 Via Dolorosa (corner of Al-Wad Rd)

Accommodation price codes

Throughout this chapter, hotel accommodation is graded on a scale from ❶ to ❾. The numbers represent the cost per night of the cheapest double room in high season, though remember that many places will have more expensive rooms and even suites. Where dorm beds are available the price is given, in the currency used by the hostel (which may be shekels, US dollars or euros). Note that all prices are likely to have risen slightly since this book went to press. The rates quoted are for bed only unless otherwise stated (for example, if we specify that breakfast is included).

❶ US$40 (160NIS) and under
❷ US$41–59 (161–245NIS)
❸ US$60–89 (246–365NIS)
❹ US$90–119 (366–490NIS)
❺ US$120–149 (491–610NIS)

❻ US$150–199 (611–815NIS)
❼ US$200–249 (816–1020NIS)
❽ US$250–299 (1021–1220NIS)
❾ US$300 (1221NIS) and over

☏02/626 5800, ⓦwww.austrianhospice.com. An imposing and beautiful hostel with thirteen-bed single-sex dorms, and quite large, immaculately kept en-suite rooms. The roof terrace has great views, taking in the Church of the Holy Sepulchre in one direction, the Dome of the Rock in another, and the Damascus Gate in a third. There are also two lovely small coffee terraces overlooking the street at the front, as well as a Viennese coffee house and an ornate chapel complete with mosaics and a red marble altar. Payment must be in euros or US dollars, cash or traveller's cheques. Breakfast included; dorms €18, doubles ❹

Golden Gate Hostel 10 Souq Khan al-Zeit (but actually just up Aqabat al-Batikh) ☏02/628 4317, ⓔgoldengate442000@yahoo.com. Very spick and span, and a cut above the other cheap hostels, though the dorm beds are slightly more expensive. There's also a range of private rooms, the best of which have a/c and en-suite bathrooms. It's quieter than the other hostels, and a higher proportion of its clientele are Palestinian (usually families). The only part of the hostel which isn't scrupulously clean is the roof terrace, which is nonetheless large with decent though not classic views. Alcohol is banned, and there's a midnight curfew, but such rules do keep out the riff-raff. Dorms 50NIS, doubles ❶

Hashimi Hotel 73 Souq Khan al-Zeit ☏02/628 4410, ⓦwww.hashimihotel.com. This Muslim-run hotel is spotless spiritually if not always physically (check the sheets), with single-sex dorms and private rooms, marble floors, beige and white decor, and a family atmosphere. There's also 24hr room service, and a great rooftop terrace, but alcohol is forbidden, and unmarried couples may not share a room. Its popularity with large Muslim groups can also make it noisy, and the generally pious atmosphere may not appeal to the non-religious. Prices are fixed in euros, and the exchange rate tends not to be favourable if you want to pay in shekels or dollars. Dorms €20, doubles ❹

Hebron Hostel (formerly the Tabasco Inn) 8 Aqabat al-Taqiya (off Souq Khan al-Zeit) ☏02/628 1101 ⓔashraftabasco@hotmail.com. Best value of the cheap Old City hostels, with wonderful cool stone dorms, plus small private rooms on the roof, which can be sweltering at the height of summer and cold in the depths of winter, but are fine in between. The bathrooms are clean, and the hot water reliable, but the roof terrace lacks a view. Dorms 30NIS, doubles ❶

Old City near Jaffa Gate

If coming into the Old City through the Jaffa Gate with your baggage, beware of commission touts who hang around in Omar Ibn al-Khattab Square accosting tourists and offering to help find a hostel – if you do accept their help, they will take you to an establishment which pays them a commission and adds it to your room rate.

All of these are shown on the maps on p.48 and p.56.

Citadel Hostel 20 St Mark's Rd ☏02/628 4494, ⓔinfo@citadelhostel.com. In an old stone house – 700 years old, they claim – on the edge of the Armenian Quarter, with three dorms (single-sex and mixed) and some private rooms. It's a bit cramped, but makes up in charm what it lacks in spaciousness. Facilities include a kitchen (with free tea and coffee), satellite TV, free wi-fi (or use of the one computer) and a terrace with good views of the Holy Sepulchre. The cheapest private rooms (which need to be booked well in advance) are shack-like affairs on the roof, so it's worth paying a bit extra for an inside room. Doors close at midnight but guests can get in with daily entry codes for the keypad lock. Dorms 55NIS, doubles ❶

Jaffa Gate Hostel Off Omar Ibn al-Khattab Square (down an alley beside the Christian Information Centre) ☏02/627 6402, ⓔjaffa_gate_hostel @yahoo.com. This place gets very mixed reports. It's pricey for what you get, whether in dorms (65NIS) or private rooms. There's wi-fi coverage and a small terrace with a view of the Church of the Holy Sepulchre, but bathrooms are rather grubby, and it isn't great value compared to other Old City hostels, which offer similar facilities at lower rates. ❷

New Swedish Hostel 29 David St ☏02/627 7855, ⓦwww.geocities.com/swedishhostel. A cramped little place, with poky private rooms and ten-bed dorms (35NIS), plus a TV room, where they claim to offer Premier League and European football coverage. The staff are generally friendly and helpful, but it's still really a fall-back option for when other hostels are full. ❷

Petra Hostel 1 David St ☏ **02/628 6618,** ✉ **petrahtl@netvision.net.il.** A great place to stay, with an American manager, but pricey compared to other Old City hostels. The building once housed the oldest hotel in Jerusalem, the *Mediterranean*, whose guests included Mark Twain, Herman Melville, Edmund Allenby and Tsar Nicholas. Under the Mandate, the breakfast area was a ballroom, and Eliezar Ben Yehuda, the inventor of modern Hebrew, held his son's bar mitzvah here. The hostel is big and roomy, with a well-equipped kitchen, a safe, laundry service and private rooms. The balconies of the dorms give great views of the citadel, or you can sleep on the roof (30NIS), which has one of the best views in the city (non-residents can enjoy it for 5NIS), taking in the Dome of the Rock, the Church of the Holy Sepulchre, Mount Scopus and the Mount of Olives and, less excitingly, the neighbouring Hezekiah's Pool (now a rubbish dump; see p.50). Dorms 45NIS (plus 10NIS for a locker), doubles ❷

East Jerusalem

All of these are shown on the map on p.109.
Faisal Hostel 4 HaNeviim ☏ **02/628 7502.** Now rather run-down, this long-standing travellers' hostel still has a few things going for it, including a pleasant Middle Eastern café, free wi-fi coverage, reasonable dorms and a couple of private rooms. In its heyday, it was so political that even staying here felt like an act of defiance against the Israeli occupation, and it's still the place to stay if you want a chinwag about Palestinian politics, but it really could do with a lick of paint. Dorms 30NIS, doubles ❶
Metropole 6 Salah al-Din ☏ **02/628 2507,** ℻ **5134.** A creaky old place, but it does the job, with sombre rooms and rather thin carpets, this hotel is a remnant from the days of Jordanian rule, and still caught in a 1950s time warp. It's a little drab but good value for the price, and it does have a certain old-fashioned charm. ❷
Palm Hostel 6 HaNaviim ☏ **02/627 3189,** ✉ **newpalmhostel@yahoo.com.** A very friendly place, and an old backpackers' favourite, with dorms and private rooms, slightly ramshackle, and not very organized (don't bother to book ahead), but it all adds to the

homely feel, as does the lobby café area, where there's free tea and coffee, and even free evening meals on occasion. The hostel also has free wi-fi coverage (or join the queue for the one computer), and there's a fruit and veg market downstairs (see p.226). Not for the fussy, but old-school travellers will love it. Dorms 30NIS, doubles ❷

West Jerusalem

All of these are shown on the map on p.127.
Jerusalem Hostel 44 Jaffa Rd ☏ **02/623 6102,** ⊛ **www.jerusalem-hostel.com.** Centrally located on Zion Square in the heart of downtown West Jerusalem, this modern hostel opened as the *Warshavsky Hotel* in 1928, and Irgun leader Menahem Begin (see p.138) harangued the crowds, generalissimo-like, from its balcony in his first official speech after independence in 1948. Private rooms have a/c in summer, heating in winter, and all have attached bathrooms. Rooms facing Zion Square also have a balcony and view but are on the other hand noisier than those at the back. Dorms are well kept but single-sex. There's free wi-fi in the lobby, and guests have use of a well-equipped kitchen. Note that reception is open only 8am–10pm, and closed for Shabbat. Breakfast included; dorms 70NIS, doubles ❸
YHA Agron 6 Agron ☏ **02/621 7555,** ⊛ **www .iyha.org.il.** Well situated within easy reach of downtown West Jerusalem and the Old City, the four- or five-bed dorms are clean and well equipped, and there are squeaky-clean en-suite double and single rooms. On the downside, the atmosphere is a little institutional and it is often full up with groups, so you'll need to book well ahead. The reception is closed 11pm–7am, and during Shabbat or Jewish holidays, so you cannot check in then except by prior arrangement. Facilities include a theatre-style convention hall and a synagogue with 45 Torah scrolls. Breakfast included; dorms 130NIS, doubles ❹

The suburbs

Notre Dame de Sion Convent 23 HaOren, Ein Karem ☏ **02/641 5738,** ⊛ **www.sion-ein-karem .org; bus #17 from Egged Central Bus Station.** Out where the air is clear in the beautiful former Arab village of Ein Karem (see p.153), this is a retreat for those who prefer a calm, spiritual atmosphere to the hustle and bustle of town. It's also a good place to get a feel for the monastic life, staying in a community of nuns, who are happy to chat about Jerusalem and religious matters. The convent dates from 1863, and there's a beautiful garden where you can take afternoon tea. Breakfast included ❸

Mid-range hotels and guesthouses

Jerusalem has a wide variety of very interesting and often quite quirky hotels and guesthouses. As with hostels, the Old City and East Jerusalem tend to offer the best value for money, though there are some good-value private B&Bs in West Jerusalem too. Many of the best places are hospices run by religious institutions, originally intended for pilgrims; those listed here will take anybody, but they do ask guests to respect their religious nature.

Old City

Unless otherwise stated, these are shown on the map on p.56.

Casa Nova Casa Nova St between Jaffa Gate and New Gate ☎02/628 2791, ⓦwww.custodia .org/casanovaj. A Franciscan pilgrims' hospice, with bed and breakfast or full- or half-board in simple but clean, safe surroundings in a grand 100-year-old building with a wonderful interior garden courtyard and rooftop terrace with panorama of the city. It's worth booking ahead as the hospice is often full, especially around Christmas and Easter. 11pm curfew. Breakfast included ❸

Christ Church Guest House Omar Ibn al-Khattab Square ☎02/627 7727, ⓦwww.cmj-israel.org (see map, p.48). Clean and quiet Christian-run guesthouse attached to Jerusalem's first Protestant church. The old wing was Jerusalem's original British consulate and has larger and more atmospheric rooms than the new wing, though rooms in both are spotless and bright. Optional religious activities emphasize the Jewish roots of Christianity, and include Friday night Shabbat dinner. Guests can also explore a subterranean Herodian tunnel room discovered when Christ Church was originally built in the 1840s. Because of the guesthouse's religious nature, unmarried couples cannot share rooms, and there's an 11pm curfew. Car parking facilities available. Breakfast included ❹

HaKotel Hurva Square, Jewish Quarter ☎02/627 6277 (see map, p.85). Small hotel, actually an apartment, with a small choice of slightly different rooms. The reception's in a food shop on the south side of Hurva Square.

You get a fridge, a/c, and a kitchenette with a kettle and tea bags. It isn't great value compared with other Old City hotels, but it's the only place in the Jewish Quarter if that's where you want to stay. Rooms cost substantially more at weekends (Friday and Saturday nights) than weekdays. Breakfast included ❻

Gloria Hotel 33 Latin Patriarchate St (first left inside Jaffa Gate) ☎02/628 2431, ⓦwww .gloria-hotel.com. Charming family-run hotel that's ancient downstairs, pretty modern upstairs, and remarkably quiet despite its proximity to the Jaffa Gate. The entrance and lobby areas are all arched vaults, but the rooms, though not huge, are cosy and well appointed, with TV, a/c and heating. The rooftop terrace has a splendid view of the Old City. Limited car parking facilities available. Breakfast included ❺

Lutheran Guest House St Mark's Rd, Armenian Quarter ☎02/626 6888, ⓦwww.guesthouse -jerusalem.com. A haven of tranquility in a cool nineteenth-century stone building (on Crusader foundations) with a ravishing courtyard garden, tastefully renovated to provide modern facilities while retaining a classic Jerusalem feel. Parts of the building were designed by German architect Conrad Schick (see p.132). There's a roof terrace with excellent views, and a dining room serving European and Middle Eastern cuisine, and the rooms are spotless. It's advisable to book in advance, and if you stay ten nights, you get the eleventh free. Early (10.45pm) curfew. Breakfast included ❹

🏃 **New Imperial Hotel** Omar Ibn al-Khattab Square, just east of the Jaffa Gate ☎02/628 2261, ⓦwww.newimperial.com.

A magnificent ramshackle old place, full of character and eccentricity complete with old photographs on the walls, sweeping staircases and towering rooms, though these are not always as clean as they ought to be. Built in 1885, it hosted Kaiser Wilhelm and his entourage on their visit in 1898, and other former guests include T.E. Lawrence (of Arabia). During World War II, it was used by the British as a hospital. The balconied rooms at the front overlook the square and Citadel, and the roof has stupendous views of the Jaffa Gate, the Church of the Holy Sepulchre and the Dome of the Rock. Beneath the hotel (and unfortunately inaccessible) is the Pool of Bathsheba, where King David's beautiful neighbour supposedly bathed while the lecherous monarch played peeping Tom (II Samuel 11:2–3), though he'd need to have had good eyesight since his palace was on Temple Mount, clean across town. ❸

East Jerusalem

All of these are shown on the map on p.109.
Ambassador Nablus Rd, above Sheikh Jarrah ☏02/541 2222, ⓦwww.jerusaelmambassador .com. A reasonable four-star hotel, not quite deluxe (no pool, for example), but it tries. There's a fitness centre, a patisserie and a good restaurant for French, Italian or Middle Eastern cuisine. The rooms are a decent size and well serviced, with a/c, satellite TV, internet connection and a minibar, and if they aren't spacious enough, there are junior suites for not much more. The main downside is the hotel's location, which isn't tremendously convenient for the Old City or the west side of town. Breakfast included ❻
Azzahra 13 Al-Zahra, down a short alley ☏02/628 2447, ⓦwww.azzarhahotel.com. A quiet jewel of a place in a beautifully restored old Jerusalem building, previously frequented by the likes of Jordan's former king Abdullah. The large, high-ceilinged rooms are simple but comfortable, and make up in charm for what they lack in mod cons. Some have balconies, a/c and heating, and they all have a TV and fridge. Communal areas preserve the building's architectural features, making effective use of the stone walls to give a cool but classic feel. There's also a wonderful garden and good restaurant (see p.188). Breakfast included ❺

Capitol 17 Salah al-Din ☏02/628 2561, ⓦwww .jrscapitol.com. The public areas are getting rather shabby in this once quite upmarket establishment, but the rooms are fine, and for a mid-range hotel it's more than adequate. There's a/c and satellite TV in the rooms, a café and restaurant, and they may well offer discounts (especially off season) if you stay for more than a couple of nights. Breakfast included ❺
Christmas Hotel 1 Abu Taleb ☏02/628 2588, ⓦwww.christmas-hotel.com. A modern hotel that doesn't look much from the outside, but is cool and stylish within. The staff are sweet as pie, the rooms are tastefully done out with blue soft furnishings and wooden fittings, and there's a lovely garden restaurant and bar. Breakfast included ❻
Jerusalem Hotel off Nablus Rd, beside the bus station, ☏&⒡ 02/628 3282, ⓦwww.jrshotel.com; toll-free booking UK ☏0800/328 2393, US ☏1-800/657-9401. Far and away the best of Jerusalem's mid-range hotels, very popular, with only 14 rooms, so booking is essential. The hotel is in a nineteenth-century mansion done out in classic Arabic decor, featuring beautiful stone floors and archways, and rooms are supplied with fine traditional wooden furniture specially imported from Egypt. Modern conveniences include satellite TV, wi-fi and a/c. The staff are friendly and informative and the owner is a mine of information. Tours of the West Bank are available, for residents and non-residents alike, and there's a delightful vine-covered garden restaurant (see p.188). Breakfast included ❻
Legacy 29 Nablus Rd ☏02/627 0800, ⓦwww .jerusalemlegacy.com. The former YMCA hostel reborn as a spanking new and rather impressive establishment, with wooden floors, tasteful furnishings and a choice of royal or executive rooms or suites (the executive rooms and the suites have balconies with Old City views). All rooms have LCD cable TVs, and there's a fitness centre, jacuzzi, restaurant and bar – really quite impressive for the price. Breakfast included ❻
Meridian 5 Abu Taleb ☏02/628 5212, ⓦwww .jerusalem-meridian.com. A 74-room hotel popular with pilgrim groups offering two types of room: club rooms, which are small but comfortable, with en-suite bathrooms, central heating and a phone; and executive

rooms, which are larger with satellite TV, a minibar, two phone lines and a/c. There are also apartments for long-term stays, and for families, two executive rooms can be taken together as a suite. There is a roof garden coffee shop with a view of the Mount of Olives and Mount Scopus, and a spacious, comfortable lobby lounge, as well as a bar and dining room. Breakfast included ➏

Mount of Olives 53 Mount of Olives Rd, Al-Tur ☏02/628 4877, ⊛www.mtolives.com. Homely and rather well-worn family-run hotel, very friendly and located in the Palestinian village of Al-Tur, up on the Mount of Olives overlooking the Old City, offering clean air and classic picture-postcard views, especially in the mornings when the sun is in the right direction (one problem of the location is that there have been reports of sexual harrasss-ment of women tourists on the Mount of Olives, so it is not a good area for women to wander around alone here, especially at night). Only the rooms at the front have Old City views, so you should specify that you want a room at the front when making your reservation. Breakfast included ➌

Mount Scopus Nablus Rd, Sheikh Jarrah ☏02/582 8891, ✉mtscopus@netvision.net.il. A quiet hotel, overlooking the city from above East Jerusalem. The rooms are cosy, carpeted and well kept, with a/c, TV (on request if not already installed), a bathroom with a full-sized tub, and a balcony. It's worth insisting on a south-facing room, preferably on an upper floor, as the view takes in East and West Jerusalem and the Mount of Olives, though the Old City is largely hidden. Breakfast included ➎

New Metropole 8 Salah al-Din ☏02/628 3846, ℻27 7485. Don't be put off by the jarring blue and yellow painted windows on the stairs leading up to the lobby: this modern-ized 1950s hotel is not the snazziest in town, but it's friendly, and good for the price. The rooms are drab but cosy, with a/c and heating, and there's a roof terrace with good views of Mount Scopus and the Mount of Olives. Breakfast included ➍

Ritz 8 Ibn Khaldoun ☏02/626 9900, ⊛www .jerusalemritz.com. Not as ritzy as you might expect from the name, but modern and well done out, with good-size, airy rooms, a cool lobby space and unobtrusive, efficient staff. Breakfast included ➏

Rivoli 3 Salah al-Din ☏02/628 4781, ℻627 4879. There's a choice of noisier but brighter

front rooms (overlooking the police station and post office) or quieter but darker back rooms at this unexceptional but decent enough hotel. The rooms all have high ceilings and fans, but no a/c, and there's a lounge and breakfast room on the first floor. Breakfast included ➌

St George's Cathedral Pilgrim Guest House 20 Nablus Rd, left inside the entrance to the cathedral ☏02/627 7232, ⊛www.j-diocese.org /archive?ct=guest houses. A peaceful clois-tered retreat owned by the Anglican Church. The simple but impeccable modernized rooms (all with a/c, TV, en-suite bathrooms and wi-fi) once formed part of the cathe-dral's choir school, and are set around a courtyard garden decorated with archeolog-ical finds that have been unearthed here. There is also a dining room (open to non-residents) serving European and Middle Eastern food, and a cosy lounge and gift shop. Breakfast included ➎

Seven Arches Mount of Olives ☏02/626 7777, ⊛www.7arches.com. Opened in 1963 as a deluxe Jordanian hotel on the Mount of Olives, the *Seven Arches* is visible from virtually anywhere in Jerusalem, and the views over the Old City from in front of the hotel are classic (see p.118) but sadly only a few rooms in the hotel share it, so be sure to insist on one when you book. The rooms are well designed and spacious, but not very well kept, and service can be poor. Displayed in the entrance is a Byzantine mosaic that was unearthed when the hotel was built. One disadvantage of the hotel's position is that it is pretty remote from anywhere except the neighbouring Palestinian village of Al-Tur, which has little in the way of shopping facili-ties or posh restaurants, other than the hotel's own, of course, which apart from serving high-class Middle Eastern food, offers excellent Old City views while you dine (there's also a bistro if you fancy a change). Breakfast included ➎

West Jerusalem

All of these are shown on the map on pp.126–127.

Avital 141 Jaffa Rd, Mahane Yehuda ☏02/624 3706, ⊛www.itsik-hotel.co.il. It's a little out of the way for the sights, but handy for Mahane Yehuda market (see p.129 & p.226) and reasonably near the Egged bus station, with a bicycle rental place next door (see p.208). It's also quite good value for a West Jerusalem hotel, but not as well kept as it might be. You get quite a large room, with a sitting area, sink, stove and microwave, a poky little bathroom, and an internet café downstairs. Breakfast included ❹

Beit Shmuel 6 Shema'a ☎02/620 3455, @www.merkazshimshon.com. Clean, bright and modern, and run by the World Union for Progressive Judaism (but open to all). It has two sections. The cheaper rooms (in what they call the "hostel"), are simple but spacious, sleeping up to six, all en suite with a/c, and most have balconies and great views across what used to be no-man's-land to the Old City. There's also a "guest house" in a newer wing of the building, whose rooms are cosier and have slightly more facilities (bathtub, wi-fi), again with excellent Old City views from most. It gets very full, so worth booking well ahead, and it's worth specifying a room with a balcony and Old City view if possible. Breakfast included ❺

Dan Boutique 31 Hebron Rd ☎02/568 9999, @www.danboutiquejerusalem.com. A well-run little hotel that's handy for the German Colony, and the bars and clubs in the old railway station compound, though it's a bit of a schlep from downtown, and even from the Old City. The gold and black decor in the rooms is bright and modern, in an unobtrusive kind of way, and though there's no pool, the hotel does have a fitness room, and a scenic terrace with Old City views. Breakfast included ❻

Eldan 24 King David St ☎02/567 9777, @www.eldanhotel.com. Not the city's most exciting hotel, but efficient, well run and adequate in all respects. There's a/c, TV, a minibar and a line for laptop internet use in all rooms, it's well located for West Jerusalem and the Old City, and the staff are friendly and helpful. Breakfast included ❻

Habira 4 HaHavatzelet (entrance in Frumkin) ☎02/625 5754, @www.hotel-habira.co.il. A good fall-back option if the neighbouring *Kaplan* (see below) is full, containing a lot more rooms than you'd expect from the outside, all carpeted and en suite, with a/c, wi-fi and TV, and some with balconies, either over the noisy Jaffa Rd, or the quieter back alley. It's plain and simple, but well located, clean, quiet and easy-going. There aren't many communal facilities, but there is a sun roof. Breakfast included ❹

Harmony 6 Yoel Salomon ☎02/621 9998, @www.atlas.co.il. Bright new hotel from the same firm who run the *Cinema* in Tel Aviv (see p.256). It has friendly, efficient staff, snazzy, modern rooms, TV, a/c, wi-fi coverage throughout, free afternoon tea (including snacks), and a reputation for service, on top of an excellent modern design ethic that makes it feel fresh and exciting. Conveniently located in the heart of downtown West Jerusalem, it's already putting neighbouring establishments well in the shade. Breakfast included ❻

Holiday 2000 2 HaHistadrut ☎050/268 3008, @www.holiday2000.net. You need to stay for a minimum of two nights to take one of these "apartments" (actually bedrooms with a kitchenette, but only the larger ones have a stove as opposed to just a microwave). They're very central, pretty good value, and they get cleaned, with a change of towels daily, and a change of sheets twice weekly. The larger ones have a balcony, and they all have cable TV, a/c and free wi-fi. Breakfast included ❹

Jerusalem Inn 7 Horkanos ☎02/625 2757, @www.jerusalem-inn.com. The rooms at this popular city-centre guesthouse are jolly and bright, and all but two have French windows opening onto a small balcony. The management advise asking for a newly refurbished room, but the non-refurbished rooms are almost as good, and rooms on the second floor are larger than those on the first. It isn't the best value in the city centre, but it's a decent enough choice at the lower end of mid-range. Breakfast included ❺

Jerusalem Tower 23 Hillel ☎02/620 9209; @www.inisrael.com/jth/jerusalem. The location of this hotel is excellent, but the rooms, though comfortable, with TV, a/c and attached bathrooms, are small (skilful use of mirrors makes them look a bit bigger), and they don't have very big windows, which makes them rather dark. Even so, it's still worth asking for an upper-floor room with an Old City view, especially as lower floors are rather noisy. Don't expect great service here – it's not that kind of place – but if you're looking for somewhere reasonably comfortable to lay your head and keep your baggage while you check out the city, it isn't a bad choice. Breakfast included ❻

Kaplan 1 HaHavatzelet ☎02/625 4591, @natrade@netvision.net.il. A friendly little *pension*-style hotel in the centre of West Jerusalem with small but bright and breezy rooms supplied with a TV, phone and small bathroom. Guests have free use of a kitchen much like they might have in their homes, with free tea and coffee, and there's wi-fi coverage and washing facilities. The atmosphere is so homely, it's almost like staying in someone's house. ❸

Kikar Zion 25 Shamai, off Zion Square ☎02/624 4644, ℱ4136. Friendly but rather tired city-centre hotel, catering largely for package tour groups. To get in, you have to take an elevator from the rather scuzzy entrance round the back of Zion Square. Rooms vary in size, so when booking it's worth asking for a large one, and also for one on the top floors, since not only do you then get a view, but you are also out of range of noise from the square below. Breakfast included ❺

Mishkenot Sha'anim Yemin Moshe ☎02/629 2220, ⓦwww.mishkenot.org.il. A lovely place to stay, in what former mayor Teddy Kolleck tried to promote as Jerusalem's "culture mile", from the Khan Theatre (see p.203) and Cinemateque (see p.204) to the Arts and Crafts Lane (see p.225), but this is "a special guesthouse for artists, intellectuals and academics", so ordinary folk need not apply. What makes it worth a try, if you can persuade them that you are an artist, a scholar or a VIP, is that the rooms are in Moses Montefiore's original Yemin Moshe almshouses (see p.137), and offer great views of the Old City as well as the pleasure of staying in a historic milieu. Guests have included Simone de Beauvoir, Umberto Eco, the Dalai Lama, Saul Bellow and Herman Wouk. Breakfast included ❼

Montefiore 7 Shatz ☎02/622 1111, ⓦwww .montefiorehotel.com. A three-star hotel that makes a good mid-range choice, tucked away in a quiet corner of downtown West Jerusalem, its rooms are cosy and well looked after, with TV, a/c and heating, and suites are available. The staff are efficient and courteous, and the buffet breakfasts are more than adequate, though slightly less so on Saturday because the hotel observes Shabbat, which means no cooking. One minus point is its position on a steep pedestrianized street, which means that taxis cannot drop you right outside, but this is a minor inconvenience as it's a short distance from the main road. Breakfast included ❺

Noga 1st and 2nd floors, 4 Betzalel ☎02/566 1888, ⓦwww.hotelnoga.com. A small, family-run place in a quiet but reasonably central location and with big, airy rooms, and three kitchens for use of guests with essentials (tea, coffee, sugar) supplied, and three terraces, very homely and also very popular with those in the know. There's no reception, so you can only check in by calling the owner in advance and arranging an arrival time. ❸

Notre Dame Center 3 Paratroopers Rd ☎02/627 9111, ⓦwww.notredamecenter.org. The Roman Catholic Church's main pilgrim centre in Jerusalem (but open to all), this historic building (see p.135) is ideally positioned for the visitor, handy for both East and West Jerusalem and across the street from the Old City. The rooms are spotless, carpeted and restful, with en-suite bathrooms (some with shower, some with tub), and with great views of the Old City walls from those in the south wing. There's also an attractive stone-walled chapel and a library, as well as a great terrace café in summer (see p.183) and a very fine restaurant (see p.190). Book well in advance. Breakfast included ❹

Palatin 4 Agrippas ☎02/623 1141, ⓦwww .palatinhotel.com. A friendly, family-run hotel decorated with modern art posters and very convenient for central West Jerusalem. The rooms are rather poky (the bed takes up most of the space), and a bit dusty in the corners, but they all have a TV, a phone, a/c, central heating and an en-suite bathroom, and the atmosphere is homely and easy-going. Breakfast included ❹

St Andrew's Hospice 1 David Remez ☎02/673 2401, ⓦwww.scotsguesthouse.com. Immaculate guesthouse run by the Church of Scotland and attached to St Andrew's Church (look for the Scottish flag flying aloft), very clean and modern, with a relaxed atmosphere. The rooms are bright and airy, with en-suite bathrooms, free use of a kettle and tea bags, shared balconies and great views across to Mount Zion and the Old City (the guesthouse itself looks quite impressive when seen from the Jaffa Gate, especially at night).There's also the excellent Sunbula gift shop (see p.228) on site. The downside is that, although it is within walking distance of the Old City, the walk involves rather a steep climb, and there is rather farther to traipse if coming from downtown East or West

Jerusalem (though you can take bus #18). No curfew. Breakfast included ❻

YMCA, Three Arches 26 King David St ☎02/569 2692; ⓦwww.ymca3arch.co.il. A Jerusalem landmark (see p.137), with its imposing tower and cupolas, and a cut above the usual "Y". Rooms are comfortable and tasteful though not massive, and guests have access to all sports facilities, which include a fitness centre and swimming pool. The *Three Arches* was built by the same company that constructed the Empire State building, and its magnificent lobby, with vaulting reminiscent of Crusader constructions, is well worth visiting even if you don't stay here. The decor does at times give a slightly churchy atmosphere, but this is a Christian organization after all, and the surprisingly successful mix of Art Deco and traditional Middle Eastern styles is very easy on the eye. In the front, a tiled panel quotes Edmund Allenby's 1933 dedication speech, "Here is a place whose atmosphere is peace, where political and religious jealousies can be forgotten, and international unity be fostered and developed," high ideals which the Y really does try to live up to. Breakfast included ❻

Zion 10 Dorot Rishonim ☎02/625 7585, ⓦwww.zionhotel.co.il. An attractively renovated hotel in a nineteenth-century building. The medium-sized rooms are cosy and carpeted, with original features preserved, but containing all modern conveniences such as a TV, fridge, phone, heating and a/c

(though not tremendously well looked after), and some rooms also have a balcony. The location, directly above the popular *Rimon* café (see p.183) in West Jerusalem's *midrahov* (pedestrian precinct), makes it extremely handy for downtown West Jerusalem, but also rather noisy. ❸

The suburbs

Little House in the Colony 4a Lloyd George, German Colony ☎02/566 2424, ⓦwww.o-niv.com/melonit (see map, pp.126–127). A homely B&B guesthouse out of the centre of town but not too far out to be walkable if you fancy a long stroll (or take bus #4, #14, #15, #18 or #24 if not). Located in the trendy German Colony, it boasts a sunny breakfast room, small but bright and clean rooms with wooden floors and TV, and a family atmosphere. There's even a little garden. Rooms adjoining the neighbouring Smadar cinema are especially cheap (❸), to compensate for the noise. Breakfast included ❻

YHA Yitzhak Rabin 1 Nahman Avigad, Givat Ram ☎02/678 0101, ⓦwww.iyha.org.il (see map, p.127). Modern spacious rooms, built with school and seminar groups in mind, at this modern guesthouse out by the Hebrew University campus, handy for the Israel Museum and handy-ish for Yad VaShem, but a lot less so for the Old City and downtown East or West Jerusalem (buses #9 and #17 can take you into town, except on Shabbat of course, when it's a long but healthy walk). Breakfast included ❹

Expensive hotels

West Jerusalem has the lion's share of the upper end of the market with plenty of modern five-star hotels scattered around its suburbs. The older and more established hotels, however, tend to be closer to the centre, and you'll also find a few luxury options east of the Green Line.

East Jerusalem

All of these are shown on the map on p.109.

Addar Suite Nablus Rd, opposite the American Colony ☎02/626 3111, ⓦwww.addar-hotel.com. Guests at this low-key deluxe hotel include diplomats and business people from the West and the Arab world, and the decor is plush and modern with lavish furnishings, catering perhaps a little more to Middle

Eastern than to Western tastes. The bathrooms, complete with jacuzzi, are done out in white marble, and there are more suites than simple rooms. Guests include diplomats and Israeli parliamentarians; the most famous name on the "stayed here" list is former Irish president Mary Robinson. Breakfast included ❼

American Colony Nablus Rd ☎02/627 9777, ⓦwww.americancolony.com.

▲ High-end luxury at the American Colony hotel

More an institution than a hotel, this former pasha's palace has become the meeting place for local and international diplomats, VIPs and journalists, and is Jerusalem's most stylish hotel by far. The decor is exquisite, the service punctilious, and the atmosphere tranquil and refined. Former guests include Allenby, Churchill, Chagall, Graham Greene, John Le Carré, Ingrid Bergman, Lauren Bacall, Lawrence of Arabia and Peter O'Toole (who played Lawrence in David Lean's film). It has all the modern conveniences you would expect from a five-star hotel, including two restaurants, most famously the *Arabesque* (see p.188), plus a cellar bar (see p.195), and a delightful inner patio. The cheaper rooms are a lot less interesting than the more expensive ones, so you may want to pay extra to have somewhere more atmospheric. Breakfast included ❽

Golden Walls (Pilgrim's Palace) Sultan Suleiman St, near Damascus Gate ☎ 02/627 2416, ⓦ www.goldenwalls.com. Well located in the heart of East Jerusalem just outside the Old City, with friendly and efficient staff, and pleasant modern rooms, but not really as plush as they ought to be for the price. Facilities include TV, a/c, and individual room safes, and there's round-the-clock room service. The lounge has a panoramic view of the Old City walls, the roof garden has an even better one, and the dining room serves excellent Middle Eastern food. Breakfast included ❼

Olive Tree 23 St George St ☎ 02/541 0410, ⓦ www.olivetreehotel.com. Slick new hotel with classic Jerusalem stone decor belonging to the Royal Plaza chain, and supposedly built on the site of an ancient caravanserai located next to an olive tree under which King David played his harp. It's got banqueting halls, a lobby bar, tastefully done-out rooms and an atrium, and caters mainly for upmarket tour groups, though the service is a cut above that of your average tour group hotel. On the other hand, at rack rates, you'd be better off paying less and taking a room at the *American Colony*. Breakfast included ❽

West Jerusalem

All of these are shown on the map on p.127.
David Citadel 7 King David St ☎ 02/621 1111, ⓦ www.thedavidcitadel.com. The preferred choice of the super-rich these days (pending completion of the *Palace* across the street – see ⓦ www.thepalacejerusalem.com for latest details), and if you've got money to spend on the most deluxe facilities in town, then this is the place to stay: cool, modern and immaculate, part of the Mamilla development, complete with chocolates on your pillow, Ahava cosmetics in the bathroom and Frette cotton bathrobes, though you don't exactly get three bags full from the

staff, as some might expect given the hefty price. There's a large pool, Thai and shiatsu massage, facials, aromatherapy, Mediterranean and Japanese restaurants, executive and presidential suites, and a capacious function room. In some ways it's plusher than the *King David* or the *American Colony*, but it doesn't of course have their character or history, though it's building up a portfolio of famous former guests, including US president Bill Clinton and fashion designer Jean-Paul Gautier. Breakfast included ❾

Inbal 3 Jabotinsky, by Liberty Bell Park ☎02/675 6666, ⓦwww.inbalhotel.com. This deluxe establishment bills itself as "the finest hotel in Jerusalem", and the trappings are all there, but it's corporate rather than posh. The rooms are plush, but they could be hotel rooms anywhere, and they aren't huge; the decor is elegant, but it somehow lacks character. Really it's a hotel for upmarket package tourists. You'll certainly be looked after in the lap of luxury and comfort while you're here, but it isn't a hotel to remember, and it's also not tremendously well located. On the other hand, if it's luxury you're after, and bland doesn't bother you, then you might just prefer it to the *King David* or the *American Colony*. Breakfast included ❾

🏃 **King David** 23 King David St ☎02/620 8888, ⓦwww.danhotels.com. Israel's spraunciest and most famous hotel, built for the Jewish Egyptian Mosseri family in 1931 and now run by the Dan Hotels chain, the *King David* is getting a bit long in the tooth but still has bags of character and a list of former guests that reads like *Who's Who*, including Churchill, Sadat and Haile Selassie, Gorbachev, Thatcher and Kissinger, Liz Taylor and Richard Burton, Kirk Douglas and Paul Newman, among scores of assorted royals, presidents and film stars. Its south wing was famously bombed by the Irgun in 1946 (see p.137). The rooms are super deluxe, and nothing if not tasteful, and there are no less than 36 luxury suites. Even if you don't take one of those, you may well want to pay a little extra to get an east-facing room with a view of the Old City. The lobby and other public areas are done out in local stone with marble floors and biblical motifs, and there's a lovely, old-fashioned reading room. On the downside, the service is a bit creaky where

it matters – the soap in your room gets changed daily but actual problems can take a long time to sort – and the food is rather mediocre. Breakfast included ❾

King Solomon 32 King David St ☎02/569 5555, ⓦwww.kingsolomon-hotel.com; toll-free booking from the US ☎1-800/606-9593. Formerly the *Sheraton* (the present-day *Sheraton* is reviewed below), this is still quite a classy hotel and good value for a five-star. Guests are greeted in the lobby by a spherical Frank Meisler sculpture of Jerusalem, and the rooftop pool (open in summer only), offers fine views of the Old City. The rooms are smart and tastefully done out, and it's worth asking for one with an Old City view when you book (the price is the same). Breakfast included ❼

Mount Zion 17 Hebron Rd ☎02/568 9555 ⓦwww.mountzion.co.il. An unusually sited hotel, built into the side of a hill facing Mount Zion, with the lobby on the top floor. It boasts the biggest hotel pool in Jerusalem, and full four-star facilities. The old wing was built as a hospital back in 1882, the new wing added in 1986, but both have been renovated with large comfy rooms. Along with the pool, fitness room and other standard facilities, there is also a hot pool in the original water cistern under the hotel's old wing. A room with a view costs a bit extra, but if you're going to stay here it's worth the difference. Breakfast included ❾

Prima Kings 60 King George St (entrance on Ramban) ☎02/620 1201, ⓦwww.prima.co.il. An unremarkable but reasonably well-located and good-value four-star hotel at the junction of King George St with Agron, not tremendously central, but pretty handy for both West Jerusalem and the Old City. The rooms are not massive (and some travellers have reported bad smells so check first) but the beds are very grand, with padded headboards, and the staff generally very accommodating. It isn't Jerusalem's top address, but it's good value by West Jerusalem standards. Breakfast included ❼

Sheraton 47 King George St ☎02/629 8666, ⓦwww.sheraton.co.il; toll-free booking from the US & Canada ☎1-800/325-3535; toll-free booking from the UK & Ireland ☎0800/3253 5353. Standing tall on the edge of downtown West Jerusalem, but also handy for the Old City (over which some rooms have great views), the *Sheraton* is essentially a business hotel, but known for its service and great dining, so popular with upmarket tourists too. There's an Italian restaurant, *La Primavera*, plus of course the full range of faclities including sauna, health club and pool. The rooms are done out in wood, with a small sitting area including leather chairs and a coffee table. The white marble bathrooms even have a phone. Breakfast included ❾

The suburbs

Ramat Rahel Kibbutz Hotel Kibbutz Ramat Rahel (bus #7 from Egged Central Bus Station) ☏ 02/670 2555, ⓦ www.ramatrachel.co.il. An upmarket kibbutz inn of the sort common in rural Israel, offering a relaxed setting with fine views of Bethlehem and the desert beyond, and the unusual combination of staying on a kibbutz and staying in Jerusalem. Don't expect to find the rural socialist idyll of kibbutzim from Israel's pioneering days: they've come a long way since then, and this is a wealthy suburban community, though it's still a whole lot more relaxed and agricultural than staying in town. Guests can use kibbutz's fitness centre and tennis courts for a small charge, and the pool, sauna and jacuzzi are all free. Since the kibbutz also has a popular conference centre, the hotel may be booked up if there's a big conference on, so it's wise to book ahead. Breakfast included ❼

⑩

Eating

E ast meets West in Jerusalem, food-wise as in so many other ways. For Western and international food, Jerusalem's **restaurants** don't quite match New York or London, and for Middle Eastern food they are not quite equal to Beirut or Damascus, but in both cases they come pretty damn close. **Israeli food**, as eaten on the west side of town, is essentially Middle Eastern (hummus, falafel and so on), but with the addition of Jewish and Western elements, and there's also an extraordinary variety of **international cuisine**, including Thai and Chinese, French and Italian, Moroccan and Ethiopian, even South African and South American (but note that the term "oriental" usually means Middle Eastern rather than East Asian). Strangely, what Westerners usually think of as **Jewish cooking** – chicken soup, gefilte fish, *latkes* and so on – is surprisingly thin on the ground. In fact these dishes are peculiar to Ashkenazi (East European) Jews; the Sephardim who make up the majority of the Jewish community eat food that is much the same as those of their Arab neighbours.

In East Jerusalem, traditional **Middle Eastern food** dominates entirely, and restaurants are especially strong on **mezze** (mixed hors d'oeuvres) and **kebabs** including *shawarma*, *shashlik* and kofta (which is what you'll get if you just ask for "a kebab").

Café and **street stall foods** such as hummus, falafel, corn on the cob, pulses and sweets are available everywhere. In fact you could spend weeks in Jerusalem eating well and healthily without ever going into a restaurant. Breads, cheeses and yoghurts, pickles, olives, fresh vegetables and fruit are freely available and cheap. Also common are shops selling what are known in Arabic as *bizr*, in Hebrew as *bitzuhim* – nuts, seeds, salted roast chick-peas and the like – while bakeries supply *burekas*, Israel's second most popular finger food (after falafel), consisting of a puff-pastry triangle stuffed with cheese, spinach or potato.

Junk-food junkies in need of a fix will find *McDonald's* at 4 Shamai in downtown West Jerusalem or *Burger King* at 7 Ben Yehuda. Israeli shoppping **malls**, scattered around the outskirts of town like Malha's Kanyon Yerushalayim (see p.222), all have a food court where a number of fast-food outlets surround a common eating area.

Bread

Local **breads** include both Middle Eastern and Western varieties, the latter far more common in bakeries on the West side of town. The most famous local bread is **pitta**, a round, flat, hollow bread, into which falafel or shawarma are

> Under Israeli law, **smoking** is banned in cafés and restaurants, but some nonetheless have an area set aside for smokers.

▲ Juice bar/café inside the Damascus Gate

stuffed, along with the requisite salad or pickles, for street eating. In West Jerusalem on a Friday, you'll also come across **halla**, a yeasty plaited loaf made with egg and used to celebrate Shabbat and Jewish festivals.

Though **bagels** are famously Jewish, you'll be hard-put to find a decent one in Jerusalem. That is because the bagels here are not boiled before baking (some are steamed, but it isn't the same), so they don't get that chewy texture vital for a proper Yiddische bagel. Exceptions – where the bagels are shiny and chewy as they should be – include *Tal Bagels* at 64 Emek Refaim in the German Colony, and *Bagel Bite* at 84 Bethlehem Rd (on the corner of Yehuda in the Baka neighbourhood, almost in Talpiot), both American in origin, and both rather far from the city centre. The nearest approximation you'll get downtown is at *Holy Bagel* (34 Jaffa Rd). The sesame-covered bagel-shaped but elongated bread rolls sold in East Jerusalem are called **ka'ak**, and usually eaten with *za'atar* (see p.180), of which you should be given a small amount in a twist of paper when you buy one.

Breakfast

Breakfast is generally provided in hotels (see p.165), but if you're staying somewhere where it isn't, you might want to pop out for some bread and something like yoghurt, cheese, cold cuts or a hummus-type salad. Alternatively, if self-catering isn't your thing, hummus bars (see p.184) are a good bet, opening early and serving good solid food to set you up for the day. The downside is that they don't always do tea or coffee. A full **Israeli breakfast** consists of salad, fruit juice, eggs, and tea or coffee. Many West Jerusalem cafés serve them and good ones can be found at *Aroma* (see p.183) and *Rachela* (see p.183). For a more Western-style breakfast, try *Riff-Raff* (see p.192). In the Old City, *Pizzaria Basti* (see p.187) does decent breakfasts. If a Continental breakfast will do you, any café can drum you up a coffee and croissant; especially recommended are those which bake their own, notably *Aroma* (see p.183), *Café Hillel* (see p.183) and *Patisserie Suisse* (see p.183).

Kosher food

Most, but not all, Israeli restaurants are **kosher**, and certified as such by a religious authority such as the Beth Din (a certification which the restaurant pays for). The Hebrew term for kosherness is *kashrut*. Places that are kosher will have a sign to that effect in the window or on the menu. It means, among other things, that meat and dairy dishes are not served in the same establishment, and that the restaurant is closed on the Sabbath (but often open until shortly before Shabbat begins on Friday, and after Shabbat on Saturday evenings). Kosher establishments do not serve pork or shellfish, among other things, and meat must be slaughtered in a specific way (for the exact criteria, see p.277), but there are degrees of kosher; Glatt or Lamehadrin are stricter forms, and restaurants or food manufacturers adhering to those must, for example, have only religious Jews preparing the food. Kosher restaurants may not mix meat and dairy products, so they must be either meat, dairy or *pareve* (neither). They also have to close for Shabbat, which means at least an hour before sunset on Fridays and the eve of Jewish holidays, but may open after nightfall on Saturdays. Restaurants which are kosher are described as such in the listings in this chapter.

The rules for what meat is allowed (*halal*) in Islam are similar, but simpler: meat must be killed in the same way, and pork is prohibited, but other non-kosher foods such as rabbit and shellfish are allowed.

Restaurant prices

Throughout the listings in this chapter, we've given restaurants a **price rating**, describing them as cheap, moderate, or expensive. Obviously, these terms are subjective, and prices will depend on what you eat, but roughly speaking, a typical meal (excluding wine) in a restaurant described as "cheap" will cost less than 70NIS (£12/$20); you can expect to eat for 70–150NIS (£12–25/$20–40) per head in restaurants described as "moderate", and more than that in restaurants described as "expensive". Note that these price descriptions refer to evening à la carte eating – some places may nonetheless have set menus, special offers or "business lunches" (see p.186) which will cost substantially less.

Local specialities and food terms

For ordinary food vocabulary, see p.297.

atayef small pancakes stuffed with cheese or nuts and drizzled with syrup, a Palestinian Ramadan speciality.

blintzes pancakes, usually stuffed with sweet cheese; an Ashkenazi Jewish speciality but much the same as Russian *blinis*.

bureka puff pastry triangle stuffed with cheese, spinach or potato; a Sephardi Jewish speciality, though Turkish in origin.

borscht red beetroot soup, served hot or cold; a Polish dish that's become an Askhkenazi Jewish favourite.

cholent the traditional Shabbat stew of beef brisket, beans, barley, potatoes, dumplings and vegetables, all cooked slowly overnight.

denis fish sea bream, formerly farmed intensively on the Red Sea, causing serious damage to the ecosystem until a 2008 victory by Israeli environmentalists halted it.

falafel deep-fried chickpea (garbanzo bean) balls, Israel's national dish.

fuul Egyptian brown fava bean stew.

gefilte fish sweet minced fish balls, an Ashkenazi Jewish speciality that was originally the stuffing for a carp.

hummus chickpea (garbanzo bean) paste, mixed with tahini, olive oil, lemon juice and garlic; a *mezze* dip that's common across the Levant, and a mainstay of both Israeli and Palestinian cuisine.

kofta lamb minced with coriander, usually served as a kebab (if you just ask for "kebab", this is what you'll get); it's Palestinian but common across the Middle East.

kubbe minced lamb enclosed in a case of burghul (cracked wheat) and deep fried; essentially a Lebanese speciality, but popular in Palestinian cooking too.

latke fried potato cake (not unlike Swiss *rösti*); a typical Ashkenazi Jewish speciality.

maqluba Palestinian signature-dish, consisting of layers of meat or chicken, vegetables and rice, with tomatoes at the bottom, cooked in a casserole and then inverted onto a plate (hence the dish's name, which means "upside-down").

masabaha whole cooked chickpeas (garbanzo beans) in *tehina*; like hummus, very much a Levantine dish.

meorav yerushalmi (literally, "Jerusalem meats") mixed meats in a pitta, an Israeli dish that's local to West Jerusalem.

mezze Middle Eastern hors d'oeuvres, mainly consisting of dips (such as hummus) or salads (such as tabbouleh), though all are called "salads" in Arabic.

musakhan The Palestinian national dish, consisting of chicken with sumak, onions and pine nuts, baked in a flat *taboon* bread called a *shrak*.

muttabal a typical *mezze* dip consisting of baked eggplant mashed with *tehina*; also known as *babaghanouj*.

pitta hollow flatbread.

ruz falastini "Palestinian rice": rice cooked with fine pasta, fried pine nuts and saffron.

sfiha Palestinian "pizza", baked with minced meat, tomatoes and onion.

shawarma marinated meat kebab (usually lamb, sometimes chicken or turkey) on a vertical spit, carved and generally served in a pitta; looks like a doner kebab, but is insulted by the comparison.

shakshuka vegetable stew based on tomatoes and green peppers, often served with an egg on top; common to all Middle Eastern cuisine.

shashlik lamb and vegetable kebab grilled on a skewer over charcoal, a dish that's typical of both Palestinian and Sephardi Jewish cuisine.

shish tawouk chicken kebab grilled on a skewer over charcoal.

schnitzel veal, chicken or turkey steaks covered with matza meal (the Jewish equivalent of breadcrumbs) and fried.

St Peter's fish a variety of tilapia from the Sea of Galilee.

sumak a lemony-flavoured red spice made from the dried berries of a Middle Eastern shrub.

taboon traditional Palestinian oven (not unlike an Indian tandoor).

tabbouleh parsley salad with bulghur wheat, essentially Lebanese, but popular in Palestinian cooking too.

tehina tahini (sesame seed paste) mixed with lemon juice and garlic.

za'atar a condiment consisting of thyme, hyssop, sumak, sesame seeds and salt, all pounded together.

Cafés

European-style **cafés** are mostly to be found in West Jerusalem, though there are one or two in the East, including the Old City, where there's also a small but waning number of traditional *qahwas* (Arabic coffee houses; see box, p.182). Israelis love Mediterranean-style café culture, and will often hang out and meet up in cafés rather than bars. The German Colony has become extremely trendy for this, and people from all over West Jerusalem can be found in its café-restaurants and espresso bars, though lately the cognoscenti have been gravitating to the smaller but hipper café scene on the Gaza Road (also known by its Hebraicized name, "Azza Street").

Israeli cafés generally serve very good espresso **coffee**. Cappuccino and caffè latte are much as in the West; *afukh* means espresso with just a little milk (like an Italian *macchiato* or Spanish *cortado*). Instant coffee (known universally as Nescafé, or just "Nes") is also normally available (quite a few Israelis actually prefer it), and comes with milk unless you specify "no milk" (*bliy halav* in Hebrew, *bidoun halib* in Arabic). Arab establishments, and some Israeli ones, also serve Turkish coffee, usually with cardamom (*bi-hel*); if you don't like cardamom, ask for it without (*bidoun hel*).

Tea can be a bit hit and miss. It's generally served black, often with a sprig of mint (in which case it is known in Arabic as *shai bi-nana* and in Hebrew as *tay binana*), or sometimes with a slice of lemon, but all too often it consists of a meagre tea bag dunked in a cup of vaguely hot water, or served in a saucer accompanied by a cup of lukewarm water (the latter a favourite in Israeli restaurants). Arab *qahwas* (see box, p.182) are more likely – but by no means certain – to make it properly, with boiling water, and occasionally even loose-leaf tea. They may also serve it with other herbs such as sage (*shai bi-maramiya*).

Cafés may also offer **infusions**, usually just camomile (*kamamilya* in Hebrew or Arabic), but sometimes peppermint (*menta*) or verbena (*louiza*). The other alternative to tea and coffee in West Jerusalem coffee houses is **hot chocolate**

▲ The Rimon café in West Jerusalem

(*shoko*); the chocolate often appears in concentrated pill form at the bottom of a glass of hot milk, which needs to be stirred in to release the flavour.

Old City

Bint al-Balad Frères St, next door to Melia handicraft shop, Christian Quarter ☎02/628 1377 (see map, p.56). A lovely little pie and coffee house, run by a women's co-op. The coffee itself isn't actually very good here (Turkish is better than espresso), but the cakes and pies are great, and they serve wonderful home-style Palestinian food too, though only if they have an advance order (call to enquire). Mon–Sat 8am–7pm.

Gate Café On the left as you enter from Damascus Gate (see map, p.73). A covered open-air terrace café with a ringside seat overlooking the activity on the plaza inside the Damascus Gate, but set-back from it. Has been known to serve food, but nowadays only does coffee, tea, juices and *sfiha* (Palestinian "pizza"). Daily 8am–8pm (closes later in summer).

Geo's 124 Souq Dabbagha (main entrance on Muristan Rd), Christian Quarter (see map, p.56). Full of tourists, as you'd expect in this location, between the Jaffa Gate and the Church of the Holy Sepulchre, but they have good espresso and espresso-based cappuccinos, lattes and so on, plus sandwiches, salads, breakfasts and free wi-fi coverage, and pretty standard prices. Mon–Sat 8am–7pm.

R. Himo Café On the right as you enter from Damascus Gate (see map, p.73). A small café

right on the plaza inside the Damascus Gate, where you can sit amid the hubbub with a hubble-bubble, or just a coffee or freshly squeezed fruit juice. Overpriced and something of a tourist trap, but the location's unbeatable. Daily 7.30am–10pm.

The Quarter Café 11 Tiferet Israel, Jewish Quarter (see map, p.85). The real draw at this café is the wonderful view over the Mount of Olives, though you'll need to bag one of the four tables by the window to enjoy it. As well as coffee, they serve (rather pricey) food – blintzes, borscht, *latkes*, even salmon steaks – and, unusually for an Old City café, it's wheelchair accessible. Sun–Thurs 9am–6pm, Fri 9am–2.30pm. Kosher.

East Jerusalem

All of these are shown on the map on p.109.

El Dorado 19 Salah al-Din. Run by a family that started importing coffee from Mocha in Yemen in 1922. Head upstairs to find some space and enjoy their fine espresso made with, naturally, their own imported coffees (no longer mocha, but still excellent), and check out their range of high-class imported chocolates while you're at it, or take some away wrapped in coloured cellophane. Sat–Thurs 8.30am–8pm.

Gossip 9 Shimon HaTzadik. Cool, modern café offering the best of east and west

Qahwas

Arab coffee houses, or **qahwas**, in Jerusalem as throughout the Middle East, are traditionally the exclusive domain of men, who will sit for hours playing backgammon (*tawla* or *sheshbesh*) or cards, and smoking waterpipes (*argila* or *sheesha*). Qahwas usually serve tea with mint, and strong Turkish coffee (*qahwa* means coffee as well as coffee house) spiced with cardamom and sweetened to your taste. Hookah pipes (*argila*) are served with plain tobacco (*tombak*, which is rather rough) or flavoured tobacco (*ma'azil*, which strictly speaking should mean with molasses, but in practice is usually flavoured with fruit). A woman's presence will be considered somewhat strange (you won't often see a Palestinian woman in one), but is more likely to be accepted in places in the Old City where the regulars are used to tourists of both sexes stopping by. One such is on Aqabat al-Saraya at the southern end of Souq Khan al-Zeit, by Souq al-Attarin, and there are a couple more on the west side of the Muristan off the passage leading down from the barbers' shops to Christian Quarter Road. Other *qahwas*, less used to tourists, include the *Café Karkour* just inside Herod's Gate, and *Café Jabler*, 50m down the road, plus two more just outside the walls on HaNeviim.

Something between a drink and a sweet, **sahlab**, available in winter from street vendors in East Jerusalem and the Old City, and also from some *qahwas*, and even in West Jerusalem cafés on occasion, is a warming concoction of sweet hot milk, thickened in principle with the root of a species of orchid (but in practice with arrowroot or even cornflour), and served with cinnamon, coconut and raisins.

– espresso, and permutations thereof, plus salads, sandwiches and banana split if you want to be western, or Turkish and a *sheesha* if you want to be eastern (or, should you wish to go multicultural, espresso with a *sheesha*, or Turkish with a banana split). Daily noon–midnight.

Patisserie Suisse 13 Salah-al-Din, beside Capitol Hotel. A popular (and a/c) East Jerusalem hideaway, selling beer, tea, camomile and espresso coffee. Formerly a pastry shop, its range of cakes is now rather limited, though it does have fresh croissants every morning. Savoury snacks on offer include grilled chicken breast, hamburgers and cheeseburgers, hot dogs, chicken nuggets and roast beef pastrami sandwiches, with ice cream for afters. Mon–Thurs & Sat 9am–7pm.

Central West Jerusalem

All of these are shown on the map on pp.126–127.

Aroma 18 Hillel ⊛aromae.aroma.co.il. Popular espresso bar (now a chain, but this is the original branch) with excellent Italian-style coffees and a trendy clientele in the heart of downtown West Jerusalem. It is also known for its tasty and filling sandwiches, made with a choice of breads which are baked on the premises, as are the croissants. Numerous branches elsewhere in the city include 38 Emek Refaim in the German Colony. Daily 24hr.

Bohlinat 6 Dorot Rishonim (in the Ben Yehuda Street midrahov). A convivial and rather trendy café with wooden furniture and earthy terracotta-style walls, where bright young things pop in to have a coffee, read a newspaper or play backgammon by day, or hang out and have a drink by night. As well as coffee, they serve beer, wine, salads and sandwiches. The music is a mixture of dance styles including trip-hop and (inevitably) trance. Daily 24hr. Licensed.

Café Hillel 8 Hillel. Another Hillel St coffee bar that's become a nationwide Israeli chain, with further Jerusalem branches at 1 Heleni HaMalka and in the German Colony at 54 Emek Refaim. Here at its original branch there's a cool, a/c, inside space, with a terrace and wicker chairs outside. You could be sensible and take a quiche or a salad with your coffee, but can you really resist the truffles or the triple-layered chocolate cream cake? Sun–Thurs 6.30am–midnight, Fri 6.30am–Shabbat, Sat Shabbat–midnight. Kosher.

Nocturno 7 Betzalel. A small café on the corner where Betzalel meets Ben Yehuda and becomes a major road. Despite its size, this place is not unlike a San Francisco coffee bar, with a notice board and leaflets advertising local events, and a mellow, arty clientele. There's also free wi-fi. Sun–Thurs 7am–11pm, Fri 7am–Shabbat, Sat Shabbat–11pm. Licensed. Kosher.

Notre Dame Coffee House Notre Dame, Paratroopers Rd. In the summer, you can take your coffee on the rooftop terrace, an excellent vantage point over the city; in winter, you're confined to the indoor café and the small terrace out front, both serving tea, coffee, beers and sodas as well as snacks, salads, soups and toasties. Daily 9am–10pm.

Rachela 5 HaHavatzelet. A quiet and congenial little café, an oasis of tranquility in the city centre, serving Israeli and Middle Eastern breakfasts (the latter based on *shakshuka*), and what they call an English breakfast (scones with cream and jam), as well as fish dishes (65–80NIS), and their own home-made marmalade. Sun–Thurs 10am–11pm, Fri 10am–2pm. Kosher.

Rimon 4 Lunz, in the Ben Yehuda St midrahov. A Jerusalem institution, going since 1954, very popular, rather commercial, and rather overpriced, it's nowadays more a restaurant than a café, serving everything from blintzes and pasta to fish steaks, but no meat. Always busy and a favourite meeting spot for middle-aged Jewish women shopping in town. There's a second branch in the Mamilla shopping centre. Sun–Thurs

8am–1am, Fri 8am–Shabbat, Sat Shabbat–1am. Kosher.

Tmol Shilshom 5 Yoel Salomon (round the back – entrance via the alley by no.11) ⓦ www.tmol-shilshom.co.il. A comfy lounge with a bookish but homely atmosphere serving coffee and a variety of herb teas, in a popular downtown café that doubles as a secondhand bookshop (though the selection of books in English is small), named after Shai Agnon's novel (published in English as *Only Yesterday*; see p.288). Literary events include readings by Israeli authors, and there's free wi-fi. Food includes blintzes, salads, omelettes and sandwiches, plus banana bread, cakes and pies. Sun–Thurs 9am–midnight, Fri 9am–sunset, Sat Shabbat–midnight. Kosher.

German Colony

In addition to these, *Aroma* (see p.183) and *Café Hillel* (see p.183) both have branches on Emek Refaim. All are shown on the map on p.127.

Caffit 35 Emek Refaim. Choose from a cool terrace or smart indoor space at this overblown café which also serves hefty portions of food (pasta, bagels, salads or fish, main dishes 44–88NIS). Sun–Thurs 7.30am–11pm, Fri 7.30am–Shabbat, Sat Shabbat–11pm. Kosher.

Masaryk 31 Emek Refaim ⓦ www.masaryk .co.il. A covered terrace where you can take coffee, or fish and pasta dishes (56–95NIS), with breakfast served in the mornings. Sun–Thurs 7.30am–midnight, Fri 7.30am–Shabbat, Sat Shabbat–midnight. Wheelchair accessible. Licensed. Kosher.

Tahanat HaCafé (Coffee Mill) 23 Emek Refaim. A wide choice of coffees, teas and infusions at this old-fashioned coffee house done out in wood. In the morning, they do bagels and sandwiches. Sun–Thurs 7.30am–11pm, Fri 7.30am–Shabbat, Sat Shabbat–11pm. Kosher.

Gaza Road (Azza Street)

All of these are shown on the map on p.127.

HaLekhem shel Tomer 28 Gaza Rd. Small and quiet café, with just a couple of tables, both out on the forecourt. As well as coffee, they have wonderful tarts and cream pastries, not to mention tiramisú, and they sell cheeses, bread, and high-class Czech or German lager to take away. Sun–Thurs 7am–9.30pm, Fri 7am–Shabbat. Kosher.

Rehavia 19 Gaza Rd. A cool café-bar with a young crowd, serving Israeli breakfast all day, plus salads, sandwiches, Mediterranean antipasti, pasta and fish – but who cares about main courses when the afters include vanilla ice cream with brownie chunks and *silan* (date syrup), or frozen nougat with chestnut cream and mascarpone? Sun–Thurs 7.30am–midnight, Fri 7.30am–Shabbat, Sat Shabbat–midnight. Licensed. Kosher.

Shokolah 8 Arlozoroff. A café-cum-chocolate shop, where you can stop for an energy boost (or, put it another way, pile on the calories) in the form of dreamy and creamy creations from three of Israel's finest chocolatiers; luckily for your waistline, they're also rather pricey. Alternatively, take a chocolate cream pastry with your coffee or *shoko*, into which they'll slip a cheeky shot of liquor as well if you like. Sun–Thurs 9am–8pm, Fri 9am–2.30pm. Serves spirits in coffee only. Kosher.

Sigmund 29 Gaza Rd (at the corner of HaAri). A curious little place that looks like a shack with an umbrella on top, named after Dr S. Freud, the founder of psychoanalysis. It's a community centre of sorts, with information leaflets and fliers on the bar, but it doesn't have much space – there are a couple of tables, and a couple more outside, but most of the hip clientele just squeeze round the bar. Coffee aside, there are crêpes and milk shakes, even soup and couscous. Sun–Thurs 7.30am–9pm, Fri 7.30am–3pm. Kosher.

Hummus and falafel places

Chickpeas (garbanzo beans) form the basis of Jerusalem's two most common foods, whose popularity across the city brings Israelis and Palestinians together in a shared passion. **Hummus**, which consists of chickpeas mashed with tahini (sesame paste), olive oil and sometimes garlic and/or lemon juice, is eaten as a dip (often referred to as a "salad"), with pitta bread to scoop it up. In restaurants, it may be offered as a starter, but low-priced **hummus bars** serve it up for breakfast, and this is how working people here traditionally set themselves up for the day. Most hummus establishments – certainly those on the east side of town – should be able to find you a cup of tea or coffee too, and most also serve falafel.

Falafel, which consists of deep-fried chickpea balls, usually spiced with cumin, is ubiquitous, but not always very good. On the east side, large falafels with an onion centre are available, but the small plain ones are usually better. Either way, they've absolutely got to be freshly made – falafel that is left out to get cold loses its outer crunchiness and inner lightness and is not worth buying, so if they don't fry it in front of you, don't bother. West Jerusalem tends to beat the east in the falafel stakes, and serves them up in a pitta with a big selection of salads, pickles and sauces, while in the east, you usually just buy the balls. Falafel joints are invariably takeaways: if you want to sit down and eat your falafel, find a street bench. In addition to the places listed here, Mahane Yeuda market has a large number of stalls selling excellent falafel, and is also a good place to get mixed meats in a pitta (*meorav yerushalmi*), considered a West Jerusalem speciality (at *Sima*, for example; see p.191).

Old City

Abu Shukri 63 Al-Wad Rd, Muslim Quarter (see map, p.73). An Old City institution, whose tip-top hummus draws diners from all sides of town. As well as your plate of hummus and pitta bread, they'll give you a side plate of pickles and falafels, and if you fancy a change from hummus, they do a pretty mean *fuul* as well. Daily 8am–5.30pm. Cheap.

Hummus Lina 42 Aqabat al-Khanka, by the Eighth Station of the Cross (see map, p.56). A traditional and popular hummus joint, serving tasty hummus with pitta, pickles, onions, and hot peppers; also *fuul*, *masabaha*, salad and cold drinks. Daily 8.30am–4pm. Cheap.

Uncle Moustache Al-Qadisha (inside Herod's Gate, just round to the left; see map, p.73). The best falafel in the Old City, either small and plain, or large and stuffed with onions, at this perennially popular little diner, which also makes excellent *kubbe*, but don't let them palm you off with falafels that have been lying around rather than freshly cooked ones. There's a *qahwa* (traditional café; see p.182) just across the street to supply tea or coffee for breakfast. Sat–Thurs 9am–6pm, Fri 9am–1pm. Cheap.

East Jerusalem

Abo Ali In the little alleyway between nos.10 and 12 Salah al-Din (see map, p.109). Basement restaurant serving excellent hummus and delicious Palestinian home cooking, especially handy for breakfast. Daily 6am–4pm. Cheap.

Falafel al-Bakri 5 Salah al-Din (see map, p.109). Unassuming but reliably good no-nonsense straight falafel joint, eat in or take out. Sat–Thurs 8am–7pm. Cheap.

West Jerusalem

All of these are shown on the map on pp.126–127.

HaSabiykh 24 Ben Yehuda. Excellent falafel shop in the Ben Yehuda *midrahov*, serving up fresh fried falafels in a pitta with copious amounts of your choice of salads, or alternatively, *sabiykh* (fried slices of eggplant with a hard-boiled egg), in a pitta with the same salads. Sun–Thurs 10am–8pm (9pm in summer), Fri 10am–2pm. Kosher. Cheap.

HaTimani 48 HaNeviim, opposite the end of Monbaz (sign in Hebrew only). Pictures of rabbis deck the walls of this superb falafel shop, where there are leaflets on the counter with the Hebrew grace after meals prayer printed on them so that you can give thanks to God for your falafel, which, having tasted it, you may well be inclined to do. Sun–Thurs 9.30am–9.30pm. Fri 9.30am–2pm. Kosher. Cheap.

Pinnati 13 King George St. Small, packed, and very popular downtown hummus joint, where you'll probably have to share a table. The atmosphere is frenetic but the hummus, and similar dishes such as *masabaha*, are outstanding. Sun–Thurs 8am–6.30pm, Fri 8am–3pm. Kosher. Cheap.

Shalom Betzalel St, opposite the end of Ussishkin, Popular local hole-in-the-wall falafel stand, now with a bigger and more convenient city-centre branch at 27 Yoel Salomon, which has sit-down space and does shawarma, kebabs and a 37NIS "business meal". Sun–Thurs 10am–10pm, Fri 10am–Shabbat, Sat Shabbat–10pm (Yoel Salomon branch open till midnight). Kosher. Cheap.

Restaurants

Restaurants in **East Jerusalem** and the Old City are almost invariably Middle Eastern, starting you off with a selection of *mezze* (salads and dips) before progressing on to a main course of lamb or chicken, or possibly fish such as Denis (bream) or St Peter's (tilapia), washed down with Turkish coffee and a sweet such as *baklawa*. In **West Jerusalem**, there's a much wider choice of international cuisine, sometimes limited by the strictures of *kashrut* (see p.179), but generally more akin to the sort of restaurants you'd find at home. Prices are also rather higher in West Jerusalem than on the east side of town, but wages are low and staff depend on **tips**, which are usually in the twelve to fifteen percent range.

Some West Jerusalem restaurants offer a **lunchtime business menu**, usually available from noon to 4pm. This allows you to choose from a selection of dishes for a set rate, generally quite a bit cheaper than you'd get paying à la carte. At one time, business menus used to be quite ubiquitous, and a huge bargain; that's no longer the case, but they're still worth looking out for.

In many places in the Muslim Quarter and East Jerusalem, you won't be able to drink **alcohol** with your meal. Restaurants serving alcohol in the listings that follow are described as "licensed" unless they serve only beer, in which case that is noted. Restaurants in West Jerusalem, especially more upmarket places, serve wine, which may be Israeli or imported, and will be priced roughly on a par with the wine in equivalent restaurants in Western countries. For more on Israeli and Palestinian wines, see p.195.

Old City

Al-A'elat (Families Restaurant) 77 Souq Khan al-Zeit (see map, p.73). A large, cool and rather cavernous restaurant specializing in shashlik, shish kebab, lamb chops and chicken, all served with chips, salad and bread. Also on offer are various kinds of salad and *mezze* including *labaneh* (sour cream cheese balls in olive oil). Daily 9am–9pm in summer, 6pm in winter, later on special occasions. Cheap.

After-hours eating

Once upon a time, the only place you could get anything to eat after midnight was the *Green Door* bakery on Aqabat al-Sheikh Rihan, off Al-Wad Road in the Muslim Quarter (see map, p.73). You can still get pizzas of a sort made up there at any time of the day or night (with your own ingredients if you like), but standards of hygiene are not all they should be, and most people prefer to patronize the 24-hour bakeries on HaNeviim, outside the Damascus Gate (*Mussarah* at no.10 and *Al-Amien* at no.14) which, as well as assorted breads, stock soft drinks and other foodstuffs (*Al-Amien* is more or less a supermarket nowadays). *Al-Ayed*, almost on the corner of HaNeviim with Sultan Suleiman (see opposite), is also open 24/7. A number of places stay open round the clock in central West Jerusalem too, though some of them close Friday sunset to Saturday nightfall to stay kosher. Among the latter is a bakery at 28 Jaffa Rd (next to Hen; see map, p.127) which sells *burekas* and filled bagels. Places open twenty-four seven rather than twenty-four six include *Zuni* (see p.192), *Aroma* (see p.183) and *Bohlinat* (see p.183).

Al-Tawfiq 21 Al-Wad, Muslim Quarter (see map, p.73). Kebabs, shashlik, grilled chicken and the usual range of salads and dips served up in a tunnel-like space amid jarring bright blue and white decor with mirrors that make it rather like eating in a fairground house of fun. Daily 8am–6pm. Cheap.

Armenian Tavern 79 Armenian Patriarchate Rd, Armenian Quarter ☎02/627 3854 (see map, p.48). A basement restaurant in a former Crusader church, beautifully decorated with Armenian tiles. The menu features delicious Armenian dishes such as *khaghoghi derev* (stuffed vine leaves), *soujuk* (spicy sausages) and *lahmajun* (Armenian "pizza"), and there's a special menu on Friday nights (reservations particularly recommended then and on Saturday). The background music is Armenian folk. Mon–Sat non–10pm. Licensed. Moderate.

Amigo Emil Aqabat al-Khanqah, Christian Quarter (see map, p.56). Top marks to this excellent little restaurant, in a trio of stone arches near the Eighth Station of the Cross. The ambience is classic Old City, decorated with old photos from Elia (see p.227), and the food is fresh and well prepared, whether kebabs, chicken or fish. You can start with a plate of mixed *mezze*, and for mains try a *sayadiyeh* (fish fillet in spicy coriander sauce with rice) or a fish fillet in honey and mustard sauce with mash. Daily 11am–9.30pm. Licensed. Moderate.

Four Brothers Latin Patriarchate Rd off Omar Ibn al-Khattab Square, Christian Quarter (see map, p.56). Great turkey shawarma, good hummus and, in the morning, falafel, by, as its name suggests, four brothers. Daily 9am–10pm, or until the shawarma runs out. Cheap

Nafoura 18 Latin Patriarchate Rd, Christian Quarter (see map, p.56). Good-sized portions of Middle Eastern food, including *mezze* or a falafel platter, served in a small but pleasant garden with a fountain. Some dishes are available in small or large sizes, and the 75NIS set menu will fill you right up. Daily noon–10pm. Licensed. Moderate.

Papa Andrea's 64 Souk Aftimos, in the Muristan (see map, p.56). Rooftop or indoor eating, the latter offering views over the Old City, especially the neighbouring Church of the Holy Sepulchre. The food is Middle Eastern, with *mezze*, grills, shashlik and steak on the menu. The house speciality is *musakhan*, served with a glass of

araq (local spirit). There's also a diner downstairs for shawarma and snacks. Mon–Sat 9am–11pm, Sun noon–5pm. Licensed. Moderate.

Pizzaria Basti 70 Al-Wad, opposite the Third Station of the Cross (see map, p.73). A 90-year-old family-run business offering reasonable pizzas (it claims to have been the first restaurant in Palestine to serve pizza) as well as kebabs, hamburgers and schnitzel, all with chips and salad. They also do a good-value breakfast. Daily: summer 7am–11pm (depending on custom), winter 8am–6pm. Cheap.

Rossini's 32 Latin Patriarchate Rd, Christian Quarter ☎02/628 2964 (see map, p.56). Upmarket French-Italian restaurant, though the ambience is a little bit bar-like. There's nothing pubby about the food however, with smoked breast of goose among the starters, and main courses such as pork cutlets in calvados sauce, or roast duckling breast in orange sauce (or a vegetarian casserole if you don't eat meat). Licensed. Expensive.

East Jerusalem

All of these are shown on the map on p.109.
Al-Ayed 6 HaNeviim. Just outside the Damascus Gate, and very convenient if you're taking a bus or service taxi from there, serving shawarmas and other Palestinian grills. The interior gets a bit grubby during the day, but you can sit outdoors and eat it in the little square in front, though that is right in the middle of the bustle surrounding the neighbouring service taxi station. 24/7. Cheap.

Al-Mehbash 21 Nablus Rd. A very laid-back lounge-style restaurant in a lovely old building with a scenic roof terrace (where you can also eat), serving Palestinian dishes (the house speciality is *maqluba*), with *mezze* for starters and home-made sweets for dessert. On Saturday nights they have dance parties with a local DJ, and on Friday nights an *oudh* (Arabic lute) player to soothe you with Arabic classical music. Daily noon–10pm. Licensed. Moderate.

Al-Shuleh Grill 16 Salah al-Din, opposite Capitol Hotel. An unpretentious diner, popular among East Jerusalemites for its traditional snacks (hummus, falafel and salads) and roast meats (shawarma, kebabs, liver and chicken). Sat–Thurs 9am–8pm. Cheap.

Ramadan

During the holy month of **Ramadan** (see p.211), observant Muslims do not eat between sunrise and sunset. As a result, many restaurants in East Jerusalem and the Old City (especially the Muslim Quarter) will alter their schedules. Some will actually close up for the whole month (and even in the run-up), but most will simply remain closed until just before sunset, and may stay open late. Also during Ramadan, you will find that stalls selling falafel and other snacks spring up on the streets of East Jerusalem and the Muslim Quarter shortly before sunset, selling all sorts of delicious goodies to break the fast. Establishments run by Christians or Jews are unlikely to be affected, while those catering mainly for tourists may open up regardless. Given that many local people are committed to fasting during Ramadan, you may feel it is considerate not to eat or smoke in the street during the day in this period.

Arabesque American Colony Hotel, Nablus Rd ☎02/627 9777. The most upmarket restaurant in East Jerusalem, serving French and other European haute cuisine. The Saturday all-you-can-eat buffet lunch (noon–3pm; US$50) is ever-popular, and the hotel also has a less expensive brasserie (daily 6pm–midnight), serving English-style cream teas from 3pm, plus a jasmine-scented garden restaurant for snacks and coffees. Daily 6.30am–10pm (meals served noon–3pm & 7–10pm). Licensed. Expensive.

Askadinya 11 Shimon HaTzadik, Sheikh Jarrah ☎02/532 4590. Excellent French- and Italian-style food, at this classy establishment, popular with the *American Colony* crowd. There's a good choice of soups and salads, and steak with a variety of sauces, or fish, veal, lamb or pork, as well as pasta and pizza. Background music is classical, with a live *oudh* (Arabic lute) player on Thursday and Saturday evenings. Daily noon–midnight. Licensed. Expensive.

Azzahra 13 Al-Zahra ⊛ www.azzahrahotel.com. Belonging to the hotel of the same name, this restaurant features a classy indoor section and a delightful garden. It serves charcoal-grilled meats and kebabs and good pizzas, as well as special dishes like *mansaf* and *mousakhan*, with hot and cold appetizers to start and Arabic sweets to finish. Daily except Wed, noon–11pm. Licensed. Moderate.

Café Europe 11 Al-Zahra. Rather an odd kind of place: a café-restaurant done out with girly pink ribbons and drapes, and serving such unlikely dishes as ham and eggs, fish and chips, pepper steak or pork chops. It isn't East Jerusalem's most renowned eatery, but it makes a change from the usual fare. Mon–Sat 10.30am–8pm. Licensed. Cheap to moderate.

Kan Zaman Jerusalem Hotel, off Nablus Rd beside the bus station. In the open air, under a grapevine pergola, with occasional live music, you can sample good, homely Palestinian grub such as *musakhan*, or less traditional dishes such as "chicken yalla yalla" (stuffed with mushrooms and other vegetables), or "bee sting" (a honey and caramel dessert). Daily noon–10pm. Licensed. Moderate.

Lotus and Olive Garden Abu Taleb St ☎02/628 5212. The restaurant of the *Meridian Hotel*, though not inside the hotel itself, it's actually quite a sophisticated bar-restaurant in a former private residence dating from 1905. As well as the usual grills and fish dishes, it has quite a few good vegetarian selections, but it's the starters that most impress, with the likes of honey and mustard chicken tenders, or four-cheese stuffed mushrooms to get you salivating. Sun–Wed 4pm–midnight, Thurs–Sat 4pm–12.30am. Licensed. Moderate to expensive.

Pasha's 13 Shimon HaTzadik, Sheikh Jarrah ☎02/582 5162, ⊛ www.borderlinerestaurant .com. A restaurant in an early twentieth-century villa, specializing in barbecued meats and Lebanese-style cooking. Lebanese dishes are basically the same as Palestinian ones, but they're more delicately spiced and cooked with a finesse that reflects the French influence on Lebanese cuisine – widely recognized as the finest in the Middle East. There's also terrace eating, and you can even order an *argila* (hookah pipe) after your meal. Daily noon–10pm. Licensed. Moderate.

Philadelphia 9 Al-Zahra ☎02/628 9770. This long-established place, which claims to be "the most popular restaurant in Palestine", has fed movie stars, and

US President Jimmy Carter, among other VIPs, but prices are well within reach of the hoi polloi too. A lengthy menu includes red mullet, stuffed pigeon, meat with *tehina*, plus a fifteen-plate *mezze* and six kinds of stuffed vegetables to start. The *musakhan* is particularly good, and for afters there's an assortment of *baklawa*. It isn't named after Pennsylvania's City of Brotherly Love, by the way: Philadelphia was the Roman name for Jordan's capital, Amman. Daily 11am–midnight. Licensed. Moderate.

West Jerusalem

All of these are shown on the map on pp.126–127.

Ashkenazi Jewish

Deutsch 32 Mea Shearim. Comfort food for *Haredim*, wonderful *cholent* (the traditional slow-cooked Shabbat stew, pukka *kneidel* soup (chicken soup with dumplings), the menu's in Yiddish only, but they'll tell you what they've got. Sun–Thurs noon–9pm, Fri noon–3pm. Serves beer. Kosher. Cheap to moderate.

Heimishe Essen 19 Keren Kayemet, Rehavia ☎02/563 9845. It's a far cry from the hole-in-the-wall Yiddische eateries of Tel Aviv, but this is the best restaurant in Jerusalem for the likes of chopped liver, gefilte fish, *cholent*, *tzimmes* (sweet carrot stew), kugel (savoury potato pudding) and other traditional Ashkenazi Jewish cuisine. Sun–Wed 9am–10pm, Thurs 9am–2am, Fri 9am–2pm. Licensed. Kosher. Moderate.

Hen 30 Jaffa Rd (sign in Hebrew only). Jewish and Middle Eastern specialities such as Yiddische chicken soup, chopped liver,

stuffed vegetables or goulash combine to make this little place really rather wonderful in its own unassuming little way. The food is good but service can be a bit slapdash. There's also a bakery next door for *burekas*, cakes and juices. Sun–Thurs 10am–5pm, Fri 10am–3pm. Kosher. Cheap.

East Asian

Mandarin 2 Shlomzion HaMalka, 1st floor ☎02/625 2890. The first Chinese restaurant in Israel, in operation since 1956, serving Cantonese and Szechuan cuisine. Beef, chicken and duck dishes cost substantially less than those rare non-kosher delicacies, pork, prawns and squid, and there are also dim sums, and reasonably priced set meals for two or three people. Daily noon–3.30pm & 6.30pm–midnight. Licensed. Moderate.

Sakura Feingold Court, between 31 Jaffa Rd and 22 Rivlin. Jerusalem's first and best sushi restaurant, offering not a huge variety of sushi, but good quality, and supplemented by sashimi, tempura and noodle soup, plus choya, sake and Japanese beer. Business lunches are also available. Daily noon–midnight. Licensed. Moderate.

Thai Sandwich Bar 25 Jaffa Rd (sign in Hebrew, with "Thai Food" in English). Classic Thai cuisine it certainly isn't (do they put their stir-fry into a baguette in Bangkok?), but it does have wokfuls of filling fast food at low prices to eat in or take out. Sun–Thurs 11am–midnight, Sat Shabbat–midnight. Kosher. Cheap.

Ethiopian

Megenanya 17 Jaffa Rd. A small but cosy Ethiopian restaurant offering a choice of

Shabbat eating in West Jerusalem

To maintain their kosher status, most places in West Jerusalem close on Shabbat (sunset on Friday till nightfall on Saturday). The following restaurants, and bars or cafés serving food, are exceptions.

Aroma (see p.183)
Barood (see p.196)
Bohlinat (see p.183)
Cielo (see p.190 – not Friday night)
Focaccia (see p.190)
Jan's (see p.191 – evening only)
Mandarin (see above)
Mike's Place (see p.196)
Notre Dame Coffee House (see p.183)

Riff-Raff (see p.192)
La Rotisserie (see p.190 – evening only)
Sakura (see above)
Sea Dolphin (see p.190)
Shanty (see p.196 – evening only)
Shegar (see p.190)
Sol (see p.197 – evening only)
Spaghettim (see p.190)

mainly beef dishes such as *tibs* (spicy beef stew) served with *injera* (a kind of sourdough flatbread). It's interesting, too, to see dreadlocked or *kippa*-topped Ethiopian-Israeli customers exchange greetings with Ethiopian Christian clergy from the Old City as they pass by. Sun–Thurs 10am–midnight, Fri 10am–Shabbat, Sat Shabbat–midnight. Serves beer. Kosher. Moderate.

Shegar In the alley between 65 Jaffa Rd and 10 Agripas. A little bit of Africa in Jerusalem, and a favourite meeting place for members of the city's Ethiopian-Israeli community, this small diner is as much a bar as a restaurant (they sometimes have Ethiopian beer), where you can mop up staple Ethiopian dishes such as *tibs*, *doro wat* (chicken stew) or *kay wat* (lamb stew) with your *injera* (there's no cutlery) while checking out the latest Ethiopian news in Amharic on the telly. Serves beer. Daily noon–midnight. Serves beer. Cheap to moderate.

Fish

Sea Dolphin (Dolfin-Yam) 9 Ben Shetakh ☎02/623 2272. Very fine fish and seafood restaurant in a beautiful old house in Nahalat Shiv'a. Start with the likes of grouper carpaccio before launching into a main course of scallops in creamy crab sauce, tuna steak in spicy tomato, or simply your choice of fish in your choice of sauce. It's especially advisable to book ahead on Fridays and Saturdays. Daily noon–11pm. Licensed. Expensive.

Ticho House 7 HaRav Kook ☎02/624 4186. Very pleasant indoor and outdoor dining in a fish and dairy restaurant attached to the museum (see p.128), and an excellent place for a light lunch. As well as fish, there's pasta, soup and salad, set breakfasts (10am–noon only) and special menus for junior and senior citizens, plus live jazz on Tuesdays, folk on Thursdays (reservations required for both). Sun–Thurs 10am–11.45pm. Fri 10am–2pm, Sat Shabbat–11.45pm. Licensed. Kosher. Moderate.

French

La Guta 18 Rivlin ☎02/623 2322, ⊛www.rol .co.il/sites/la-guta. Small, upmarket French restaurant serving steak, beef, duck, goose, and plenty of *foie gras*. There's an excellent wine list too, *naturellement*. Sun–Thurs noon–4.30pm & 6.30–11.30pm, Fri noon–3pm, Sat Shabbat–11.30pm. Kosher. Expensive.

La Rôtisserie Notre Dame, Paratroopers Rd ☎02/627 9111. The best and poshest French restaurant in town, specializing in carved meats and steaks. Beef, veal, lamb, pork, duck and fish are all on the menu, along with steaks of all varieties and a selection of fine wines. Daily 7–10pm. Licensed. Expensive.

Rivlin 7 Rivlin. Bistro-style restaurant serving European cuisine in pleasant surrounds with starched white tablecloths. The best deal here is the lunchtime business menu, which is extremely reasonable at 65NIS. Sun–Thurs noon–11pm, Fri noon–2.30pm, Sat Shabbat–11pm. Licensed. Kosher. Moderate to expensive.

Italian

Angelo's 9 Horkenos ☎02/623 6095. Great home-made pasta, Roman Jewish specialities, including ravioli stuffed with salmon, or with mushrooms, and penne in vodka sauce. There's also a soup freshly made daily. Desserts include tiramisú. Fish and dairy products are served, but no meat. Sun–Thurs noon–11pm, Sat Shabbat–11pm. Licensed. Kosher. Moderate.

Cielo 18 Ben Sira ☎02/625 1132. Authentic Italian food, and a menu that doesn't overreach itself. Starters include *calamari alla siciliana* or palm hearts in cream sauce, followed by tournedos in marsala and cognac, chicken breast in lemon and tarragon, or trout with lemon and capers, with rich chocolate mousse for afters. Sat–Thurs noon–11pm, Fri noon–2.30pm. Licensed. Moderate to expensive.

Focaccia 8 Rabbi Akiva. Italian food in a lovely old building with an outside terrace. There's pizza and pasta, and of course, the house speciality, focaccia (Italian flatbread with toppings), baked in the restaurant's own *taboon* (Middle Eastern bread oven – they also bake their own pittas in it). The building's a fine old stone house with a terrace out front for *al fresco* dining. Daily 1pm–midnight or later. Licensed. Moderate.

Spaghettim 35 Hillel. Spaghetti with a choice of more than forty different sauces including old favourites such as napolitana, bolognese, carbonara or pesto, along with new-fangled (and not very Italian) sauces such as salmon and walnut, or gorgonzola with spinach. Daily noon–midnight. Licensed. Moderate.

Meat

In addition to these, another restaurant specializing specifically in meat dishes is *La Rôtisserie* (see opposite).

El Gaucho 22 Rivlin. Part of an Israeli chain of Argentinian-style steak restaurants, it does serve things other than steak (kosher chorizo, for example, made from beef), but it's the chargrilled doorsteps of sliced steer you come here for. They come thick and juicy in sizes to match any stomach, done to whatever turn you choose, from show-it-the-pan rare to tourist-on-the-beach well done. Sun–Thurs noon–11.30pm, Sat Shabbat–11.30pm. Licensed. Kosher. Moderate to expensive.

Hess 9 Heleni HaMalka ☎02/625 5515, ⓦwww .hess-restaurants.com. Glatt kosher Swiss meat restaurant, serving up large hunks of veal, beef and *wurst* in various permutations, plus a veritable cornucopia of pork-free cold cuts. For 130NIS, you can get a "King's gourmet platter" featuring a huge range of meats, and if that isn't enough, you can add 90NIS on top for an extra assortment of pâtés and meat parfaits. There's also a business lunch or supper menu deal available. Mon–Thurs 11am–11pm, Sun 4pm–11pm. Licensed. Kosher. Expensive.

Sima 82 Agripas, Mahane Yehuda. Small diner and takeaway selling kebabs, chops and steaks. It's particularly renowned for its *meorav yerushalmi*, which connoisseurs consider the best in town, served in a pitta, or on a plate with salad and chips. There isn't much seating space so you may have to settle for a takeaway at busy times. Sun–Thurs 9am–11pm, Fri 9am–1pm, Sat Shabbat–11pm. Kosher. Cheap.

Middle Eastern and North African

Darna 3 Horkanos ☎02/524 5406, ⓦwww .darna.co.il. Succulent lamb or chicken tajines, excellent couscous, and glorious Fez-style *pastilla* (sweet poultry pie with cinnamon) are among the treats on offer at this top-notch Moroccan restaurant done out in fine North African style. Sun–Thurs

noon–3pm & 6pm–midnight, Sat Shabbat–midnight. Licensed. Kosher. Expensive.

Okhlim BaShuk 8 HaTapuah, Mahane Yehuda. Solid Persian and Sephardi Jewish cooking at this small restaurant in the middle of Mahane Yehuda market, with the sign and menu in Hebrew only. Dishes on offer include couscous, *meorav yerushalmi* (Jerusalem-style mixed meats), stuffed vegetables and a turmeric-flavoured chicken soup that's quite unlike its Ashkenazi equivalent. Sun–Thurs 10am–8pm, Fri 10am–3pm. Kosher. Moderate.

Vegetarian

As well as hummus and falafel joints (see p.184), and the three vegetarian restaurants listed in this section, dairy kosher restaurants cannot also serve meat (though they may serve fish). Among restaurants that are not specifically veg, *Angelo's* (see p.190), *Rimon* (see p.183), *Spaghettim* (see opposite), *Ticho House* (see opposite) and *Tmol Shilshom* (see p.184) all cater well for herbivores.

HaMarakiya 4 Koresh. A soup bar, serving hearty veg soups, *shakshuka* and alcoholic beverages, sometimes with live acoustic music. It's all very homely, with a friendly and easy-going vibe, and it attracts a young, informal crowd, but it's small and can get quite crowded (come early to avoid the rush). Sun–Thurs 7pm–late, Sat Shabbat–late. Licensed. Kosher (but not certified). Cheap.

Jan's 5 Chopin (by Jerusalem Theatre). Candlelight, low tables and cushions, old European paintings and classical music give this romantic hideaway the feel of an Ottoman salon in an orientalist fantasy, and the food is as decadent as veggie food can be, with a big choice of pies or stuffed vegetables among the offerings, and banana pancakes with *dolce de leche* for dessert. Sat–Thurs 5pm–2am, Fri 7pm–3am. Licensed. Moderate.

Te'enim 12 Emile Botta ☎02/625 1967, ⓦwww.rest.co.il/teenim. Not easy to find, tucked away off the road behind the *King*

The vegetable known as a **Jerusalem artichoke** is not an artichoke and has nothing to do with Jerusalem. The rootstock of a variety of sunflower, thought by some to taste like an artichoke, it gets the Jerusalem part of its name from a corruption of the Italian for sunflower, *girasole*.

▲ Clay pot dish at the Little Eucalyptus

David Hotel in a Centre for Holocaust Studies, but worth seeking out for wholesome veg bakes, tofu and mushroom dishes, salads and soups. Sun–Thurs 10am–11pm. Fri 9am–2pm. Kosher. Moderate to expensive.

Village Green 33 Jaffa Rd ⓦ www.village-green .co.il. Vegetarian self-service with cockle-warming soups, generous vegetable pies, baked potatoes, vegan stuffed veg, tofu bakes and a salad bar. Sun–Thurs 9am–10pm. Fri 9am–3pm. Kosher. Cheap to moderate.

Miscellaneous

Little Eucalyptus 7 Horkenos ☏ 02/623 2864. One of Jerusalem's more interesting restaurants, trying to create a modern Israeli cuisine, and also to recreate some biblical dishes. Specialities include Jerusalem artichoke soup, *za'atar* salad, figs stuffed with chicken breast in tamarind sauce, an assortment of stuffed leaves, including mallow, which, as an edible wild plant, was an important food source

during the 1948 Arab blockade of West Jerusalem. Desserts include tahini with *silan* (date syrup). Sun–Thurs noon–3pm & 6–10pm, Fri noon–3pm, Sat nightfall–10pm. Licensed. Kosher. Expensive.

Riff-Raff 16 Yoel Salomon. Big sandwiches, salads, omelettes, pizzas, pasta and – unusually for Jerusalem – bacon and egg breakfasts make this defiantly non-kosher restaurant a favourite with travellers and Jerusalemites alike. Sun–Thurs 9am–midnight, Fri & Sat 9am–1am. Moderate.

Zuni in the alley by 15 Yoel Salomon. It's not entirely clear whether this cool, modern locale is a restaurant, a bistro, a brasserie or a bar, but the important thing is, you can eat and drink here, and it's open round the clock. Starters include carpaccio, or squid with ginger and lemon, followed by sea bass with fennel comfit, or a fine risotto. They also do good breakfasts till noon. Daily 24hr. Licensed. Moderate to expensive.

Sweets, waffles and ice cream

In East Jerusalem and the Old City, shops selling sweets usually have tables where you can sit down with the sticky confection of your choice. Among specialities worth trying at Palestinian sweet shops are **kanafe** (white cheese topped with crunchy orange sweet pastry), **baklawa** (layers of filo pastry stuffed with chopped nuts and drenched in syrup), and **burma** (sweet shredded wheat stuffed with pistachios or other nuts). The other local sweet specialities are halva and sheets of tangy dried apricot paste, for more on which see p.223.

For more Western-style sweet treats, such as ice cream or waffles, West Jerusalem is the place to go, and you'll certainly find plenty of choice. Most of the cafés listed on pp.182–184 serve their own pastries, often very good indeed, but one or two eateries also specialize in fine chocolate, waffles or ice cream.

Aldo 40 Jaffa Rd, West Jerusalem; 21 Ben Yehuda, in the midrahov; 46 Emek Refaim, German Colony (all on the map on p.127). The best ice cream in town. Flavours incude Twix, Snickers or Ferrero Rocher on the one hand, or blueberry, passion fruit, or lemon and mint on the other. They also stock high-class confections by Israeli chocolatier Max Brenner. Kosher. Sun–Thurs 9am–midnight, Fri 9am–Shabbat, Sat Shabbat–midnight.

Babette 16 Shamai, West Jerusalem (see map, p.127). A tiny hole-in-the-wall serving sinfully delicious Belgian-style waffles, with a range of toppings from chocolate to chestnut cream, and you can sit in with a coffee or hot chocolate drink to accompany your waffle. Kosher. Sun–Thurs noon–midnight, Fri noon–Shabbat, Sat Shabbat–midnight.

Eiffel Sweets Sultan Suleiman St, East Jerusalem (see map, p.109). A good place to buy burma and baklawa by weight, and they also have kanafe (but check the price before you order it) and various cream desserts including eclairs. Daily 8.30am–9pm.

Ja'far Sweets 42 Souq Khan al-Zeit, Old City (see map, p.56). The best place in town to buy kanafe, which you can eat in or take out. It's always freshly made, warm and delicious – just sweet enough, and never sickly. There's also excellent burma and baklawa, wrapped up to go. Daily 9am–6pm.

Sweets, waffles and ice cream

Drinking and nightlife

Jerusalem is not really the place for exciting **nightlife**. If it's pubs, clubs or discos you want, then Tel Aviv is the place to be and many will take a *sherut* or drive to the coast for a night out.

Drinking cultures are vastly different on the two sides of Jerusalem, though neither Israelis nor Palestinians tend to be big drinkers. **West Jerusalem** has a large number of bars, mainly frequented by hip young Israelis, which get going late and keep on until the early hours, and a number of nightclubs down in the suburb of Talpiot. In Arab **East Jerusalem** and the Old City, it's mainly the Christian minority who drink, plus non-religious Muslims of course, but it's much more discreet and there aren't really many bars.

Bars

Bars in West Jerusalem are concentrated around Yoel Saloman, Rivlin and Ben Sira streets – **Rivlin** in particular gets very lively of an evening – and many stay open until the last person leaves, which may be 2am or so midweek in winter, and around 5 or 6am on Friday nights/Saturday mornings in summer. Bars which close when the last person leaves are listed here as closing "late". Many West Jerusalem bars have a **happy hour**, which varies from bar to bar, both in what time it starts and finishes, and what's on offer; the usual deal is two beers for the price of one, and this may extend to other drinks, but usually only Israeli rather than imported spirits.

If you'd rather go drinking with a group, Sandemans New Europe Tours (Ⓦ www.newjerusalemtours.com) run a nightly **pub crawl**, starting 8pm outside Poalim Bank on Kikar Zion in West Jerusalem, costing 40NIS plus drinks (the price covers entry into some clubs, and also gets you some drink discounts).

Old City

Bulghourji 6 Armenian Patiartchate Rd, Armenian Quarter (see map, p.48). A sophisticated bar in a lovely old stone building with a pleasant beer garden and lots of lounging space, serving draught Taybeh and other beers, wines, spirits, soft drinks and coffee, plus snacks such as *soujuk* (Armenian sausage)

and *lahmajun* (Armenian "pizza"). Daily noon–10pm.

Varsavee in the arcade beneath the New Imperial Hotel, off Omar Ibn al-Khattab Square and Greek Orthodox Patriarchate Rd, Christian Quarter (see map, p.56). A small bar with a discreet, relaxed atmosphere, serving drinks, hookahs, and food (the food section is open from 8am for a good-value 25–35NIS breakfast). Daily 3pm–midnight.

Alcoholic drinks

Beer

The two main brands of Israeli **beer** are Maccabee, a decent but bland light lager, and Goldstar, which is darker and more flavoursome. The cheapest beer, Nesher, is tasteless and insipid. Microbreweries such as Dancing Camel (Ⓦwww.dancingcamel .com) surface now and again, but their beers tend to be on the sweet side. Taybeh (Ⓦwww.taybehbeer.com), from Ramallah on the West Bank, is an excellent German-style lager made according to the German beer law, with only four ingredients (barley, hops, yeast and water), which quite correctly claims to be the finest beer in the Middle East. Unfortunately, Taybeh is hard to come by in West Jerusalem, and Israeli microbrewery beers take some tracking down too, but imported beers such as Heiniken, Baltika, and even Newcastle Brown, are readily available.

Wine

Among **local wines** worth checking out are the Latrun monastery's Cabernet Sauvignon, and Cremisan monastery's (Ⓦwww.cremisan.org) Merlot, Cabernet Sauvignon and David's Tower, the last of which is made from a local variety of grape grown around Bethlehem. Domaine du Castel's (Ⓦwww.castel.co.il) Castel Grand Vin, Blanc du Castel and Petit Castel are tasty wines made from grapes grown in the Jerusalem region, and in the same area, west of Jerusalem, Tzora Vineyards (Ⓦwww.tzorawines.com) produce much-acclaimed Judean Hills and Neve Ilan reds, and Shoresh Blanc white. Many of **Israel's best wines** in fact come from the Golan Heights (Israeli-occupied Syria), most notably the Yarden range (Ⓦwww .golanwines.co.il). Other major Israeli wine labels include Barkan (Ⓦwww .barkan-winery.com), Carmel (Ⓦwww.carmelwines.co.il) and Tishbi (Ⓦwww.tishbi .com), of which the last is generally better value for cheap and mid-range wines than the other two. If you're serious about your wine, you might want to check Daniel Rogov's annual *Guide to Israeli Wines*, which is available at Steimatsky (see p.218) and other bookshops.

Spirits

The one local firewater to try is *araq*, an aniseed drink similar to Turkish *raki* or Greek *ouzo*; Ramallah-produced Arak Extra Fine, with a green and gold label, is by far the best brand.

East Jerusalem

In addition to the bars listed here (shown on the map on p.109), one or two restaurants also double as bars, notably the *Lotus and Olive Garden* (see p.188).

Borderline 13 Shimon HaTzadik, Sheikh Jarrah ☏02/532 8342, Ⓦwww.shahwan.org. Beer (Taybeh, Guinness and Heineken, all on tap) plus coffee, water-pipes and good food at this classy bar-restaurant attached to *Pasha's* (see p.188), which often hosts live bands (call for details). It's a popular haunt for liberal East and West Jerusalemites as well as foreign NGO workers. The name derives from its proximity to the Green Line, just 100m up the street. Daily 5pm–2am or later.

The Cellar Bar American Colony Hotel, Nablus Rd. East Jerusalem's most serious drinking venue, a dark, low-ceilinged and conspiratorial cavern, popular with expats, diplomats and journalists. The atmosphere is intimate and sophisticated with the feel of a real drinking den. There's also a summer bar in the Palm House Garden for those who prefer the open air during the balmier months. Daily 6pm–3.30am.

West Jerusalem

Because many West Jerusalem cafés serve alcohol, and bars often serve coffee, the distinction between a café and a bar can often get blurred, and some cafés double up as bars. Of the cafés listed in this book, this particularly applies to *Bohlinat* (see p.183) and *Rehavia* (see p.184).

All these bars are shown on the map on p.127.

Barood Feingold Court (between 31 Jaffa Rd and 22 Rivlin) ☎02/625 9081. A wine bar that's as much a restaurant as a bar, warm and inviting, its walls well cluttered with pictures, serving Balkan and Sephardi Jewish cuisine, with starters such as *pastel-ikos* (bread stuffed with meat and pine nuts), and main courses such as beef and leek stew with plums. As a result, a lot of people come here for dinner, and you may need to reserve a table, especially on a Friday or Saturday night. Mon–Sat noon–3am.

Besht Pundak 12 Yoel Salomon (in the alley). Coffee, pie and live blues (as opposed to beer, pretzels and pop music) are the theme at this small, dark underground cellar bar, all rather restrained and serious in the heart of Jerusalem's party zone, and featuring live performances of not only blues but also bluegrass, country and jazz. Sun–Thurs 6pm–3am.

Birman 8 Dorot Rishonim (in the Ben Yehuda St midrahov). Next-door to *Bohlinat* (see p.183), and bigger than it looks from the outside, this "music bistro bar" serves food and drink, and has live music from 8pm, generally involving its house pianist accompanying various styles of soft music, mainly at the jazz end of the spectrum, to a sophisticated clientele. Kosher (but not certified). Sun–Thurs 5pm–late, Sat Shabbat–late.

Blue Hole 12 Yoel Salomon (round the back). Low-ceilinged cellar bar with an intimate subterranean atmosphere and continual free refills of olives or pretzels to eat with your beer. The crowd is very mixed – one table could be discussing the football match they're watching on TV, while the next analyse the Talmudic text they have open in front of them – but the atmosphere is always very relaxed and congenial. Sat–Thurs 6pm–3am, Fri noon–3am (happy hour till 9.30pm).

Capricorn 18 Shlomo HaMelekh. Once upon a time this place was almost New Age (they used to give out cards with readings for your star sign). They keep it dark and, like so many Jerusalem bars, it's quite small, which makes it pretty cosy in its own quiet way, until about midnight, when it becomes a karaoke bar, and a decidedly tacky one at that – lovers of Japanese karaoke establishments, for example, will not be impressed – but it can be a laugh if you aren't fussy about these things. Daily 8.30pm–late.

Colony Bar 7 Bethlehem Rd, Old Station Compound. One of the more upmarket locales around the old train station, attracting politicians, diplomats and other people you might prefer not to mix with, but very comfortable, with a lounge bar and discreet dining area. Sun–Thurs 6pm–late, Fri & Sat (well, strictly speaking, Sat & Sun mornings) 12.30am–late.

Gotham Feingold Court (between 31 Jaffa Rd and 22 Rivlin). Not as gothy as you'd expect from the name, but this dance-bar is darkly done out and prefers dark musical sounds. There are live bands here on Tuesday nights (indie rock), and other times the music is electronic, drum 'n' bass, or anything bassy. There's usually a 20–40NIS entry charge and it doesn't get going until well after midnight. Mon, Tues, Thurs, Fri & Sat 11.30pm–late.

Mia 18 Hillel ⓦ www.mia-bar.co.il. A classy cocktail bar done out in classic American style, with a rare stock of high-quality liquors (even – for those who drink such things – raspberry-flavoured Belgian beer) and bartenders who know how to make a cocktail. Daily 7pm–late.

Mike's Place 37 Jaffa Rd (entrance round the back in an alley off Yoel Saloman) ⓦ www .mikesplacebars.com. A long-standing Jerusalem institution, formerly a poky cellar bar, that's been reborn in a new location as something like an American college student bar, attracting a crowd to match. There's food (burritos, burgers, and other American and Tex-Mex fast food staples), assorted international beers on tap, an easy-going atmosphere, a pool table, and more English spoken than Hebrew or Arabic, happy hour daily 4.30–9.30pm, and live music nightly at 11pm. There's also a branch in Tel Aviv (see p.264). Daily 11am–4am.

Nadin 5 Rivlin. Very popular with young, *kippa*-clad Jerusalemites, out for a drink but somewhere respectable. Beer, hookah pipes, sandwiches and salads, seats in the street and music, but nothing your mum wouldn't want you to listen to. Daily 4.30am–3am (happy hour till 9.30pm).

Shanty 4 Ma'alot Nahalat Shiv'a (between Rivlin and Yoel Salomon, next to Mike's Place). A restaurant-bar that's on the small side and gets quite packed, but it all adds to the atmosphere. There's a wide range of wines, spirits and cocktails (a whole menu of the latter), and the good food includes blintzes, pizzas, toasties and salads. Daily 7pm–3am.

Sira 4 Ben Sira (between Shlomzion HaMalaka and Hillel). Laid-back bar with a punky feel and a ravey crowd, seats spreading out into the entrance and the street in front, good electronic music or indie bands, a small dancefloor, great atmosphere and no airs or graces. Daily 7pm–3am.

Sol 15 Shlomzion HaMalaka. A tapas bar, but rather more chic than most you'd find in Spain, and rather more expensive too. There are over seventy tapas to choose from, some Iberian (such as mushroom *empanadas*), some more Middle Eastern (eggplant with tehina and pomegranate sauce), others hybrid (squid with feta cheese), and others neither (smoked duck breast with Dijon mustard). People come here to eat rather than drink, but obviously you don't eat a tapa without a beer, though you can be posh and drink Spanish or local wine instead. Daily 7pm–late.

Stardust 6 Rivlin, ⊛www.pubstardust.com. A poky little bar that's like a regulars' local (HaPoel Jerusalem FC supporters in particular favour it), and refreshingly unpretentious on a street full of trendy nightspots. The venue has hosted a succession of legendary Jerusalem bars since the 1970s, and past customers at this one include Johnny Greenwood (of Radiohead), John Cale (of the Velvet Underground), Nick Cave and Natalie Portman. Sat–Thurs 4.30pm–5am, Fri 1pm–5am. Happy hour 4.30–9.30pm.

The Record 7 Heleni HaMalka. A tiny but friendly little place, good for casual drink anytime, but especially handy for catching English Premier League and European football matches (for which it will open early if necessary – a list of games they'll be showing live is posted outside). Sat–Thurs 4.30pm–late, Fri noon till late.

Triple 16 Rivlin. Three floors (hence the name) – a bar and small dancefloor at the bottom, a bigger dancefloor in the middle, and a rooftop seating area above that. The crowd is young, the atmosphere hedonistic, the music poppy. There's sometimes a 40NIS cover charge, which includes your first drink. Kosher. Sun–Thurs 7pm–late, Sat Shabbat–late.

Uganda 4 Aristobolus ⊛www.uganda.co.il. Away from Jerusalem's main bar area and on the intellectual end of the underground scene, with interesting electronic sounds (on sale on CD at the back, along with comics and mags; schedule of forthcoming DJs in Hebrew on the website) and a hip but restrained vibe, named, with heavy irony, after the country Theodore Herzl originally wanted for a Jewish homeland. One of the few West Jerusalem bars to serve Taybeh. Sun–Fri noon–late, Sat 6pm–late.

Yankee's Bet David (behind Yoel Saloman by the Blue Hole). A very informal hangout, with a makeshift look and slightly disreputable air, and a variety of music, plus Guinness, Carlsberg and Tuborg on tap, and live bands on Wednesdays and Thursdays (DJs other days). A good place to let your hair down, relax and enjoy the sounds. Daily 8pm–4am.

Zabotinski 2 Ben Shatach. Hangout of the young, rich and beautiful, complete with fashion police on the door, happy hour till 9pm, and live music (usually folk) later. The bar is named after Ze'ev Jabotinsky (spelt slightly differently, but the same guy),

Juice bars

Juice bars can be found on both sides of town but those in the west, such as *Tutti-Frutti* at 23 Ben Yehuda and *Magic Fruit Juice* opposite, offer a far wider choice of fruits than those in the east, quite often including things like melon, persimmon (sharon fruit), prickly pear (*sabra*), kiwi fruit, strawberry and pawpaw.

East of the Green Line, the prices are lower, but you'll be confined largely to orange, grapefruit and carrot. In season (Oct–Dec), you'll also get pomegranate (but note that this is simply halved and pressed, which means the unpleasant bitter taste of the pith is not removed), plus the traditional Palestinian drinks of almond milk ("asir louz) and tangy tamarind cordial (*tamar hindi*) – one of Jerusalem's great tastes; *Alarz* on Sultan Suleiman, a little to the east of the *Golden Walls Hotel*, is one of the best addresses for sampling those. In summer, *tamar hindi* is also available from itinerant sellers, much in evidence on the piazza outside the Damascus Gate.

(see p.151), who, in 1920, was arrested by the British in this very building for his part in Arab–Jewish riots. Despite its name and history however, the bar is not particularly themed on Jabotinksy, but it's very spacious as Jerusalem bars go, and its dark colours give quite a classy feel. Daily 5.30pm–late.

Clubs

The best Jerusalem clubs are found in the industrial zone of **Talpiot**, out to the south of town, invariably on HaOman Street. These don't get going until at least midnight, mostly on Thursdays and Fridays, with not very much happening midweek. Night buses #101, #102, #103, #105 and #106 run half-hourly from midnight to 3am on Thursday night/Friday morning and Saturday night/Sunday morning, and daily in July and August (except Friday night/Saturday morning). The other big area for nightlife (aside from the bar scene in town) is the **old railway station compound** off the Hebron Road, where trains used to terminate before they got shunted out to Malha (see p.24).

Clubs appear and disappear with dizzying speed, and those listed here may well have been superseded by the time you read this, so keep your ear to the ground. The latest trend to hit the city is **mega-bars** (basically a large bar with a small dancefloor, serving food as well as drinks).

Bass 1 HaHistadrut (entrance in the alley) ⓦ www.bassjerusalem.com **(see map, pp. 126–127).** Something between a bar and an underground nightclub, with resident and guest DJs (typically techno or hip-hop), and usually a cover charge (20–30NIS) to get in. The mostly Hebrew website lists who's playing and which days. Times vary, but usually Wed–Fri 10pm–late.

Campus 30 HaOman, Talpiot industrial zone ☏ 02/648 3888. As the name suggests, this club is favoured by students (take your ISIC card if you have one: it will usually get you a discount), and is generally less pretentious and less snooty about clothes than the nearby *HaOman* (see below). There are two dancefloors, one for house, techno and trance, the other for 1980s and Israeli disco sounds. Entry is 30–80NIS. Thurs & Fri 11.45pm–dawn.

HaOman 17 17 HaOman, Talpiot industrial zone ☏ 02/678 1658, ⓦ www.17jerusalem.com. Jerusalem's biggest and most famous club, now with offshoots in Tel Aviv (see p.264) and Haifa, has been reborn as a mega-bar, with the emphasis on drinks, rather than electronic music and big-name DJs, and it's even more about seeing, being seen and dressing to impress than it was before (so make sure your schmatters are well sharp if you want to be sure of getting in). While events are obviously subject to change, Monday is currently student night, Tuesday is Israeli night (Israeli pop classics and singalong), Thursday is the big night, with top house, techno and trance DJs, Friday is army night (for Israelis doing their one- to three-year military service), and Saturday is disco classics night for a slightly older crowd. Entry is 70NIS. Tues, Thurs & Sat 9pm–3am, Fri 11pm–5am.

Izen 7 Bethlehem Rd, Old Station Compound (see map, p.127). A chic and trendy mega-bar (it claims to have been the city's first), with good food, a wide range of drinks, a varied menu of music, and a sophisticated crowd, that's at the very epicentre of the station compound nightlife scene. *Izen* sometimes hosts live music, in which case there may be an entry fee, but usually it's free to get in. Mon–Sat 9pm–late.

Entertainment

Jerusalem is as conservative culturally as it is politically, and lovers of **classical music** are generally better served here than clubbers or pop fans, but there's something for everyone and you can spend the night, drinking beer and taking in the latest rock, hip-hop or dance music just as you can spend it sipping wine and listening to Brahms and Liszt.

For up-to-date **listings** and information on events in Jerusalem, see the Friday supplement of *Ha'Aretz* (with the *Herald Tribune*) or the *Jerusalem Post*. The big problem with all of these is that they tend to omit mention of anything in East Jerusalem, for which you will have to make your own enquiries – the Palestinian National Theatre (see p.203) is a good place to start, and the free pamphlet *This Week in Palestine* (see p.43) contains limited listings for East Jerusalem.

Tickets for concerts and theatres in West Jerusalem can be obtained from Bimot at 8 Shamai (℡02/623 7000, ⑩www.bimot.co.il), Klayim at 12 Shamai (℡02/625 6869, ⑩www.klaimonline.co.il), and Ben Nayim at 38 Jaffa Rd (℡02/625 4008).

Live music venues

Israel's music centre is Tel Aviv, and Jerusalem is provincial by comparison, but it has a good selection of venues, both great and small, and there's always something on. In addition to the venues listed here, some **bars** often put on live music, among them: *Borderline* (see p.195; mainly rock and hip-hop), *Besht Pundak* (see p.196; mainly blues and country), *Birman* (see p.196; soft jazz and piano), *Gotham* (see p.196; indie rock), *HaMarakiya* (see p.191; acoustic guitar music), *Izen* (see opposite; varied dance music), *Mike's Place* (see p.196; mainly rock and jazz), *Sira* (see p.197; indie rock and electronica), *Yankee's* (see p.197; mainly rock and hip-hop) and *Zabotinski* (see p.197; mainly folk). The *Music House* (see p.227) also puts on gigs from time to time.

Artel Jazz Club 9 Heleni HaMalka, West Jerusalem ℡077/962 0165 **(see map, p.127).** There's music almost every night at 9pm in this laid-back little club, sometimes with a small admission charge. Weekends are the busiest but it's always worth dropping by. There's Czech and German lager on tap, so you can even just treat it as a bar with live music. Daily 7pm–2am. Happy hour 8–10pm.

Beit Shmuel 6 Shema'a, West Jerusalem ℡02/620 3455, ⑩www.merkazshimshon.com **(see map, p.127).** On Friday evenings there is an "Oneg Shabbat" (Sabbath celebration) featuring Israeli pop singers. It isn't so much a concert as an informal gathering of a religious nature, its main aim being to encourage Jewish people to see Shabbat as a joyous rather than an onerous occasion.

Bible Lands Museum Museum Row, Ramat Gan ☎02/561 1066, ⓦwww.blmj.org (see map, p.127). The museum puts on concerts with wine and cheese every Saturday at 8.30pm, but you never know what you'll get: one week it might be jazz, the next a classical recital. The museum's website will have full details. Entry to the concert costs the same as entry to the museum, which concert-goers can look around before and after the performance.

Jerusalem Centre for Arabic Music Al-Nuzha St, behind the Palestinian National Theatre, East Jerusalem ☎02/627 4774. A small venue hosting occasional performances of Arabic folk, pop and classical music, from both Palestine and abroad. The Centre is dedicated to promoting Arabic music in general, and it hosts quite an eclectic range of performers.

Pargod Theatre 94 Betzalel, West Jerusalem ☎02/623 8819, ⓦwww.pargod.org (see map, p.126). A theatre (see p.203) which hosts various musical performances, the only regular one of which is the Friday afternoon jazz jam session (1.30–4.30pm), that has been going for over thirty years now. The session is free, though you're expected to buy at least one drink. Other musical events tend to concentrate on folk, country, jazz, blues and Israeli "ethnic" music (a develop-ment of Israeli folk), but there are rock performances too, including covers of 1960s and 1970s sounds. In short, the Pargod is as innovative in the field of music as it is in theatre.

Sultan's Pool (Merrill Hassenfeld Amphitheatre) Hativat Yerushalayim on the corner of Hebron Rd, West Jerusalem (see p.127). Jerusalem's biggest live music venue, and in the open air, so mainly used in summer. The pool has hosted the likes of Sting, Neil Young and other assorted rock legends and dinosaurs,

and it's a pretty dramatic venue with the city walls and citadel forming the backdrop. For the latest on who's playing, check Klayim or Bimot in Shamai Street (see p.199), or the listings in Friday's *Ha'Aretz* or the *Jerusalem Post*.

The Lab (HaMa'abada) 28 Hebron Rd, in the old station compound, West Jerusalem ☎02/629 2001 (see map, p.127). Styling itself a labora-tory for performing arts, this is Jerusalem's most happening venue of the moment, and offers a wide range of performance arts including theatre and dance, but its mainstay is live music, mostly rock and jazz. Mon–Sat 10pm–late.

Ticho House 7 HaRav Kook, West Jerusalem ☎02/624 4186 (see p.128 and see map, p.126). Jazz performances with wine and cheese on Tuesdays at 8.30pm, light music and singing on Thursdays at 8.30pm, and what they call "Jewish soul music" (Jewish folk music, in fact).

Yabous Culture Center Al-Zahra St, East Jerusalem (see map, p.109). A much-needed cultural centre for East Jerusalem, expected to open in 2009 in the premises of the long-defunct Al-Quds Cinema. For further information, check the Yabous Productions website at ⓦwww.yabous.org.

Yellow Submarine 13 HaRekhavim, New Industrial Area, Talpiot ☎02/679 4040, ⓦwww .yellowsubmarine.org.il. This is Jerusalem's main pop venue, hosting a range of live music from rock to rap, and artists from Israel and abroad. They seem to have something on most nights of the week, and details should be published on their website and in the Friday supplements. The big disadvantage of this place is its distance from the city centre, down among the night-clubs in Talpiot's industrial zone. Prices range from 30NIS to 100NIS, depending on the event.

Classical music

European **classical music** is big in Jerusalem, which probably has the highest number of classical aficionados per head of population of any city in the world. Three venues – the Henry Crown Symphony Hall, the International Confer-ence Centre and Sultan's Pool – offer full orchestral performances and you'll also find plenty of small concerts, with at least one on almost any day of the week. Some of these are one-off performances in places that are not normally music venues, while others are occasional or regular events held in smaller venues, churches or museums. As with pop music, it's worth checking the Friday supplements of *Ha'Aretz* and the *Jerusalem Post*.

▲ A concert at the Henry Crown Symphony Hall

In addition to places listed here, the Israel Museum (☎02/670 8811, ⊛www .english.imjnet.org.il; see p.144) and the YMCA in King David Street (☎ 02/625 7111; see p.204) very occasionally host classical concerts, as do the Gerard Behar Center (see p.203) and the Khan Theatre (see p.203).

Ascension Church Augusta Victoria Hospital, Mount of Olives ☎02/628 7704, ⊛www .evangelisch-in-jerusalem.org (see p.122 and map p.109). The church hosts occasional choral and classical music concerts, a programme of which (together with those in the Lutheran Church of the Redeemer) can be found on the website.

Bible Lands Museum Museum Row, Ramat Gan ☎02/561 1066, ⊛www.blmj.org (see map, p.127). Concerts with wine and cheese every Saturday at 8.30pm, sometimes classical (see opposite).

Dormition Abbey Mount Zion ☎02/565-5330 (see map, p.127). The church organ here is used for public recitals of liturgical or classical music, particularly on Saturday mornings at 11am.

Henry Crown Symphony Hall Jerusalem Centre for the Performing Arts, 20 Chopin, Talbiya ☎02/560 5755, ⊛www.jerusalem-theatre.co.il (see map, p.127). The home of the Jerusalem Symphony Orchestra (⊛www.jso.co.il), and venue for most of their concerts, this superb auditorium, part of the Jerusalem Theatre complex, also occasionally hosts visiting orchestras and the Israel Camarata (⊛www .israel-camerata.org), as well as the popular

(and free) *Etnakhta* concerts on Monday evenings for the Voice of Music radio station (tickets available from 4pm, doors open 5pm). Smaller concerts are held at the Rebecca Crown Hall in the same building. Concerts are frequently booked out, especially those of the Jerusalem Symphony Orchestra, so it's wise to book ahead if possible.

International Conference Centre (Binyanei HaUma) Jaffa Rd near Herzl Blvd (up past the Egged Central Bus Station; see map, p.126) ☎02/655 8558, ⊛www.iccjer.co.il. Jerusalem's main concert hall, Binyanei HaUma hosts performances by the Israel Philharmonic Orchestra, and classical musicians from at home and abroad including occasional appearances by the Jerusalem Symphony Orchestra, who usually play at the Henry Crown Symphony Hall (see above). Even performances of Indian classical music are not unknown here, and the centre has also hosted the Eurovision Song Contest. Under one of its foyers there's a pottery factory built by the Roman Tenth Legion which is open to the public.

Jerusalem Centre for Arabic Music Al-Nuzha St, behind the Palestinian National Theatre, East Jerusalem ☎02/627 4774 (see map, p.109).

Sometimes holds concerts of Arabic classical music.

Jerusalem Music Centre Mishkenot Sha'ananim ☎02/623 4347, ⓦwww.jmc.co.il. Part of what aims to be an arts colony in Yemin Moshe, the Music Centre is dedicated to encouraging young Israeli musicians and giving them a space to perform. It also puts on concerts (tickets typically 30–100NIS) both at the centre and also at the YMCA.

Lutheran Church of the Redeemer 21 Mauristan St, Christian Quarter ☎02/626 6800, ⓦwww.evangelisch-in-jerusalem.org (see p.70 and map p.56). Though not exactly a concert hall, the Lutheran church, in the heart of the Old City does host occasional concerts of classical and choral music, usually of a religious nature. The website has a programme of concerts.

Music Center Hinnom Valley, off Hebron Rd behind the Cinemateque ☎02/565 2111, ⓦmusic-center.jerusalem.muni.il (see map, p.127). Run by the city council, with the aim of promoting musical talent in Jerusalem and providing a resource for would-be musicians, the Music Center offers classes and runs a number of inter-ethnic projects for Jewish and Palestinian Jerusalemites to bring together elements from both their cultures. It also puts on concerts from time to time. Daily 2–9pm.

Notre Dame de Sion Convent 23 HaOren, Ein Karem ☎02/641 5738, ⓦwww.sion-ein-karem .org (see p.167). Hosts occasional concerts.

Sultan's Pool (Merrill Hassenfeld Amphitheatre) Hativat Yerushalayim on the corner of Hebron Rd. In addition to pop concerts (see p.200 and map pp.126–127), classical concerts are also put on at the Pool, again particularly in summer since it's an open-air venue and, if anything, even better suited to classical music than to rock. For full details, check the listings in Friday's *Ha'Aretz* or the *Jerusalem Post*.

Targ Music Centre Ein Karem ☎02/641 4250, ⓦwww.klassitarg.org.il. A pleasant suburban locale that often puts on concerts of chamber music and other non-orchestral classical music, especially Friday evenings and Saturday lunchtimes. The centre, founded in 1968 by pianist duo Bracha Eden and Alexander Tamir, tries to nurture new Israeli talent and promote musical excellence. Concert tickets are usually around 30–80NIS.

Ticho House 7 HaRav Kook, West Jerusalem ☎02/535 6954, ⓦwww.pearl-music.co.il /english/Ticho.html (see p.128 and map p.126). A "concerticho" of live chamber music is held in the gallery on Friday mornings at 11am [40NIS].

Theatre, dance, poetry and comedy

Most **plays** by Israeli or Palestinian authors are, naturally enough, written and performed in Hebrew or Arabic (or occasionally in Yiddish). For those who don't speak any of those languages, that is a pity, since both Israeli and Palestinian **modern drama** are dynamic and controversial, with a much wider influence

The Jerusalem Centre for the Performing Arts

With such a highly cultured population, post-independence West Jerusalem felt keenly the lack of a dedicated venue for theatre and classical music. Thus it was that, in 1958, a Jewish Venezuelan steel magnate by the name of Miles Sherover and his wife Gita, friends of then mayor Teddy Kolleck, decided to endow the city with a world-class theatrical venue, which opened its doors as the 900-seater **Sherover Theatre** in 1971.

Meanwhile, Chicago entrepreneur Henry Crown wanted to pay for a football stadium in Jerusalem, but when the ultra-orthodox lobby opposed the plan, Kolleck persuaded him to spend his money instead on an extension to the Sherover Theatre, which opened in 1986 as the **Henry Crown Hall**, with perfect orchestral acoustics and 750 seats. To complete the complex – commonly known as the **Jerusalem Theatre**, but officially the **Jerusalem Centre for the Performing Arts** – a smaller 110-seat **Little Theatre** were incorporated, along with the medium-sized, 450-seat **Rebecca Crown Auditorium**, named after Henry's wife.

than theatre in most English-speaking countries, and well worth going to see if you can understand them. There are, however, some good English-language productions to be found in Jerusalem too, as well as English stand-up **comedy** and **dance**, the latter obviously breaking through the language barrier. One of the most recommended dance events is put on by the Tzabarim Folklore Ensemble at the YMCA (see p.204).

Gerard Behar Center 11 Betzalel, West Jerusalem T 02/625 1139 (see map, p.126). A modern venue hosting dance performances, occasional concerts, and most importantly, the Jerusalem English-Speaking Theatre (JEST; T 02/642 0908, W www.geocities .com/jest-theatre), who put on musicals, comedies, dramas and some classics, as well as plays in English. The centre was closed at last check for renovation, but should be up and running again by the time this book comes out.

Khan Theatre 2 David Remez (by the old station compound) T 02/671 8281, W www.khan.co.il (see map, p.127). A great venue in a nineteenth-century Ottoman caravanserai (merchants' hostel), this is the city's first repertory theatre. Unfortunately the plays are all in Hebrew, though there are very occasional concerts, and a café if you just want to pop in and check out the building.

Off the Wall Comedy Basement 34 Ben Yehuda, West Jerusalem (by HaMashbir department store) T 02/624 3218, W www.israelcomedy .com (see map, p.127). Stand-up comedy in English some nights, Hebrew others, at Jerusalem's first comedy club. The style of humour is mostly Jewish-American, and typically deals with issues of interest to "Anglo" Israelis (that is, Jewish immigrants of English-speaking origin), but you'll still be laughing, even if one or two of the jokes do go over your head. Entrance is 30–45NIS, with a small discount for students.

Pargod Theatre 94 Betzalel, West Jerusalem T 02/623 8819, W www.pargod.org (see map, p.126). A Jerusalem institution, the tiny, tunnel-like Pargod theatre was set up in a refurbished ex-water cistern by its founder Arye Mark in 1969 as a step forward from holding performances in his flat, and has survived on the thread of a shoestring largely thanks to Mark's perseverance in the face of adversity. Performers have often started as members of the audience who drift into helping out and then acting, but unfortunately all plays as such are almost all in Hebrew (the website, however, is in Hebrew, English and Russian – not Arabic of course),

though there are regular concerts (see p.200) and occasional dance performances.

Palestinian National Theatre Al-Nuzha, East Jerusalem (off Nablus Rd) T 02/628 0957, W www.pnt-pal.org (see map, p.109). The first Palestinian arts centre in the country when it opened in 1984, the theatre puts on plays in Arabic and English, as well as folklore evenings, exhibitions, conferences and other events. A lot of the plays are quite political, and the theatre has faced occasional closure by Israeli military authorities in the past (even detention of its performers is not unknown), and is now of course cut off from much of its audience by the Separation Wall, but despite all these difficulties it is still going strong, and indeed continues to expand its activities.

Psik Theatre T 02/651 3663, W www.psik.org.il. A theatre company producing new plays with present-day relevance, for adults, and also for children and young people, mostly in Hebrew. The Psik doesn't currently have its own venue, but hopes to have in the near future.

Sherover Theatre Jerusalem Centre for the Performing Arts, 20 David Marcus, Talbiya T 02/560 5755, W www.jerusalem-theatre.co.il (see map, p.127). This is Jerusalem's most prestigious mainstream theatre, the original part of the Jerusalem Theatre complex, but the plays here are almost always in Hebrew. Dance performances take place here every couple of months or so, and it's always worth checking the press to see what's on. There's also a Little Theatre in the complex for smaller performances.

Tmol Shilshom 5 Yoel Salomon, West Jerusalem (round the back – entrance via the alley by no. 11) W www.tmol-shilshom.co.il (see map, p.127). This café-restaurant-bookshop (see p.184) holds regular English book readings and discussions, occasionally even poetry slams, a fast, furious and free-for-all poetry reading session.

Train Theatre Liberty Bell Park, West Jerusalem T 02/561 8514, W www.traintheater.co.il (see map, p.127). Originally in an old rail car (hence the name), this small theatre puts on shows and story readings specifically for children. Note however that they are all in Hebrew.

YMCA King David St, West Jerusalem ☎050/523 3210, ⓦjerusalemdance.com (see p.137 and map p.127). The "Y" hosts a 2hr folklore show called "Jerusalem of Gold" in its auditorium, usually on Mondays, Thursdays and Saturdays (but not necessarily every week) at 9pm, consisting of Arab and Jewish traditional dances performed by Tzabarim Folklore Ensemble, a mixed troupe of Israeli and Palestinian dancers. Tickets can be booked online, by phone, or at the YMCA box office from 6pm on the evening of the performance.

Film

Whatever your taste in **film**, you should be able to find a cinema in Jerusalem that's showing something you like, and there'll always be something in English (American films are shown with Hebrew subtitles, though Israeli films do not usually have English subtitles). The *Ha'Aretz* and *Jerusalem Post* Friday supplements have up-to-date listings. All of the **cinemas** currently operating are in West Jerusalem; the Old City doesn't have any, and the two that existed in East Jerusalem have long been closed, though one of them should reopen in the future as part of the planned Yabous Culture Centre (see p.200). The two art-house theatres (the Smadar and Cinemateque) are far preferable to the two mainstream cinemas (the Globus and Rav Hen), which are out of town, have long, slow-moving queues to get in, and audiences who chat and even talk on the phone during the movie. In addition to the cinemas listed here, there is also a film on the history of Jerusalem shown in a converted cinema with roller-coaster special effects at the Time Elevator (see p.125). Most cinemas close for Shabbat – the Smadar is an exception.

Cinemateque Hebron Rd ☎02/565 4333, ⓦwww .jer-cin.org.il. Comfortable art-house cinema showing three or four different films daily, some old, some new, some foreign, some Israeli, and quite a few independent. The seats are plush, the sound perfect, and you can even watch shorts and documentaries. There's also an attached café-restaurant with Old City views, and in July, the Cinemateque runs a Jerusalem Film Festival (see p.215).

Globus Malha Mall (Kanyon Yerushalayim) ☎02/678 8448. Multiplex out in Malha (see p.155) showing a selection of the latest movies on general release to a frequently rowdy, mainly teenage audience; arrive early if you want to see the beginning of the film, as queues are long and there never seem to be enough ticket windows open to manage them.

Rav Hen Lev Talpiot Mall,17 HaOman, Talpiot industrial zone ☎02/679 2799, ⓦwww.rav-hen .co.il. Inconveniently located and often with long queues, but the main screen here is the place to watch new releases if you want a big picture and loud acoustics. This cinema tends to split the latest releases with the Globus, so chances are you won't be able to choose which theatre to go to for the Hollywood blockbuster of your choice anyway.

Smadar 4 Lloyd George, German Colony ☎02/566 0954. The oldest cinema in town, screening an interesting selection of Israeli and foreign movies, a mix of art-house, cult and mainstream. It was founded in 1928 to serve British troops by a German resident of the Colony. As anti-Semitism in Germany worsened, he gave it over to Jewish management to avoid a boycott by Jewish Jerusalemites, and after 1948, it was taken over by a former Israeli soldier who sold the tickets and ran the projector himself, with help only from his wife. Though snapped up by a cinema chain in 1993, it still has the feel of a local independent cinema, laid-back and unpretentious, with a bar-restaurant attached (you can take drinks into the theatre), and open seven days a week.

Third Ear 8 Emek Refaim, German Colony ☎02/563 3093, ⓦwww.third-ear.com. Strictly speaking this is a DVD rental shop, but they also have a screening hall, with comfy chairs and good acoustics, where they show a selection of interesting productions; if you read Hebrew, you can check the schedule on their website.

⑬

Sports and activities

J erusalem is not the sportiest town on earth, not compared with Western cities, and not compared with Tel Aviv, but you can still take in a match or get some exercise should you so wish. Jerusalem's main **spectator sports** are football (meaning soccer, of course, but American football exists too) and basketball, which was until recently more popular. **Participation sports** and outdoor activities available in or around town include swimming, climbing, hiking, cycling and horseback riding.

Football (soccer)

In **football** terms, Israel and Palestine are not just (like England and Scotland) separate countries, but they even play on different "continents", with Palestine affiliated to the Asian Football Confederation, while Israel belongs to UEFA. This means that Israeli clubs play in European competitions, and Israel can in theory qualify for the European Championship.

Israeli football teams tend to have political affiliations, with those called HaPoel ("workers'") generally having Labour- or Meretz-voting fans, while supporters of teams called Maccabi usually vote for the right. In Jerusalem, the clubs' political affiliations are even more entrenched than elsewhere, with Beitar Jerusalem affiliated to the right, while HaPoel Jerusalem and HaPoel Katamon are associated with the Israeli left.

All three Jerusalem clubs play their home games at **Teddy Stadium**, opposite the shopping mall in Malha (see p.155; buses #4 and #18 from King George Street, #6 from Jaffa Road). Named after former mayor Teddy Kolleck, the ground opened in 1992 and holds a 21,600-strong crowd. Though it's a multi-sport stadium, the Teddy is mostly dedicated to football, and the atmosphere is excellent, with stands right down to the pitch, and great acoustics too. Beitar fans call it *Gehinom* ("Hell"), which is what they try to make it for away teams. You'll rarely need to get **tickets** in advance – just turn up and buy them on the gate – but should you want to be sure of a seat (it's an all-seater stadium), it is possible to buy tickets in advance from Klayim, Bimot or Ben Nayim (see p.199). Israel's football season kicks off at the end of August, and ends in May.

Beitar Jerusalem ⓦ www.bjerusalem.co.il. Jerusalem's top team and Israel's biggest club, six times league champions. Beitar play in the twelve-member Israeli Premier League, whose members meet each other three times during the season. Home league matches tend to be played on

Saturday evenings – click on their name at ⓦeng.football.org.il/clubs for forthcoming fixtures. Grudge match of the year is against the mainly Arab side Bnei Sakhnin from Galilee, when racist chanting and crowd violence (from both sides) are pretty much guaranteed. For a match where the football itself is more the attraction, Maccabi Haifa and Maccabi Tel Aviv are the best opponents to watch Beitar play. Against HaPoel Tel Aviv there is still some political rivalry, but not as bitter, nor as violent, as against Sakhnin. Beitar's only ever match against a Scottish or English side was in the 1998 UEFA cup, when they held Rangers to a one-all draw in Jerusalem, going out 5–3 on aggregate after the return match at Ibrox.

HaPoel Jerusalem Beitar's former deadly rival, once the most important Haganah, Labour Party and trade union supporting club in Israel, but currently languishing in the second tier of Israeli football (*Liga Leumit*), with a fan base that has severely waned over the years and continues to do so. **HaPoel Katamon** Ⓦ www.katamon.co.il. Originally formed by a merger of clubs from Abu Ghosh (see p.252) and the Jerusalem suburb of Mevaseret Zion, it was bought up in 2007 by disaffected HaPoel Jerusalem fans upset that their club had been taken over by businessmen running it into the ground for profit. Katamon play in the southern division of the country's fourth tier (*Liga Aleph*), and are mostly of note for being Israel's first fan-owned club.

American football

As well as soccer, Israel also has American football, but it's a much more low-key affair. Schedules can be found on the American Football in Israel (AFI) website at Ⓦ www.israelfootball.net (click on "AFI" and then on "schedule").

Big Blue Jerusalem Jerusalem's American football team, whose home ground is the Kraft Family Stadium on Sederot Ben Zvi near Nahla'ot (not far from Egged Central Bus Station; see map, p.126). The stadium was built with money donated by New England Patriots owner, business tycoon Robert Kraft.

Basketball

Until recently, **basketball** was bigger as a spectator sport in Israel than football, and it still has a massive following. If you want to **play** a bit of informal basketball, there are courts at Liberty Bell Garden, which are free to use and especially busy on Fridays. There's also an indoor court at the YMCA on King David Street (see opposite), which can be booked when not otherwise in use.

HaPoel Jerusalem Ⓦ www.hapoel.co.il. In basketball, unlike football, it's HaPoel who are the main club. Their most exciting opponents are Maccabi Tel Aviv, usually the league champions, and runners up to HaPoel in the final on three out of the four occasions that the Jerusalem side have won the State Cup. As in football, basketball's top flight, called the Super League (*Ligat HaAl*), has twelve clubs, but they only meet twice each during the season, which lasts from October to April. Matches are usually played on a Saturday evening, after Shabbat. In 2004, HaPoel won the European ULEB Cup, beating Real Madrid 83–72 in the final (the same year, Maccabi Tel Aviv won the more prestigious Euroleague, making it an Israeli double). HaPoel play in the 2,800-seater Malha Arena, half a kilometre west of Teddy Stadium and the Malha Mall at 3 Avraham Stern (☎02/643 1331). Tickets on the door, or in advance from Klayim, Bimot or Ben Nayim (see p.199).

Baseball

The Israel Baseball League (@www.israelbaseballleague.com), launched in 2007 to much enthusiasm from Jewish American baseball fans, proved a complete fiasco, with players left unpaid, investors out of pocket, bats that kept breaking and facilities that would shame an amateur Sunday league. As a result, the 2008 season was cancelled. If baseball does return to Israel, Jerusalem's team, the **Jerusalem Gold**, are expected to use the Kraft Family Stadium (see opposite) as their home ground.

Fitness centres

Many upmarket hotels have fitness rooms, sometimes open to non-residents for a small fee. There are also a number of **private gyms** and fitness centres around town, but not many in the city centre.

Giraffe 10 Lunz, West Jerusalem (in the Ben Yehuda St midrahov) ☎02/624 1956. The most centrally located gym, a little bit poky but not bad value and open to both sexes.
Iron Gym 19 Keren haYesod, West Jerusalem ☎02/625 2829, @www.irongym.co.il. Friendly, reasonably well-equipped gym that's open to both sexes.
Ramat Rachel Fitness Centre Kibbutz Ramat Rachel ☎02/670 2555. @www.ramatrachel.co.il (bus #7 from Jaffa Rd/King George St; see p.157). Well-equipped, with a steam bath, sauna and spa as well as a swimming pool and gym, but pricey, and rather a haul from town.

Razim 9 Diskin, Rehavia ☎02/563 2946, @www.razim.org. Clean, friendly, women-only fitness centre.
YMCA King David St, West Jerusalem ☎02/569 2673 or 84, @www.jerusalemymca.org. Has a sports centre, with a fitness room, swimming pool, squash courts, basketball court and sauna.
YMCA Nablus Rd, East Jerusalem ☎02/628 6888, @www.ej-ymca.org. Has a swimming pool, fitness room, sauna and squash court, as well as outdoor courts for basketball or tennis, and a football field.

Tennis

Israel Tennis Center 1 Elmaliakh, Gonen Tet, Katamon ☎02/679 1866, @www.tennis.org.il. Eighteen courts for hire.
Jerusalem Sports Club 32 HaTzefira, German Colony ☎02/563 2125. Courts for hire.
Sir Arthur Gilbert Tennis Club Hebrew University, Mount Scopus ☎02/588 2796. Ten courts. Open

until 10pm (floodlit if necessary) except Fridays and Saturdays.
YMCA Nablus Rd, East Jerusalem ☎02/628 6888, @www.ej-ymca.org. The most central locale with tennis courts for hire.

Swimming pools

Many upmarket hotels have **swimming pools**, as do the two Ys (see above), but the biggest pool in town is the Olympic-sized Jerusalem Pool at 43 Emek Refaim in the German Colony (☎02/563 2092; bus #4 or #21 from King George Street, or #18 from Jaffa Road and King David Street), open Mon & Wed 5.30am–5.45pm, Tues & Thurs 5.30am–9.45pm, Fri 8am–4.30pm, Sat 8am–5.45pm, Sun noon–9.45pm. Entrance is 50NIS, or 500NIS for eleven sessions.

Cycling

Though Jerusalem and the surrounding area are quite hilly, this should not deter any serious cyclist. One of the few places you can **rent bikes** is Nitzan Bike at 137 Jaffa Rd (by the *Avital Hotel*) ☎02/625 2741, which charges 50NIS per day.

Ten-pin bowling

Jerusalem has two **bowling alleys**, both in shopping malls in Talpiot (bus #30 from Jaffa Road or Shlomzion HaMalka).

Jerusalem Bowling Center Third floor, HaAhim Israel Mall, 18 Yad HaRutzim ☎02/673 2195. Israel's first bowling alley, and a little bit long in the tooth, but still fun.

Strike Top floor, Lev Talpiot Mall, 17 HaOman ☎02/678 2000. New, eighteen-lane bowling alley in a revamped mall.

Festivals and holidays

As a city holy to three religions, Jerusalem is never short of festivities of one sort or another, but be aware that **religious festivals** are generally celebrated here in a pious and sober manner. Generally speaking, it is Christians who go in for processions and public festivity, while Jews and Muslims are more likely to celebrate at home or inside synagogues or mosques. The sheer number of religious festivals and holidays celebrated in Jerusalem is further complicated by the fact that Jewish and Muslim holidays are dated according to **lunar calendars**, in which each month begins and ends at the new moon. To make up the difference between a year of twelve lunar months and a solar year of 365–366 days, the **Jewish calendar** adds an extra month every three or four years. The **Muslim calendar** does not have such leap years, and consequently regresses against the Western (Gregorian) calendar by approximately eleven days a year. What this means in practice is that Jewish and Muslim festivals will fall on different days of the Gregorian calendar every year

Christian holidays don't escape complication either, being celebrated on different dates by different denominations: Roman Catholics and Protestants follow the Gregorian (Western) calendar, but the Eastern Orthodox churches use the Julian calendar (thirteen days later than the Gregorian), while the Armenian Church operates a further twelve days on. Palestinian secular holidays (celebrated in PA-controlled areas, and by some Palestinian shopkeepers in Jerusalem) do, however, follow the Gregorian calendar.

In addition to the religious feasts and fasts, there are a number of **cultural festivals**, dedicated to things like music, cinema and theatre.

Jewish festivals

Jewish festivals are of two sorts. Serious religious holidays (*yom tov*, pronounced "yonteff" in Yiddish) are specified by the Torah and subject to the same kind of strictures as the Sabbath (see p.276), with all forms of work forbidden. As public and religious holidays they involve shutdowns of shops and public services, including transport, but little celebration as such. Other celebrations, such as Hannukah and Purim, are religious in origin, but allow work to continue, and are generally more joyous occasions, though not public holidays. While Jewish people in English-speaking countries may greet each other with a "Good yonteff" on religious holidays, the expression to use in Hebrew is "*Hag sameakh*," which has the advantage that it can be used for occasions like Hannukah and Purim as well as proper *yomim tovim*.

Jewish festivals follow the Jewish calendar rather than the Western (Gregorian) one. Exact dates are given in the box on pp.212–213.

▲ Jewish children in fancy dress during Purim

Religious festivals and fast days

Tu Bishvat 15 Shevat (Jan or Feb). The "new year for trees", a minor celebration marked by tree-planting activities.

Purim 15 Adar (Early spring). Commemorates events recorded the biblical book of Esther, when a Jewish Queen of Persia saved her people from the empire's anti-Semitic prime minister Haman. Purim is held a day later in Jerusalem (and other walled cities) than elsewhere, and is particularly a festival for children, with fancy dress, games, clowns and street activities, especially in the Ben Yehuda *midrahov*. In synagogues it is marked by a public reading of a scroll (*megilla*) of the book of Esther. Festive foods include three-cornered cakes stuffed with poppy-seed paste, called *hamantashen*.

Passover (Pesah); 15–22 Nissan (usually in April or at the end of March, around Easter time). Commemorates the biblical Exodus from Egypt, no leavened bread may be eaten for a week, though only the first and last days are public holidays.

Omer Seven-week Lent-like period between Passover and Shaevuot, during which celebration is generally discouraged and various calamities that befell the Jewish people are remembered. Punctuated by a number of commemorative days (see opposite) and also by:

Lag beOmer 18 Iyyar (the 33rd day of the Omer). A lull in the Omer period of restraint and a popular day for marriages.

Shavuot (Pentecost); 6 Sivan (seven weeks after Passover, usually in May). Commemorates the giving of the Torah to Moses on Mount Sinai, and also the spring harvest. A public holiday, it is traditionally celebrated with the eating of cheesecake.

Tisha beAv 9 Av (July or Aug). Fast commemorating the destruction of the First and Second Temples, which are held to have occurred on the same Hebrew date.

Rosh HaShannah (Jewish New Year); 1 Tishri (Sept or Oct). Two-day public holiday marked with the consumption of apple dipped in honey, honey cake and new fruits (traditionally you eat a fruit which you haven't eaten during the preceding year). The way to wish Jewish people a happy New Year is "*Shana tova*".

Yom Kippur (Day of Atonement); 10 Tishri (nine days after Rosh HaShannah). The most serious and solemn day of the Jewish calendar, observed with a 25hr fast, during which the whole of Israel more or less shuts down. The purpose of the fast is to atone for all the sins you may have committed during the previous year. Some people may wear sackcloth during Yom Kippur as a sign of penitence.

Sukkot (Tabernacles); 15–22 Tishri (two weeks after Rosh HaShannah). A harvest festival which also commemorates the fact that the Israelites in the wilderness lived in temporary accomodation. During the eight days of the festival (of which the first and last are public holidays), observant Jewish people build a roofless temporary structure (*sukkah*), in which they eat and sometimes sleep, and in the synagogue, a palm frond (*lulav*) is held with branches of myrtle and willow and waved in four directions and up and down while praying. The last day of Sukkot (*Simhat Torah*), on which the annual cycle of reading weekly portions of the Torah in the synagogue is finished and restarted, is the one Jewish festival whose celebration traditionally involves alcoholic inebriation. *Simhat Torah*, the first day of Sukkot and the first day of Rosh HaShannah will all fall on the same day of the week.

Hannukah 25 Kislev–3 Tevet (usually in Dec). A winter solstice festival of lights to commemorate the Maccabees' 164 BC rededication of the Temple in Jerusalem after its profanation by the Seleucids. Hannukah lasts for eight days, during which Jewish homes light candles, starting with a single one on the first day, and building up to eight on the last.

Yom HaShoah (Holocaust Day); 27 Nissan (12th day of Omer). Mourns the victims of the Holocaust with a 2min silence at 11am and the closure of cinemas, theatres, nighclubs and concert halls.

Yom HaZikaron (Remembrance Day); 4 Iyyar (19th day of Omer). Honours Israel's war dead and victims of terrorist attacks with prayers, cinema, theatre and nightclub closures, and an 11am 2min silence.

Yom Ha'Atzma'ut (Independence Day); 5 Iyyar (the day after Yom HaZikaron). Public holiday celebrating Israel's 1948 independence from British rule. Like a Jewish religious holiday, it begins the evening before, running from sunset to sunset.

Yom Yerushalayim (Jerusalem Day not to be confused with the Iranian one; see p.214); 28 Iyyar (usually in May). Commemorates Jerusalem's 1967 reunification when Israeli troops occupied its eastern half. Celebrations include prayers at the Wailing Wall and processions in West Jerusalem.

⑭

Muslim holidays

Muslim holy days follow the Islamic calendar, which consists of exactly twelve lunar months and so regresses against the solar year by about eleven days annually. Predicted dates are given in the box on pp.212–213.

Al-Hijra (Islamic New Year); 1 Muharram. Commemorates the 622 AD flight of the Prophet Mohammed and his followers from Mecca to Medina, from which the Islamic era is dated. Shops and businesses remain open, but families hold a celebration dinner.

Moulid al-Nabi 12 Rabi al-Awwil. The Prophet Mohammed's Birthday, not a holiday but a day of celebration.

Leilat al-Miraj 27 Rajab (33 days before Ramadan). The night on which Mohammed made his Night Journey from Mecca to Jerusalem and to Heaven (see p.103), celebrated mainly in the mosque, with scriptural readings and discussions.

Ramadan Dates vary (see box, pp.212–213). The month of Ramadan is the most important event in the Muslim calendar with fasting from dawn to dusk and much

celebration at night. Muslim shops and businesses stay open as usual but close before sunset so that people can eat; cafés and restaurants are shut sunrise to sunset but may open after dark, though some will close up altogether.

Eid al-Fitr 1 Shawwal. Three-day holiday to celebrate the end of Ramadan. A particularly festive time among Muslim Jerusalemites, lasting for three days, but it tends to be celebrated in the home or in the mosque rather than on the streets. Typical activities involve visiting friends and family, and eating sweetmeats.

Eid al-Adha (Eid al-Kabir, Bakr-Id) 10 Dhul Hajja. Two-day feast and holiday to commemorate Abraham's willingness to sacrifice his son to God (here in Jerusalem, of course; see p.102), and also the time of pilgrimage to Mecca. Largely a

Holiday and festival dates 2009–2013

Variable dates

Festival	Status	2009
Jewish		
Purim	festival, not holiday	11 March
Passover (1st day)	holiday 1st and 7th days	9 April
Yom Ha'Atzma'ut	holiday	29 April
Yom Yerushalayim	celebration, not holiday	22 May
Lag beOmer	low-key festival, not holiday	12 May
Shavuot (Pentecost)	holiday	29 May
Rosh HaShannah (New Year)	two-day holiday	19 Sept
Yom Kippur	very strict holiday	28 Sept
Sukkot (1st day)	holiday 1st and 7th days	3 Oct
Hannukah	eight-day festival, not holiday	19 Dec
Muslim (subject to confirmation of new moon sighting)		
Moulid al-Nabi	festival not holiday	9 March
Ramadan (1st day)	one-month fasting period	22 Aug
Eid al-Fitr	three-day holiday	20 Sept
Eid al-Adha	two-day holiday	27 Nov
Al-Hijra (New Year)	low-key festival, not holiday	18 Dec
Christian (movable)		
Catholic Easter Sunday	holiday (Fri and Mon)	12 April
Eastern Orthodox Easter Sunday	holiday (Fri and Mon)	5 May

Fixed dates

Christian holidays		
Catholic and Protestant Christmas		25 Dec
Eastern Orthodox Christmas		7 Jan
Armenian Orthodox Christmas		19 Jan
Palestinian secular holidays		
New Year and Fatah Day		1 Jan
Labour Day		1 May
Independence Day		14 Nov

family affair at home, it involves the purchase, slaughter and communal consumption of a sheep in remembrance of Abraham's eventual sacrifice of a ram in place of his son.

Christian holidays

In Jerusalem, Christian holidays are much more religious affairs than their counterparts in most Western countries. They are also rather spread out because of their celebration on different dates by different churches, each working according to a different calendar. As an example, **Christmas** is celebrated by the Western churches on December 25, by the Eastern on January 7, and by the Armenians on January 19.

Palm Sunday A week before the Catholic Easter. Marks Jesus's triumphant arrival in Jerusalem, and is celebrated with a procession led by the Franciscan friars from Bethpage (see p.160).
Easter Movable (see box above for dates). The crucifixion and resurrection of Christ, marked

2010	2011	2012	2013
29 Feb	21 March	9 March	25 Feb
30 March	19 April	7 April	26 Mar
19 April	9 May	26 April	16 April
12 May	1 June	20 May	8 May
2 May	22 May	10 May	28 April
19 May	8 June	27 May	15 May
9 Sept	29 Sept	17 Sept	5 Sept
18 Sept	8 Oct	26 Sept	14 Sept
23 Sept	13 Oct	1 Oct	19 Sept
2 Dec	21 Dec	9 Dec	28 Nov
26 Feb	15 Feb	4 Feb	24 Jan
11 Aug	1 Aug	20 July	9 July
10 Sept	30 Aug	19 Aug	8 Aug
16 Nov	6 Nov	26 Oct	15 Oct
7 Dec	26 Nov	15 Nov	4 Nov
4 April	24 April	8 April	31 March
19 April	4 April	24 April	15 April

with pilgrims arriving en masse to follow Jesus's footsteps along the Via Dolorosa. Greek Orthodox Easter is celebrated with the miracle of the Holy Fire (see p.69).

Ascension On a Thursday, five and a half weeks after Easter. Marks Jesus's departure from earth to heaven.

Christmas Dates vary (see box above). The anniversary of the birth of Christ. The Roman Catholic/Protestant Christmas on December 25 is biggest in Bethlehem, of course, with visitors from around the world coming to celebrate, and buses laid on from Jerusalem (arrangements vary year by year; check with the Christian Information Centre).

Epiphany (Twelfth Night); Twelve days after Christmas Day, when the three kings came to visit the infant Jesus in Bethlehem, and also when Jesus was baptized, followed twelve days later by the visit of the Magi bearing gifts. For many Christians, this rather than Christmas Day is the time for giving presents.

Secular Palestinian holidays

Of the main secular Palestinian holidays and commemorations (see box above for dates), all of which follow the Gregorian calendar, most commemorate political events (usually tragic from the Palestinian point of view) and only two are official **public holidays**: Fatah Day, and Independence Day.

213

Fatah Day 1 Jan. Marks the founding, in 1965, of Fatah, the PLO's largest political faction, but of course a holiday for the new year anyway.

Land Day 30 March. Marks the 1976 shooting of six unarmed demonstrators by Israeli forces in Galilee during protests against land seizures from local Palestinian communities by the Israeli state; it is mostly commemorated in Galilee, but sometimes marked by demonstrations or shop closures in East Jerusalem.

Deir Yassin Day 9 April. Commemorates the infamous 1948 massacre (see p.153), marked by private mourning and a procession to the site of the village.

Naqba Day 14 May. The anniversary of Israel's independence, which was, for the Palestinians, their great national "catastrophe" (*naqba*).

Jerusalem Day Late Oct (exact date varies). Declared in 1979 by Iran's Ayatollah Khomeni to protest the city's occupation by Jews, and celebrated more in Iran than in Jerusalem. Not to be confused with Israel's Yom Yerushalayim (see p.211).

Independence Day 14 Nov. Celebrates the (premature) declaration of a State of Palestine by the Palestine National Council in 1988.

Palestine Day 29 Nov. The anniversary of the 1947 UN vote for partition of Palestine (see p.272), now declared by the UN a day of solidarity with the Palestinian people, but celebrated more by anti-Israel protestors elsewhere than by Palestinians in Jerusalem.

Cultural festivals

In addition to the various religious and national holidays celebrated in Jerusalem, there is a smattering of **cultural events**. Most are musical, one way or another, but there are also events featuring arts and crafts, music, theatre, or the sampling of alcoholic beverages. The majority are held over the summer, particularly in August. Tickets for most events are available from Bimot, Klayim or Ben Nayim (see p.199).

Music festivals

Abu Ghosh Music Festival Ⓦ www.agfestival .co.il; held twice a year – at Shavuot and Sukkot – in the village of Abu Ghosh (see p.252), mainly in the Notre Dame de l'Arche de l'Alliance Church. The main focus of the festival is vocal music, but that can mean anything from choral to folk, and there's always a bit of non-vocal classical music anyway, but in the vocal sessions, the audience frequently join in. Tickets are available in Jerusalem at Klayim and Bimot (see p.199).

Israel Festival Ⓦ www.israel-festival.org.il; end of May and early June. Israel's main celebration of the performing arts, featuring events at venues across the west side of town, with a couple outside Jerusalem too. Performers come from around the world to take part, and there's a huge variety of performances, including theatre, dance, classical music and world music. The Israel Festival also incorporates the Jerusalem Jazz Festival, a series of concerts held mainly at Yellow Submarine (see p.202).

Sounding Jerusalem Chamber Music Festival Ⓦ www.soundingjerusalem.com; three weeks in June and July. Set up in 2006 by Austrian cellist Oskar Hütter, who hopes that it will help bridge divides across the city. For that reason it is deliberately spread across venues in West Jerusalem, East Jerusalem and elsewhere in the West Bank. The musicians are Israeli, Palestinian and European, and the venues include Old City churches, West Jerusalem historic sites, and West Bank villages.

East Jerusalem Music Festival July. Held at the Tombs of the Kings (see p.112), drawing performers from around the world as well as local artists, playing an eclectic range of music, including jazz, choral, and European and Arabic folk and classical music. Sponsored by the UN and European consulates and put on by Yabous Productions (2 Ibn Jubair ☎ 02/626 1045, Ⓦ www .yabous.org), who are the people to contact for further information and tickets.

Mishkenot Sha'ananim Music Festival End of Aug. A series of concerts featuring a mixture of Israeli pop music from crooners to funk bands, held over five evenings on the roof of the Mishkenot Sha'ananim almshouses in Yemin Moshe (see p.137). Information and tickets from the Mishkenot Sha'ananim institution (℡02/629 2220, Ⓦwww.mishkenot.org.il).

Jerusalem International Chamber Music Festival Ⓦwww.jcmf.org.il/en; beginning of Sept, usually also catching the very end of Aug. A series of concerts held in the auditorium of the YMCA on King David St (see p.204) every evening for two weeks. The concerts include old favourites as well as less well-known and original new works, performed by great artists from Israel, the Palestinian Territories and around the world (Daniel Barenboim is a regular). Tickets go on general sale from June, and can be bought at the YMCA or booked by phone.

International Harp Contest Ⓦwww .harpcontest-israel.org.il; Oct, every three years (2009, 2012, 2015). Though often thought of as a Celtic instrument hailing from Wales or Ireland, the harp has a long biblical pedigree – King David, for example, famously played one (I Samuel 16:23), and the earliest known depiction of a harp, dating from the fourth millennium BC, comes from Megiddo (Armageddon) in northern Israel. This competition is usually held in Tel Aviv, but usually with concerts in Jerusalem too (at the Jerusalem Centre for the Performing Arts; see p.202).

Cinema and theatre festivals

Jerusalem Film Festival Ⓦwww.jff.org.il; July. Put on by the Cinemateque (see p.204), and spread over ten days, showcasing feature films, documentaries and shorts from across the world. Some films are shown on big screens in the old train station compound (see p.198) for free, with others at Sultan's Pool (see p.200), the Smadar cinema (see p.204) and the Cinemateque itself. Tickets can be bought at the Cinemateque box office or on line at the festival's website.

International Puppet Festival Early Aug. Five-day festival held some years in the Palestinian National Theatre (p.203), but lately in the Train Theatre (see p.203), should appeal particularly to children in the two- to twelve-year-old range, with puppet shows from around the world. For further details, contact the Train Theatre on ℡02/561 8514.

Jewish Film Festival Ⓦwww.jff.org.il; During Hannukah, usually in Dec (see pp.212–213). Put on by the Cinemateque (see p.204), featuring Jewish movies from Israel and around the world. Many important film directors have been Jewish (Stanley Kubrick, Steven Spielberg, Billy Wilder, Sidney Lumet, John Schlesinger and David Cronenberg, to name but a few), but the films showcased here have a specifically Jewish theme. Tickets are available from the Cinemateque box office.

Beer and wine festivals

Israel Museum Wine Festival July. Held over three evenings in the Israel Museum, featuring unlimited tasting of Israeli wines plus workshops on winemaking and wine tasting. Tickets and information are available from the museum (see p.144).

Jerusalem Beer Festival Ⓦwww.jerusalembeer .com; late Aug. Held in the old train station compound, where you can sample some fifty different beers from around the world. Actually, most of the beers are available from shops in town anyway, and Israeli and Palestinian microbrewery beers seem to be notable by their absence, but why let that dissuade you from joining a good old booze-up? Admission is usually free until 7pm, an incentive to get there early.

Arts and crafts festival

International Arts and Crafts Fair Ⓦartfair .jerusalem.muni.il/eng; mid-Aug. Two week festval in the Sultan's Pool (see p.200), which has been going since 1976. There's an Israeli pavilion showcasing crafts from around Israel and an international pavilion for crafts from countries around the globe, plus concerts, international food stalls and craft demonstrations. It's an evening event, but closed on Fridays for Shabbat, and you have to pay to get in.

Shopping

J erusalem can be an expensive place to shop and there are plenty of tacky souvenir places aimed squarely at tourists. However, there are bargains to be had, and there are things here that you won't find at home such as olive oil soap from Nablus, contemporary Israeli art and high quality judaica (Jewish religious items). You'll also find Dead Sea cosmetic products a lot cheaper than at home and a good range of antiques and second-hand books. The city's markets are sights in themselves and a great place to try local delicacies. For opening hours see p.41.

Antiques

Some of Jerusalem's antique shops display incredible pieces that you might be surprised to see on sale rather than in a museum, and if you are prepared to fork out hundreds of dollars, you can pick up some amazing finds. Roman and Byzantine oil lamps and coins, on the other hand, which are really not all that rare, go for ridiculous prices. You should also be wary of "ancient pottery" sold on the streets of the Old City. Reputable establishments (including those listed here) will have a certificate from the Israeli ministry of antiquities, indicating that the pieces they sell are not only genuine, but legal to export as well. See also "Bric-a-brac" on p.219.

Aweidah Gallery 4 Via Dolorosa, Old City
ⓦ www.aweidah-gallery.com (see map, p.73).
Ancient artefacts that it's worth popping in just to see, though your eyes may pop out when you see the prices. At the lowest end of the scale, Byzantine oil lamps start at around $50. There are also Roman and Byzantine coins, Egyptian, Canaanite and Israelite sculptures, and works of art dating

well back into pre-Christian times.
Sat–Thurs 10am–5pm.
Baidun & Sons 20 Via Dolorosa, Old City
ⓦ www.baidun.com (see map, p.73). Just down the street from Aweidah, and very similar – high-class antiques dating from Canaanite through to early Islamic. Again, prices are high but so is quality. Daily 10am–6pm.

Art and sculpture

There are quite a lot of **galleries** in Jerusalem, and some very fine paintings and sculptures if your wallet will stretch to them. There's also a lot of overpriced tat aimed quite shamelessly at foreign Jews sentimental for Israel, but it's worth doing the rounds of the serious galleries if you do have an interest in modern art, particularly modern art with a Jewish theme. *Art & Judaica*, a free pamphlet found in the lobbies of upmarket West Jerusalem hotels, advertises a number of

▲ Shopping in the Central Souqs, Old City

art studios. The largest concentration of **art shops** is in West Jerusalem, along the northern end of King David Street and on Shlomzion HaMalka.

Al-Hoash (Palestinian Art Court) Zeituna Mansion, 7 Al-Zahra, East Jerusalem ⓦwww .alhoashgallery.org (see map, p.109). Conceived as the core of a Palestinian national gallery, Al-Hoash has built up quite a portfolio of modern Palestinian artists. A calendar of exhibitions can be found on the website.
Anadiel 20 Frères, Old City (see map, p.56). Attached to the Al-Ma'mal Foundation, whose office is round the corner, this is one of very few galleries exhibiting contemporary Palestinian art. Owing to restrictions on bringing in art from the West Bank the gallery is now open for occasional exhibitions only. For information on forthcoming events, check the Al-Ma'mal Foundation's website (ⓦwww.almamalfoundation.org), or call them on ☎02/628 3457.
Archie Granot 1 Agron, West Jerusalem ⓦwww .archiegranot.com (see map, p.127). Multi-layered papercuts by talented British-born artist Archie Garnot. Some pieces include refreshing new treatments of traditional Jewish themes, especially inscriptions and geometric designs as well as documents (such as a *ketuba* or Jewish wedding certificate), and *mezuzot* (see p.234). Granot has spawned a gaggle of imitators, but this is the original. Sun–Thurs 10.30am–7pm, Fri 10.30am–2.30pm.

Art Time 18 Shlomzion HaMalka, West Jerusalem ⓦwww.art-time.co.il (see map, p.127). Light, bright, modern art in a gallery dedicated to finding and promoting new Israeli talent. Prices are high, but it's usually worth popping in for a look round anyway. Sun–Thurs 10am–3pm & 4–7pm, Fri 10am–4pm.
Bet HaOmenim (Artists' House) 12 Shmuel HaNagid, West Jerusalem ⓦwww.art.org.il (see map, p.126). The place for up and coming Jerusalem artists to exhibit their work, with studios used by artists working in a range of forms and materials. Always worth having a look if you are interested in what's new on the local art scene. Sun–Thurs 10am–1pm & 4–7pm, Fri 10am–1pm, Sat 11am–2pm.
Eden Fine Arts 10 King David St, West Jerusalem ⓦwww.eden-gallery.com (see map, p.127). Bright, expensive, modern art, much of it pop-art-inspired. The artists are all Israeli, but their work sells well to the American market, and the gallery now has a branch in New York, as well as one in Tel Aviv (at the *Hilton Hotel*, no less). Sun–Thurs 9am–9pm, Fri 9am–4pm.
Lucien Krief Gallery King David Hotel annexe, 21 King David St, West Jerusalem ⓦwww .lucienkrief.co.il (see map, p.127). High-quality contemporary and fine art collected

by artist and sculptor Lucien Krief. Paintings are the mainstay, and there are some very impressive ones, but you'll also find sculpture and judaica. Sun–Thurs 10.30am–10.30pm, Fri 10.30am–2pm, Sat Shabbat–11pm.

Royal Collection 22 King David St, West Jerusalem, by Eldan Hotel (see map, p.127).

An upmarket shop with lots of expensive art and sculpture, but most notable for being the Jerusalem outlet of renowned Tel Aviv sculptor Frank Meisler (www.frank-meisler.com), and his distinctive statuettes of caricatured Jewish stereotypes, including Hassidic musicians, rabbis, fiddlers and matchmakers. Sun–Thurs 10am–8pm, Fri 10am–3pm.

Books

Jerusalem has an excellent selection of **bookshops**, especially if you are after titles on religion, Jewish history or Middle Eastern politics. Stalls all over town sell newspapers and magazines in English (see p.35 for a rundown of what's available) – the unnamed newsstand at the corner of Nablus Road with Sultan Suleiman, opposite the Damascus Gate (daily 5am–1.30pm), carries a comprehensive range. Steimatzky (see below) also has a good selection.

New

American Colony Bookshop American Colony Hotel, Nablus Rd, East Jerusalem (see map, p.109). Specializes in Middle Eastern literature, but also has a wide selection of books on Palestinian issues, and particularly on Jerusalem itself. Daily 9am–8pm.

Educational Bookshop 22 Salah al-Din, East Jerusalem (see map, p.109). A small but well-stocked East Jerusalem bookstore specializing in books on Jerusalem's history and politics, and the best source for publications by Palestinian and Human Rights groups. Also good for maps and newspapers. Daily 8am–7pm.

Franciscan Corner Omar Ibn al-Khattab Square at the corner of Greek Catholic Patriarchate Rd (inside Jaffa Gate; see map, p.56). Run by the Franciscans, this little place has some surprisingly interesting publications by them on religious issues, and also on archeology. Mon–Fri 8am–6pm, Sat 8am–5pm.

Gur Arieh 8 Yoel Salomon, West Jerusalem (see map, p.127). A small bookshop selling new and used titles in English, and open long after all the other bookstores have gone to bed. Sun–Thurs 10am–11pm, Fri 10am–Shabbat, Sat Shabbat–11pm.

Jordan Books 42 Jaffa Rd, West Jerusalem (see map, p.127). Most of the titles at this downtown bookstore are in Hebrew, but there's a small selection in English, and it includes some good reads, especially Israeli novels about Jerusalem. Sun–Thurs 10am–11pm, Fri 10am–Shabbat, Sat Shabbat–11pm.

Ludwig Meyer 4 Shlomzion HaMalka, West Jerusalem (see map, p.127). A small but well-chosen selection of books in English on Jerusalem, the Middle East, Jewish philosophy and other subjects. Sun, Mon, Wed & Thurs 9am–1pm & 3–6pm, Tues & Fri 9am–1pm.

SPNI (Society for the Protection of Nature in Israel) Sergei Building, 13 Heleni HaMalka St, West Jerusalem (see map, p.127). As well as survey and trekking maps (most of them unfortunately only available in Hebrew), SPNI's shop stocks books on wildlife (mostly in Hebrew) and some on Jerusalem. Sun–Thurs 9am–6pm, Fri 8.30am–1pm.

Steimatzky 39 Jaffa Rd, West Jerusalem www.steimatzky.co.il (see map, p.127). Jerusalem's main branch of Israel's biggest bookstore chain, with the largest collection of new books in English, and a good selection of British and American magazines too. It's also the best place to look for maps of the city. There are more downtown branches at 7 Ben Yehuda, 9 King George and in the Mamilla Shopping Centre. Sun–Thurs 8.30am–8pm, Fri 8.30am–2pm, Sat Shabbat–8pm.

Secondhand

In addition to the shops listed here, Gur Arieh (see above) has some secondhand titles, and *Tmol Shilshom* at 5 Yoel Salomon (see p.184) is a café that also sells a few secondhand books.

The Book Gallery 6 Shatz, West Jerusalem
W www.bookgallery.co.il (see map, p.126).
An Aladdin's cave of secondhand and
antiquarian books, concentrating on
subjects of Jewish interest. The website
allows you to browse online. Sun–Thurs
9am–7pm, Fri 9am–2pm.

The Bookshelf Southern end of Jewish Quarter
Rd, Jewish Quarter, Old City (see map, p.85).
A jumble of used books, but a good place
to look for (relatively) cheap secondhand
paperback fiction in English. Sun–Thurs
10am–6.30pm, Fri 10am–2.30pm.

Moffet 1 Alliance Israelite (off Jaffa Rd opposite
the junction with HaNeviim), West Jerusalem
(see map, p.126). A mixed bag of secondhand
titles, not a great selection, and not all that
cheap, but you might find something interesting. Sun–Thurs 9am–7pm, Fri 8am–3pm.

Sefer VaSefel Upstairs at 2 Ya'avetz, by 40 Jaffa
Rd, West Jerusalem (see map, p.127). Jerusa-
lem's best selection of secondhand books in
English, as well as new books, and even a
small café where you can sit and read them.
Sun–Thurs 9am–7pm, Fri 8am–2pm.

Stein 43 King George St, West Jerusalem
(see map, p.127). Hidden away inside an
apartment building, this doesn't look like a
shop from the outside, but its dense shelves
are well worth a browse if you like secondhand book stores. Most of the books are on
Jewish subjects, or by Jewish or Israeli
authors, but there are some unexpected
odds and ends in the mix, and they may
have books you can't find elsewhere.
Sun–Thurs 9am–7pm, Fri 9am–2pm.

Trionfo 9 Dorot Rishonim, West Jerusalem
W www.trionfo.novoya.com (see map, p.127).
Antiquarian books and old prints, mostly
nineteenth-century impressions of the holy
land and depictions (often hostile) of Jewish
subjects from non-Jewish books and
magazines. They also have old maps and
posters, and a few archeological antiquities
for good measure. Sun–Thurs 10am–7pm,
Fri 10am–2pm.

Bric-a-brac

Petit Musée 80 Mea Shearim, West Jerusalem
(see map, p.126). Old and new silver judaica,
jewellery and silverware, including some odd
and interesting pieces, plus beads, cameos,
tiles, brooches and pendants. Not a huge
selection, but well chosen. Sun–Thurs
noon–6pm.

Syriac Silver Exhibition 5 Christian Quarter Rd,
Old City (see map, p.56). An odd mix of stuff:
new and secondhand jewellery, silverware,
old keys and all sorts of religious medallions
– no real bargains, but worth a browse.
Mon–Sat 9.30am–6pm.

Ceramics

Arman Darian 12 Slomzion HaMalka, West
Jerusalem W www.darianart.com (see map,
p.127). Unlike the Armenian potters in the
Old City and East Jerusalem, Arman Darian
is a recent immigrant from Armenia, and his
designs are generally more modern. Aside
from bowls, cups and table sets, most are
on hand-painted tiles and large panels,
often with Jewish themes. Sun–Thurs
10.30am–7pm, Fri 10.30am–3pm.

Cadim 4 Yoel Saloman, West Jerusalem
W www.israelartguide.co.il/cadim (see map,
p.127). A potters' cooperative, selling
modern, very Israeli pieces in predominantly
naive rustic styles. As well as crockery,
the range includes utensils, judaica and
pieces for decoration only. Prices are high.
Sun–Thurs summer 9am–10pm, winter

9am–8pm, Fri 9am–2.30pm, Sat (summer
only) Shabbat–10pm.

Danny Azoulay 5 Yoel Saloman, West Jerusalem
(see map, p.127). Dainty, delicately painted
porcelain judaica (especially *mezuzot*), plus
a fair few small and more affordable trinkets
such as napkin rings, thimbles and bottle
stoppers. Sun–Thurs 10am–7.30pm, Fri
9.30am–2pm.

Jerusalem Pottery (Karkashian Brothers) 15
Via Dolorosa, Old City (see map, p.56).
Armenian-style ceramics, often featuring
Christian themes, some very jolly,
especially wall plaques, but also crockery
(bowls, plates, cups and so on). Some
of the pieces betray a Persian influence.
Prices are fixed and displayed. Mon–Sat
9am–5pm.

Palestinian Pottery 14 Nablus Rd, East Jerusalem ⓦ www.armenianceramics.com (see map, p.109). Despite the name (it's also known as Balian Armenian Ceramics), this place sells handmade and hand-painted Armenian ceramics. Its founders were brought over from Armenia by the British in 1917 to restore the tilework on the Dome of the Rock, and the family of one of them still runs the firm. They specialize in tile murals (large pictures made up of a number of tiles), but they also produce single tiles, plates and coffee cups. Mon–Sat 9am–4pm.

Sandrouni's Armenian Art Centre 84 Armenian Orthodox Patriarchate Rd, Old City ⓦ www .sandrouni.com (see map, p.48). Some of the most spectacular and original Armenian ceramics in the Old City: a wide selection of good-quality traditionally made crockery, vases and tiles. Beware of imitators such as the place at no. 87, which has no connection with this one. Mon–Sat 9am–7pm.

Clothes and accessories

Clothes are not especially cheap in Jerusalem but there are some good designer boutiques, and a couple of items of headgear may be of particular interest (see box opposite).

In addition to the shops listed here, Sunbula (see p.228) sells **textiles** and embroidered items, as does Rikma Yafa (see p.225), and you'll find quite a lot of fashion boutiques in the Kanyon Yerushalayim (see p.222). Jersusalem is also a good place to pick good-quality **outdoor gear**, much of it army surplus.

Traditional clothes

Abu Khalaf 98 Christian Quarter Rd, Old City (see map, p.56). A wide range of sumptuous fabrics from right across the Middle East and as far afield as India and Afghanistan. Best buys include cushion covers, which start at just 35NIS. Daily 10am–7pm.

Gold 14 Spitzer, Mea Shearim, West Jerusalem (see map, p.126). If you've ever wanted one of the old-fashioned black hats worn by the *Haredim*, this is the place to buy them. They're quite pricey at 500NIS a snip and the shop is obviously aimed at Orthodox Jews rather than casual shoppers but if you're serious about headwear, you might

▲ Embroidered kippot (Jewish skullcap)

Keffiyas and kippot

Among the traditional items of clothing you can buy, two items of headwear stand out, the Palestinian *keffiya*, and the Jewish *kippa*.

The **keffiya** headscarf, a symbol of Palestinian resistance, is ever popular if a little old hat (so to speak) back home nowadays, and it won't go down tremendously well if you wear it in West Jerusalem. The colour of a *keffiya* has a certain political significance: black and white tends to indicate support for Fatah, the party of Yasser Arafat and the Palestinian establishment, while red and white tends to indicate support for left-wing (and hardline) Palestinian parties such as the PFLP and the DFLP.

On the Israeli side of town, knitted **kippot** (Jewish skullcaps, also called *yarmulkas*) are available in all sorts of colours – Ethiopian Israelis often sport red, gold and green ones – but of more interest to non-Jewish or non-religious tourists might be the larger and even more colourful embroidered *kippot* worn by Yemeni Jews, which are more like a hat than a skullcap. As with *keffiyas*, there's a kind of code associated with *kippot*: black velvet ones tend to be used by ultra-orthodox *Haredim*, while little knitted ones, held on with hairclips, may indicate support for the religious right, though obviously that doesn't apply so much to ones with smileys or Premier League football club badges on them. Less observant Jews keep a cotton or nylon one at home for use on religious occasions only.

just want to pop in anyway. Sun–Thurs 5–9pm, Fri noon–1pm.

Jerusalem Yarmulka 21 Mea Shearim, West Jerusalem (see map, p.126). Not only does this shop stock more different types of dark velvet *kippot* than you could shake a *lulav* at, but they'll embroider a message of your choice upon them in Hebrew or English; and they'll do the same on a baseball cap or a *halla* cover. Sun–Thurs 10am–7.30pm, Fri 9.30am–2pm.

Kippa Man 5 Ben Yehuda, in the midrahov, West Jerusalem (see map, p.127). Attractive large, embroidered Yemeni-style *yarmulkas*, or little knitted ones with a variety of designs (including football club logos as well as smileys and cartoon characters), and a selection of non-religious hats including the traditional kibbutz hat, which provides excellent protection from the sun. Sun–Thurs 9am–7.30pm, Fri 9am–2pm.

Melia 14 Frères, near the New Gate, Christian Quarter, Old City (see map, p.56). A women's cooperative selling authentic Palestinian handicrafts, including shawls, dresses, purses, bags and cushions, all embroidered in traditional Palestinian designs. The co-op trains women in traditional embroidery techniques and provides an outlet for their products, allowing them to work from home. Mon–Sat 8.30am–7pm.

Modern fashion

Belt In 31 King George St, West Jerusalem (see map, p.127). Leather belts made on the premises of this small shop and tailored to your specifications. If you pop in and tell them what you want, they should have it ready for you in 24 hr or even less. Sun–Thurs 9.30am–7.30pm, Fri 9.30am–2.30pm.

Claire 1 HaSoreg, by Havilio Square at the bottom of Rivlin, West Jerusalem (see map, p.127). An eclectic range of Israeli designer ladies' wear, modern rather than classic, but quite chic nonetheless. Sun–Thurs 10am–8pm, Fri 10am–2pm.

Leprechaun in the alley by 17 Ben Yehuda, in the midrahov, West Jerusalem (see map, p.127). A tiny little boutique tucked away down a grubby little alley, selling snazzy clubwear, including jackets, hoodies, T-shirts and bags. Sun–Thurs 11am–8pm, Fri 11am–3.30pm.

Shesh 6 Hillel, West Jerusalem (see map, p.127). A cool and attractive selection of modern Israeli designer clothes for women, mostly dresses, but also jackets, tops, skirts and trousers. Sun–Thurs 9am–8.45pm, Fri 9am–3.45pm.

TishArt 6 Shatz, West Jerusalem (see map, p.126). Designer clubwear T-shirts, not a huge selection, but what they have is generally a little bit avant-garde with a hint

(15)

SHOPPING | Clothes and accessories

of psychedelia. Sun–Thurs 10am–8pm, Fri 10am–2pm.

Outdoor gear

Camping Lematayel 5 Yoel Salomon Ⓦ www .lametayel.com (see map, p.127). Downtown branch of an Israel-wide camping supplies chain; their main Jerusalem branch is at 20 Pier Kenig in Talpiyot. Sun–Thurs 10am–8pm, Fri 10am–2pm.

Defence 21 Ben Yehuda, West Jerusalem, in the midrahov (see map, p.127). Army surplus, store selling backpacks, army kit bags, cotton hats (great for sun protection) and even bullet-proof vests and gas masks Sun–Thurs 9.30am–8pm, Fri 9.30am–2pm.

Steve's Packs 11 Mordekhai Ben Hillel, in the Ben Yehuda St midrahov, West Jerusalem (see map, p.127). A small downtown outlet for a firm that makes good backpacks, bags and body-belts. They have a slightly larger branch in Malha's Yerushalayim Mall (see below). Sun–Thurs 10am–7pm, Fri 9am–3pm.

Department stores and malls

HaMashbir 20 King George St, West Jerusalem (see map, p.12). A bog-standard department store, but it does have a reasonable range of perfumes and clothes, and a food section that's as good as any supermarket. Sun–Thurs 9am–8pm, Fri 9am–3pm.

Kanyon Yerushalayim Malha. Way out in the southern suburb of Malha (see p.155), this is Jerusalem's biggest shopping mall, three floors full of chain stores and boutiques (260 shops in all), plus a cinema (see p.204), a gym, a synagogue, and a food court (including a branch of *Pinnati*; see p.185). Two shops on the top floor will be of particular interest if you're travelling with kids: Shilav, Israel's main children's wear chain and immediately next door, Yaldonim, which sells children's clothes and soft toys. The mall also has a branch of Steimatsky (see p.218), Tower Records (see p.227) and Steve's Packs (see above). Sun–Thurs 9.30am–10pm, Fri 9.30am–2.30pm.

Food and drink

Jerusalem is a great place to buy **food** with plenty of local specialities and fresh fruit and vegetables packed with flavour. As with most things the west side of town has higher prices but more variety than the east. In the Old City, Souq Khan al-Zeit, and the stalls along al-Wad Road are excellent for groceries. Mahane Yehuda market (see p.226) also has a great range and the food department at HaMashbir (see above) isn't bad either. The bottom end of HaNeviim (see p.226) is the best place to get fruit and veg. For farmhouse cheeses, check Avi Ben (see opposite) and HaLekhem shel Tomer (see p.184). For sweets, see opposite and p.192. Israeli **wine** and Palestinian Taybeh **beer** (see also p.195) are also well worth trying and make excellent gifts.

Supermarkets

Super 24 13 Shamai, West Jerusalem (see map, p.127). A small supermarket, mostly of note for being both central and open round the clock, as are the bakeries on HaNeviim (see p.186). Daily 24hr.

Supersol 1 Agron, West Jerusalem (see map, p.127). The main Jerusalem branch of a major Israeli supermarket chain, well stocked with fruit, drinks, confectionery and delicatessen at reasonably low prices. Sun–Wed 8am–midnight, Thurs 7am–1am, Fri 7am–2.30pm, Sat Shabbat–midnight.

Spices

Al Quds Grocery 71 Souq Khan al-Zeit, Old City, by Hashimi Hostel (see map, p.56). A good place to stock up on *sumak*, *za'atar*, toasted sesame, and other Palestinian spices that you won't get at home. Ground cardamom seed might be worth buying if you've developed a taste for it in Turkish

Local food specialities

Locally grown **fruit** includes Jaffa oranges of course, but also exotic fruits such as fresh dates, persimmons (sharon fruits), custard apples (sweetsops) and even starfruits (the best quality is to be found in the street markets rather than supermarkets). Lovers of **olives** will have a field day, with untold different varieties available, all of them packed with flavour. Olive oil is also good quality, usually cold pressed, but not as cheap as you might expect. Better value are the **nuts and seeds** known in Hebrew as *bitzukhim*, in Arabic as *bizr*; these include sunflower and pumpkin seeds, walnuts and almonds, and – a real treat – candied pecans. Other local sweet specialities (see also p.192) include **halva** (crushed sesame bar), of which the best – or at least the crunchiest – tend to be Israeli brands such as Elite. Supersol (see opposite) does its own brand, not quite as good as Elite, but available in half-kilo blocks, or packets of individually wrapped bitesize portions. Also available in packets, in East Jerusalem, are sheets of **dried apricot paste**, tangy, gummy, and a lot healthier than most sweet snacks; there are two brands, of which Kamardin Camel (with a camel on the front) is rather better than Al-Louard (with orange cellophane and a picture of apricots); note that many Old City stores will try to charge tourists as much as double the local rate (which is currently 7–10NIS). For a change from honey, **date syrup** (*silan*) is available at some food stores in Mahane Yehuda and the Old City, but only it seems in rather large 900g jars.

coffee, but other spices will probably be lower-priced at home. Note that what they call "saffron" is in fact safflower or turmeric. Daily 8am–8pm.

Sweets and nibbles

For eat-in sweet shops, see p.192.
Al-Amad 119 Souq Khan al-Zeit, on the corner of Aqabat al-Taqiya, Old City (see map, p.56). A small shop making a range of different halvas, cut straight from the block and sold by weight. Daily 9am–5.30pm.
Mo'aqet 15 Salah al-Din, East Jerusalem (see map, p.109). The best *bizr* business in East Jerusalem, where you'll find all sorts of salted seed and nut snacks, from pumpkin seeds to roasted chickpeas, not to mention candied pecans, and that's aside from the sweets, spices, herbs, oils, and sheets of dried apricot paste which they also sell. Daily 8.30am–8pm.

Wines, beers and spirits

Avi Ben 22 Rivlin, West Jerusalem (see map, p.127). The foodie's liquor store of choice, an upmarket wine merchant with a good selection of Israeli, Palestinian and imported wines, a small range of imported spirits, plus Taybeh and whatever Israeli microbrewery beers they can get hold of. Also in stock are a few excellent but pricey Israeli olive oils, and some interesting Israeli farmhouse cheeses. Sun, Mon, Wed & Thurs 9am–8pm, Tues 9am–10pm, Fri 9am–4pm.
Citadel Liquors 35 Latin Patriarchate St, by Jaffa Gate, Old City (see map, p.56). It doesn't look as posh as the wine shop across the street, but this is a much better place to find monastery-produced wines (such as Latrun and Cremisan), Taybeh beer, and Ramallah *araq*. Their selection of Israeli wines is small, but not too bad either. Mon–Sat 10am–8.30pm.
Mashka'ot Agripas 48 Agripas, Mahane Yehuda, West Jerusalem (see map, p.56). Well-stocked liquor store selling a wide selection of Israeli wines, and a good selection of Israeli and imported beers, including one or two from Israeli microbreweries. Sun–Thurs 8am–8pm, Fri 8am–4pm.

Jewellery

For costume jewellery try Nahalat Shiv'a market (see p.226). Also worth trying are Petit Musée (see p.219), Syriac Silver (see p.219) and Zion Zakaim (see p.225).

The Cardo Charm 23 The Cardo, Old City Ⓦ www.mysilverart.com (see map, p.85). Beautiful handmade silver filigree pieces, be it jewellery or judaica, made on the premises and available off the shelf or made to order in traditional Jewish style. The most popular pieces are bracelets, but they also have rings, *kuddush* cups and other items. Prices are extremely high (US$300–700 for a silver bracelet, for example), but each piece is handmade and unique. Sun–Thurs 10am–6pm, Fri 10am–2pm.

Danny Eliav 19 King David St, West Jerusalem (see map, p.127). Very chic and exclusive designer jewellery, mostly gold, with lots of diamonds, pearls, emeralds and rubies. The same family has been making jewels in Jerusalem since 1890. Sun–Thurs 10am–7pm, Fri 10am–3pm.

Judaica

For china and porcelain judaica see "Ceramics" p.219. Some of the stores listed under "Art and Sculpture" and "Souvenirs and Gifts" also sell pieces of judaica,

15

SHOPPING | Judaica

Judaica

The practice of the Jewish religion involves the use of a number of ritual objects or "judaica", whose design has become an art form in itself, somewhat akin to jewellery-making, and often made of silver. Many of these pieces are used in every observant Jewish home, but the most magnificent examples are those used in the synagogue. Items commonly sold include:

Havdala sets Shabbat is bid farewell on Saturday night with a ceremony called *havdala*, which requires another blessing over wine, the lighting and extinguishing of a plaited candle, and a spice shaker for the participants to smell.

Kippa (*kippot* in the plural, *yarmulka* in Yiddish) Jewish skullcap; actually rather a modern creation, *kippot* only became *de rigueur* in the nineteenth century, before which Jewish men quite commonly attended synagogue and prayed with their heads uncovered. There's a kind of code to *kippot*, much like that associated with *keffiyas* (see box, p.221).

Menorah The seven- or nine-branched candelabra that has become a symbol of the Jewish faith. The nine-branched version (correctly called a Hannukiya) is used to celebrate the festival of Hannukah, when one candle is lit on the first day, two on the second and so on up to eight – one candle, called the *shamas* (meaning the synagogue equivalent of a church beadle) is used to light the others.

Mezuza (plural *mezuzot*) A box containing passages from the Torah written out by hand on parchment and nailed to the doorposts of every Jewish home (see p.227).

Passover plate When the family celebrate the Passover feast, a dish is used which has places for all of the special foods used in the service, including green herbs, bitter herbs, a symbolic meat offering, a roasted egg, and an apple and nut confection called *haroset*.

Shabbat candlesticks The woman of the house lights two candles just before nightfall on Friday to welcome in the Sabbath, and the same is done on the eve of festivals. Every observant Jewish home has a pair of candlesticks for the purpose.

Talit A white prayer shawl, bordered with black or blue, donned by men when praying in the synagogue.

Tefilin Boxes containing biblical passages on parchment (see p.277).

Tzitzit Four-cornered, tasselled garment (see p.277).

Wine goblet Each Sabbath and festival is welcomed with a blessing over wine (*kiddush*), which is passed around the household for each member to take a sip, and Jewish households invariably keep one or more goblets especially for making *kiddush*.

as does The Cardo Charm (see opposite). For *kippot* try Jerusalem Yarmulka (see p.221) or Mr Kippa (see p.221). The more expensive places advertise in the free pamphlet *Art and Judaica*, available in the lobbies of upmarket hotels.

Min Hastami 15 Mea Shearim, West Jerusalem (see map, p.126). Everything you need to be a practising Jew, including *tefilin*, junior-size Torah scrolls, a large selection of *mezuzot*, *kippot* (black velvet ones of course – this is Mea Shearim), and even modern designer *tzitzit*. Sun–Thurs 10am–6pm, Fri 10am–1pm.
Rikma Yafa 41 Mea Shearim, West Jerusalem Ⓦ www.rikma-yafa.com **(see map, p.126).** Beautiful hand-embroidered wall hangings, bags (designed to carry Jewish religious items, but good for plenty of non-religious uses too) and cloths designed for covering loaves of Shabbat bread at the table. Pricey (they start at around 400NIS), but each one is an individual work of art. Sun–Thurs 10am–8pm, Fri 10am–1pm.
Tiferet 39 Mea Shearim, West Jerusalem (see map, p.126). Classic silver judaica

– candlesticks, *havdala* sets, *menorahs* and the like – some of it very fine indeed. Sun–Thurs 10am–8pm, Fri 10am–1pm.
Yaakov Greenvurcel 28 Hutzot Hayotzer (see p.226) and 27 Yoel Saloman, West Jerusalem Ⓦ www.greenvurcel.co.il **(see map, p.127).** Sleek, modern judaica pieces, particularly Hannukah *menorahs*, but also Shabbat candlesticks and *mezuzot*. Some of the designs are a bit silly, but others are very stylish. Sun–Thurs 10am–5pm, Fri 10am–2pm.
Zion Zakaim 8 King David St, West Jerusalem (see map, p.127). A fascinating mix of judaica and jewellery, some old some new, plus some amazing pieces of furniture of Syrian Jewish origin. Sun–Thurs 9.30am–9pm, Fri 9.30am–1pm.

Markets

The most exciting market area is in the Old City, but there are markets outside the walls too, in both East and West Jerusalem.

Arts and Crafts Lane (Hutzot HaYotzer) Hativat Yeushalayim, below Jaffa Gate Ⓦ www .jerusalem-art.org **(see map, p.127).** A "lane" of studios in restored buildings that from 1948

to 1967 stood derelict in the no-man's-land between Israel and the West Bank. Studios include painters, sculptors, potters, jewellers and silversmiths, and the standards are

▲ Service with a smile, Mahane Yehuda market

almost as high as the prices. Among the more interesting are Uri Ramot at no.14 (ⓦwww.uri-ramot.com), who makes jewellery and small sculptures from ancient Roman glass, and Yaakov Greenvurcel at no. 28, who makes modern judaica (see p.225). Sun–Thurs 10am–5pm, Fri 10am–2pm.

Fruit and vegetable market 6 HaNaviim, opposite Damascus Gate (see map, p.109). This is one of the few places in Jerusalem where you can buy proper fruit and veg, as opposed to the big, shiny supermarket-style products that you get almost everywhere else. Flavourwise it's the best in town.

Mahane Yehuda Between Jaffa Rd and Agrippas St, West Jerusalem (see map, p.126). West Jerusalem's liveliest food market (see p.129), specializing in fruit and veg, pastries, olives and *bitzuhim* (nuts and seeds), falafel and *meyarot yerushalmi* (mixed fried meats), at its busiest on Fridays before Shabbat comes in. Sat–Thurs roughly 9am–7pm, Fri 9am–3pm.

Nahalat Shiv'a market Havilio Square, at the southern end of Rivlin, West Jerusalem (see map, p.127). A small, hippyish night market (but a morning market on Fridays), selling clothes, costume jewellery, embroidered *kippot*, rolling papers and pipes. Sat–Thurs 5–11pm, Fri 9am–3.30pm, weather allowing.

Old City Souqs Much of the Old City is a market area, often referred to by Israelis as "the Arab market" or just "the *shuq*"; main market areas include Souq Khan al-Zeit (see p.75) and the Central Souqs (see p.76), which sell mainly workaday goods, especially food, and the Via Dolorosa (see p.58), David St (see p.50) and Christian Quarter Rd, which sell mainly souvenirs and religious items, often rather tacky ones. Best buys include Palestinian sweets (see p.192 & p.223), Arabic cassettes and CDs (see below), blue glassware from Hebron, and carved mother-of-pearl or olive wood from Bethlehem. Daily roughly 9am–5pm.

Music

Alam al-Fan in the Damascus Gate, Old City (see map, p.73). One of a number of small Old City shops selling CDs, cassettes and DVDs. The music is mainly by Egyptian and Lebanese popular artists, but there are some Palestinian performers too, mostly folk, but also modern sounds, including Palestinian hip-hop. Daily 9am–6pm.

Alam al-Naghm 1 Souq Khan al-Zeit, Muslim Quarter, Old City (see map, p.73). A similar selection to Alam al-Fan, just 50m away. Further down Souq Khan al-Zeit, there is also Al-Amad at no. 119, and Nejoum al-Fan at no.144, the second of which has a slightly larger selection than the others. Daily 9.30am–6.30pm.

GalPaz 5 Malkhei Israel, Mea Shearim ⓦwww .alpaz.co.il (see map, p.126). This is where the *Haredim* (ultra-Orthodox Jews) come for their sounds, and it has Jerusalem's best selection by far of Jewish liturgical music, *kletzmer* (Ashkenazi Jewish folk music, a living tradition with many excellent modern and fusion artists), Yiddish folk songs, and traditional Jewish music in general. Sun–Thurs 9am–10pm.

Hatav Hashmini 2000 12 Shamai, West Jerusalem (see map, p.127). A varied mixture of sounds, including rock, Israeli folk, hip-hop and electronic, especially good for Israeli trance. Sun–Thurs 8.30am–9pm, Fri 8.30am–3pm.

How to haggle

Bargaining is the name of the game in the Old City, particularly when shopping for souvenirs, but it's not common practice in shops, stores or restaurants, nor so much in Israeli markets. Bargaining should always be good-humoured – never haggle for something you don't really want, nor mention a price you're not prepared to pay. You should always have an upper limit in mind before you start, but contrary to popular belief, there's no magic figure to aim for, such as half or a third of the asking price: you could end up paying as little as a tenth or almost as much as the starting price. You can also bargain for accommodation in some hotels and hostels, especially in low season and depending on how business is at the time.

Music House 25 Keren HaYesod, West Jerusalem ☎02/624 1377 **(see map, p.127).** All sorts of music from classical symphonies to experimental electronic and Israeli psychedelic trance. The shop also doubles up as a record label, and even hosts gigs on occasion. Sun–Thurs 9am–7.30pm, Fri 9am–3pm.

Tower Records 1 Mordekhai ben Hillel, West Jerusalem (see map, p.127). The Jerusalem branch of the American chain, with a good selection of CDs by Israeli and foreign

artists, including *kletzmer*, Israeli folk music (generally rather corny – the local equivalent of country and western), "oriental" music (meaning Middle Eastern-style music, but in Hebrew rather than Arabic, again with many good modern and fusion artists), and of course Israel's favourite electronic sound, trance, in all its various sub-genres. Also DVDs of Israeli and American films, but check that the language, subtitles and DVD region are appropriate to your needs. Sun–Thurs 10am–9pm Fri 10am–2.30pm.

Photography and posters

For original old posters, try Trionfo (see p.219).

Agfa Photo Schwartz 11 Mordekhai ben Hillel, in the Ben Yehuda St midrahov, West Jerusalem (see map, p.127). The best address in town for camera equipment and repairs, film and film developing, camera battery charging, and prints from film or digital. Sun–Thurs 8.30am–7pm, Fri 8.30am–2pm.

🏃 **Elia Photo Service 14 Aqabat al-Khanqah, Christian Quarter, Old City** ⓦwww .eliaphoto.com **(see map, p.56).** A unique and fascinating collection of Jerusalem photographs dating back to the nineteenth century, collected (and often taken) by the owner's father, a refugee from Armenia. Prices are high but it's worth going in just for a look. The best of the photos taken by the owner's father are now available in a book called *Jerusalem Through My Father's*

Eyes by Kevork Kahvedjian. Mon–Sat 9am–6pm.

Israeli Poster Center 29 King George St, West Jerusalem ⓦwww.israeliposters.co.il **(see map, p.127).** All kinds of Israeli posters including reproductions of Mandate-era Zionist propaganda, photographs (notably of Israeli soldiers at the Wailing Wall in 1967), caricatures of Israeli life (army camp, Mahane Yehuda market, Ben Yehuda Street, the Wailing Wall), images of Jerusalem (doorways of, windows of, Old City gates, Old City streets), and lots more. Sun–Thurs 10am–7pm, Fri 10am–3pm.

Varouj Photos 36 Aqabat al-Khanqah, Christian Quarter, Old City (see map, p.56). A smaller selection of photos than Elia, not original, not as sharp or clearly dated, nor as well mounted as Elia's, but a lot cheaper. Mon–Sat 8am–7pm.

Soap and skincare

Square blocks of **olive oil soap** from Nablus (*sabon baladi Nablusi*) can be found in certain Old City grocery stores, especially on Souq Khan al-Zeit. There are two qualities, of which white (*abiad*) is for bathing, and green (*akhdar*) for washing clothes. Several different brands are sold in Nablus itself, but in Jerusalem, the only white Nablusi soap available is *Al-Jamaal* (camel brand), with a picture of a camel on the packet.

Ahava 17 Jaffa Rd, West Jerusalem (on the corner of King Solomon St; see map, p.127). A tiny little place, by West Jerusalem standards, but the best outlet for Ahava's Dead Sea mud and mineral cosmetics, including mudpacks, mud and mineral

soaps, and all sorts of other sulphurous, smelly concoctions to cleanse your skin and open your pores. There's another official outlet at 5 Ben Yehuda, but prices are higher there. Sun–Thurs 10.30am–3.30pm, Fri 10.30am–1.30pm.

Souvenirs and gifts

Of things sold as tourist **souvenirs**, those worth considering include olive wood and mother-of-pearl carvings from Bethlehem, and blue hand-blown glass from Hebron. Also popular are the multicoloured round Jerusalem candles that are lit up from within by their flame as they burn. Hookah pipes (*argila*) are better-made than in neighbouring Egypt, but also several times the price; fine as ornaments, they are a little impractical to smoke since they require special tobacco, and have to be lit with charcoal, although charcoal tablets that can be ignited with a lighter are now available.

Domari Centre Shuafat Rd, Shuafat, East Jerusalem (opposite Al-Hayat medical centre) ℡02/532 4510, ⓦdomarisociety.googlepages .com/gypsyboutique. This community centre belonging to Jerusalem's Domari Gypsy community (see p.83) has a small shop selling traditional Domari crafts. Items include jewellery and embroidered textiles, and a book of photos of Domari life. In principle the shop is open daily 10am–5pm, but it's best to call in advance to be sure someone is there.

Gans 8 Rivlin, West Jerusalem ⓦwww.gans.co.il (see map, p.127). Gift items made by ninety different artists, all but one Israeli. The goods on sale include candle holders, ceramics and other nick-nacks. Originally Gans was a Vienna quilt maker, forced to relocate to Palestine in 1939; the firm broadened its range to sell fabrics, then gift items, and finally gave up its original business altogether so that now it is only a gift shop. Sun–Thurs

10am–5pm, Fri 10am–2pm, but will have longer hours when construction of the light railway (see p.25) is completed.

Sunbula St Andrew's Church, 1 David Remez, West Jerusalem ⓦwww.sunbula.org (see map, p.127). Embroidery, carvings, olive oil and soap are among the products on sale at this non-profit outlet selling handicrafts made by various Palestinian community groups. Quality is high, and the money goes to the people who did the work. Mon–Sat 10am–5pm.

Yad Lakashish 14 Shivtei Israel, West Jerusalem ⓦwww.lifeline.org.il (see map, p.127). Non-profit organization providing an outlet for handicrafts by 300 elderly and disabled Jerusalem artisans. Products include jewellery, judaica, children's toys and clothes, greetings cards and other gift items. It is also possible to arrange a visit to their workshop. Sun–Thurs summer 9am–6pm, winter 9am–4pm, Fri 9am–1pm.

Excursions

Excursions

Bethlehem and around.. 231

Hebron... 241

Jericho... 243

The Dead Sea and Masada.. 248

Heading west: Abu Ghosh 252

Tel Aviv and Jaffa 253

16

Excursions

There's no shortage of interesting places within striking distance of Jerusalem, and a lot of them make excellent day-trips. On the West Bank side, the most obvious excursion is the nearby town of **Bethlehem**, the birthplace of Jesus. Beyond it, **Hebron** is equally fascinating, but something of a flashpoint between Jewish settlers and Palestinian residents – at present most Western governments are advising their nationals not to go there, but when it is safe to visit, it really is a must-see. Also strong on biblical resonance, **Jericho** is where, according to the Bible story, the walls came tumbling down, and you can check out remains of what some people believe to be those very walls. Nearby is the bizarre salt lake known as the **Dead Sea**, and not far away, the amazing rock fortress of **Masada**, last bastion of the Jewish rebellion against Rome, whose Zealot defenders committed suicide rather than surrender. Heading in the other direction, the bright lights of **Tel Aviv**, Israel's brash and exciting commercial capital, beckon enticingly. On the way, the restaurants of **Abu Ghosh** make it a good stop, or an easy excursion from town.

The **Separation Wall** (see box, p.234) cuts Jerusalem off to some extent from the West Bank, and it is illegal under Israeli law for Israeli citizens to travel to PA-controlled areas, but as a foreigner, you are largely immune to these restrictions, so long as you have a valid passport. Note however that checkpoints sometimes close on Jewish festivals such as Rosh HaShannah and Yom Kippur.

Bethlehem and around

Bethlehem, the birthplace of Christ, is just 10km south of Jerusalem. A major tourist attraction, despite now being cut off from its larger neighbour, it seems to struggle at times to cope with all the pilgrims who flock here, but it's a charming little town, with friendly people, and Christian monastics of various sects going about with a dignified air of quiet devotion. The religious institutions here represent every shade of Christianity, and Christmas is celebrated three times: on December 25 by the Catholics and other Western churches; on January 7 by the Greek Orthodox and other Eastern churches; and on January 19 by the Armenians (see p.213 for more on visiting at Christmas).

Getting there

Getting to Bethlehem from Jerusalem involves passing through the Separation Wall (see box, p.234). Bus #124, from East Jerusalem's central bus station on

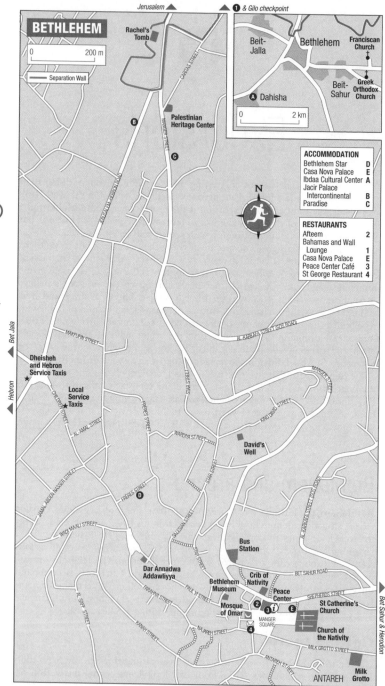

BETHLEHEM

0   200 m

Separation Wall

ACCOMMODATION

Bethlehem Star	D
Casa Nova Palace	E
Ibdaa Cultural Center	A
Jacir Palace Intercontinental	B
Paradise	C

RESTAURANTS

Afteem	2
Bahamas and Wall Lounge	1
Casa Nova Palace	E
Peace Center Café	3
St George Restaurant	4

Jerusalem

1 & Gilo checkpoint

Beit-Jalla

Bethlehem

Franciscan Church

Beit-Sahur

Greek Orthodox Church

A Dahisha

0   2 km

Rachel's Tomb

CARDS STREET

MANGER STREET

Palestinian Heritage Center

B

C

N

BEIT JALA-HEBRON ROAD

Bet Jala

Hebron

MAKRUFIN STREET

AL KARKAFA STREET (SOS ROAD)

Dheisheh and Hebron Service Taxis

Local Service Taxis

CHILDREN STREET

AL AMAL STREET

FRERES STREET

JUBUS STREET

WARDYA STREET

KING DAVID STREET

MANGER STREET

JAMAL ABDEN NASSER STREET

SHAR STREET

David's Well

FRERES STREET

D

WADI MAALI STREET

SALOMAN STREET

STAR STREET

Bus Station

AL KARKAFA STREET (SOS ROAD)

Dar Annadwa Addawliyya

FARAHYA STREET

PAUL VI STREET

Bethlehem Museum

Crib of Nativity

Peace Center

BET SAHUR ROAD

SHEPHERDS STREET

St Catherine's Church

Bet Sahur & Herodion

AL SAFF STREET

KANAH STREET

NAJAREH STREET

Mosque of Omar

2

3 i E

MANGER SQUARE

4

Church of the Nativity

ANTAREH STREET

MILK GROTTO STREET

Milk Grotto

ANTAREH

Sultan Suleiman Street, will drop you at the Gilo checkpoint where you will need to show your **passport**. Mornings (3–9am) and afternoons (2–5pm) at the checkpoint are very busy with Palestinians coming to and from Jerusalem, however foreign tourists may be fast-tracked if there's a queue. Note that Israeli law prohibits entry to Israeli citizens, including those with dual nationality.

On the other side of the checkpoint, taxi drivers await to take you into Bethlehem. Some offer deals for a tour of the sights, and you will obviously need to negotiate the price. There may be service taxis into town (*servees*; 2.50NIS a place), but private cab drivers will try to head you off before you reach these (follow Palestinians coming through if you want to take a *servees*). Otherwise, the fare in a "special" (privately hired cab) is 10–15NIS to Manger Square, and you will need to haggle for this (find out the current rate in advance if you can), but it's more interesting to walk, as this will take you past some of the wall's best graffiti. It's about a kilometre from the checkpoint to Manger Square, reached most directly by forking left up Star Street when Manger Street veers off to the right.

Arrival and information

Bethlehem centres around **Manger Square**, on whose east side is the Church of the Nativity, which is what most visitors have come to see. The **tourist office** is in the Peace Center, a large, modern building on the square's north side (Mon–Thurs & Sat 8am–3.15pm; ☎02/276 6677). It has maps of the town and can offer practical advice on visiting Bethlehem's sights and those in the surrounding area. The Cairo-Amman **Bank**, on the square's west side, has an ATM, and there are **moneychangers** on and just off the square, and along Manger Street. The **post office** (Sat–Thurs 8am–2pm), also on the west side of Manger Square, is an ideal place to send Christmas cards, but remember that the PA issues its own stamps, and Israeli ones are not valid here (as neither are PA-issued stamps in Jerusalem or Israel). The town **market** is just west of Manger Square, between Paul VI and Najareh streets. In late October, there's an **Olive Harvest Festival**, essentially consisting of stalls selling olives, oil and other agricultural products in Manger Square.

For **bus** #124 to Jerusalem, you'll have to go back through the checkpoint. For Bet Sahur, buses leave from the lowest level (B4) of the bus station on Manger Street, just north of Manger Square, as do **service taxis** to Ramallah. Service taxis for Hebron and Bet Jala hang out at the junction of Paul VI Street with the Hebron Road.

Accommodation

Most people take in Bethlehem as a day-trip from Jerusalem, but there are plenty of **hotels** here if you want to stay, and they're very good value compared to Jerusalem hotel prices, although they get well booked-up over Christmas, when prices rocket as a result.

Bethlehem Star Frères St ☎02/274 3249, ⓔhtstar@palnet.com. A friendly little place; the rooms are small but cosy, en suite, carpeted and clean, but the hotel's real draw is its panoramic top-floor restaurant, with 360-degree views of Bethlehem and the surrounding countryside, including Jerusalem. Breakfast included ❷

Casa Nova Palace Manger Square, next to St Catherine's Church ☎02/274 2798, ⓦwww .casanovapalace.com. Run by the Franciscans with a central location and well-kept rooms, but often full with pilgrim groups, so worth booking ahead. The main part was formerly the *Orient Palace Hotel*, and is still pretty smart for a pilgrims' guest house, with a/c,

The Separation Wall

The idea of building a wall around the West Bank to cut it off from Israel goes back to 1994, when Yitzhak Rabin had a similar barrier built around the Gaza Strip. From 2000, the Second Intifada gave the idea new impetus, and as suicide bombings and other attacks by West Bank Palestinians in Israel increased, pressure for some kind of barrier grew.

Construction of the wall – known variously as the Separation Barrier, the West Bank Wall, by Israelis as the

▲ The Separation Wall near Bethlehem

Security or Anti-Terrorist Fence, and by Palestinians as the Segregation or Apartheid Wall – began in earnest in 2002. The wall – more accurately a barrier, as it is not actually a wall as such along its entire length – does not exactly follow the Green Line (the West Bank's official border), but deviates into it, putting Jewish settlements, water supplies and a lot of farmland on the Israeli side, and often cutting off Palestinian villages from their fields (one school on the outskirts of Jerusalem even found itself cut off from its playground). Palestinians accuse the Israelis of using the Wall to annex territory – seven percent of the West Bank will be on the Israeli side – and it certainly makes life very difficult for residents of Bethlehem, who cannot now go shopping in Jerusalem, for example, unless they have a permit, which few can get. East Jerusalem, the West Bank's capital, will eventually be surrounded completely, cutting it off from its hinterland.

On the other hand, the wall seems to have done exactly what Israeli public opinion wanted it to: suicide bomb attacks have almost entirely ceased. In West Jerusalem, the difference is striking. Just a few years ago, there were searches at every store and guards at every bus stop, and the feeling of insecurity was palpable. Now all that has eased off. For a time, Jewish Israelis were even afraid to enter most of the Old City, but now they are returning. Ordinary common crime is also down. Israel's extreme right are upset because they see the wall as an abdication of the ideal of annexing the whole of Palestine, but most Israelis are very pleased, and you need only to look at the litany of Palestinian bomb attacks before the wall was built (see for example p.125, p.260 & p.264) to see why.

The wall has unhappy historical echoes. "Ich bin ein Berliner", somebody has painted prominently on it, and graffiti artists such as Banksy (see box, p.238) have had a field day adding subversive images. Most foreigners who see the wall find it unsettling but some would say it is only a more extreme version of the West's own increasingly draconian immigration barriers, and it is perhaps with this in mind that the international community has declined to put any real pressure on Israel to stop building it. For the Israeli government's commentary on the wall, see ⓦ www.securityfence.mod.gov.il or ⓦ securityfence.mfa.gov.il. For a United Nations report on it, see ⓦ www.ochaopt.org /documents/ocha_specialfocus_barriergates_2007_11.pdf.

satellite TV and 24hr room service, though you have to check out at 8am. If you want to take full-or half-board, the prices for meals are an excellent deal. Breakfast included ❸

Ibdaa Cultural Center Guesthouse
Jerusalem–Hebron Rd, Dheisheh ☎02/277 6444, ⓦ www.ibdaa194.org. Quite a different

place to stay, this is the guesthouse of a widely acclaimed cultural centre and community project in the refugee camp at Dheisheh, 2km southwest of Manger Square, whose inhabitants fled Israel in 1948 and, unable to return, ended up in this overcrowded camp, one of nineteen on the West Bank. A stay at the guesthouse is a chance to see what life in the camp is like (the Center runs tours) and to see the Center's work in practice (volunteers are also welcome). Beds are 60NIS per person in double rooms or dorms. ❶

Jacir Palace Intercontinental Jerusalem–Hebron Rd (Yasser Arafat St) ☎02/276 6777, Ⓔjacir@interconti.com. Bethlehem's top address, its lobby and main public areas occupying the 1910 mansion of the Jassirs, one of Bethlehem's leading families, with wonderful painted ceilings. The rooms themselves are in two modern wings, and there's a pool and a lovely covered patio café. Breakfast included ❻

Paradise Manger St, at the northern end of town ☎02/274 4542, Ⓦwww.paradise bethlehem.com. Originally constructed in 1980, this medium-sized hotel was once Bethlehem's best offering, and has hosted diplomats and other dignitaries. It was badly damaged during a 2001 incursion by Israeli troops, who burned it out before leaving, but it has now been rebuilt and, though not deluxe, it's comfortable enough, with modern conveniences, and certainly a bargain compared with equivalent hotels in Jerusalem; the rooms all have a/c, heating and satellite TV and there's room service 6am–midnight daily, as well as good deals for full- and half-board. Breakfast included ❸

The Church of the Nativity

Looking more like a fortress than a church, the **Church of the Nativity** (daily Feb–March & Sept–Oct 5.30am–6pm, April–Aug 5.30am–7pm, Nov–Jan 5.30am–5.30pm; free), entered from Manger Square, holds pride of place in the town. The tradition that this is the **site of Christ's birth** is based on the fact that, after the Second Jewish Revolt against the Romans in 135AD, the Roman Emperor **Hadrian** paganized all the main Jewish and Christian sites, building a shrine to Adonis over the Grotto of the Nativity, which is how Constantine's mother, **St Helena**, identified the site two hundred years later and ordered the building of a church to mark the spot, which opened in 339 AD. The church was completely rebuilt under the Byzantine Emperor **Justinian** in the sixth century, and was expanded in Crusader times by the addition of several chapels and monasteries. Inside, the different **rival churches** with rights over it – Greek Orthodox, Armenian Orthodox and Roman Catholic – maintain a precarious coexistence through an intricate schedule of worship and division of responsibilities (called the Status Quo, as in Jerusalem; see p.65). Disputes over control of the church have more than once erupted into violence, and were one of the causes of the **Crimean War** (see p.236).

As for resembling a fortress, the church actually ended up performing that function in a 2002 **siege** after Israeli forces invaded Bethlehem looking for Palestinian militants. After fierce fighting, over 200 Palestinians, including about forty militants, took refuge in the church. After a 39-day standoff, the siege finally ended when Western diplomats and Christian clergy negotiated a deal in which the militants were allowed to leave Palestine for exile abroad.

The entrance and main hall

The **entrance** was once grand (you can still see the shape of the original arch) but it was lowered by the Crusaders and again by the Ottomans to prevent mounted horsemen entering the church. As a result, most people have to stoop to enter, and the entrance is therefore known as the **Door of Humility**. The vestibule behind the entrance leads into the **main hall**, divided into a central nave and two aisles by golden-coloured columns of local stone, many of them decorated with pictures of saints; **mosaics** on the side walls and under the current floor (revealed under lifted-up wooden panels in the middle of the vestibule), belong to Constantine's original fourth-century construction. The ceiling

CHURCH OF THE NATIVITY

0   20 m

contains oak donated by England's King Edward IV for roof repairs in 1480.

The octagonal marble **font**, with its clover-shaped basin, now hidden away behind the pillars on the church's south side, was part of Justinian's sixth-century church, and originally stood next to the high altar. It was moved in the Middle Ages so that prospective converts might enter the church and be baptized here in the southern aisle before approaching the altar to take communion.

The Grotto of the Nativity

Stairs on the right of the altar lead down into the **Grotto of the Nativity** (closed Sunday mornings), the site of Jesus's birth, where a fourteen-pointed silver star marks the exact spot. The star was installed by the Catholics in 1717 and removed by the Greeks in 1847, but France, against Russian opposition, pressured the Ottoman authorities into letting the Catholics replace it in 1853. Greek Orthodox monks tried to stop them, and in the ensuing fracas, a number were killed. Russia responded by attacking Turkey, thus starting the **Crimean War**. The star bears the inscription, *Hic de Virgine Maria Jesus Christus natus est* – Here Jesus Christ was born to the Virgin Mary. Of the fifteen lamps burning around the recess, six belong to the Greeks, five to the Armenians and four to the Roman Catholics.

Down three steps opposite the **Altar of the Nativity**, is the **Chapel of the Manger** where Christ was laid. Behind the marble manger (on the right) is a painting of the nativity scene showing him in an altogether different type of manger. Facing it, the **Altar of the Adoration of the Magi** marks the spot where the Wise Men (the Bible doesn't actually say that there were three of them) are believed to have adored the infant Jesus (Matthew 2:11).

The Church of Saint Catherine

A small door in the north wall of the basilica leads to the adjoining Roman Catholic **Church of Saint Catherine** (daily March–April & Sept–Oct 4am–6pm, May–Aug 4am–7pm, Nov–Feb 4am–5.30pm; free), where Christ appeared to St Catherine of Alexandria. Built in 1881, it incorporates remains of Crusader buildings discovered during construction. It is from here the **Christmas Eve Midnight Mass** is televised and beamed worldwide. Special buses run from Jerusalem (check with the Christian Information Centre inside Jerusalem's Jaffa Gate for details and tickets); the square is packed out and it gets pretty cold standing around, so take warm clothes. The daily **procession of Franciscan Fathers** from the church to the basilica (at noon, or 1pm during daylight saving) is also well worth watching.

From the church, medieval stairs lead down into a complex of **caves and tombs** (often closed for no apparent reason) linked to the Grotto of the Nativity, although there's no public access from one to the other. The main altar in this impressive subterranean complex is devoted to **Saint Joseph**, the earthly father of Christ, and is said to be where he had the dream in which an angel warned him to flee to Egypt to safeguard the baby Jesus from Herod's anger. Next to it, the **Chapel of the Innocents** commemorates the children who were slaughtered by Herod after the Holy Family had left (Matthew 3:16). Also off St Joseph's chapel is the **Tomb of Saint Jerome**, a Dalmatian priest who translated the Old Testament from Hebrew to Latin. The cell where St Jerome executed his mammoth task is now a chapel, and his statues stands in the middle of the church's cloistered courtyard.

The Milk Grotto

Five minutes' walk southeast of Manger Square you'll find the **Milk Grotto** (daily 8–11.45am & 2–5pm; free). Here, the Holy Family hid from the Slaughter of the Innocents or during the flight to Egypt, and Mary let a drop of her milk fall while nursing Jesus, so turning the rock from red to chalky white. Ever since, Christians and Muslims have believed that the rock increases a nursing mother's milk and fertility; pilgrims used to chip off pieces of the rock to take home, and women hoping to conceive still come to pray here. The cave-like interior, a cool and serene escape from the summer heat outside, is also wheelchair accessible (ring the bell for access).

Milk Grotto Street, which leads to the church, is lined with shops selling the olive wood and mother-of-pearl carvings for which Bethlehem is famous. A few of them are workshops where you can see the articles being made.

The Bethlehem Museum

Right off Paul VI Street, just 100m from Manger Square, the **Bethlehem Museum** (Mon–Wed, Fri & Sat 8am–noon & 2–5pm, Thurs 8am–noon; 8NIS), was established in 1971 by the Arab Women's Union. Household articles are displayed in a traditional house, with a reconstructed *diwan* (living room) complete with carpets and charcoal stove, and a kitchen with pottery, wood, brass and straw utensils. The stable is subterranean, as was usual in Bethlehem houses, which is why the Grotto of the Nativity is underground. There's also embroidered clothing and traditional jewellery, and lots of fascinating old photos of the town. Visitors are given a guided tour in English (or Arabic, if you prefer), and a small showroom upstairs sells hand-embroidered items made by local women in traditional style.

The Crib of Nativity

If you're tired of worthy, educational museums, or have kids in tow who are getting bored, the **Crib of Nativity** (daily 9am–9pm; $15; ☎02/276 0876, Ⓦwww.cribofnativity.com) – slogan: "every day is Christmas in Bethlehem" – is a glorious piece of over-the-top kitsch featuring a fifteen-minute puppet show, and a collection of 31 mini dioramas showing biblical scenes. The show is only put on when there is a large enough audience (over fifty at least), and can be in any of seven languages, so call ahead to see when there will be one in English.

King David's Well

North of Manger Square in King David Street, though also accessible from Manger St up a steep flight of stairs, **King David's Well** (daily 7am–noon & 3–7pm; free) is the only monument in Bethlehem – "royal David's city" – to

English street artist Banksy (Ⓦwww.banksy.co.uk) has made a huge name for himself by producing satirical and often quite subversive street murals, mostly created using stencils. Attitudes to his work vary – some is simply painted over as graffiti or "vandalism", while other pieces have sold for hundreds of thousands of pounds. In 2005 and 2007, he left several images on the Separation Wall around Bethlehem. One of them, featuring a soldier questioning a donkey, raised the ire of local people who felt the donkey was supposed to be them, and has since been painted over; another gives a vestige of hope to the local population "Nothing lasts forever" it says. You'll see a couple of Banksy murals on the wall itself on the way into town, and another near the Palestinian Heritage Center (see below). Two of his best works are the mural of a soldier being frisked by a little girl opposite the *Jacir Palace Hotel*, and one of a rioter throwing a bouquet in Bet Sahur (see opposite).

Taxi drivers have already cottoned on that the murals are tourist sights, and those waiting at the checkpoint will offer to take you round all of them for an inflated price, but most Bethlehemites – including the tourist office – have never heard of Banksy, so the chances of them preserving his work are unfortunately slim.

the famous king who was crowned here (I Samuel 16:1–13), and is assumed to have been born here to a local family (Ruth 4:11 & 17; I Samuel 16:1). It marks the site where his soldiers broke through Philistine lines in order to fetch him drinking water from a well after he cried, "O that one would give me drink of the water of the well of Bethlehem which is by the gate!" (II Samuel 23:15). David was so awed by this that he offered the hard-gotten water as a libation to God. The "well" is in fact three large cisterns.

Cultural Centres

At the junction of Manger Street with Caritas Street, the **Palestinian Heritage Center** (Mon–Sat 11am–6pm; free; ☎02/274 2381, Ⓦwww.phc.ps) is something between a museum and a gift shop, with the wares at the front and the exhibits – costumes, items from traditional life, and a reconstructed Bedouin tent – at the back. Next to it is one of Banksy's (see above) best-preserved local murals, featuring a dove in a bullet-proof vest.

The large, modern building on the north side of Manger Square is the **Bethlehem Peace Center** (Mon–Sat 11am–6pm; free; ☎02/276 6677, Ⓦwww.peacecenter.org). Aside from housing the tourist office, it hosts exhibitions and has an archeological museum under construction. It also hosts concerts and other cultural events, and its café (see opposite) is an excellent spot to take a breather in between sightseeing. In 2002, it served as the venue for negotiations to end the Church of the Nativity siege (see p.235).

The Lutheran-run **Dar Annadwa Addawliyya** (aka the International Center) at 109 Paul VI St (daily 8am–9pm; free; ☎02/277 0047, Ⓦwww.annadwa.org) also hosts" cultural events, as well as a café-restaurant and guesthouse, and is always worth popping into if you want to know what events are on in town over the next few days.

Eating and drinking

Afteem 40 Manger Square (just off the square, in fact, on the north side). Gleamingly spotless falafel and hummus joint with stone walls and some of the best falafel in Palestine, always freshly cooked, piping hot, and served with a side dish of salad and pitta (or stuffed into the pitta, if you prefer, along with the salad). Daily 8am–10pm. Serves beer. Cheap.

Bahamas and Wall Lounge Caritas St, opposite the Wall. A fish restaurant and adjoining lounge bar, up near the checkpoint and amongst the Wall's most striking graffiti. The restaurant serves shrimp, squid, mullet and bream, each with appropriate sauces, and at prices that don't even come near to what you'd pay for the same food in Jerusalem. The lounge bar serves salads, sandwiches, coffee, cocktails (alcoholic or not), beer or fruit juice, and hookah pipes with a choice of tobaccos. Daily 11am–11pm. Licensed. Moderate.

Casa Nova Palace Manger Square, opposite St Catherine's Church. Indoor or garden eating at the Franciscan guesthouse is open to non-guests, and far from the ascetic food you might expect from monks or pilgrims, it features dishes such as salmon steak in

orange sauce, or mussels with garlic and cheese, all washed down with wine, beer or drinks of your choice. Daily noon–3pm & 6–9.30pm. Licensed. Moderate.

Peace Center Café Peace Center, Manger Square. A light, airy, modern space, carefully designed, with minimalist decor and blue Hebron glass tableware. It looks like a place that would charge silly prices, but actually the salads, sandwiches, tea and coffee are all at ordinary café rates, and the *sahlab* (see p.183), *zhourat* (an invigorating mixed herbal infusion), and juices – including tamarind, licorice and carob – go for similar amounts. Mon–Sat 10am–8pm.

St George Restaurant Manger Square, southwest corner. A fine selection of grilled meat, fish and poultry in comfortable surroundings, with a well-stocked bar. Specialities include *shashlik* or lamb chops, or you can order a complete fish or meat dinner (65NIS). Daily 9am–5pm. Licensed. Moderate.

Bet Sahur and the Shepherds' Field

In the village of **Bet Sahur**, which adjoins Bethlehem to the east, the **Shepherds' Field** (2km from Bethlehem; take a left at the far end of the village), has been identified since at least the seventh century as the place where the Angel of the Lord visited the shepherds to tell them of Christ's imminent birth (Luke 2:12). Several rival sites claim to mark the exact spot, with the weight of tradition centring on two: Der al-Ra'wat (Mon–Sat 8am–3.30pm; free), operated by the Greek Orthodox Church, and Siar al-Ghanem (Mon–Sat 8am–5.30pm, Sun 8–11.30am & 2–5.30pm; free), which belongs to the Roman Catholics.

The 1989 **Greek Orthodox Church** was erected near the traditional site of the Grotto of the Shepherds. Marking the scene of the apparition, the subterranean chapel here dates from the fourth century and contains frescoes and traces of a Byzantine mosaic pavement. The modern, tent-shaped 1954 **Franciscan Church of the Angels**, designed by Antonio Barluzzi (see p.121), is built over a cave where the shepherds are supposed to have lived. On the altar, fifteen panels show scenes from the annunciation to the arrival of the Holy Family in Egypt, though neither the people nor the sheep look very Middle Eastern.

The **Field of Ruth**, immediately north of the Greek Orthodox Church, is where Boaz saw and fell in love with the biblical heroine gleaning in his field (Ruth 2:2–12). The couple married and became great-grandparents of David and ancestors of all Judah's kings. On the main road, just east of the turn-off to the Greek Orthodox Church, Graffiti artist Banksy (see opposite) has painted a **mural** on the side of a garage, depicting a rioter throwing a bouquet of flowers.

Most people walk to Bet Sahur from Bethlehem, though you can take a bus from the bottom level (B4) of the bus station on Manger Road.

Herodion

Eleven kilometres southeast of Bethlehem, on the summit of an extraordinary flat-topped, cone-shaped hill, lie the remains of **Herodion** (Sat–Thurs

8am–5pm, Fri 8am–4pm; 23NIS) perhaps the most outstanding of all Herod's architectural achievements. A strategic fortress built around 30 AD as a secure refuge for the king from his enemies, it is also thought to be his burial site, though his tomb remains undiscovered. Now that the fortified walls are long gone, the structures remaining are sunk below the rim of the mound, making it look rather like a volcano with a crater. In the First Revolt (66–70 AD), it was one of the last strongholds to fall to the Romans and, as at Masada (see p.250), its defenders took their lives before the Romans could. The remains of three Byzantine chapels with rich decorative mosaic floors show that the site continued to be inhabited during the fifth and sixth centuries.

The mound on which the fortress stands is artificial, originally reached from the north via "200 steps of the whitest marble", traces of which can still be seen. Today the way up is a winding path from the car park southwest of the mound, a fifteen-minute climb. The fortress and palaces that once stood here are long gone, but excavations have uncovered a circular enclosing wall with four round watchtowers which once guarded Herod's living quarters, and the remains of a bathhouse, hot baths, arcades, synagogue, and an immense banqueting hall. The view is also magnificent. At the base of the mound, excavations have revealed a pool built by Herod, surrounded by a reconstructed parade of colonnades, a bathhouse and a trio of Byzantine churches.

Herodion cannot be reached from Bethlehem by public transport: Egged bus #166 from Jerusalem to the nearby Jewish settlement of Teqoa passes the access road for Herodion, but services are sparse (8 daily). A taxi from Bethlehem should cost around 100NIS for a round trip including a reasonable waiting time; if you're really fit (and so long as the political situation doesn't make it dangerous), you could even walk from Bethlehem, but be sure to take sun protection and water.

Rachel's Tomb

Next to Route 60, 3km north of Manger Square, **Rachel's Tomb** (Sun–Thurs 1.30am–10.30pm, Fri 1.30am–Shabbat; free; ☎ 1800/580 0863, Ⓦ www.keverrachel.com) is the burial place of the biblical matriarch, Jacob's favourite wife. There has been a succession of synagogues on the site: the building which houses the tomb today was originally erected by the Ottoman Turks in the 1620s, although the dome over it was commissioned by Sir Moses Montefiore (see p.137) in 1860. The all-new structure surrounding it was built in 1997.

Barricaded off from both Bethlehem and Jerusalem by the Separation Wall, the tomb can be visited **only on bus #163**, which is armoured and runs three times daily from Egged Central Bus Station and the junction of Shivtei Israel with Mea Shearim, plus once at 1am for men only. The bus runs to meet Jewish prayer times and is not intended for non-religious or non-Jewish sightseers.

Inside the tomb, there's little to see in any case: just a velvet-draped tomb in a synagogue. Jewish women come to pray here for children or to ask "Mother Rachel" to intercede with God on their behalf – a highly dubious practice theologically, given that the concept of saintly intercession is frowned upon by Judaism.

Kfar Etzion

Some 13km out of Bethlehem, the road passes the Jewish West Bank settlement area of Gush Etzion, now numbering seventeen settlements. The oldest settlement,

Kfar Etzion, was established in 1935, abandoned the following year in the face of Arab hostility during the Palestinian revolt, and then revived in 1943, along with three others, to form a "bloc" (*gush*) of four. It was the last of the four settlements to fall to Arab Legion troops (supported by local "irregular" volunteers) in 1948, having been under siege for five months – most of those who surrendered were machine-gunned down by the irregulars in revenge for (or in imitation of) the previous month's massacre at Deir Yassin (see p.153). Re-established in 1967, it became the first Jewish settlement to be built on the West Bank after its occupation, and some of its members are children of original pre-1948 settlers.

The settlement's history is recounted in a **museum** and a **sound and light show** (20NIS; call ☎02/993 5160 to arrange visit), recounting the events of 1948 from the settlers' point of view. Should you wish to **stay**, there is a YHA Youth Hostel (☎02/993 5162; Sun–Thurs with breakfast ❸, Fri & Sat full-board only ❷). You will not be able to travel directly between Kfar Etzion and Bethlehem, but the settlement can be reached from Jerusalem's Egged Central Bus Station on buses #161 and #164 (approximately hourly; 20min).

Hebron

Seventeen kilometres south of Bethlehem, **Hebron** (Al-Khalil in Arabic, Hevron in Hebrew) is holy to Muslims, Jews and Christians alike as the burial place of most of the biblical patriarchs and matriarchs, whose tombs, and Hebron's old city, are among the region's most fascinating sights. Sadly, Hebron is also known for its history of **violence**, particularly two terrible massacres: in 1929, when an anti-Semitic Arab mob attacked the town's ancient Jewish community, killed 67 of them and drove the rest out of town; and in 1994, when a Jewish settler shot dead 29 Muslim worshippers in the Tomb of the Patriarchs. Today Hebron is the most contentious West Bank town, with a militant Palestinian community and a group of the most extreme Jewish settlers right in the town centre under Israeli military protection.

Visiting Hebron

The barbed wire and armed troops are proof enough of the **tension** in Hebron, and you should always check the latest situation before making a visit. Currently, most Western governments are advising their nationals against visiting Hebron. There is nothing to stop you getting into a service taxi from Bethlehem (or the settlers' armoured bus #160 from Jerusalem's Egged Central Bus Station to the Jewish side of town), and you could probably get away with seeing the Haram and wandering round the city without any problem. But we wouldn't advise this and you should really join an **organized tour** (see below) if you are determined to go. Bear in mind that if your government advises you not to come here and you disregard that advice, you will not be covered by travel insurance. For current information about the situation in Hebron, check the website of the UN's Temporary International Presence in Hebron (TIPH) at Ⓦ www.tiph.org.

Hebron tour operators

Alternative Tours ☎052/286 4205, Ⓦ www .alternativetours.ps. A political tour, visiting the Tomb of the Patriarchs and the old city; excelllent insight into the current situation but very much a Palestinian take (no mention of the 1929 massacre, for example). Leaves from the *Jerusalem Hotel* (see p.169); 140NIS.

Breaking the Silence Etours2hebron@gmail
.com, ⓦ www.shovrimshtika.org. Former Israeli
soldiers opposed to current policy offer a
liberal take on the situation in Hebron,
including a visit to a Palestinian family. Tours
are held irregularly (see the website for
dates) and leave from Binyanei HaUma,
near the Egged Central Bus Station
(see p.201); 40NIS.
Jewish Community of Hebron ☎052/431 7055,
ⓦ www.hebron.com. Settler-run tour in an

armoured bus, also visiting Rachel's Tomb
(see p.240), as well as settler-held buildings
and Jewish sites in Hebron. Profits fund
settler activities. Leaves from the *Sheraton
Hotel* (see p.175); US$40.
Tours in English ☎02/277 2151, ⓦ www.atg.ps.
Palestinian political tour of Bethlehem and
Hebron every Thursday. Leaves from *Olive
Tree Hotel* (see p.174); 230NIS.

The Haram al-Khalil (Tomb of the Patriarchs)

The main sight in Hebron is the **Haram al-Khalil** or **Tomb of the Patriarchs**
(Sun–Thurs 8am–4pm, except during prayer times), just east of the souq. It is
believed to stand above the Cave of Makhpela, bought by Abraham to bury his
wife Sarah (Genesis 23), it is also Abraham's burial place and that of his son Isaac
and grandson Jacob, their wives Rebecca and Leah, as well as Adam and Eve and,
according to some, Joseph. The Haram is for Jews second in holiness only to the
Wailing Wall, and for Muslims second in Palestine only to the Dome of the Rock.
Monolithic and austere, it dominates the city and, even without the heavily armed
Israeli soldiers enforcing security, looks more like a fortress than a tomb.

The walls and the pavement of the Haram are unmistakably Herodian, built
with huge, perfectly hewn stone blocks; the later Crusader and Mamluk additions
further add to its impressiveness. Until the 1994 massacre, Jews and Muslims
shared the space, with prayers at different times, but it has now been divided. If
you want to go in, you will have to show your passport and state a religion. Jews
are allowed only to enter the Jewish side, except on Jewish holidays, when they
can enter the Muslim side too, and for six hours on the Muslim Maulid festival,
when they are excluded. Muslims may enter only the Muslim side, except on
Jewish holidays, when they are excluded, and for six hours on the Prophet's
birthday (Maulid), when they can enter the Jewish side. Christians and others may
enter both sides, but don't say you are an atheist or have no religion as this will
not be accepted. Anybody entering either side must present ID (a passport is fine),
and pass through a metal detector. Cameras are allowed, but photography is
banned on the Jewish side during Shabbat and festivals.

Entrance to the **Muslim section** is up the Mamluk stairway on the northwestern wall, which leads around the building to the Al-Is'haqiyya or the Great
Mosque. Inside, the decor is notably Mamluk, with loads of *ablaq* (stone in
alternating colours) and a beautiful painted ceiling. Central to the mosque are
the cenotaphs of Isaac and Rebecca, which in their present form date from
1332 and are supposed to lie directly above the tombs in the Cave of Makhpela.
The platform at the back of the prayer hall, opposite the *mihrab* (the niche
indicating the direction of Mecca), was in 1994 where American settler Baruch

Hebron's blue glass

Politics and religion aside, Hebron is famous for its ceramics and its **blue glass**, and
you'll see ornaments made from Hebron blue glass all over the West Bank. They are
also on sale in Bethlehem and Jerusalem, but if you want to track them down to
source, and see them being made, head for Midan al-Quds, a road junction at the
very northern end of town, where you'll find three glass factories nearby.

Goldstein, wearing Israeli army uniform and carrying an M-16 rifle, shot dead 29 worshippers before being overpowered and beaten to death. More people died in the aftermath, most of them shot by panicking Israeli troops; although numbers vary it's thought that a further ten people were killed, perhaps more. Shockingly, Goldstein is still regarded as a hero by some people on Israel's far right, particularly among the settlers.

Entering the **Jewish section**, round the other side of the complex, you come into the calm interior of what was until 1994 part of the mosque, but is now hived off as a synagogue. To the right as you enter are the rooms containing the ninth-century cenotaphs of Abraham and Sarah, opposite which are those of Jacob and Leah, dating from the fourteenth century.

The Old City

Around the Haram, Hebron's once thriving **old city** is all but a ghost town, strewn with barbed wire and barriers, and patrolled by uneasy Israeli troops. The town is divided into two zones: H1 (under PA control) and H2 (under Israeli control), the latter a patchwork of small areas occupied by settlers, which takes up a fifth of the town in total, but cuts right across the old city. There are only 400 settlers, defended by 350 Israeli soldiers. They are not ordinary Israelis, but militants of mainly American origin. Liberal Israelis detest them, but they have a certain level of support among right-wingers, who see them as reclaiming the city for Judaism and avenging the 1929 massacre.

Needless to say, the Palestinians and the settlers hate each other, the conscript soldiers hate being there, and the tension is almost palpable. Visit, if you must, on a guided tour; don't under any circumstances wander around on your own.

Jericho

Claiming to be the oldest city on earth, **Jericho**, the "City of Palms" (Ariha in Arabic), lies in the south Jordan Valley, 40km east of Jerusalem. At 250m below sea level, it's the lowest town in the world, which makes it extremely hot in summer, and warm in winter. This has long made it a favourite winter resort, but it also means that Jericho can be roasting hot, especially in summer, when temperatures frequently top 45°C. Even in November and February, the heat can take it out of you, especially as Jericho's tourist sights are quite a long way apart. Always therefore take sun protection and water – the dangers of dehydration, sunstroke and heatstroke (see p.38) are very real here.

History

The oldest of some twenty successive settlements excavated here dates back to around 8000 BC, but the event for which the city is best known occurred around 1200 BC, when **Joshua** and the invading Israelites crossed the Jordan River, sounded their trumpets, and as the song tells it "the walls came tumbling down", or, as the more prosaic biblical version has it (Joshua 6:20), "the wall fell down flat". The city was rebuilt in the ninth century BC (I Kings 16:34) and, later, Elisha purified the water of the spring after being lobbied by local residents who complained that it made the land barren (II Kings 2:19–22). **Jesus** visited the town several times; he restored the sight of a blind beggar

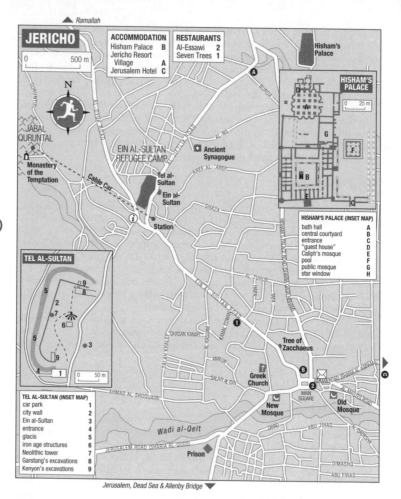

JERICHO

ACCOMMODATION		RESTAURANTS	
Hisham Palace	B	Al-Essawi	2
Jericho Resort Village	A	Seven Trees	1
Jerusalem Hotel	C		

▲ Ramallah

0   500 m

N

JABAL QURUNTAL

Monastery of the Temptation

Cable Car

EIN AL-SULTAN REFUGEE CAMP

Ancient Synagogue

Tel al-Sultan

Ein al-Sultan

Station

Hisham's Palace

HISHAM'S PALACE

0   25 m

HISHAM'S PALACE (INSET MAP)	
bath hall	A
central courtyard	B
entrance	C
"guest house"	D
Caliph's mosque	E
pool	F
public mosque	G
star window	H

TEL AL-SULTAN

0   50 m

TEL AL-SULTAN (INSET MAP)	
car park	1
city wall	2
Ein al-Sultan	3
entrance	4
glacis	5
iron age structures	6
Neolithic tower	7
Garstang's excavations	8
Kenyon's excavations	9

Tree of Zaccheus

Greek Church

MAIN SQUARE

New Mosque

Old Mosque

Wadi al-Qelt

JERUSALEM ROAD ISHARIA AL-QUDSI

Prison

DIMASHQ

ABU FIRAS

Jerusalem, Dead Sea & Allenby Bridge ▼

(Luke 18:35–43) and on Jebel Quruntul, the Mount of Temptation, he spent forty days in meditation (Luke 4:1–3). The centre of population shifted from Tel al-Sultan to the site of the present town during the Byzantine period.

Arrival and information

There is no direct **transport** from Jerusalem to Jericho, and Israeli citizens cannot by law go there, so you cannot take a direct taxi unless the driver is a Palestinian national. Hotels such as the *Jerusalem Hotel* (see p.169) and the *Palm Hostel* (see p.167) can arrange tours to Jericho, sometimes taking in Qumran and Masada as well, but the easiest way to get there under your own steam is to take bus #36 from East Jerusalem's central bus station on Sultan Suleiman Street to Abu Dis, just past Bethany (see p.158), and pick up a service taxi from there.

On the way to Jericho, you'll pass the **Inn of the Good Samaritan**, some 10km east of Jerusalem, on the spot where the hero of Jesus's famous parable against racism (Luke 10:30–36) came to the aid of the injured traveller despite their membership of mutually hostile ethnic groups. A little further, a large sign by the roadside marks your descent below **sea level**.

There is a PA **tourist office** north of town near Tel al-Sultan (℡02/992 2935), but it's rarely open and has little information anyway. Service taxis take you to Jericho's main square, where you'll find the Cairo–Amman Bank, and a moneychanger. **The post office** (daily 8am–2.30pm) is just off the main square, on Al-Karamah Street (the Amman Road) – stamps sold here can only be used in PA-controlled areas. One of the best ways to see the sights, which are quite scattered, is to rent a bicycle from Abu Sama'an on the east side of the main square (℡02/232 4070; 4NIS per hr, 15NIS per day).

Accommodation

Hesham Palace Hotel Ein al-Sultan St, just off the main square ℡02/232 2414. This rambling, ramshackle 1920s hotel has – to put it mildly – seen better days, and parts of it look like a building site, but it's still an atmospheric place, and the town's best low-budget option. Once a favourite gambling haunt of Jordan's King Hussein, it is very gradually being renovated, and the rooms in use are not too bad, with en-suite bathrooms, ceiling fans, and even a/c. ❷
Jerusalem Hotel Amman Rd, about 2km from the main square ℡02/232 2444, ⓦwww .jerusalemhotel-jericho.com. Jericho's only mid-range option, offering a motley mix of en-suite a/c rooms, some with nice balconies overlooking citrus groves, some bigger than others, some brighter than others, most with slightly ill-fitting carpets, though, unlike the corridors, they don't seem to have any chunks missing from the walls. There are also a few much cheaper second-class rooms with a shared bathroom downstairs. ❷
Jericho Resort Village 2km north of town, near Hisham's palace ℡02/232 1255, ⓦwww .jerichoresorts.com. A four-star hotel, out of town but handy for Jericho's main sights, with the full range of facilities including a pool, children's pool and playground, and a rooftop spa. Rooms have a/c, phone, satellite TV and a wall-safe, and there are three restaurants (one in a Bedouin-style tent), a tearoom, cocktail bar and drinks terrace. Breakfast included ❻

The Tree of Zacchaeus

The only sight actually in town is the **Tree of Zacchaeus** on Ein al-Sultan Road, a two-thousand-year-old tree which Zacchaeus, a rich tax collector, climbed to see Jesus en route to Jerusalem (Luke 19:4). Spotting Zacchaeus, Jesus asked him for an invitation to his home, and, once there, so inspired him that he forthwith gave half his wealth to charity.

Tel al-Sultan (Tel Jericho) and around

Tel al-Sultan, the *tel* (mound) of ancient Jericho (daily 8am–5pm; 10NIS) is 2km northwest of the modern town. The excavations (mostly below ground level, so you'll be looking down at them) reveal numerous settlements built upon the ruins of their predecessors. Standing on top knowing that there are ten thousand years of civilization under your feet can be an awesome sensation, and there's a magnificent view from the **observation point** – oasis greens against a backdrop of parched, stark desert.

One of the site's major archeological discoveries is a seven-metre-high **neolithic tower** dating from around 7000 BC. Its size and construction – with a central stairway – is unrivalled anywhere in the world at that period. Just to its north lay what seems to be a religious **shrine**, the earliest structure at the site, though little remains of it today.

The walls

The oldest **city walls** that have been uncovered date from the Early Bronze Age (around 2600 BC). Centuries later, a Middle Bronze Age fort was protected by a **glacis** (sloping wall). John Garstang's 1930 excavations here revealed that mud-brick walls from this period did indeed "come tumbling down" into the glacis, apparently vindicating the famous biblical story (Joshua 6), but Kathleen Kenyon's 1952 dig showed that the collapse happened in the Middle Bronze Age, around 1600BC and too early for Joshua. Since then, it has been suggested by controversial Egyptologist David Rohl (who has made something of a career out of trying to tie archeological finds to biblical stories) that the Bronze Age in Palestine was actually 350 years later than its conventional dating, in which case the Bible could still be right.

Ein al-Sultan (Elisha's Spring)

One reason for the original location of the ancient city of Jericho was its proximity to a constant source of water – **Ein al-Sultan**. The spring, opposite Tel al-Sultan, still provides a lifeline for Jericho, gushing water at the rate of 1000 gallons per minute, and distributed throughout the oasis by a complex system of gravity-flow irrigation. Early tradition identifies this spring with the one the prophet Elisha purified by throwing salt into it (II Kings 2:19–22), giving it its other name: Elisha's Spring.

The Ancient Synagogue

Three hundred metres north from Ein al-Sultan, to the right of the road leading to Hisham's Palace, a sign points to an **ancient synagogue** dating from the fifth or sixth century, a rectangular building divided into three by two rows of columns. In principle, the synagogue is open to the public (daily 8am–4pm; 10NIS), but it was closed at last check, with no news on when it might reopen. When it does, you can pop in to see the synagogue's beautiful mosaic floor, decorated with floral and geometric patterns. Beneath the image of a *menorah* (Jewish candelabra), the Aramaic inscription reads "Peace Upon Israel".

Jabal Quruntul and the Monastery of the Temptation

Three kilometres northwest of Jericho, **Jabal Quruntul** is the mountain where Jesus fasted for forty days and was tempted by the devil with the words: "If thou be the Son of God, command that these stones be made bread" (Matthew 4:3–4). The cave where this happened is now a chapel inside the Greek Orthodox **Monastery of the Temptation**, which seems to cling precariously to the sheer rock face.

It is possible to reach the monastery by climbing up the bare, rocky slopes, a trek of only fifteen to thirty minutes (depending on your fitness), but most people take the **cable car** or *télépherique* (daily 8am–5pm; 55NIS round-trip; Ⓦ www.jericho-cablecar.com). The station for this is opposite the entrance to Tel al-Sultan. The cable car was built in 1999 by an Austrian firm, and claims to be "the longest cable car below sea level". The cars travel in groups of three, and give a bird's-eye view of Tel al-Sultan as they pass over, stopping at the halfway mark to let passengers at the top and bottom get on or off the next group of cabins.

At the top is a **café** whose terrace affords a magnificent panoramic view over Jericho and the surrounding area, including the Dead Sea. When it's clear (usually only after rain), you can see right into Jordan. From here it's still quite a steep climb up a stairway to the **Monastery of the Temptation**, whose present building dates from the nineteenth century. Entrance is at the whim of the monks, but generally speaking, and so long as you are "modestly" dressed, they will let you in between 10am and 4pm if you ring the bell, and will show you the chapel where Jesus was tempted by Satan, but they may choose not to, especially if you arrive at lunchtime (1–3pm), so it's wise to turn up early if possible. The chapel itself is not in any case tremendously exciting, though it's still just about recognizable as a cave, despite the icons, screens and frescos which decorate it.

Hisham's Palace (Khirbet al-Mafjar)

The splendid ruins of **Hisham's Palace** (daily 8am–5pm; 10NIS) around 2km from Jericho town centre and a similar distance northeast of Tel al-Sultan, are all that's left of one of the finest examples of Ummayad architecture in the country. The palace was built as a hunting lodge in 743 AD, during the reign of the Ummayad caliph Hisham ibn Abd al-Malik, though historians now believe that it was actually commissioned by his nephew and successor, Walid ibn Yazid. Three years after its construction, it was all but levelled in an earthquake, and was only excavated in the 1930s. Many of its reconstructed fittings are now in the Rockefeller Museum in Jerusalem (see p.110).

At time of writing, a **refurbishment** of the site is under way, financed by the US government, which involved the installation of walkways that will make at least most of the site wheelchair accessible, and there will also be a small **museum**, to the right of the entrance, exhibiting finds from the site.

The site

In the central courtyard, through the imposing stone entrance to the left of the forecourt, is the amazing **star window**, which has become an emblem

▲ The Star Window at Hisham's Palace

of the city and appeared on Palestinian postage stamps. Not a glass window as in a European church, the window is a circular aperture to provide light, originally set in the wall in one of the rooms. Within it sits a geometric six-sided star decorated with bands and patterns that could almost be Celtic. The window is surrounded by columns and the remains of the general living quarters. To its left is a **small mosque**, probably reserved for the caliph's personal use, and behind it, steps lead down to a **small bathhouse**, well preserved with an arched ceiling and mosaic floor.

From the northwest corner of the courtyard, a paved path leads to the imposing remains of the massive **bath hall**, with thirty-six panels of pink and blue mosaic in its floor (only a few of them on view – the rest are covered for their own protection).

To the north of the hall, the building labelled "guest room" houses the palace's greatest treasure: a superb and undamaged **mosaic**; to see it you have to go round to the back and climb the stairs. The mosaic depicts a lion and a group of gazelles in an allegory relevant to the function of the room: the two gazelles beneath the tree on the left are diplomats or guests that have good relations with the kingdom and are therefore welcome; the gazelle on the right, however, represents a visitor who wishes the ruler harm, and is therefore being savaged by the lion, representing revenge. The mosaic is unusual in Islamic art, which usually eschews representations of animals as smacking of idolatry, though its style is echoed in the mosaics of the Ummayad Mosque in Damascus.

Next to the building with the mosaic is the **bathhouse**, where parts of the terracotta piping can still be seen in the walls.

Eating and drinking

Al-Essawi Restaurant Main square (east side). A little grubby, but it does very low-priced chicken, kebabs and hummus, and is conveniently situated, bang in the centre of town. Daily 6.30am–11pm. Cheap.

Seven Trees Ein al-Sultan St, between the centre of town and Tel al-Sultan ☏ 02/992 2781. Like Jericho's other *muntzaats* (park restaurants), the *Seven Trees* has fallen on hard times since the Second Intifada took away most of the tourists – Israeli, Palestinian and foreign – who used to come here. They can still whip you up a meal, and you can still enjoy it in the garden, but you'll need to call ahead and arrange it. Daily 10am–7.30pm. Moderate.

The Dead Sea and Masada

The salt lake known as the **Dead Sea**, 27km from Jerusalem as the crow flies, and 295m below sea level, is one of the natural wonders of the world. The lowest point on the earth's surface, the water is so dense – twenty-five percent solids – that it is practically impossible to swim in. Instead you can bob about on your back and even read a newspaper. It's also renowned for its black, mineral-rich mud, which is claimed to cure everything from acne to arthritis.

Towering above the Dead Sea, the craggy hilltop fortress of **Masada** is famed for both its spectacular views and its tragic history. Here the last die-hard rebels of the First Revolt held out against the might of imperial Rome for three hard years before choosing death rather than defeat.

Dead Sea practicalities

The Dead Sea has its own ecosystem and sauna-like microclimate. Pleasantly warm in winter, the area becomes a steam bath during the summer, with temperatures regularly exceeding 40°C, exacerbated by exceptional humidity – if visiting at that time of year, you'll need to bring water, sunglasses and a hat for protection. There are three public bathing **beaches** along the shore that have freshwater taps for rinsing off the sticky salt solution and, should the need arise, full-time **lifeguards**. The water's salinity gives it a strange oily feel, and layers of salt start to crystallize on your skin (it's best not to jump in straight after shaving and any cuts or grazes will sting like crazy). If you swallow even a mouthful of the foul-tasting liquid, let someone know immediately (though you'll probably bring it straight back up again), as swallowing such a high concentration of minerals can be dangerous.

Ein Gedi

Of the Dead Sea's bathing sites, the most popular is **Ein Gedi** which can be reached by bus from Jerusalem (12 daily; 1hr 30min), Qumran (12 daily; 1hr) and Masada (9 daily, or 14 the other way; 30min). Along with its beach, Ein Gedi boasts a hugely popular **nature reserve** (April–Sept 8am–5pm, Oct–March 8am–4pm; 23NIS; ☏07/658 4285), covering two valleys, with waterfalls, a spring and a variety of possible hikes ranging from simple one-and-a-half-hour walks to difficult five-hour treks which should be attempted only if you're fit and properly kitted out. Adjacent to the park are the remains of a **Byzantine-era synagogue** (April–Sept 8am–5pm, Oct–March 8am–4pm; 12NIS, combined ticket with the nature reserve 26NIS). The synagogue's beautiful mosaic floor bore an inscription (now in Jerusalem's Rockefeller Museum; see p.111) warning darkly against revealing "the town's secret" to gentiles – the secret in question was probably the technique for making a perfume derived from the balsam plant, which grew wild only in this region, and for which Ein Gedi was famous.

There's also a **health spa** at the neighbouring kibbutz (daily: winter 8am–5pm; summer 8am–6pm; 70NIS; ☏08/659 4813, ⓦwww.ngedi.com/spa .htm), where you can bask in sulphur bathing pools or wallow in the famous mud. If you need to stay, there's a YHA Youth Hostel (☏08/658 4165, ⓦwww .iyha.org.il) with private rooms (❹, includes breakfast) or single-sex dorms (114NIS), and a kibbutz guesthouse (☏08/659 4220 or 1, ⓦwww.ein-gedi.co .il; ❽, halfboard [double $200 half-board]), whose guests have free use of the spa.

Qumran

The archeological site of **Qumran** (daily: April–Sept 8am–6pm; Oct–March 8am–5pm; 18NIS) 37km north of Ein Gedi, can be reached by bus from there or from Jerusalem, or by taxi from Jericho. Here in 1947, a young Bedouin shepherd accidentally discovered the Dead Sea Scrolls (see p.145) while looking for a lost sheep. The scrolls are thought to be written by an ultra-devout monastic Jewish sect, the Essenes, who lived here in a **monastery**, until its destruction by the Romans in 68 AD. Remains of a tower, kitchens, dining hall and a **scriptorium**, where supposedly the scrolls were written, can be seen, together with various cisterns, aqueducts and channels – evidence both of the importance of water in the desert, and of the role ritual bathing played in the life of the Essenes. At the far side of the site you can look out to the start of the gorge and the caves where the first scrolls were found. There are numerous possibilities for **walks** into the surrounding Judean hills, with well-marked routes taking you into the still and somewhat surreal desert. The site also has a small shop and cafeteria.

Any **bus** on the highway will stop if you signal it; there are twelve daily to Jerusalem (1hr), and the other way to Ein Gedi (1hr). There is no direct public transport between Qumran and Jericho; you could hire a private taxi (a "special"), but expect to pay a good 300NIS for the round trip with waiting time.

Masada

Towering over the Dead Sea, the rugged rocky crag of **Masada**, 17km south of Ein Gedi (April–Sept: Sat–Thurs 8am–5pm, Fri 8am–4pm; Oct–March: Sat–Thurs 8am–4pm, Fri 8am–4pm; 23NIS; ☎08/658 4207 or 8), is the single-most visited archeological site in Israel. Masada is best known for its role in the 66–70 AD **Jewish War**, when it was last outpost of Jewish resistance against the Romans. Visitors traditionally make the pilgrimage to watch dawn break from the summit, the dramatic landscapes of the Dead Sea, deserts and mountains providing ample tonic for tired eyes – and once your senses are fully warmed up, you can begin to contemplate the dramatic fate of those brave souls who fought and died here so long ago.

Jonathan the Maccabee first had a fortress built here in 150 BC, and it was strengthened and enlarged under **Herod the Great**, who chose it for its virtual impregnability as a potential refuge from the subjects who hated him so. The elaborate system of dykes and channels directed the sparse rainfall into twelve reservoirs hewn out of the mountainside, whose 40,000m^3 capacity allowed its defenders to withstand a siege for years.

Masada practicalities

Most people visit Masada on one of the **excursions** which can be booked from Jerusalem (at the *Palm Hostel* or *Citadel Hostel* for example, or with firms such as Egged or United Tours). These usually set off at 3am to reach the site for dawn and the summit for sunrise, and they generally visit a couple of other sites, often with a very brief whizz round Jericho on the way back. Otherwise, Masada is connected to Jerusalem by **bus** #486; there are only ten daily buses for the two-hour journey – the first at 8.25am, the last at 1pm – but for the return journey there are fifteen daily buses, the last at 7.50pm. **Cable cars** serve the summit approximately every fifteen minutes (daily except Fri 8am–4pm; 61NIS round-trip including site entry).

Staying the night has the advantage of letting you see the site while it's still relatively cool and uncrowded. The *YHA Isaac Taylor Youth Hostel* at the bottom of the mountain (☎08/995 3222; ❹, includes breakfast) offers simple but decent rooms, and is the only accommodation for miles around, as a result of which it is often full. Cafés and restaurants at the site are expensive.

The site

The exposed stone **remains** at the site are magnificent in their rocky isolation. Approaching from the Dead Sea side, either by serpentine path or on the cable car (see above), you'll enter through the east gate, after passing some of the reservoirs on the way up. To your right are large **storehouses**, and beyond them, at the northern tip of the hill, Herod's fabulous **palace**, clinging to the cliff edge. From here, and indeed from vantage points all

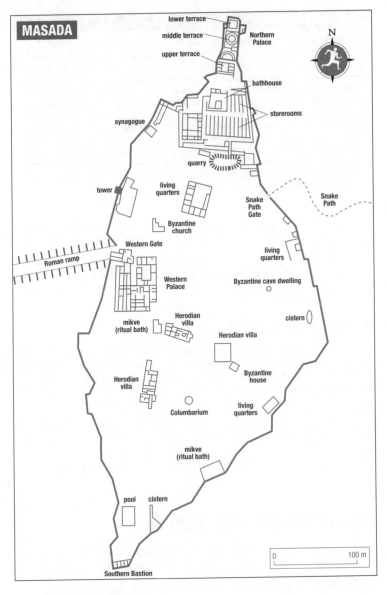

MASADA

lower terrace
middle terrace
upper terrace

Northern Palace

bathhouse

storerooms

synagogue

quarry

tower

living quarters

Byzantine church

Western Gate

Roman ramp

Snake Path Gate

Snake Path

living quarters

Byzantine cave dwelling

cistern

Western Palace

mikve (ritual bath)

Herodian villa

Herodian villa

Byzantine house

Herodian villa

Columbarium

living quarters

mikve (ritual bath)

pool   cistern

0   100 m

Southern Bastion

N

around the summit, the **Roman wall** surrounding the mountain, and some of the eight Roman army camps from which the siege was managed, are clearly visible. Heading back across the site from the palace, a **synagogue** built by the Zealots can be seen against the western wall, and there are a couple of ritual baths nearby. Further west, in the middle of the site, are Byzantine buildings and a church built when Masada was briefly occupied by a group of monks in the fifth century. Beyond these you come to the west

The siege of Masada

During the 66–70 AD Jewish War, Masada was occupied by a thousand-strong group of Jewish rebels known as the Zealots. Under siege by the Roman Tenth Legion, they managed to hold out for three years but in AD 73, with the enemy scaling the steep cliff and capture imminent, they chose death over slavery, and carried out an elaborate **mass suicide pact**. First, each man executed his wife and family with a sword. Then ten men were selected to kill the other men and, finally, lots were drawn to determine the man who would complete the ritual slaughter, before falling on his own sword. Two women and five children, who had hidden themselves in a water channel, lived to tell the tale to the Romans, who broke through the following morning to find 960 bodies. This heroic act of defiance in the face of defeat has become a potent symbol in modern Israel: today, every Israeli schoolchild and army recruit is taken up to Masada to absorb the lesson, with the recruits taking an oath of allegiance that "Masada shall not fall again".

palace and west gate (through which you'll enter if you come from Arad and up the Roman ramp), where you'll find some fine Roman **mosaics**, and Zealot living quarters.

A comprehensive and inexpensive **booklet**, available at the site, describes all the ruins in detail. If you're wondering what the painted **black line** that adorns most buildings is, it's the dividing line between the excavated walls and sections that have been reconstructed.

Sound and light show

Masada has a **sound and light show** (March–Oct on the western side of the mountain; show starts nightly 8pm but arrive by 7.30pm; 41NIS; ☎08/995 9333) which tells the story in Hebrew (simultaneous translation available) of the Jews' last stand against the Romans. Unless you have your own transport, however, it is extremely difficult to get to – from the Dead Sea side of Masada, it's about an hour's drive (around 400–500NIS by taxi, if you can find one). The nearest town is Arad, which is served by Egged bus #384 or #385 (4 daily; 1hr 30min) from Ein Gedi via Masada, but even from Arad, there is no public transport, and a taxi would cost 150–200NIS, still leaving you with the problem of getting back again afterwards. There is no direct public transport between Arad and Jerusalem.

Heading west: Abu Ghosh

Fourteen kilometres west of Jerusalem, just north of Route 1, **Abu Ghosh** is a Christian village named after an early nineteenth-century bandit chieftain licensed by the Ottomans to extract "taxes" from passing travellers. In the 1948 war, Abu Ghosh remained neutral and even helped the Israelis, as a result of which its inhabitants have been labelled "collaborators" by other Palestinians. At the top of the village, the 1924 **Church of Notre Dame de l'Arche de l'Alliance** ("Our Lady of the Ark of the Covenant") is said to occupy the site of the house of Abinadab where the Ark of the Covenant rested for twenty years (I Samuel 7:1–2) until taken by David to Jerusalem. It is built on the site of a fifth-century Byzantine church, whose floor mosaics are still visible. At the bottom of the village are a khan and a

Crusader Church put up by the Knights Hospitaller in the twelfth century, the latter restored by Benedictine monks at the end of the nineteenth century, who also added a small monastery.

Abu Ghosh is most popular, however, for its **restaurants**. Gourmets, and Jerusalemites starved by Shabbat closing, flock here to sample the excellent Palestinian cooking at the *Caravan Inn*, founded in 1947, on the village's main drag at 27 HaShalom (℡02/534 2744; daily 10am–11pm; moderate), which gets particularly packed out on Saturday lunchtimes, or at the village's hummus joints, of which the most renowned are the two *Abu Shukris* (daily 8am–6pm; cheap). The original *Abu Shukri* is at 4 Mahmoud Rashid on the way into the village on the left, with a breakaway establishment across the street, founded by a disaffected relative; both are equally good, and equally packed out of a Saturday lunchtime. The other notable restaurant in the Abu Ghosh area is the *Elvis Inn*, by Neve Ilan fuel station just off the freeway at the next junction west (℡02/534 1275; daily 7.30am–12.30pm; moderate), graced with a large gold statue of Elvis Presley outside, and Elvis memorabilia within. You can order a burger and fries or a hummus and pitta, or just a coffee, but it's the kitsch 1950s American diner-style decor you come for, and possibly the music (no prizes for guessing who they play), rather than the food, which is OK, but nothing special. They also hold regular Elvis impersonation contests – call them for details.

Abu Ghosh can be reached from Jerusalem on bus #185 (1–2 hourly; 20min).

Tel Aviv and Jaffa

In contrast to Jerusalem, **Tel Aviv** is a brash modern city, hip, cosmopolitan and secular ("Jerusalem prays, Tel Aviv plays," as they say). Located by the sea, it entices pleasure seekers with beaches, bars, clubs, and for those of that preference, a lively gay scene. To its south, the ancient town of **Jaffa**, now inside Tel Aviv's municipal boundaries was once Palestine's main port, and remains largely Palestinian, though with Jewish and mixed neighbourhoods too.

Jewish immigrants founded Neve Zedek, now part of Tel Aviv, as a suburb of Jaffa in 1887. Tel Aviv was officially inaugurated in 1909 as the world's first all-Jewish city, and was soon the centre of Palestine's Jewish community. In World War I, the British garrison set up camp here, and in 1921 it received its own town council. The same year, anti-Semitic riots by Arabs in Jaffa drove most of that city's Jewish population up to Tel Aviv, expanding and consolidating the city still further.

When the State of Israel was proclaimed in 1948, Tel Aviv became its first capital, and even after the government's move to West Jerusalem in 1949, it remained the diplomatic centre. Most embassies remain here, along with the defence ministry and the main representatives of Israel's fashion, commercial, culture and entertainment industries.

Arrival

Getting to Tel Aviv from Jerusalem is a piece of cake. Bus #405 leaves four or five times an hour, except on Shabbat, taking around an hour and a quarter. Alternatively you can take a *sherut* (service taxi) from HaRav Kook, just off the Jaffa Road in downtown West Jerusalem which saves the trek out to the bus station. *Sheruts* run 24/7 including Fridays and Saturdays (though on Shabbat

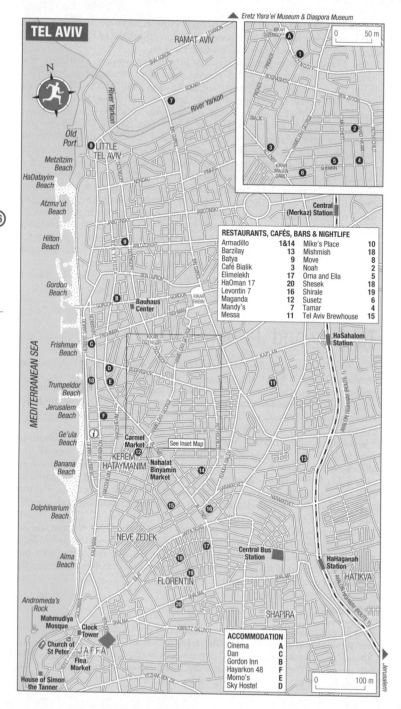

TEL AVIV

RAMAT AVIV

Eretz Yisra'el Museum & Diaspora Museum

0   50 m

KIKAR
DIZENGOFF A
1
DIZENGOFF
PINKAS
BOGRASHOV
BEN ZIYYON
BIALIK
2
HAMELEKH GEORGE
3
MELCHETT
KING GEORGE
KIKAR
MAGEN
DAVID
6   SHENKIN
5
4

River Yarkon

River Yarkon

Old
Port

LITTLE
TEL AVIV

Metzitzim
Beach

HaDatayim
Beach

Atzma'ut
Beach

Hilton
Beach

Gordon
Beach

Bauhaus
Center

KIKAR
RABIN

Central
(Merkaz) Station

RESTAURANTS, CAFÉS, BARS & NIGHTLIFE

Armadillo	1&14	Mike's Place	10
Barzilay	13	Mishmish	18
Batya	9	Move	8
Café Bialik	3	Noah	2
Elimelekh	17	Orna and Ella	5
HaOman 17	20	Shesek	18
Levontin 7	16	Shirale	19
Maganda	12	Susetz	6
Mandy's	7	Tamar	4
Messa	11	Tel Aviv Brewhouse	15

HaSahalom
Station

Frishman
Beach

Trumpeldor
Beach

Jerusalem
Beach

Ge'ula
Beach

Banana
Beach

Dolphinarium
Beach

Alma
Beach

MEDITERRANEAN SEA

Carmel
Market

See Inset Map

KEREM
HATAYMANIM

Nahalat
Binyamin
Market

NEVE ZEDEK

Central Bus
Station

HaHaganah
Station

HATIKVA

FLORENTIN

SHAPIRA

Andromeda's
Rock

Mahmudiya
Mosque

Clock
Tower

Church of
St Peter

JAFFA
Flea
Market

House of Simon
the Tanner

ACCOMMODATION

Cinema	A
Dan	C
Gordon Inn	B
Hayarkon 48	F
Momo's	E
Sky Hostel	D

0   100 m

Jerusalem

N

16

EXCURSIONS

they leave from the west side of Heil HaHandassah, just south of HaNeviim), and make the journey in just over an hour. It is even possible to go by train (10 daily; 1hr 40min), though Jerusalem's station is now inconveniently located in Malha (see p.27).

In Tel Aviv, buses and *sheruts* leave you at the **Central Bus Station** (☎03/694 8888), southeast of the city centre on Levinsky. To get into town from here, take city bus #4 or #5 from the fourth floor (platform 417 & 418 respectively), or the *sherut* minibuses on the same routes from Tsemakh David, on the other side of the same floor. For Jaffa, take bus #46, also from the fourth floor. Alternatively, it's a thirty-minute walk into town; leave by the Levinsky exit on the third floor, turn left down Levinsky and then right up HaAliya which leads into Allenby.

The **Central Train Station** (also called Merkaz or Savidor; train information ☎03/611 7000) is 2km out of town at the eastern end of Arlozoroff, which is also the way into town if you're walking. The bus stand is to your right as you exit the station: #10 runs to Ben Yehuda and Jaffa, #18 to Dizengoff and Allenby, #32 to Allenby and Ben Yehuda. On foot, HaShalom station (served by bus #23 to Allenby and Shenkin) is actually nearer to the city centre. The bus **back to Jerusalem** (#405) leaves from platform 605 on the sixth floor of the bus station, *sheruts* from Tsemakh David, by the bus station's fourth floor.

Information, tours and transport

The Tel Aviv–Jaffa Tourism Association's **tourist information office** is at 46 Herbert Samuel ☎03/516 6188, ⓦ www.visit-tlv.com (Sun–Thurs 9.30am–5pm, Fri 9.30am–1pm, Sat 10am–4pm), stocks free maps of Tel Aviv and Jaffa, plus various free booklets. They also run free **walking tours**: Tel Aviv by night (Tues 8pm starting at Rothschild with Hertzl), Old Jaffa (Wed 9.30am, starting at Jaffa's clock tower) and Tel Aviv Bauhaus (Sat 11am, starting at 46 Rothschild).

The centre of Tel Aviv is best negotiated on foot, but the reliable and well-developed **city bus** network, operated by the Dan transport cooperative, is the easiest way to get from one end of the city to the other. Services run frequently from approximately 6am to midnight, except Friday evenings and daytime Saturday. Inside the city there's a flat fare of 5.30NIS, or a one-day travelcard (*hofshi yomi*) will cost you 12NIS (both can be purchased on board). Route maps are displayed on many bus stops, or a good map in Hebrew is available infrequently from the Dan information kiosk (☎03/639 4444) inside the Central Bus Station; better still, check ⓦ www.dan.co.il/english for routes and timetables. Some of the more poplar routes (such as #4 and #5) are also plied by **sheruts** (minibuses), which charge 5.50NIS. **Taxis** patrol the city day and night – always insist on the meter, as you'll certainly be overcharged if it's not switched on.

Dan also run a two-hour **panoramic bus tour** of Tel Aviv and Jaffa (route #100), costing 45NIS for a single trip, or 65NIS for a day ticket allowing you to get on and off as you please, with free travel on other city buses for the day thrown in. The tickets can be bought on the bus, which runs seven times a day (five times on Fridays, none on Saturdays).

Accommodation

Downtown Tel Aviv has dozens of hotels and hostels to suit all tastes and budgets, and you shouldn't have any problems finding a bed, except perhaps in July and August.

🏃 **Cinema** 1 Zamenhoff, on Kikar Dizengoff ☎03/520 7100, ⓦwww.cinemahotel.com. If you want somewhere special to stay in Tel Aviv, this is the place. It isn't the most deluxe hotel in town, but service is extremely professional, and probably better than in most Tel Aviv five-stars. The rooms aren't huge but they're very well designed, and the whole place has a dual Bauhaus/ movie theatre theme based on it being both a former cinema (hence the projectors in the lobby) and a fine example of Tel Aviv's International Style architecture. In fact, it's worth popping in for a look even if you don't stay here. Breakfast included ❻

Dan 99 HaYarkon ☎03/520 2525, ⓦwww .danhotels.com US toll-free ☎1-800/223-7773, UK toll-free 0800/731 2789. Beachside five-star with two pools, a fitness centre, sauna, jacuzzi, smart rooms, snappy service, all mod cons, tasteful furnishings, and everything you'd want from a luxury hotel, but if that isn't enough, you can take an executive sea-view room, or a suite, and get to use a special extra-deluxe lounge that other guests are excluded from. Breakfast included ❾

Gordon Inn 17 Gordon ☎03/523 8239, ⓔgordonin@gmail.com. Not exactly in the thick of things, but central enough, quiet and clean, its airy rooms, some en suite, are each equipped with a kettle, fridge, TV and a/c, and it's a cut above the scuzzier hostels at the southern end of town, though it does have dorm accommodation too (90NIS). Rather than breakfast as such, the room price (or 20NIS extra in the dorm) includes a voucher for a free meal at a beachside restaurant, be it breakfast, lunch or supper. ❷

Hayarkon 48 48 HaYarkon ☎03/516 8989, ⓦwww.hayarkon48.com. This somewhat institutional hostel is less fun than *Momo's* (see below) but it's cleaner and brighter, offering a choice of dorms – ordinary (72NIS) or a/c (90NIS). It also has a range of private rooms, some en suite with a/c and balconies though it's lacking a bar. The hostel stakes its reputation on its cleanliness and the reliability of its hot showers; the included breakfast, on the other hand, (coffee and toast) isn't anything to write home about. ❸

Momo's 28 Ben Yehuda ☎03/528 7471, ⓦwww .momoshostel.com. Long-standing travellers' favourite, and your best bet for a budget bed in Tel Aviv (though you might possibly save a few shekels at *Sky Hostel*, a block north), *Momo's* is the place to meet other travellers, exchange stories and advice, ask about work possibilities, sink a few beers, and generally be gregarious. Most people take a dorm (68NIS), but private rooms of varying size and facilities are available. Breakfast (included in price) consists of just coffee and a cake. ❶

The downtown area

Tel Aviv centres on **Kikar Dizengoff** (also called Zina Square), a pedestrianized plaza raised above the road which is named after the city's first mayor. Its avant-garde **Fire and Water Fountain** was designed in 1958 by Israeli artist Yaacov Agam. Four times a day (11am, 1pm, 7pm and 9pm), it does a twenty-minute music and light show which is definitely worth stopping by for if you're passing.

A few minutes' walk to the south of Kikar Dizengoff is a secondary centre in the form of **Kikar Magen David**. Magen David is a six-way junction, its name (usually rendered in English as "Star of David", though *magen* actually means "shield") refers to the six-pointed hexagram star which supposedly adorned King David's shield; the most common symbol for the Jewish religion, it also appears of course on the Israeli flag.

The place to start investigating Tel Aviv's Bauhaus architectural heritage (see box, opposite) is the **Bauhaus Center** at 99 Dizengoff (Sun–Thurs 10am–7.30pm, Fri 10am–2.30pm; ☎03/522 0249, ⓦwww.bauhaus-center.com), essentially a shop stocking books, maps, postcards and souvenirs relating to Bauhaus in Tel Aviv, but it also has free exhibitions, and runs tours of the city's International Style highlights (Fri 10am; 50NIS) – then again, so does the tourist office (see p.255), and theirs are free.

International Style architecture in Tel Aviv

Much of downtown Tel Aviv, particularly the area around Kikar Magen David is dominated by buildings of the **International Style** of architecture which were built in the 1930s and 1940s. Highly influenced by the German **Bauhaus** school under the motto "form follows function", the style is characterized by clean lines, right angles and minimal decoration consisting only of protruding balconies and occasionally flanged edges designed to cast sharp shadows in the harsh Mediterranean sunlight. This went especially well with the whitewashed concrete buildings that Tel Aviv's founders had in mind when they dreamed of it being a gleaming white city by the sea.

There are over 1500 International Style buildings in Tel Aviv. The richest hunting ground for classic examples of the style is on Sederot Rothschild, and also surrounding streets, particularly Bialik, Ahad Ha'Am, Engel and Melchett. A map sold at the Bauhaus Center shows them all. We've listed some of the best examples below, but you're sure to discover more on any wander around town:

Rothschild 63, 67, 71, 79, 82, 83, 84	**Levanda** 56
Ahad Ha'Am 57	**Arlozoroff** 1
Melchett 5, 15	**Maze** 56
Bialik 6, 16, 18, 21	**Ben Gurion** 32
Bilu 6	**Trumpeldor** 39
Kikar Dizengoff *Hotel Cinema*	**Frug** 34
Gordon 9	**Hess** 1, 4

Rehov Shenkin

East off Kikar Magen David, **Rehov Shenkin**, once the haunt of ultra-orthodox *Haredim* and lefties, is now Tel Aviv's trendiest street. By day the young and beautiful "Shenkinai" hang out in its cafés or wander round its once hippyish, now chic shops full of concept items and designer ware. At night, the same crowd meet up here before hitting the city's clubs (see p.264). **Café Tamar** at no. 57 (see p.263) is Tel Aviv's answer to *Les Deux Magots* on the Left Bank – a long-time hangout of Israeli Labour Party hacks and assorted intellectuals, leftists and journos, and one of the most atmospheric cafés in the city.

With time to spare, continue along Shenkin and turn on to **Sederot Rothschild** for a rare glimpse of 1930s charm. An air of dignity pervades its tree-lined pavements and a wander along its length reveals several International Style buildings (see box above).

Carmel Market

Carmel Market (Shuq HaCarmel), west across Allenby from Shenkin, is Tel Aviv's main market (Sun–Thurs sunrise to sunset, Fri till late afternoon) – a vibrant and always lively market where you'll find anything from Eastern European delicatessen, household goods, T-shirts, and cheap cassettes, to an abundance of fruit and vegetables, live fish and chickens. The first section, coming from Allenby, is mainly for clothes, but this soon gives way to the market's real heart: the food section, where the stalls purvey not only fresh fruit and veg, but also falafel, pastries and pickles. As a kind of offshoot from Shuq HaCarmel, the parallel **Nahalat Binyamin market** is Tel Aviv's main arts and crafts market. It's all a bit twee, especially compared to its brasher, more workaday neighbour, but it's definitely worth a wander.

The pedestrianized area in front of the markets, on the west side of Kikar Magen David, often attracts **buskers** who play an interesting and quite eclectic mix of sounds.

The Yemenite Quarter

To the west of Shuq HaCarmel, **Kerem HaTaymanim** – or the Yemenite Quarter – is a maze of narrow lanes and alleys and cramped buildings, with a collection of popular cafés and restaurants. The quarter was founded in 1904 by Jews from Yemen, and is known for its delicious Yemeni Jewish cuisine. A very large number of the quarter's inhabitants today are still descended from its original Yemeni founders.

Neve Zedek

The **Neve Zedek** neighbourhood, just south of the Yemenite Quarter, dates from 1887 when it became the first area to be settled by former Jewish residents of Jaffa. Now one of Tel Aviv's trendiest quarters, its Arab-style houses, built almost on top of each other, are highly sought after, and many have been renovated by the artists and well-heeled bohemians who now live here.

Florentin

From Neve Zedek, Rehov Herzl leads south into **Florentin**, a district dating back to the 1920s and yet another one to have undergone something of a renaissance. Its dilapidated International Style buildings (1 Frenkel is a fine example) are gradually undergoing redecoration (if not restoration). Its streets are still lined with shops and small businesses, but Florentin has become the centre of Tel Aviv's "alternative" scene, and its southern reaches host many of the city's hippest nightclubs.

Bet Yair at 8 Stern (Sun–Thurs 9am–3pm; 10 NIS; ☎03/682 0288) is the house where British police in 1942 arrested Avraham Stern, leader of a small, extreme right-wing Zionist paramilitary group, called LEHI but more commonly known after him as the Stern Gang, who was trying to forge an alliance against Britain with Nazi Germany during World War II. Rather than put him on trial, the British simply shot him dead. The house is now a museum, run by the Defence Ministry and dedicated to Stern's memory, his apartment preserved as it was in his lifetime, with personal effects such as his Bible and *tefilin* (phylacteries; see p.277), and displays and multimedia presentations on LEHI's activities and Stern's death.

North of downtown

North of Kikar Dizengoff, **Rehov Dizengoff**, the city's main boulevard, heads north towards the Yarkon River. Running parralel to it are **Ben Yehuda** and **HaYarkon** to the west, and, rather further away, **Ibn Gvirol** to the east. All are lined with cafés and foodstalls, so you won't go short of a drink or a falafel on any of them. The fact that Tel Aviv's main boulevards run north–south, parallel with the shore, is a result of the city's direction of growth, but something of a planning blunder in that it blocks the sea breezes which cool most other Mediterranean cities.

Kikar Yitzhak Rabin

Tel Aviv's rather ugly City Hall is on **Kikar Yitzhak Rabin**, formerly Kikar Malkhei Yisra'el (Kings of Israel Square), which was renamed following the

1995 assassination here of Prime Minister Yitzhak Rabin, shot during a peace rally by a young right-wing extremist who objected to the Oslo Accord that Rabin had signed with PLO leader Yasser Arafat.

Behind City Hall, at the spot where Rabin fell, a **monument** to his memory consists of a section of pavement seeming to rise up in revolt against the murder committed on it. Israel was of course deeply shocked by the assassination – public opinion strongly backed Rabin – but it seems to have had the desired effect: after Rabin's death, the peace deal gradually fell apart.

The Tel Aviv Museum of Art

The **Tel Aviv Museum of Art** (Mon, Wed & Sat 10am–4pm, Tues & Thurs 10am–10pm, Fri 19am–2pm; 42NIS; ☏03/607 7020, ⓦwww.tamuseum.com) is a fifteen-minute walk southeast of City Hall at 27 Shaul HaMelekh. It is home to an impressive collection of Impressionist and Post-Impressionist artworks with a roll call of famous names including Picasso, Dalí, Monet, Cézanne, Chagall (look out for his Wailing Wall), Lichtenstein, Munch, Rodin and Moore. Permanent and temporary exhibitions of Israeli and Jewish artists and sculptors are also held here.

The Old Port

A kilometre north of Kikar Dizengoff, HaYarkon, Ben Yehuda and Dizengoff meet at the misleadingly named **Old Port**, a rejuvenated seafront area where people come to eat, drink and hang out. Opened by Tel Aviv's Jewish City Council in 1936 in response to the closure of Jaffa's port by Palestinian Arabs during their uprising against the British, the Old Port never really saw much commercial traffic, and closed in 1965 when the new port of Ashdod opened further south.

Behind the Old Port, the area known as **Little Tel Aviv** was once a rather down at heel and hip neighbourhood. Inevitably, in the nature of such areas, it has become wealthy and conventional, but the scores of bars and restaurants crammed into its area still manage to give a truly laid-back Mediterranean atmosphere.

The beaches

The further you go north or south from town, the less crowded Tel Aviv's **beaches** become, but those in town each have their own character. Because of undertow currents, swimming can be dangerous and you should always check the safety flags before attempting it: white means it's safe; red means it's dangerous; black means it's so dangerous that it's illegal. Lifeguards are on duty on some beaches, sometimes in summer only. A popular beach game is *matkot*, something like a game of beach tennis played with giant table tennis bats and a ball, and considered by some to be Israel's unofficial national sport.

At the northern end of town, **HaDatiyim Beach**, also called Nordau Beach, is where the religious crowd disport – men and women are allocated different days (women Sun, Tues & Thurs; men Mon, Wed & Fri). Non-orthodox women also enjoy the hassle-free nature of women's days here. On Shabbat, with the orthodox safely inside their synagogues, the beach is open to everyone else. South from here, **Atzma'ut (Independence) Beach** is popular with the gay community (as well as straight women after a more relaxed atmosphere). **Hilton Beach**, by the *Hilton Hotel*, is very popular, with a beach bar, and a calm swimming area protected by breakwaters; it's also the best beach for surfing, and there are kayaks and pedalos for rent. Continuing south, **Gordon Beach** and **Frishman Beach** both have good facilities including bars and cafés and are very popular for sunbathing, volleyball and strolling along the prom. **Jerusalem Beach** was jokingly presented by the mayor of Tel Aviv to the mayor of Jerusalem on a TV show, hence the name. **Dolphinarium Beach** is named after a dolphinarium which used to be here and a nightclub of the same name. The club was the target of an infamous suicide bombing in 2001 which killed 21 and injured over 100, most of them teenage revellers. Today the beach is used for watersports including surfing, windsurfing and kayaking; swimming as such is banned. Friday afternoons see a free-for-all jam session with musicians and performers all joining in. The last beach before Jaffa, **Alma Beach** is far enough from town to be free from the crowds, and gives great views of Old Jaffa, but the currents are treacherous and there are no lifeguards, so do not go swimming here.

Ramat Aviv

Tel Aviv's two most exciting museums lie some 3km north of the city centre, across the Yarkon River in the quiet suburb of **Ramat Aviv**. Both museums are served by buses #27 and #127 from the seventh floor of the Central Bus Station, or by #25 from Dizengoff with HaMelekh George.

The Eretz Yisra'el Museum

The sprawling site of the **Eretz Yisra'el Museum**, or HaAretz Museum, at 2 Levanon (Sun–Wed 10am–4pm, Thurs 10am–8pm, Fri & Sat 10am–2pm; 38NIS; ☎03/641 2408, ⓦ www.eretzmuseum.org.il), encompasses an immensely varied collection displayed in a number of small specialist exhibitions. Most important among them is the Glass Museum housed in the green circular building at the top of the hill, which relates the history of glass-making and contains one of the finest collections of ancient glassware in the world. Relics from the copper mines at Timna near Eilat (also known as King Solomon's Mines) are housed in the Nehustan Pavilion, with other buildings devoted to stamps, coins, folklore and ethnography, ceramics and the alphabet.

The complex also contains **Tel Qasila** – one of the few archeological sites to have been preserved in Tel Aviv. Excavations here have revealed evidence of occupation in the area for the past 3000 years, although the only substantial remains are the outlines of two Philistine temples from the twelfth century BC. Some scholars believe it could be the site of ancient Jaffa, or at least its port in the pre-Christian era.

The Diaspora Museum

A kilometre further north up Levanon, on the Tel Aviv University campus, the **Diaspora Museum**, or Bet Hatefutsot (Sun–Tues & Thurs 10am–4pm, Wed 10am–6pm, Fri 9am–1pm; 35NIS; ☎03/745 7880, ⓦ www.bh.org.il), features a well-presented assortment of maps, models, videos and displays exploring the history of the Jewish people, their traditions, religion and settlement throughout the world. There's plenty to keep you interested, from an introduction to the Hassidic way of life to models of synagogues, exhibits on Jewish communities and a section on Jewish music. There's also a massive library of films on different Jewish communities available for viewing, and Jewish visitors can trace their ancestry by computer.

▲ The view from Jaffa's walled city

Jaffa

In a reversal of fortune, **Jaffa**, once Palestine's main port and second largest city, is now little more than an appendage of Tel Aviv, its former suburb, but being much older, it has some historical sites of tourist interest, and even a few biblical connections – the prophet Jonah sailed from here, for example (Jonah 1:3). The Crusaders took Jaffa three times, but its bloodiest moment came in 1799 when Napoleon captured it from the Ottomans, killed over four thousand captured soldiers, and left the town in ruins. From central Tel Aviv, it's less than thirty minutes' walk along the seafront, or down Derekh Yafo (Jaffa Road), to the impressive 1906 **clock tower** on Rehov Yefet, which marks the heart of tourist Jaffa. To its west lies the formerly walled city of **Old Jaffa**.

Rehov Ruslan

Directly opposite the clock tower, on Rehov Ruslan, the **Mahmudiya Mosque**, with its elegantly slender minaret, was built, like much of Old Jaffa, in the early nineteenth century following the destruction wrought by Napoleon. The open interior is decorated with classical stonework brought from Roman sites up the coast, but unfortunately it's closed to non-Muslims.

Across Ruslan from the mosque, a small alley leads to the unassuming **Jerusalem Gate** at the beginning of Rehov Hatsorfim – until 1869 this was the only entrance into Jaffa. In the neighbouring coffee shops, Jewish men originating from Arab countries sit around drinking mint tea or Turkish coffee and playing backgammon – on the surface at least, not so different from their Palestinian neighbours.

Old Jaffa

Kikar Kedumin, Old Jaffa's main square, is dominated by the Italian-style Roman Catholic **Church and Monastery of St Peter** (March–Sept daily 8–11.45am & 3–6pm, rest of year till 5pm) with its attractive bell tower. In the middle of the square a staircase (there's a ramp for wheelchairs) leads down to a well-labelled excavation of remains dating from the third century BC to the third century AD (Sun–Thurs 9am–10pm, Fri 9am–2pm, Sat 10am–10pm; free).

Opposite the church entrance, a terrace by *Ella* restaurant offers a good view of **Andromeda's Rock**, just out to sea. According to Greek legend, Perseus, son of Zeus, rescued the beautiful princess Andromeda from the rock as she was being sacrificed to a sea monster – the grooves in the rock are said to have been made by the chains that tied Andromeda down.

Off Kikar Kedumin, at 8 Simtat Shimon HaBurski, the **House of Simon the Tanner** is where, according to legend, St Peter stayed after being summoned to raise from the dead one Tabitha, aka Dorcas, "a woman full of good works and almsdeeds" (Acts 9:36–43), and where he subsequently had a vision on the roof in which animals descended from heaven accompanied by a voice telling him to kill and eat them (Acts 10:9–19). Once a mosque, it is now a private house, but it actually dates from the nineteenth century and not from biblical times at all.

The flea market

Across Rehov Yefet from Old Jaffa is the flea market, **Shuq HaPishpeshim**, run primarily by Sephardi Jews and reached from any of the streets to the left of the clock tower. Festooned with rugs and baubles, this is arguably Israel's most colourful street market, thronging with locals in search of bargains and tourists looking for antiques; genuine, high-quality antiques do turn up here, but with prices to match.

Eating and drinking

Even more than West Jerusalem, Tel Aviv is a **café society**. You'll find the trendiest hangouts in Shenkin, Florentin and Little Tel Aviv. The city's **restaurants** offer every conceivable type of international cuisine, and you can eat extremely well here, but what really sets it apart from Jerusalem are its Ashkenazi and Yemeni Jewish eateries.

Cafés

Café Bialik 2 Bialik ⓦ www.bialikcafe.co.il. An excellent café-bar, with food, coffee and draught beer (Pilsner Urquell and Newcastle Brown on tap), wi-fi coverage and occasional live music or stand-up comedy. A suicide bomber seriously damaged the café in 2002, injuring twenty people, and the 2007 smoking ban put a hefty dent in its business, but it soldiers on, remaining one of the most congenial places in town to relax with a coffee or a beer. Daily 8am–1am. Licensed.

Noah 93 Ahad Ha'Am. Bohemian hangout popular with literary, artistic and cinematic types, not to mention musicians, getting a bit trendy of late. Food includes salads, sandwiches and carrot cake, there's a small garden, and jazz concerts are not unknown

(usually on Sundays and Tuesdays). Sun–Thurs 7.30am–midnight.

Shirale 18 Frenkel, Florentin ⓦ www.2eat.co.il /shirale. Styling itself an "espresso art bar" this cosy vegetarian café serves organic salads, sandwiches and juices as well as coffee. It also doubles as an art gallery, getting more and more like a bar rather than a café as the evening progresses, but it's always laid-back and congenial. Sun–Thurs 9am–12.30am, Fri 9am–Shabbat. Kosher. Licensed.

Susetz 20 Shenkin. At the heart of the Shenkin scene, its outside tables are the key vantage point over the street to see, and of course be seen. As well as the usual range of espresso-based coffee concoctions, you can snack on bagels, salads and pasta dishes, and you can come in the morning, when it isn't crowded, to eat breakfast. Sun–Fri 7am–midnight, Sat 9am–midnight. Licensed.

Tamar 57 Shenkin. Long-standing hangout of the city's lefty intellectuals and journalists, one of the most atmospheric cafés in the city, and the only place in Tel Aviv that really feels like a local. Sun–Fri 7am–8pm.

Restaurants

Batya 197 Dizengoff ☎03/522 1335. Saturday is the busiest time at this homely Yiddische (but not kosher) café-restaurant, established in 1941, where *cholent* (slow-cooked bean and brisket Shabbat stew) is the signature dish, typically preceded by a starter of chopped liver or chicken soup, and followed by apple strudel for afters. Daily noon–midnight. Licensed. Moderate.

Elimelekh 35 Wolfson, Florentin. Going since 1936, and much loved by a devoted clientele for its old-school Ashkenazi Jewish home cooking, including *cholent*, stuffed *kishke* (a kind of sausage), gefilte fish, *tzimmes* (sweet stewed carrots), borscht, *kreplakh* (the Jewish answer to ravioli) and all the goodies your *bubbe* used to make. Sun–Thurs 11am–midnight, Fri & Sat 11am–5pm. Serves beer. Cheap to moderate.

Maganda 2 Rabbi Meir, Kerem HaTaymanim ☎03/561 1895. Quite a posh Yemeni restaurant whose specialities include stuffed vegetables, turkey heart, and kebabs. Daily noon–midnight. Licensed. Sun–Thurs noon–midnight, Sat Shabbat–midnight. Kosher. Licensed. Moderate to expensive.

Mandy's 2 Rokakh ☎03/699 6404, ⓦwww.2eat .co.il/eng/mandys. Elegant restaurant cum bar overlooking the Yarkon River. It's owned by Mandy Rice-Davies who may be familiar to British readers from her role in the 1960s Profumo affair. Since then she has established herself as a novelist and restaurateur in Israel (she wrote *The Scarlet Thread*, a love story set in Palestine during World War I). The cosmopolitan bistro-style menu includes starters of beef or salmon carpaccio and main courses such as chicken wings in soy, honey and ginger, or salmon fillet in teriyaki sauce. There's also a tasty selection of bar snacks. Wed–Sun 10pm–late. Licensed. Moderate to expensive.

Messa 19 HaArba'a ☎03/685 6859, ⓦwww .messa.co.il. Very stylish (some would say overdesigned) French and Middle Eastern restaurant, considered the trendiest eatery in town, a favourite with celebs and VIPs, all done out in white, with long walnut tables, an attached bar (all done out in black), and marble floors throughout. It's very chichi, and there's a fresh menu daily, as well as some interesting and innovative cocktails, but the food doesn't always live up to the promise of the interior decor. Daily noon–3.30pm & 7–11.30pm. Licensed. Expensive.

Orna and Ella 33 Shenkin ☎03/620 4753. Very, very popular café-restaurant (worth reserving well ahead, and even then you'll probably have to wait on the sofa for a table) serving wonderful European and modern Israeli dishes. The sweet potato pancakes with sour cream and chive sauce are legendary, the home-made pasta a treat, the desserts too delicious to be true. Sun–Fri 10am–midnight, Sat 11am–midnight. Licensed. Moderate.

Bars and clubs

As in Jerusalem, the line between a café and a **bar** gets very blurred in Tel Aviv. Of the cafés we list opposite, the *Bialik* and *Shirale* in particular double as bars, as does *Mandy's* (see above). As for **clubbing,** Tel Avivians don't get started until well after midnight; the big nights are Thursday and Friday. You'll probably have to dress to impress – the clipboard mafia are out in force and you may be turned away if you're not deemed cool enough. Entry prices to clubs are frequently above 100NIS, but you can often pick up fliers for cheaper entry in the fashion and music shops on Shenkin.

Armadillo 51 Ahad Ha'Am. Comfy neighbourhood bar offering not only a friendly atmosphere but also Georgian snacks with your beer, now with a second branch at 74 Dizengoff. Sun–Thurs 6pm–2am, Fri 8pm–3am, Sat 7pm–3am.

Mike's Place 86 Herbert Samuel ⓦ www
.mikesplacebars.com. Tel Aviv branch of the
Jerusalem bar (see p.196), a die-hard tourist
trap, but that does make it a cheerfully
boozy pose-free zone, where there's sport
on the telly and no one cares what you're
wearing. The bar was the target of a suicide
bomb attack in 2003 in which three people
were murdered but it carries on undeterred,
aiming to offer "an island of sanity in a
region torn apart by conflict". There's live
music 10.30pm nightly, a decent range of
beers, American-style fast food and no
cover charge. Sun–Fri 11am–late, Sat
10.30am–late. Happy hour 3–8pm.
Mishmish 17 Lilienblum, Florentin. The name
means apricot, and this is the sister bar to

its equally fruitily named next-door neighbour
Shesek (whose name means kumquat),
playing an assortment of interesting music to
a hip crowd in orange-tinted surroundings.
Beers include Taybeh. Daily 9pm–late.
Tel Aviv Brewhouse 11 Rothschild ⓦ www.rest
.co.il/brewhouse. As its name suggests, this
place brews its own beer, with a copper tun
right in the middle of the bar area to prove
it. Truth to tell, it's more a restaurant than a
bar, but no true beer lover's going to stay
away for that. As well as a lager, an ale and
a stout (all excellent), there are steaks and
ribs, with crème brûlée for afters, and on
Friday afternoons and Sunday evenings
there's live jazz too. Sun–Fri 10am–1am, Sat
5pm–1am.

Clubs

Barzilay 13 HaRehev ☏ 03/687 8090, ⓦ www
.barzilayclub.com. The club of the moment,
though this being Tel Aviv, that could
change tomorrow. The vibe is hip and fairly
underground, the music is mainly techno
and house (with regular sets by Detroit and
Chicago names), the crowd are up for it, the
locale is an old warehouse, what more
could you want? Thurs & Fri midnight–late;
50–100NIS.
HaOman 17 88 Abrabanel, Florentin ☏ 03/681
3636. An offshoot of the Jerusalem club (see
p.198) that's outdone its parent to become
the most popular dance venue in Israel. It's
a big old place, with three dancefloors, a
state-of-the-art light show and DJ talent
from across the world playing mainly house
music, Thursday and Friday nights from
midnight till noon next day. Entry is usually
80–120NIS.

Levontin 7 7 Levontin ☏ 03/560 5084. Small
club hosting live acts as well as DJs, and
playing a wide range of sounds – anything
from hip-hop to *kletzmer*. Open most
nights but hours vary. They have a website
at ⓦ www.levontin7.com, but ⓦ www
.myspace.com/levontine7 has more
information about forthcoming events.
30–80NIS.
Move 3 HaTa'arukha, Old Port ☏ 052/665 5001.
This mini-club, as it calls itself, is small
enough for an intimate (and sometimes
sweatbox) atmosphere, though it manages
to cram in three dancefloors, with a
clean-cut (but not straight-edge) vibe,
usually playing an eclectic mix of hip-hop
and dance tunes. Tuesday is gay night.
Mon, Tues, Thurs, Fri & Sat 11.30pm–dawn.
40–80NIS.

Contexts

Contexts

A short history of Jerusalem.. 267

Religion 275

Books.. 284

A short history of Jerusalem

J erusalem has been around for well over four millennia, and for much of that time it has been the object of veneration and rivalry. It has been fought over by some of the greatest empires in history, and larger than life characters – David, Solomon, Alexander the Great, Herod, Hadrian, Saladin, and of course Jesus – have walked its streets. What follows is of necessity only the briefest of overviews; if you'd like to read more about the city's history, check out some of the books listed on pp.285–286.

Canaanite Jerusalem

Jerusalem's first mention in **the Bible** is as "Salem" (Genesis 14:18), when its king, Melchizedek, ("he was the priest of the most high God"), brings bread and wine to Abraham. Later referred to as Jebus (Judges 19:10), the city is first called "Yerushalayim" (Jerusalem) when David brings Goliath's head here in I Samuel 17:54. The name may be a corruption of Ir Shalem ("City of Salem", Salem being the city's Canaanite patron god, and presumably Melchizedek's "most high God").

Whatever the origins of its name, the site has been settled since the early **Bronze Age**, around 2600 BC, but as it wasn't on a trade route its importance was always more strategic than commercial. Ancient Jerusalem receives its first documentation on "**execration texts**" (lists of Egypt's enemies and rebellious vassal states, inscribed in hieroglyphics on bowls and figurines which were then broken) dating from the nineteenth century BC. Jerusalem features too in the **Amarna letters**, a cache of letters on clay tablets discovered at Tel Al-Amarna, Egypt in 1887, among which are six written by its Canaanite King Abdiheba to Pharaoh Akhenaten of Egypt, the last of them begging for Egyptian help against the "Habiru" who are besieging it. David Rohl, an Egyptologist (see p.246) who dates Akhenaten's reign at around 1000 BC, believes the Habiru referred to are David's forces, but most scholars date Akhenaten and the Amarna letters to around 1350 BC, making that impossible. Either way, Jerusalem was a city-state whose people, the **Jebusites**, were regarded as a nation in their own right by the early Old Testament. The Jebusites may have been an offshoot of a larger Canaanite people, the **Amorites**, originally a nomadic tribe who migrated from Arabia to Mesopotamia before spreading into Palestine, and who seem to have been the city's founders.

The First Temple period

Jebusite Jerusalem withstood the Israelite invasion under Joshua (around 1200 BC), and remained independent for the next two hundred years. Around 1000 BC, it was taken by the forces of the Israelite King **David** who made it his capital. David's City, on Mount Ophel (see p.113), was south of the modern Old City. **Solomon**, his son, extended its limits and built the **First Temple** to its north on Mount Moriah between 960 and 957 BC. He also consolidated its position as capital of a mini-empire which, in the absence of opposition from Egypt or Mesopotamia (Iraq), both in decline at the time, extended from Syria in the north to Eilat in the south, and far to the east of the Jordan River. On Solomon's death the union of the twelve Israelite tribes split and Jerusalem became capital of the smaller, southern **kingdom of Judah**. The larger northern kingdom of Israel (or Samaria) fell in 722 BC to the Assyrians who, in 701 BC under their emperor Sennacherib, laid siege to Jerusalem. For a time all seemed lost, but King **Hezekiah** wisely had a tunnel constructed from Gihon Spring to the Pool of Siloam (see p.114) to supply the city with water, and Jerusalem was able to hold out until an uprising by the Babylonians against Assyrian rule in Mesopotamia forced Sennacherib to withdraw. By Hezekiah's time, the city had expanded north and west, taking in Mount Zion, plus what became the richest part of town, the Upper City, in the area today covered by the Armenian and Jewish Quarters.

The **Babylonians** eventually triumphed over Assyria and took over its empire in 612 BC. Judah's King Joash made an alliance with Egypt against them, but was beaten by Babylonian forces under Nebuchadnezzar, who installed a puppet king, Zedekiah, on the throne of Judah in 597 BC. When Judah again joined forces with Egypt against Nebuchadnezzar in 586 BC, the Babylonians invaded and captured Jerusalem, destroyed the Temple, and drove the population into **exile** in Babylon. The city was all but abandoned for the next fifty years.

The Second Temple period

In 539 BC Babylon's empire fell to the forces of **Persia** under Cyrus the Great. An unusually enlightened ruler for his time, Cyrus reversed the Babylonian policy of forced exile and allowed the Judeans or Jews, as they were now known, to **return**. The 50,000 or so Jews who did so, led by the prophets Haggai and Zechariah, rebuilt Jerusalem on the site of David's original city, and in 515 BC constructed a smaller and more austere **Second Temple**, on the site of Solomon's original. The following century, under Judea's Persian-appointed Jewish governor, Nehemiah, Jerusalem saw a further influx of Jews from Babylon under their community's leader, Ezra, revitalizing Jewish life in the city.

But Persian rule was to last less than a century more. In 322 BC, Jerusalem surrendered to Greek forces under **Alexander the Great**. On Alexander's death nine years later, his empire split. Jerusalem at first came under his general, Ptolemy, who ruled from Egypt, but in 198 BC Ptolemy's dynasty lost the city to their rivals, the **Seleucids** (descendants of another of Alexander's generals), under whom the Temple was Hellenized and dedicated to Zeus. Many young Jews eagerly adopted Greek culture, but Jewish fundamentalists bitterly opposed it. Under the Seleucid King Antiochus IV Epiphanes, an anti-Hellenist revolt broke out in Modin, west of Jerusalem, led by a group of brothers known as the Maccabees, who took the city in 164 BC and rededicated the temple, an event still celebrated by the Jewish winter festival of lights, Hanukkah (see p.211).

The **Hasmoneans**, descendants of Simon the Maccabee, ruled Jerusalem for the next century, but fell prey in their later years to internecine strife. When the Hasmonean king Aristobulus II took the throne in 67 BC, his brother Hyrcanus tried to wrest it from him. Hyrcanus was supported by Antipater, the governor of Idumea, a kingdom to the south of Judea that had been subdued by the Hasmoneans. Hyrcanus also solicited support from the **Romans**, whose general Pompey took Jerusalem in 63 BC, installing Hyrcanus as his puppet. But 26 years later, when the next Hasmonean ruler, Antigonus, tried to ally with Rome's enemy Parthia, the Romans deposed him and installed as ruler Antipater's son, **Herod the Great**.

Roman Jerusalem

Herod embarked on a massive programme of works, crowned by his restoration and enlargement of the Temple. He expanded the city northward to include much of what are now the Muslim and Christian Quarters, with a fort, the Antonia, at the northwestern corner of Temple Mount, and a palace incorporating the Hasmonean citadel along the west side of what is today the Armenian Quarter. Because he was a Roman puppet, levied heavy taxes, and impressed labour for his construction work, Herod was widely hated, but he refurbished Jerusalem probably more than any other ruler before or since. Before his death in 4 BC, he divided his kingdom among his sons. The largest part, Judea, with its capital at Jerusalem, went to his oldest son Archelaus, but was put under **direct Roman rule** in 6 AD. The Romans were far from popular and there were numerous uprisings against them, but lack of unity prevented these from succeeding. The Jewish population was split into two main political factions: the **Sadducees**, a conservative, priestly and privileged class who held onto their position by obedience to Rome, and the **Pharisees**, who believed in strict adherence to the Jewish law, and in the coming of a Davidic heir or "messiah" who would rescue them from Roman rule. In addition to these, the **Essenes** cut themselves off and set up isolated communities in the desert, while the **Zealots** refused to accept Roman rule and began a guerrilla war against it.

This was the time of **Jesus**, who is traditionally held to have lived from 1 BC to 30 AD, though his birth has also been dated at 6 BC (it would have to be before 4BC to be within the reign of Herod the Great), and 6 AD (when the census of Cyrenius, mentioned in Luke 2:1, probably took place – the Herod of the New Testament would then have to be Archelaus, or Herod Antipas of Galilee). Of Jesus as a historical personage, almost nothing is known other than what is written in the Gospels. These appear to pit him against the Pharisaic party, but his teachings seem very much in line with theirs, and he may also have been a claimant to the throne, since he apparently claimed descent from David and Solomon (Matthew 1:6–16; Luke 3:23–31). He would have entered the city on the first Palm Sunday around 30 AD, to be crucified there a week later.

Meanwhile, the Jews fought two bloody but unsuccessful revolts against the Romans. The **First Revolt** or **Jewish War**, in 66 AD, culminated in the destruction of Herod's Temple in 70 AD by Titus, son of the Roman Emperor Vespasian. It was followed by a **Second Revolt** (132–135 AD), led by **Simon Bar Kokhba** (or Simeon ben Kosiba). Little is known about the Second Revolt, but the rebels seem to have briefly taken Jerusalem before their final defeat. This time Jerusalem was completely razed by **Hadrian** who had a Roman city, **Aelia Capitolina**, built over its ruins, and banned Jews from living in or even entering the city. Hadrian's remodelled city established roughly the shape of the Old City as we know it today. A new main thoroughfare, the Cardo, extended from a gate in the north (now the Damascus Gate, see p.75) to what are now the central souqs, with a second main street from the northern gate towards what is now the Dung Gate. The streets of today's Old City still broadly follow the pattern laid down by the Romans. What is now the Muristan was the main Roman forum, with a second one on what is now the Via Dolorosa by the Ecce Homo Arch (see p.60).

The Byzantine period

In 312 AD, the Emperor **Constantine** legalized Christianity, beginning a 300-year period of almost uninterrupted Christian hegemony over Jerusalem. Constantine's mother, St Helena, embarked on a pilgrimage to the Holy Land to identify the major Christian sites, notably that of Calvary, over which Constantine commissioned the building of the first Church of the Holy Sepulchre (see p.65). In 330 AD, Constantine moved the capital of his empire to Byzantium (modern Istanbul), and the **Byzantine period** began. Under the Byzantines, the city expanded southward, covering again the ancient City of David, as well as Mount Zion. The Cardo was also extended southward, with the construction of the excavated section that can be seen today (see p.92).

In 614 AD, during a Byzantine–Persian war, Jerusalem fell to Persian forces after a three-week siege. Palestine's Jewish community, increasingly marginalized under Byzantine rule, supported the Persians, who held the city until the Byzantines reconquered it in 627. The most terrible episode of the city's 614 fall was the **massacre** of its Christian community at Mamilla (see p.136).

Islamic rule and the Crusades

Byzantine rule came to an end in 638 with the bloodless takeover by the **Arabs**, and Caliph Omar Ibn al-Khattab came to accept the city's surrender in person. Muslims already considered Jerusalem to be their third holiest city, and it became the capital of a *jund* (province) of their empire covering most of Palestine.

The city flourished under the **Ummayad** caliphs, who ruled from Damascus (660–750) and some of its most important buildings survive from this period, among them the Al-Aqsa Mosque and the Dome of the Rock. The Ummayads were succeeded by another dynasty of caliphs, the **Abbasids**, who ruled from Baghdad (750–969), and Jerusalem under their rule was home to several prominent Muslim Sufi scholars and became a religious focal point for Christian and Jewish pilgrims. In fact it became so popular that the first recorded complaint against the tourist trade was made in the eighth century, by a local historian, Al-Muqqadasi, who wrote that Jerusalem was being overrun by pilgrims. In 969

Jerusalem was taken over by the **Fatimids**, a dynasty of Isma'ili Shi'ites who ruled from Egypt before being ousted from Jerusalem by the **Seljuk** Turks in 1073.

The Seljuks, who had swept across Asia and subjugated even the Abbasid caliphs in Baghdad, now threatened the Byzantine Empire, whose ruler Alexius Comnenus appealed to the West for help. Pope Urban II responded by calling the First Crusade to aid Eastern Christendom. In 1099, the **Crusaders** – or "Franks", as they were known, since most of them were French – put an end to the first period of Muslim rule, and heralded a Christian **Kingdom of Jerusalem**, under which the Jewish population were burned alive and its Muslims slaughtered or expelled. The Crusaders set up a Kingdom of Jerusalem under Godfrey of Bouillon, Duke of Lorraine, who had led the assault on the city, succeeded on his death the following year by his brother Baldwin I.

Saladin and the Mamluks

In 1171, the teetering Fatimid caliphate in Egypt was taken over by Salah al-Din al-Ayyubi, known in English as **Saladin**, who defeated the Crusaders in July 1187 at the battle of the Horns of Hittin (near Tiberias in the Galilee) and went on to take Jerusalem in October of that year. Saladin allowed Christians to remain and Jews to return; the city's division into four quarters dates from around this time, but it was not a rigid system, and members of all faiths and communities lived alongside each other throughout the city. Saladin's dynasty, the **Ayyubids**, continued to rule Jerusalem, until Holy Roman Emperor Frederick II negotiated a deal with them in 1229, which ceded the whole city bar Temple Mount to the Christians. Twenty-five years later, however, Jerusalem was taken by the **Khwarizmian Turks**, who proceeded to slaughter most of the city's Christian population. They in turn were ousted in 1260 by the **Mamluks** (also spelt Mamelukes), originally slaves who ran the Ayyubids' army who had eventually taken over their empire. The most renowned Mamluk sultan was Baybars the Great (1260–77), who defeated the Mongols and drove the Crusaders from most of Palestine. Buildings of his reign often bear his symbol, a pair of panthers such as those on the Lions' Gate (see p.55).

Despite their brutal politics of assassination and poisoning (few Mamluk sultans lasted long, and fewer died of natural causes), the Mamluks were great patrons of the arts who sponsored a great **building programme** in Jerusalem, ordering the construction of numerous mosques, Koranic schools, hospitals, bathhouses, drinking fountains and pilgrims' hostels. The Muslim Quarter in particular bears the stamp of their architecture, and the holy city under their rule became a centre of Muslim pilgrimage and learning. However, later Mamluk rulers neglected the city, and its decline was hastened by earthquakes and an epidemic of the Black Death in the fifteenth century.

Ottoman rule

At the end of 1516, Jerusalem was taken by the **Ottoman Empire**, the centre of power shifting to Turkey. Ottoman sultan Suleiman the Magnificent (1537–41) had the walls rebuilt and embarked on a citywide reconstruction programme, but for over three hundred relatively peaceful years Jerusalem remained a mere provincial outpost of a vast empire: Christian travellers in these years described the city as a ghost town, dusty and dilapidated.

By the nineteenth century, the Ottoman Empire had become so moribund that it could mount no serious resistance to the burgeoning economic and political strength of the northern and western European states. Foreign powers investing in the city vied with each other for a foothold as they waited for the "sick man of Europe" to die. In 1860, Mishkenot Sha'ananim (see p.137) became the first new district to be constructed outside the walls, soon to be joined by areas, often founded by foreigners, with names like the Russian Compound and the German Colony. Many of the educational and religious institutions which still exist today – Schmidt's Girls' School, the Alliance Française and St George's Anglican Cathedral – were founded at this time too.

The twentieth century

In World War I, the Ottoman Empire found itself allied with Germany against Britain. On December 11, 1917, victorious British troops, under the command of General Edmund Allenby, dismounted and marched in through the Jaffa Gate on foot (out of respect for the city's venerable status), and at the end of the war, Jerusalem became the capital of the **British Mandate** in Palestine. The city's expansion outside the walls continued under the British, as both Palestinian Arabs and new Jewish immigrants constructed new residential quarters. In many areas, Jews and Arabs lived peacefully together, but the forces of politics were already starting to come between them. Across Palestine, Zionist settlers were forcing Arab labourers off the land they worked, and in Jerusalem the Muslim religious leader, Haj Amin al-Husseini, appointed Grand Mufti by the British in 1921, preached a virulent anti-Semitism that erupted into nationwide race riots starting in Jerusalem in August 1929 (see p.90). In 1936, the Arabs launched a full-scale revolt against the British, which was put down with some brutality, and after World War II, Zionist paramilitaries launched their own campaign of often violent opposition to British rule. As well as the British, both sides also targeted each other, and sectarian murders across the city, including bomb attacks on civilians, became a daily fact of life.

Eventually the British passed the problem to the United Nations, whose 1947 **Partition Plan** proposed to divide Palestine into a Jewish and an Arab state, with Jerusalem a "corpus separatum", open to both. The Arabs strongly opposed partition, and the UN's plan sparked off riots in which mobs attacked Jewish districts. Thus, well before the British pulled out and Israel declared independence in May **1948**, both sides moved to control as much of the city as possible, and neighbourhoods that had long been mixed became polarized, with the losing community forced out. In the ensuing war, the Arabs tried to maintain a **siege of Jewish West Jerusalem**, cutting off the water supply and ambushing Jewish convoys bringing supplies from Tel Aviv. In the end, the Israelis managed to secure a supply route and the siege failed, though the Arabs did succeed in forcing the Jews out of the Old City, whose Jewish Quarter was all but destroyed in the fighting. By the end of the 1948 war, Jerusalem was **divided**, occupied by Israeli troops in the west and the Jordanian Arab Legion in the east, with an armistice line (the **Green Line**) running through the city, and large UN-patrolled areas designated "no-man's-land" between Israeli and Jordanian positions. West Jerusalem remained the seat of Israel's government but Tel Aviv became the centre of economic and cultural life, while administrative power for East Jerusalem moved to Amman. The **Six Day War** of June 1967 saw the Israeli army take East Jerusalem and the Old City, unilaterally annexing them and declaring the city the "eternal, united capital of Israel".

The Israelis immediately set about rebuilding the Jewish Quarter, and repaved most of the rest of the Old City. They also extended Jerusalem's municipal boundaries as far as Bethlehem to the south and Ramallah to the north, and

The first **Jewish settlements** east of the Green Line were established a year after the Six Day War, and were state-sponsored, despite Israel being a signatory to the Fourth Geneva Convention which rules them illegal. Most were placed on high ground around East Jerusalem, such as at Gilo and East Talpiot to the south, and French Hill and Ramot Eshkol to the south, to reinforce Israel's case for sovereignty with "facts on the ground". Modern and well provided for, the settlements are a world apart from the surrounding Palestinian neighbourhoods.

The 1991 occupation of homes in **Silwan** (see p.117), marked a new type of settlement. As in the Old City's Muslim and Christian quarters, Jewish individuals and organizations, rather than the Israeli state, started taking over homes previously occupied by Arab families. Many of the new-style settlers are funded by donations from supporters in the US and other foreign countries. Unlike the residents of state-built settlements, whose main motivation for moving in is to get a nice home at a good price, the settlers taking over houses in Arab neighbourhoods are doing so because they want to redeem the whole of Jerusalem for the Jewish people. In some cases they are also trying to re-establish Jewish communities in areas where they existed before 1948. Many Israelis regard these ideological settlers as dangerous extremists, and outside Jerusalem, Israeli troops have even occasionally been employed to remove them by force from unauthorized West Bank outposts. In East Jerusalem, however, the authorities have given over tourist sites to right-wing settler groups (see p.115 & p.123), and have been accused by Israeli peace groups of planning an unbroken band of settler-run tourist sites around the east side of the Old City.

Palestinian Jerusalemites argue that construction of new Jewish homes, and forced takeover of Arab homes, is unfair when they themselves are invariably refused planning permission to build new houses, and face demolition if they build without it. On the other hand, Israel sees the settlements as a vital reinforcement of the city's unity and its status as the country's capital, and argues that Jewish people should be entitled to live in whatever part of town they like. The biggest government-sponsored settlement expansion project under way at present is in Har Homa, on Jerusalem's southern edge, adjoining Bethlehem, but an even larger settlement was approved by the Israeli Housing Ministry in 2007 for Atarot (Qalandia), at the northern end of town. Meanwhile, independent settler groups are setting up outposts in Palestinian areas such as the Mount of Olives (see p.123) and Sheikh Jarrah (see p.113), and there are now around 200,000 Jewish settlers in East Jerusalem, alongside some 245,000 Palestinians.

more controversially started to construct three bands of Jewish settlements to surround Palestinian East Jerusalem (see box above). In fact, the city still awaits final resolution of its 1948 division. Most of the international community does not recognize Israel's jurisdiction over East Jerusalem, considering it to be a part of the West Bank, and many Western countries still maintain consulates in the east serving the Palestinian Territories. The Palestinians themselves see the city as the capital of a future independent state.

Oslo and its aftermath

Under the 1993 **Oslo Accord** between Israel and the PLO, the final status of Jerusalem was to be the last thing resolved. At the **Camp David Summit** in July 2000, Israel's prime minister Ehud Barak and PLO leader Yasser Arafat failed to reach agreement despite an Israeli concession giving a proposed

The quiet deportation

Since 1967, Israel has been faced with the question of what to do with East Jerusalem's Palestinian residents, who do not want to become Israeli citizens nor leave the city. Unwilling to face the worldwide protests that would undoubtedly ensue if they simply expelled them, and unable to persuade more than a handful to accept the Israeli citizenship which it has offered to them, Israel has fallen back on subtler methods to reduce their numbers.

One of these is the expropriation of homes on various pretexts such as that the landowner is an absentee or that the property was Jewish before 1948. Another method is to refuse planning permission for those wishing to build homes and to demolish houses built without it. Israel has also been gradually removing people's right of residence. Under 1996 regulations, if East Jerusalemites live outside of the city for seven years (and the housing shortage often forces people to move beyond the city limits), they must prove that the city is their home and "centre of life" or their resident status is revoked. Residency rights in any other country automatically ends their right to reside in Jerusalem. Other regulations disallow Palestinian residents from bringing husbands or wives from the rest of the West Bank to live in Jerusalem, and likewise children whose fathers are not legal residents, even if they are born here to legally resident mothers. Thanks to regulations like these, some hundreds of East Jerusalemites lose their resident status every year and the building of the Separation Wall (see p.234) is set to accelerate that process, as it blocks access to those who have moved out of town and even cuts into Jerusalem's municipal boundaries, shutting out Palestinian districts such as Shuafat refugee camp, Anata and Kufr Akab. Palestinian sources estimate that the wall will cut off a third of blue (Jerusalem resident) ID card holders from access to the city.

Palestinian state sovereignty over at least part of East Jerusalem for its capital (though the extent of this offer is disputed). In September, following the collapse of negotiations, **Ariel Sharon**, leader of Israel's right-wing opposition party, Likud, took a walkabout tour of Temple Mount to protest against any plan to give the Mount to a future Palestinian state. The walkabout sparked rioting by Palestinians, Israeli retaliation, a chain of violence and counter-violence, and the end of negotiations. It also marked the beginning of the **Second Intifada**, an uprising by Palestinians against Israeli occupation, with protests and strikes as in the First Intifada of 1987–93, but also bomb attacks by Palestinian paramilitaries on Israeli civilian targets, many of them in Jerusalem; one of the worst incidents came in August 2003, when a Hamas suicide bomber blew himself up on a bus, killing 23 people.

Sharon's election victory in February 2001 marked a change of tack on Israel's part, and the following year construction began on the **Separation Wall**, designed to cut off the Palestinian population of the West Bank from Israel and its main settlements, as well as from East Jerusalem. Victory by the hardline Islamic fundamentalist party Hamas in 2006 elections for the Palestinian Authority led to **civil war** in Palestine which ended with Hamas controlling Gaza while Fatah held the West Bank. Under a "road map" to peace initiated by the US, and endorsed by Russia, the EU and the UN – in which Jerusalem's status would be one of the last things to be decided – Fatah continues to negotiate with Israel, but its position is much weakened, and it looks unlikely to wrest any concessions over Jerusalem in the near future. Israel thus retains control over the whole city.

Religion

Jerusalem's fame and splendour, not to mention its status of political hot potato, are largely down to the fact that it is holy to three of the world's main religions – Christianity, Islam and Judaism. All three are monotheistic, sharing the same God and most of the same prophets, but this has seldom brought them together, least of all in Jerusalem.

Judaism

The fundamental tenet of **Judaism** is belief in a single God; its most sacred text is the **Torah**, Pentateuch, or five books of Moses (Genesis, Exodus, Leviticus, Numbers and Deuteronomy), given by God to Moses on Mount Sinai. According to tradition, the Torah is both historical record and divine law, and a complete guide to human life. It forms the first part of the Hebrew **Bible** or *Tenakh*, whose books are the same as (though in a slightly different order from) those of the Christian Old Testament. The other two parts of the *Tenakh* are the books of the Prophets (*Nevi'im*), and the Sacred Writings, or "Hagiography" (*Ketuvim*).

According to the Torah, **Abraham** (originally named Abram) founded Judaism when he rejected the "idolatrous" religion of his father and migrated from Mesopotamia to Canaan. God rewarded him for his faith by promising the land to his descendants who would be a people special to God. This promise was renewed to Abraham's son Isaac and grandson Jacob (later renamed Israel). Together, the three are known as the **patriarchs** or forefathers of Judaism. It was **Moses**, though, who was the lawgiver, and to him that the Ten Commandments and the rest of the Torah, as well as the unwritten "oral law", were given on Mount Sinai after the Exodus from Egypt.

Many of the characteristic ideas and institutions of Judaism emerged during the **Babylonian exile** after the destruction of Solomon's Temple by Babylonian King Nebuchadnezzar in 586 BC, and following the **return** of the Judeans – now called **Jews** – under Cyrus the Great some 48 years later. The Babylonian exile marked the beginning of the Jewish **diaspora** or dispersion, since many Jews remained in Babylon which, in late antiquity and the Middle Ages, had one of the largest and most important Jewish communities in the world. In Babylon, much of the Hebrew Bible was rewritten, codified, annotated and completed; the ancient Hebrew alphabet – which the Samaritans still use – was replaced by the Aramaic one in which Hebrew is written today.

After the destruction of the Second Temple in 70 AD and the razing of Jerusalem after the Second Revolt in 132–35 AD, the centre of Judaism moved to the Galilee and Mesopotamia. The **rabbis** (Jewish sages and religious authorities) codified and elaborated the "oral law"; two such compilations emerged, both called the **Talmud**. The vast Babylonian Talmud was compiled between 200 and 500 AD in the rabbinic academies of Babylon where Jews had lived continuously at least since Nebuchadnezzar's time; the second version, less complete and authoritative and often misleadingly called the Jerusalem Talmud, was compiled predominantly in Caesarea, Tiberias and Sepphoris. Both have the same starting point, a core section called the **Mishnah**, which was codified in Galilee around 200 AD, to which is added a development and commentary called the **Gemara**. Great sages who have reached middle age and are already learned in the Bible and the Talmud may then go on to study the **Kabbalah**, or Jewish mysticism, in which secret meanings are sought within the text of the Hebrew Bible and the nature of God's relationship with creation are explored.

The main internal crisis in Judaism came with the Kara'ite schism in the mid-eighth century (see p.96), but divisions also emerged in Eastern Europe in the eighteenth and nineteenth centuries with the **Hassidic** movement, which placed the emphasis on piety and prayer as opposed to the scholasticism of the Talmudic academies. The Hassidim maintained their identity, and still do, by their dress – black hats, long coats, sidelocks (*peyot*) and beards – while the less orthodox were more in favour of integrating into the societies in which they lived. A more recent split, mostly now centred in the United States and to a lesser extent Britain, was brought about by the rise of **Reform Judaism**, which began in Germany in the early nineteenth century, and which attempts to adapt traditional Judaism to the modern world. **Conservative Judaism** (also known as Masorti) is a similar movement of US origin. All of these are more restrained in their reinterpretation than Progressive or **Liberal Judaism** (known in the US as Reform), which goes a lot further. The reforms include many of the ritual laws, acceptance of modern biblical criticism, services in languages other than Hebrew, and full equality for women – even women rabbis – not to mention gay weddings. The divisions between more traditional and more modern interpretations of Judaism have recently put great strains on the religion, especially as Liberal Judaism will accept converts much more readily, and recognizes as Jewish anybody with a Jewish parent of either sex.

Judaism in practice

The most obvious features of Judaism, apart from belief in the oneness of God, and the total eschewing of any representation of God as an image (shared by Islam and by much of Protestant Christianity), are observance of the Sabbath (Shabbat), and the dietary laws (*kashrut*).

Shabbat, lasting from Friday night until Saturday night, since the Jewish day is measured from nightfall to nightfall, is not merely a holy day and a day of general rest, but a day on which no work whatsoever may be performed. What constitutes work is very closely defined. It includes lighting or extinguishing a fire, which also means turning on or off a motor, or anything electrical. A fire may be *left* on throughout Shabbat (hence the traditional Shabbat dish, *cholent*, cooked on low heat over twelve hours in an oven ignited on Friday evening and put out on Saturday evening), and setting a time switch to turn things on and off during Shabbat is also permissible. Other work prohibited during Shabbat involves carrying anything outside the home, though a walled area called an *eruv* (such as a ghetto or walled Jewish city) is considered home for this purpose, and carrying something is distinguished from *wearing* it. This kind of legalistic definition creates a few loopholes, but not many.

Similar rules apply to Jewish **holy days**. Chief among these are **New Year** (*Rosh HaShannah*), a solemn religious occasion, and, even more solemn, **Yom Kippur** (the Day of Atonement) ten days later. This is a fast day, during which nothing may be eaten, and which is observed by many Jews who keep nothing else religious. **Sukkot** (Tabernacles) is a harvest festival commemorating the Israelites' nomadic existence in the wilderness following the Exodus, when observant Jews build, and even live in, a temporary structure (*sukkah*) attached to their home for eight days. Next comes **Passover** (*Pesah*), a spring festival celebrating the Exodus from Egypt, when the fleeing Israelites had no time to leaven their bread and on which the consumption of anything that might be

The Shema

Three times daily, practising Jews recite a prayer, **the Shema**, which consists of three biblical passages. The first, from Deuteronomy 6:4–9, reads:

"Listen, Israel, to the Lord our God: the Lord is One. Love the Lord your God with all your heart, your soul and your might, and take these words that I am commanding you today to heart: instil them in your children and talk about them when you are sitting at home and when you are walking down the street, when you go to bed and when you get up. Tie them as a sign on your arm and tie them round between your eyes; write them on the doorposts of your house and on your gates."

The phrase "The Lord is One" is a basic declaration of monotheism, implying that not only are there no other gods, but also that God is indivisible and cannot be seen as a multiple entity as in the Christian trinity or the Hindu pantheon. In fact "the Lord" (*Adonay* in Hebrew) is a euphemism employed in recitation to avoid speaking the actual name of God, written יהוה in Hebrew script, and traditionally rendered in English as "Jehovah", though it was probably pronounced more like "*Yahweh*". This name was considered so sacred that even in Temple times it was pronounced only by the High Priest in the Holy of Holies, once a year, on Yom Kippur, and was otherwise never uttered. Observant Jews never attempt to pronounce this name, and some may even write the word God as "G-d" to avoid using a name of God in vain.

As commanded by the passage, observant Jewish men do indeed tie these words to their arm and between their eyes, as you will see if you go down to the Wailing Wall of a morning: those boxes strapped to their arm and forehead, called **tefilin** in Hebrew (the correct English term is "phylacteries"), contain a parchment scroll bearing the passages of the *Shema* written out by hand. Likewise, the little box called a **mezuza**, which is nailed to the right-hand doorpost of a Jewish home, and of each room bar the bathroom, contains a scroll bearing the same words.

The tassels that hang out from the clothing of Orthodox Jewish men, known as **tzitzit**, are explained by the third passage in the same prayer, which is from Numbers 15:37–41, and instructs the Israelites to put a fringe on the four corners of their garments with a sky-blue thread in it to look on and think of the sky and therefore God wherever they are. For that reason observant Jewish men wear a four-cornered garment under their shirts, with a tassel on each corner that they let hang out. The blue thread is missing because the exact dye to be used is no longer certain and the rabbis have decided that it is better to use none at all than to use the wrong one. Jewish prayer shawls (*tallit*), worn by Jewish men (and in Liberal congregations women) when praying, also have *tzitzit* on their corners.

---

construed as leavened grain, or even to have come into contact with it (food has to be specially certified as leaven-free), is prohibited for eight days; **Shavuot** (Pentecost), celebrating the giving of the Torah to Moses on Mount Sinai, is seven weeks after Passover, the intervening period being the **Omer**, when celebration and festivity are avoided, as in the Christian Lent (**Lag Ba'Omer**, on the 33rd day, is a brief respite). Other Jewish festivals, without religious strictures, are **Hanukkah**, a winter solstice festival of lights to recall the Maccabees' rededication of the Temple after taking Jerusalem from the Seleucids (see p.269), and **Purim**, in memory of Persian Queen Esther's victory over anti-Semitic Prime Minister Haman in the biblical book named after her.

The dietary laws of **kashrut** revolve mainly around restrictions on the eating of meat. The Torah (Leviticus 11) specifies that of all animals, only non-carnivorous birds, cloven-hoofed ruminants and scaly true fish may be eaten. That means that rodents such as rabbit, non-scaly fish such as eel, shark or swordfish, and all invertebrates such as shellfish are prohibited (the Torah allows certain locusts and grasshoppers, but their exact identity is now uncertain, so sky prawns are also off the menu). The eating of pork is specifically condemned – it is, according to the Torah, "an abomination". But *kashrut* does not end there: certain parts of an animal are out of bounds too, notably kidneys, and land animals must be killed in a specified manner – their throat slit and their carcass hung to drain the blood (some animal activists have condemned this as cruel, though Jewish religious authorities point out that the method is specifically defined to minimize suffering by the animal). Even then, blood must be extracted from all meat using salt before that meat can be eaten. Finally, following the biblical command "thou shalt not seethe a kid in his mother's milk" (Exodus 23:19), meat and dairy products may not be eaten at the same sitting, nor is the same cutlery used for them. Thus all kosher restaurants are classified as either meat, dairy, or *parev* (neither). If some of these strictures seem extreme compared to the original commandment, that is because observant Jews wish to avoid even the remotest possibility of breaking God's commands, and build "a wall around the law" to make sure of this.

Islam

Islam, which in Arabic means submission (to God), originated in the early seventh century in Mecca, now in Saudi Arabia. The essential creed of Islam is that there is one God, Allah, and that Mohammed is his prophet. The basis of Islamic belief and practice, and the source of its legal and social system, is the **Koran**, the literal word of God dictated through the Archangel Gabriel to the **Prophet Mohammed**, who received it over a number of years beginning around 610 AD (the first verse that he received was almost certainly 96:1: "Recite in the name of your Lord who creates: creates man from a clot of blood"). The Koran consists of 114 **suras** or chapters, arranged according to length and written in Classical Arabic. One of the suras (number 17) describes Mohammed's **Night Journey** from Mecca to **Jerusalem** (see box, p.103) in the company of the Archangel Gabriel, where he prayed and then ascended to heaven. It was towards Jerusalem that Muslims first directed their prayers, and although this later changed, Jerusalem has remained the third holy site of Islam, after Mecca and Medina, and has long been a place of Muslim pilgrimage. The revelation which prompted the change of the **qibla** (direction of prayer) is set out in the second sura of the Koran, which established the **Ka'aba** in Mecca (Saudi Arabia) as the religious centre to which all Muslims have turned in prayer ever since. Mohammed claimed **Abraham** and his son Ishmael (Isma'il in Arabic) as founders of the Ka'aba and of Arabian monotheism, thus predating and independent of both Judaism and Christianity.

Mohammed was born in 571 AD in Mecca and worked for a merchant for whom he travelled along trade routes as far north as Damascus. He met Jews and Christians, and it may be that their religions inspired him to reject Arab polytheism in favour of a single God. But the new monotheistic faith that Mohammed introduced into his native city of **Mecca** met with opposition and persecution so that, in 622 AD, he and his followers were forced to flee to **Medina**. It is from this event – the **Hegira** – that Islam is dated. Seven years after the Hegira, the new code of social justice had gained such influence that Mohammed was able to return to Mecca as a powerful political leader. After the Prophet's death in 632 AD he was succeeded by four **caliphs** (successors). It was under the third caliph, Uthman, that the revelations which had been preserved by Mohammed's followers were collected and codified.

Division and the spread of Islam

Not long after Mohammed's death, the spiritual leadership of Islam became a source of contention. The first three caliphs were all related to Mohammed by marriage, but the fourth, Ali, was not only the Prophet's son-in-law but also his cousin. A substantial minority – the **Shi'ites** – supported Ali (Shi'at Ali) and broke away from the mainstream **Sunni** Muslims. Shi'ites believe that the Islamic community should be ruled only by a direct descendant of Mohammed (and therefore of Ali), called the **Imam**, a divinely appointed ruler who possesses superhuman qualities; the Sunnis, on the other hand, supported the Ummayads, descended from Mohammed's uncle Ummaya, and later the Abbasids who deposed them in 749, as **caliphs**, responsible for the administration of justice through the **shari'a** (Islamic law) and for the defence of the realm of Islam. One of the offshoots of Shi'ite Islam is the **Isma'ilis**, who broke away from the Shi'ite mainstream over the question of succession on the death of the sixth Imam; the Fatimids, who ruled Egypt and Palestine in the eleventh century, were Isma'ilis. Non-Isma'ili ("Twelver") Shi'ites recognize twelve Imams, the last of whom, Mohammed al-Muntazar, disappeared around 873, and is considered to still be living – the Hidden Imam, who will one day reappear and be known as the **Mahdi**.

In the seventh and eighth centuries, Islam extended through the Middle East and North Africa, later spreading to sub-Saharan Africa, India, China, Southeast Asia, parts of Russia and the Balkans and Spain. Islam was brought to Palestine in 638 AD under the third caliph, Omar Ibn al-Khattab, and the land lay under Muslim rule for the next 1300 years, interrupted only by around eighty years of Crusader dominance (1099–1187).

Islam in Jerusalem

Muslims in Jerusalem are Sunni, and Palestine's Muslim community has its own religious institutions, dating back to the time of the Mandate. The **Supreme Muslim Council** consists of a president (Ra'is al-'Ulema) and four members, two representing the district of Jerusalem, one Nablus and one Acre, who are elected by an electoral college for a period of four years.

The council, based in Jerusalem, has authority over all Muslim **Waqf** (plural: Awqaf) property and shari'a courts. The Awqaf are Muslim religious endowments, whose property is dedicated to charitable uses; the Waqf Committee in Jerusalem has authority over all Awqaf in Palestine. The **shari'a** courts, each of which is presided over by a **qadi** or judge, have exclusive jurisdiction in matters such as marriage, divorce and inheritance and can adjudicate in matters concerning Waqf properties.

The Waqf administers the Muslim holy sites of the Dome of the Rock, Al-Aqsa Mosque and other Islamic institutions in Jerusalem, and often finds itself in dispute with the Israeli authorities about jurisdiction over the properties, notably over rights appertaining to Jerusalem's Temple Mount, and to adjacent properties such as the Western Wall tunnel (see p.91) and Solomon's Stables (see p.105). Even the Wailing Wall is in theory Waqf property (see p.88).

Christianity

Christianity is based on the teachings of **Jesus**, but more importantly on the belief that Jesus is the **Christ**, the Messiah prophesied by the Old Testament (Isaiah chapters 7, 11 and 12, and Micah chapter 5), and that as such he is a manifestation of God in human form, and the only conduit between humanity and God.

A Jew from Nazareth, though apparently born in Bethlehem, Jesus taught in synagogues in the Galilee, gathering around him twelve **Disciples** or **Apostles** who accompanied him to Jerusalem, which he entered in triumph on Palm Sunday. Within a week, however, Jesus was arrested, tried and **crucified**. According to Christian belief, he was **resurrected** three days later (Matthew 28, Mark 16, Luke 24, John 20). By suffering and dying on the cross, Jesus atoned for the sins of humanity, thus offering salvation to all who accept him.

The teachings of Jesus are best set out in the Sermon on the Mount (Matthew 5–7), in which he preaches a creed of love and humility, urging his followers to reject hypocrisy, to "turn the other cheek" (5:38), to love and forgive their enemies (5:43), and to store up treasures in heaven (the rewards of righteousness) rather than on earth (in the form of riches or the admiration of others – 6:19–21). All this however, radical though it may be, is still within the mainstream of Jewish rabbinical thought. What sets Christianity apart from Judaism is its belief in **Jesus's divinity** within the Holy Trinity. According to this God has three aspects: God the Father is the creator of the universe and the God of the Old Testament. God the Son is Jesus, whose life, death and resurrection enable everybody to be redeemed from the sins of which we are all guilty, so long as we accept God and truly repent. God the Holy Spirit is the form of God that is everywhere and present in all things. It was this Holy Spirit that conceived Jesus in his mother, the Virgin Mary, immaculately – that is, without sex.

The break with Judaism came soon after Jesus's death, under **St Paul**. Paul was a Jewish persecutor of Christians who converted to Christianity after Jesus appeared to him on the road to Damascus (Acts 9:1–9), making him one of the disciples. Paul separated Christianity from Judaism, moving the Sabbath from Saturday to Sunday and abandoning Jewish customs such as circumcision and *kashrut*. The last tie between the two religions was cut at the Council of Nicaea in 325 AD, which ended the coincidence of Easter with the Jewish festival of Passover. Nonetheless, Christians in most denominations echo the rituals of Passover at mass when they take **holy communion**, that is the wine and wafer, representing the blood and body of Christ, just as the disciples did at the Last Supper (Matthew 26:20–30; Mark 14:17–26; Luke 22:14–38), which was evidently a Passover feast.

The growth of the early church

Despite persecution under Nero and later emperors, Christianity spread rapidly through the Roman Empire. It arose at a time when the traditional Greco-Roman religion of the empire was in decline, and the fact that Christianity was a brotherhood in which all were equal won it many converts among the lower classes. The life and teachings of Jesus were originally disseminated by the Apostles, but soon codified in the **Gospels** of Matthew, Mark, Luke and John. These, together with the Acts of the Apostles, the Epistles (letters of St Paul to various Christian churches) and the Book of Revelation, constitute the **New Testament**, written between 60 and 120 AD. Early Christian communities under St Paul organized themselves into an international **church**. This was divided into five patriarchates – based at Antioch, Alexandria, Constantinople, Rome and Jerusalem – each independent of the others, although all recognized the primacy of Rome. Within these, the church was subdivided into dioceses, each with a bishop, who claimed the authority of **apostolic succession**, that is, appointed by someone who was appointed by someone who was appointed by someone else in a line that could be traced back to the original Apostles. The bishop and patriarch of Rome, the Pope, was thus a direct successor to St Peter, who was appointed as head of the church by Jesus Himself (Matthew 16:18–19; John 21:15–17).

Divisions within Christianity

In 312 AD, **Constantine** legalized Christianity and it eventually became the state religion of the Roman Empire, accelerating its spread, so that it is now the world's largest religion; but even by 312, it was falling into the faction-alism that has dogged it more than any other world faith. The result is that Christians do not form a single **communion**, in other words, they pray in different churches which do not all accept each other's legitimacy. The splits between these churches appear to be over fine points of doctrine, but in fact politics was usually the main factor behind them. Some dissident churches such as the Nestorians and the Arians were excluded from orthodoxy as early as the fourth century, but the first split to affect churches which you will find in today's Jerusalem came in 451.

That year, the Council of Chalcedon declared that Jesus was both fully human and fully divine, having two natures united in one person. A group of mainly eastern churches however, unwilling to accept the authority of the Greek and Roman church establishment, took the view that Jesus had a single nature which was divine with some human attributes, and were thus excluded from the Catholic church. These **Monophysites**, including the Armenian Orthodox, Syrian Orthodox (Jacobite), Ethiopian and Coptic churches, are a tiny minority of Christians worldwide, but have an important presence in Jerusalem.

With the end of the Roman Empire, Christianity went into decline. Many of the tribes that invaded the Empire were pagan, or followed the Arian heresy, and in the seventh century Islam took over from Christianity as the main religion in most of North Africa and the Middle East. Nonetheless, Christianity expanded northward, and in the eleventh and twelfth centuries it went through a revival; but strains between Rome and the other four patriarchates led to an east–west **schism** that mirrored the old Rome-versus-Constantinople rivalry of the Roman Empire.

Again, the split was largely to do with politics, the eastern churches rejecting the primacy of Rome, and the authority of the Pope. The frequent breaches between east and west became definitive in 1054, when the eastern patriarchs broke away from communion with Rome. Constantinople's 1453 fall to the Muslim Ottomans severely weakened eastern Christianity, but the **Eastern Orthodox Churches** remain dominant in Greece, Russia and other parts of Eastern Europe, and also in Jerusalem, where the largest Christian denomination is Greek Orthodox. A number of small eastern churches nonetheless continue to accept the authority of Rome, and remain in communion with the Latin (Roman Catholic) church, though they have their own liturgies. These **Uniate churches** include the Greek Catholics (Melkites), Syrian Catholics, Armenian Catholics and Lebanese Catholics (Maronites).

Western Christianity underwent its most serious division in the **Reformation** of the sixteenth century, when Christians who followed reformers such as Martin Luther and Jean Calvin became **Protestants**. Again, the origins of Protestantism were based on doctrinal points – Protestants believe that each individual has their own relationship with God which does not require the intercession of a priest – but the real impetus behind the movement was political, a desire for greater independence from Rome by the economically strong nations of northern Europe and Great Britain.

Protestantism has four main branches: **Lutheranism**, which follows the teachings of Martin Luther and is strongest in Germany and the Netherlands; **Presbyterianism**, which follows the more austere teachings of Jean Calvin, and includes the Church of Scotland; **the Baptist movement**, strong in Wales and the United States, which advocates the baptism of believers as adults by full immersion in water; and **Anglicanism**, including the Church of England and the Scottish and American Episcopal churches, which retain a hierarchy of bishops and other Catholic features, but reject the authority of the Pope and infallibility of the church. Protestants form a small minority of Christians in Jerusalem, but became important here in the nineteenth century because of the worldwide dominance of Protestant countries; the result is a number of buildings constructed and maintained by Protestant churches. By far the largest Palestinian Protestant congregation is Anglican.

Christians in Jerusalem

The vast majority of Jerusalem's Christians belong to three major churches: Greek Orthodox, Roman Catholic (also known as Latin), and Armenian Orthodox. The Greek Orthodox community are under the Greek Orthodox patriarch who claims direct succession from St James, the first bishop of Jerusalem. The Armenians are headed by their own patriarch, who was recognized under the Ottomans as the head of all the Monophysite churches. The Roman Catholic church comes under the authority of the Latin Patriarch, who is appointed by Rome.

The hierarchies of the main Christian churches have traditionally been dominated by foreigners, and the European influence can be clearly seen in icons and paintings in local churches, almost all of which depict Jesus and the Virgin Mary as light-skinned and blue-eyed, though in reality they were presumably as dark in complexion as most other local people. A blow against this European domination was struck in January 1988, when Michel Sabbah became the first Palestinian to be appointed Latin Patriarch of Jerusalem, and he was succeeded in 2008 by Fouad Twal, who hails from Jordan.

On top of these major divisions, there are a plethora of denominations from all over the world. In addition to the big three, there are also smaller congregations of Armenian Catholics, Maronites, Copts, Ethiopian and Russian Orthodox, Syrian Catholics and Syrian Orthodox. Many newer churches also claim rights to the holy sites; these include Anglicans, Presbyterians (primarily the Church of Scotland), Seventh Day Adventists, Quakers, Mennonites, Mormons and Jehovah's Witnesses. A more recent phenomenon is the arrival of fundamentalist, **born-again Christians**, mostly North American, who believe that the State of Israel is the fulfilment of biblical prophecy.

Recent years have also seen the growth of a number of **Jewish-Christian sects** stressing the Jewish roots of Christianity and attempting to link Jewish ritual and practice with an acceptance of Jesus (sometimes referred to by his presumed Hebrew name, Yeshua) as Messiah and God. While these groups are insignificantly tiny among Israeli Jews and Palestinian Christians, a number of their Western adherents have been making their way to Jerusalem of late. The movement started as a way of converting Jewish people to Christianity, but it has also led a number of Christians, especially Protestants, to take a greater interest in the Jewish origins of Jesus and his teachings.

Books

A great many books have been published about Jerusalem, mostly about its history, and most of those are pretty partisan one way or another. Obviously too, many books about Jerusalem have a strong religious angle. On the other hand, there are plenty of books that aren't about religion or politics, books that look at the city's less well-known sights, its legends and curiosities, its buildings and architecture. There are also some excellent novels set in the city, both highbrow and lowbrow. The following selection offers a good starting point with particular favourites indicated by the ✹ symbol. Good places in town to find books about Jerusalem in English include the Educational Bookshop (see p.218), the American Colony bookshop (see p.218) and Jordan Bookshop (see p.218).

Background

The Bible The obvious book to read, whether you are a believer or not, and surprisingly compelling. Parts of the Bible of particular interest to a traveller are: Genesis 12–50 dealing with the patriarchs; the "historical" books of the Old Testament (Joshua, Judges, I and II Samuel, I and II Kings, I and II Chronicles, Ezra, and Nehemiah), the Gospels, and the Acts of the Apostles. The King James (Authorized) Version is best loved for the beauty of its language, but a modern English translation such as the Good News Bible is much easier to read.

Isidore Epstein *Judaism*. A good all-round introduction, wide-ranging but concise, covering the Torah, the prophets, the Talmud and the Kabbalah, as well as Jewish philosophy and history, in accessible (and affordable) paperback form.

Robert I. Friedman *Zealots for Zion*. An examination of the West Bank settler movement, covering their history and examining their beliefs and their aim of annexing the West Bank to Israel. Written in 1992, it's dated now, but still relevant,

especially to the friction between Palestinians and Israeli settlers in East Jerusalem and Hebron.

James L. Gelvin *The Israel-Palestine Conflict*. It's very difficult to recommend a single book that gives a concise overview of the Middle East conflict. Partly, this is because so many books on the subject are busy grinding an axe for one side or the other, and partly it's because the situation changes so fast that any new book will be out of date within a couple of years. Gelvin's book is one of the best to go for as an introduction because, to start with, it tries to be neutral between the two sides, while explaining the views of both; secondly, it's relatively up to date (published in 2005); and thirdly, it presents a readable account that isn't too long or turgid, and makes plenty of suggestions for further reading if you want to look more deeply.

Justin Wintle *The Rough Guide History of Islam*. A pocket-sized mine of information about the Islamic world from the time of Mohammed through to the modern day, arranged in the form of a timeline.

Archaeology

Jerome Murphy-O'Connor *The Holy Land*. A clearly written, detailed but accessible layperson's guide by a New Testament professor and Jerusalem priest, covering all the country's main archeological sites, with historical and archeological accounts and site plans. Almost half the book is dedicated to sites in Jerusalem.

Yigael Yadin (ed) *Jerusalem Revealed: Archeology in the Holy City 1968–1974*. A collection of scholarly articles by eminent Israeli archeologists, covering excavations across the Old City, with the emphasis on what they reveal about daily life in Jerusalem during biblical and post-biblical times.

History

Karen Armstrong *A History of Jerusalem: One City, Three Faiths*. A spiritual rather than political history, concentrating more on ancient than modern times, and always with a deep sympathy and understanding for the Jews, Christians and Muslims who have lived in or come to Jerusalem over the ages, combined with a clear and extremely enlightened understanding of the theological issues surrounding the city.

K.J. Asali (ed) *Jerusalem in History*. Nine essays, each dealing with a different period, from the bronze age to the twentieth century, each by an expert on the particular period. The book is scholarly and often quite detailed, but it gives a good insight into each of the periods it covers.

Meir Ben-Dov *Historical Atlas of Jerusalem*. Lots of photos, maps and detailed plans accompany this historical description of Jerusalem from Jebusite times to the present, which not only discusses the city itself, but also shows how it fitted in with regional politics and trade routes at different times in its history.

Meron Benvenisti *City of Stone: the Hidden History of Jerusalem*. A well-balanced account of Jerusalem's history – and most especially its modern history – by an Israeli former deputy mayor of the city.

Eric H. Cline *Jerusalem Besieged: From Ancient Canaan to Modern Israel*. A very learned, generally Jewish take on the struggles to control Jerusalem (at least 118 of them in the last 4000 years), by a distinguished archeologist and historian of the region, highly critical of the way historical events have been misused as propaganda by Palestinian and other Arab politicians.

Larry Collins and Dominique Lapierre *O Jerusalem!* Well-written and-researched popular account of the 1948 struggle for Jerusalem seen through the eyes of participants, mainly from the Israeli point of view. An easy and entertaining read.

Michael Dumper *The Politics of Sacred Space: The Old City of Jerusalem in the Middle East Conflict*. An academic book which focuses on the political issues surrounding the Old City specifically, attempting to clarify the obscure workings of the Waqf and the Christian Patriarchates, and the question of Jewish settlers, as well as looking at the sensitive nature of the Old City in any Israeli–Palestinian negotiations, and the wider question of how a modern state should treat a holy city, whether it be Jerusalem, Mecca or Rome.

Roger Friedland and Richard Hecht *To Rule Jerusalem*. Among the many accounts of the Israeli-Palestinian conflict, this one stands out for placing Jerusalem at the centre of the struggle, with a clear analysis of the fault lines – Jew vs Arab, Jew vs Jew, Arab vs Arab – which divide the holy city, while the authors themselves carefully refrain from taking sides.

Martin Gilbert *Jerusalem in the Twentieth Century*. Engaging account of Jerusalem's twentieth-century history by a prominent pro-Israeli historian, who covers all the important incidents of the century, using firsthand eyewitness accounts to bring them to life.

Dore Gold *The Fight for Jerusalem: Radical Islam, the West, and the Future of the Holy City*. Unashamedly biased account of Jerusalem's history by a former Israeli ambassador to the UN, arguing that only Israel can defend the holy city against the threat to it from Islamic fundamentalism.

Flavius Josephus *The Jewish War*. An account of the 66 AD Jewish Revolt against the Romans by a rebel-turned-collaborator who was there; his account of the fall of Masada is particularly authoritative. Josephus's *Antiquities*, a history of the Jews until his day, contains information obtained from the access the Romans gave him to the Temple archives.

Amy Dockser Marcus *Jerusalem 1913: The Origins of the Arab-Israeli Conflict*. In Ottoman Palestine, Jews and Arabs rubbed along together as friends and neighbours. Then it all

went sour. Fingering 1913 as the turning point, Marcus looks at three of the people whose activities helped shape the fate of Palestine's capital, and tries to show how Jews and Arabs gradually came to realize the extent to which they were at odds over the city's future.

F.E. Peters *Jerusalem: The Holy City in the Eyes of Chroniclers, Visitors, Pilgrims and Prophets from the Days of Abraham to Modern Times*. A fascinating collection of firsthand accounts of the city from ancient times to the early nineteenth century, from a range of different viewpoints, and mostly at crucial moments in the city's history.

Bernard Wasserstein *Divided Jerusalem: The Struggle for the Holy City*. Examining the history of Jerusalem and its bitterly divided society, Wasserstein cuts through the interdenominational squabbles to the hard *realpolitik* underneath, arguing that religious fervour over the city has invariably been manipulated by politicians for their own ends.

Annabel Jane Wharton *Selling Jerusalem: Relics, Replicas, Theme Parks*. The author, an art historian, looks back over what Jerusalem has meant since the Middle Ages to people in the West, and the ways in which the city has been marketed there, whether in the form of relics, European churches modelled on the Holy Sepulchre, paintings and lithographs, or reproductions in theme parks.

Jerusalem life and legends

Tzvia Dobrish-Fried *Secrets of Jerusalem*. A whimsical compendium of curious information on little known features of the city, from an artistic manhole cover in Zion Square to the Ethiopian Compound on the roof of the Holy Sepulchre Church, covering areas like Rehavia

and the German Colony as much as downtown or the Old City.

Ronald L. Eisenberg *The Streets of Jerusalem*. Despite its name, this book doesn't tell you much about the streets themselves; what it does tell you about is their names – what they mean, and who or what they refer to. If you can't find it anywhere else, SPNI (see p.218) usually have it.

Amos Elon *Jerusalem, City of Mirrors.* An insightful essay by a prominent Israeli writer, examining Jerusalem's many aspects (the cruel city, the dangerous city, the holy city) and contrasting the very different ways in which it is seen by its inhabitants.

Adina Hoffman *House of Windows: Portraits from a Jerusalem Neighbour-hood.* An American *oleh* (Jewish immigrant to Israel) presents a series of vivid and sympathetic portraits of her neighbours in the Musrara district, giving a highly evocative portrayal of how it has changed over the years from a mixed Jewish-Arab district before 1948, to a dumping ground for poor Moroccan immigrants when it was a dead end on the Jordanian border, to a trendy area undergoing gentrification today.

Kevork Kahvedjian *Jerusalem through my Father's Eyes.* A fascinating

collection of black and white photo-graphs of Jerusalem from the 1920s to the 1950s taken by an Armenian refugee whose son now sells prints from his collection at Elia Photos in the Christian Quarter (see p.227).

Abraham E. Millgram *Jerusalem Curiosities.* A treasury of wonderful bits and pieces, quotes and anecdotes about the city in different periods of its history, from King David to King George, exploring its nooks, its crannies, and, as promised, its curiosi-ties. A fascinating read.

Zev Vilnay *Legends of Jerusalem.* An interesting collection of legends and folklore associated with Jerusalem's many sites by practitioners of its different faiths. By ferreting out the legends associated with each site, the author – a popular writer on the land of Israel – not only adds a new angle to each, but also gives a sympa-thetic insight into the superstitions that have grown around the city's holy places.

Architecture and building

Michael Burgoyne *Mamluk Jerusalem: an Architectural Study.* A detailed and scholarly study of Jerusalem's Mamluk heritage, but really for specialists in the field. Part two goes through the city's Mamluk architecture building by building, with plans, specifications and commentary on each.

Oleg Grabar *The Shape of the Holy: Early Islamic Jerusalem.* A richly illustrated account of the way Islam transformed the architecture of Jerusalem in the centuries before the Crusades, concentrating, obviously, on that masterpiece of Ummayad architecture, the Dome of the Rock.

Robert Hillenbrand *The Architecture of Ottoman Jerusalem: An Introduction.* A sequel to Michael Burgoyne's book

on Mamluk architecture, focusing on buildings that went up in Jerusalem in the sixteenth and seventeenth centuries. Specialist yes, but extremely informative if you want an extra insight into places you barely notice as you walk through the Old City.

David Kroyanker *Jerusalem Architecture.* The author, an Israeli architect and historian, has written six specialized volumes in Hebrew on the architecture of Jerusalem, but this glorious coffee-table book, with lots of colour photos, is of much more interest to a non-specialist reader, while still offering plenty of heavyweight discussion about construction and urban planning from biblical times to the present day.

Philipp Misselwitz and Tim Rieneits (eds) *City of Collision: Jerusalem and the Principles of Conflict Urbanism.* A collection of essays on the way Jerusalem's ethnic divisions are determining its shape and growth. Some of them are very interesting, but they'd be a whole lot more so if the authors could make their points in plain English rather than sociological jargon.

Simone Ricca *Reinventing Jerusalem: Israel's Reconstruction of the Jewish Quarter After 1967.* An account of how Israel conceived and executed the reconstruction of the Old City's Jewish Quarter, by an author who is very critical of its artificiality and the ideology behind it.

Fiction

S.Y. Agnon *Only Yesterday.* A young Zionist immigrant is torn between the secular world of Jaffa and the religious world of Jerusalem in this bitter-sweet portrayal of the Jewish community in early twentieth-century Palestine.

Nicholas Blincoe *The Dope Priest.* A rollicking comedy thriller featuring a retired English hash smuggler caught up in a shady Jerusalem property deal with an old Palestinian mate from Bethlehem. Silly but fun.

Batya Gur *Murder in Jerusalem.* A whodunnit from Israel's favourite spinner of detective yarns, in which her hero, police inspector Michael Ohayon, musters all his sleuthing skills to solve a spot of foul play among the rarified academics of the Hebrew University.

Simon Louvish *The Therapy of Avraham Blok, City of Blok, The Last Trump of Avram Blok.* In this trilogy, Louvish, a Scottish-born film-maker who spent his youth in Israel, portrays the surreal chaos of Jerusalem. His myriad characters rush, tumble and collide with resurrected figures from the past in a wonderfully funny, and often tragic, confusion of madness.

Matt Rees *The Bethlehem Murders* (aka *The Collaborator of Bethlehem*). A thrilling and well-informed Bethlehem detective story centred on a teacher trying to clear a student accused of collaboration with the Israelis, set against a background of Christian–Muslim tensions and frustratingly corrupt Palestinian politics.

Amos Oz *My Michael.* In 1950s West Jerusalem, a woman trapped in an unhappy marriage finds solace in a world of fantasy while, back in the real world, the Suez Crisis comes to a head. Oz, Israel's best-known novelist and a Jerusalemite through and through, sets a number of his works in the city. In his autobiographical novel, *A Tale of Love and Darkness,* a boy growing up in the city before, during and after the 1948 War of Independence looks back over the history of his family and the forces that have shaped it.

Muriel Spark *The Mandelbaum Gate.* A thoughtful tale of love and espionage by a distinguished Scottish novelist. The heroine, a half-Jewish Englishwoman on pilgimage to the Holy Land, finds herself drawn into intrigue and danger on both sides of the Green Line as she pursues an affair with a British diplomat in the divided Jerusalem of the early 1960s.

Robert Stone *Damascus Gate.* A half-Jewish American journalist gets involved in the shenanigans of a religious cult as he investigates the subject of Jerusalem syndrome. It's too slow to be a thriller, and too contrived for a serious novel, but what it does have is a strong sense of place, and sometimes you can really imagine yourself walking the same streets as the characters when you read it.

A.B. Yehoshua *A Woman in Jerusalem*. When a migrant worker is murdered in a market bomb attack, a manager at the bakery where she worked is given the task of arranging her affairs in a story that examines some of the hidden aspects of life in Jerusalem.

Poetry

Yehuda Amichai *Poems of Jerusalem*. Israel's most important poet, the first to write in colloquial Modern Hebrew, Amichai is said to be the most widely translated Hebrew poet since King David. He lived for much of his life in Jerusalem and dedicated a book of poems to the city, which is available in English translation in a single volume with his *Love Poems*.

For children

Mark Podwal *Jerusalem Sky: Stars, Crosses and Crescents*. A poetic journey through the city of three faiths, beautifully illustrated, and designed for four- to eight-year-olds (though adults will find it charming too). The pictures depict Jerusalem's Jewish, Christian and Muslim holy places, with a text recounting tales of miracles from the stories of all three religions.

Language

Language

Pronunciation, spelling and gestures 293

Useful words and phrases...294

Glossary 299

Language

Jerusalem's two official languages are **Hebrew** and **Arabic**. Both are Semitic languages closely related to each other but very different from an Indo-European language such as English. While this can make them difficult to learn for most Western travellers, making the effort to pick up a few phrases will be appreciated by both Hebrew-speaking Israelis and Arabic-speaking Palestinians. If you are not sure whether somebody is Israeli or Palestinian, it may be a good idea to stick to English in the first instance to avoid giving offence. Most people in Jerusalem will speak some English in any case and most signs are trilingual – written in Hebrew, English and Arabic. Ultra-orthodox *Haredi* Jews, especially in Mea Shearim, may also use Yiddish, a language written in Hebrew letters but actually more like German (German speakers should understand it), which has given us words like nosh, spiel, schlep and schmooze. Other Jewish Israelis may speak the language of their country of origin, most notably Russian.

For Hebrew, there are a few websites with useful phrases, including Ⓦ www.learn-hebrew-phrases.com and Ⓦ www.day12.com/phrasebook_hebrew.htm (the second of these lets you hear the words too). Arabic varies from country to country, so there is a lot less online for Palestinian Arabic specifically, but you'll find one or two useful resources at Ⓦ www.camdenabudis.net/languagelinks.html.

Pronunciation, spelling and gestures

Hebrew and Arabic contain a number of sounds which English does not have, so the **pronunciation** given here is approximate, though it should be near enough to be understood. In the transliteration in the following lists, "kh" represents the sound of the "ch" in loch, and is sometimes written as "ch" in Israel, while "gh" (used in Arabic only) is its voiced equivalent (as "g" is to "k"), a kind of gargling sound, not unlike a French "r"; a "q" is like a "k" but pronounced at the back of the throat (if that's too hard, just say it like a "k"). Letters and syllables in **bold** should be stressed. One letter, '*ayn* or '*ayin*, is notoriously difficult for Westerners to pronounce (ask a native speaker if you want to hear what it sounds like, though Ashkenazi Jews, like other Westerners, often treat it as silent).

Note that **spellings** of Hebrew and Arabic words in English may vary. Some guttural and emphatic sounds can be represented by putting a dot under letters like "h" and "t", though that has not been done in this book. '*Ayin* is usually represented by an apostrophe. It's also worth knowing that some road signs, rather than giving the English name for a town or street, may simply give the Hebrew name spelt in Roman letters, in particular Yafo for Jaffa, Azza for Gaza, and Shechem for Nablus. You may even occasionally see Hebron spelt "Chevron".

Of **gestures**, the one you should know consists of holding the fingers and thumb all together pointing upwards, and waving them up and down a little. In the Middle East – unlike Italy, where the same gesture means "for goodness sake!" – this means "bear with me" or "please wait a minute" (*rega* in Hebrew, *istanna shuwaya* in Arabic).

Useful words and phrases

English	Hebrew	Arabic

Basics

English	Hebrew	Arabic
yes	ken	**ay**wa
no	lo	la
I	a**nee**	**a**na
you (m/f sing)	a**ta**/att	**in**ta/**in**ti
she	**hee**	**hee**ya
he	**hoo**	**hoo**wa
we	a**nakh**noo	na**ha**noo
you (m or mixed/f only, pl)	a**tem**/a**ten**	**in**too
they (m or mixed/f only)	hem/hen	hoom
please (to a man/woman)	beva**ka**sha	min**fad**lak/min**fad**lik
thank you	to**da**	**shuk**ran
excuse me (to a man)	slee**kha**	law se**makht**
excuse me (to a woman)	slee**kha**	law se**makh**ti
I'm (m/f) sorry	slee**kha**	ana a**sif**/**as**fa
there is/is there?	yesh(?)	fee(?)
there isn't (any)	ayn	ma**feesh**
big/small	ga**dol**/qa**tan**	ka**bir**/se**ghir**
who?	mee?	meen?
what (is that)?	ma (ze)?	shnoo (da)?
why (not)?	**la**ma (lo)?	lay (la)?
how?	aykh?	kayf?
wait a sec	**re**ga	is**tan**na
let's go	**yal**la	**yal**la
never mind	ayn da**var**	ma'a**lesh**
thank goodness/praise the Lord	ba**rukh** ha-**shem**	alhumdul**lah**
Do you (m) speak English?	Ata mada**ber** ang**lit**?	Ta**kal**lam ing**lee**zi?
Do you (f) speak English?	At mada**ber**et ang**lit**?	Ta**kal**ma ing**lee**zi?
I (m/f) don't understand.	Ani lo me**veen**/me**vee**na.	Ana mish fa**hem**/**fah**ma.

Numbers

English	Hebrew	Arabic
half	**khet**zi	nuss
1	e**khad**	**wa**hid
2	sh**tay**im	it**neen**
3	sha**losh**	ta**la**ta
4	**ar**ba	**ar**baa
5	kha**mesh**	**kham**sa
6	shesh	**sit**ta
7	**she**va	sa**baa**
8	sh**mon**eh	ta**man**ya
9	**tay**sha	**ti**sa

10	eser	ashara
11	ekhad esray	hidash
12	shtem esray	itnash
13	shalosh esray	talatash
14	arba esray	arbatash
15	khamesh esray	khamastash
16	shesh esray	sittash
17	shva esray	sabatash
18	shmona esray	tamantash
19	t'sha esray	tisatash
20	esrim	ashreen
21	esrim ve-ekhad	wahid w-ashreen
22	esrim ve-shtayim	itneen w-ashreen
30	shloshim	talateen
40	arbaim	arbaeen
50	khamishim	khamseen
60	shishim	sitteen
70	shivim	sabaeen
80	shmonim	tamaneen
90	tishim	tiseen
100	me'a	meeya
200	matayim	meeyateen
300	shalosh me'ot	toltameeya
400	arba me'ot	arba meeya
1000	elef	alf
2000	alpayim	alfeen

Greetings

hello	shalom	asalaam aleikum
goodbye	lehitraot	ma'a salama
good morning	boker tov	saba' al-kheer
good evening	erev tov	misaa al-kheer
good night	laila tov	leila sa'ida
how are you (m)?	ma shlomkha?	keefak?
how are you (f)?	ma shlomekh?	keefik?
fine thanks	beseder	tamaam alhumdullah

Shopping

open/closed	patooakh/sagur	maftooah/masakkar
Do you (m) have (a/any)…?	Yesh lekha?	'Andak?
Do you (f) have (a/any)…?	Yesh lekh?	'Andik?
something better/cheaper	mashehu yoter tov/zol	aishay ahsan/arkhis
How much (money) (is that)?	Kama (kesef) (zeh ole)?	Qadaysh (flooss) (da)?
expensive/cheap	yakar/zol	ghali/rakheess
OK, agreed	beseder	maashi

295

Accommodation

Do you have a single /double room?	Yesh **khe**der ye**khid** /**zoo**gee?	Fee **ghor**fa li-**wa**hid/muzda **wa**ja?
(with) a double bed	(im) mi**ta** zu**geet**	bi-**wa**hid sa**reer** maz**dooj**
(with) twin beds	(im) shtei mi**tot**	bi-sari**reen**
hot water	**ma**yim kha**mim**	**ma**ya **sukh**na
bathroom	am**bat**ya	**ham**mam
air conditioning	mi**zug** a**vir**	tak**yeef ha**wa
Can I see the room?	**Esh**far li**rot** ha-**khe**der?	**Mum**kin a**shoo**fa al-**ghor**fa?

Directions

Is there a ... near here?	Yesh ... qa**rov** le**po**?	Fee ... qa**reeb** min **hi**na?
Where's the ...?	**Ay**fo ha-...?	Wayn al-...?
hotel	ma**lon**	**fun**duq
restaurant	misa**da**	mat'**aam**
bank	bank	bank
post office	do'**ar**	ba**reed**
pharmacy	bet mir**kak**hat	say**da**lia
hospital	bet kho**lim**	mus**tash**fa
toilet	shiru**tim**	twa**let**
train station	takha**nat** ra**ke**vet	ma**ha**tat at-tren
bus station/bus stop	takha**nat au**tobus	ma**ha**tat al-ootoo**bis**
service taxi station	takha**nat** she**rut**	ma**ha**tat as-ser**veess**
museum	muze'**on**	**mat**haf
church/mosque/synagogue	kene**sia**/mis**gad**/bet k**nes**set	kanee**sa**/mas**jid**/ka**neess**
tourist office	modi'**in** taya**rim**	mak**tab** as-siya**ha**
left/right	smo**la**/ya**mee**na	shi**mal**/ya**meen**
straight on	yi**shar**	**du**ghri

Time

when?	ma**tay**?	**im**ta?
now/later	akh**shav**/ye**ter** me'u**kha**	al'**aan**/baa**deen**
today/yesterday/tomorrow	ha-**yom**/et**mol**/ma**khar**	al-**yom**/**buk**ra/im**ba**rih
month/year	kho**desh**/sha**na**	**shahr**/**sa**na
day/week	yom/sha**vu**a	yom/is**bo**a
hour/minute	**sha**'a/**da**qa	sa**'a**/da**qi**qa
What time is it?	Ma ha-**sha**'a?	Qa**daysh** as-**sa**'a?
three o'clock	**sha**'a sha**losh**	**sa**'a ta**la**ta
quarter past three	sha**losh** va-**re**va	ta**la**ta wa-**ro**ba
half past three	sha**losh** va-**khet**zi	ta**la**ta wa-**nuss**
quarter to four	**re**va le-**ar**ba	ar**baa** ila **ro**ba
Monday	yom shay**nee**	yom al-it**neen**
Tuesday	yom sh**lee**shee	yom at-ta**la**ta
Wednesday	yom ra**vee**'ee	yom al-**ar**ba
Thursday	yom kha**mee**shee	yom al-kha**mees**

Friday	yom **shee**shee	yom al-**juma**'
Saturday	yom shab**bat**	yom as-**sabt**
Sunday	yom ri**shon**	yom al-**a**had

Eating and drinking

For a glossary of local specialities, see p.180.

knife/fork/spoon	sa**keen**/maz**leg**/kaf	si**kee**na/**shaw**ka/mala'a
bread	**le**khem	khubz
fish	dag	**sa**mak
meat	bas**sar**	**lah**ma
chicken	'off	djaj
eggs	beit**zim**	beid
milk	kha**lav**	ha**leeb**
oil	**she**men	zeit
vegetables	yera**kot**	khu**daar**
aubergine (eggplant)	khat**zeel**	beitin**jan**
carrots	**ge**zer	**je**zer
chickpeas (garbanzo beans)	**hum**mus	**hum**mus
courgette (zucchini)	kee**shu**	**cu**sa
haricot beans	she**'u**'it	fa**su**lia
onion	bet**zal**	ba**sal**
peas	a**fu**na	ba**sel**la
potato	ta**pu**akh a**da**ma	ba**ta**ta
rice	o**rez**	ruz
olives	zei**tim**	zei**toun**
salad	sa**lat**	sa**la**ta
fruit	pe**rot**	fa**wa**ka
apple	ta**puah**	tu**fah**
orange	ta**puz**	**bur**tuqal
lemon	li**mon**	li**moun**
apricot	**mish**mish	**mish**mish
peach	a**far**sek	khookh
dates	ta**mar**	ta**mar**
fig	**tee**na	teen
grapes	ana**vim**	**'a**nib
strawberries	tu**tim**	fa**raw**la
banana	ba**na**na	mooz
custard apple (sweetsop)	an**co**na	**ken**ya
melon	mi**lon**	sha**mam**
watermelon	ava**ti**akh	bat**tikh**
persimmon (sharon fruit)	afar**si**mon	afar**si**mon
pomegranate	ri**mon**	ru**man**
prickly pear	**sa**bra	teen **shaw**qi
starfruit	caram**bo**la	caram**bo**la
salt	me**lakh**	me**lah**
pepper	**pil**pel	**fil**fil

water	mayim	mai
(orange) juice	mitz (tapuzim)	'asir (burtuqal)
tea	tay	shai
coffee	cafay	qahwa
with (a little) sugar	im (harbeh) sukar	bi-sukar (kalil)
without sugar	belee sukar	bilesh sukar
wine	yayin	sharab
beer	bira	bira
I'm (m/f) a vegetarian	Anee tzimkhonee/tzimkhonit.	Ana nabatee/nabateeya
the bill, the check	ha-kheshbon	al-hissaab

Glossary

For food terms, see p.180.

Ablaq Decorative masonry in alternating colours (usually black and white), usually around doors or windows.

Aqaba Street in the Old City.

Area A Parts of the West Bank controlled by the PA under the Oslo Accords (Area B is under PA civil control and Israeli security control, Area C under Israeli control).

Argila Hookah pipe (also *nargila* or *sheesha*).

Ark (1) Structure containing the tablets of the Ten Commandments and used for prayer by the ancient Israelites before the construction of the Temple; (2) Cupboard on the wall of a synagogue facing Temple Mount in which the Torah scrolls are kept.

Ashkenazi Jewish of north European origin (from *Ashkenaz*, meaning the Rhineland).

Atzma'ut Israeli Independence.

Avodah Israeli Labour Party, no longer really socialist, but more liberal than Kadima.

Bab Gate or door (Arabic).

Bet or Beit House.

Derekh Road.

Fatah Main Palestinian political faction and sometime paramilitary group, currently the governing party in the Palestinian Authority on the West Bank.

Gan Park or garden.

Green Line 1949 Armistice Line between Israel and Jordan – the boundary between Israel and the West Bank.

Hadash Left-wing Israeli political party (generally Marxist) favouring equal rights for Arab Israelis.

Haganah Pre-Independence Zionist militia, forerunner of the IDF.

Halal Permitted by Islamic law.

Hallah Shabbat or festive bread made with egg, placed under a covering cloth upon the dinner table to be blessed and "broken" (as in "break bread") before eating.

Hamas Islamic fundamentalist party and paramilitary group, currently in control of the Gaza Strip, which opposes a two-state solution and aims to replace Israel with an Islamic state.

Haram Holy sanctuary or precinct, but also anything that is not *halal*.

Haredi Ultra-orthodox Jew.

Hassidism A movement within ultra-orthodox Judaism from eighteenth-century eastern Europe that emphasizes prayer and religious observance rather than Talmudic study.

IDF (Israel Defence Force) The Israeli army.

Intifada Palestinian uprising; the First Intifada (1987-91) was charcterized by strikes, rioting and civil disobedienc; the Second Intifada (2000-2006) was characterized by suicide bombings and other attacks on Israeli civilians.

Irgun Pre-1948 right-wing Zionist paramilitary group (also called *Etzel*).

JNF (Jewish National Fund) Official Israeli body controlling state land on behalf of the Jewish people.

Kadima Centre-right Israeli political party created by Ariel Sharon when he split Likud by withdrawing from Gaza.

Kakh Illegal and officially defunct racist Israeli political party (equivalent to the BNP or KKK), supported mainly among extreme settler groups such as those in Hebron.

Khan (also called a caravanserai) Inn where merchants would sleep and stable their livestock when coming into town to trade.

Kippa Jewish skullcap.

Kosher In accordance with Jewish religious law, especially food.

Kufic The original Arabic script, more angular than the modern *naskhi* script.

Likud Right-wing Israeli political party favouring free-market economics and annexation of the West Bank, Gaza and Golan to Israel.

Lulav Date frond, which is tied together with a sprig of myrtle and willow, and, along with a lemon-like fruit called an *etrog* (citron), shaken in several directions while praying during the Sukkot festival.

Madrasa Muslim religious school.

Marqana Stalactite-like decorations on the inside of a dome or doorway.

Mashrabiya Lattice-work window, usually wooden.

Meretz Centre-left Israeli political party favouring a two-state solution to the Israel-Palestine conflict.

Mezuza Box nailed to a doorpost containing Torah passages on parchment (see p.277).

Midrahov Pedestrian precinct.

Mihrab Niche in the wall of a mosque indicating the direction of prayer (towards Mecca).

Minbar Pulpit in a mosque.

Mizrahi (literally "eastern") Jewish of Arabic or Asian origin.

Naqba (literally "catastrophe") Israeli independence as seen by the Palestinians.

Oslo Accords 1993 agreement between Israel and the PLO designed to lead to a permanent two-state solution to the Israel-Palestine conflict.

PA or **PNA** Palestinian (National) Authority, an administrative body set up by the PLO to govern areas of the West Bank and Gaza ceded to it by Israel under the Oslo Accords.

PFLP (Popular Front for the Liberation of Palestine) Hardline left-wing Palestinian party and sometime paramilitary group with quite strong support in East Jerusalem.

PLO (Palestinian Liberation Organization) Umbrella organization for Palestinian political groups, including Fatah and the PFLP, but not Hamas.

Qibla Direction of Muslim prayer (towards Mecca), and the corresponding wall of a mosque.

Rehov Street.

Revisionism Right-wing tendency in Zionist thought, founded by Ze'ev Jabotinsky (see p.151).

Road Map Proposed framework for a peace settlement based on a two-state solution, originally mooted in 2002 by the US, and backed by Russia, the EU and the UN.

Sederot Boulevard.

Sephardi (literally "Spanish") Jewish of ultimately Spanish or Portuguese origin, dispersed since the expulsion of Jews and Muslims from Spain in 1492.

Sha'ar Gate (Hebrew).

Sharia (1) Road; (2) Islamic law.

Shas Sephardi and Mizrahi Jewish fundamentalist party.

Service taxi ("servees") Shared taxi or minibus following a fixed route for a fixed fare.

Sherut Israeli service taxi.

Souq Market (*shuq* in Hebrew).

Stern Gang Pre-1948 far-right Zionist paramilitary group (also called *LEHI*), a splinter from the Irgun.

Tariq Alley (usually a small Old City street).

Tefilin Boxes containing Torah passages on parchment, tied to arm and head during morning prayer (see box, p.277).

Torah The first five books of the Old Testament (five books of Moses), regarded as the source of Jewish law.

Turba Tomb.

Waqf Islamic trust administering religious sites.

Yarmulka Jewish skullcap (Yiddish for *kippa*).

Yeshiva Jewish religious seminary.

Zionism Belief in and support for the idea of a Jewish state in Israel.

Small print and

Index

A Rough Guide to Rough Guides

Published in 1982, the first Rough Guide – to Greece – was a student scheme that became a publishing phenomenon. Mark Ellingham, a recent graduate in English from Bristol University, had been travelling in Greece the previous summer and couldn't find the right guidebook. With a small group of friends he wrote his own guide, combining a highly contemporary, journalistic style with a thoroughly practical approach to travellers' needs.

The immediate success of the book spawned a series that rapidly covered dozens of destinations. And, in addition to impecunious backpackers, Rough Guides soon acquired a much broader and older readership that relished the guides' wit and inquisitiveness as much as their enthusiastic, critical approach and value-for-money ethos.

These days, Rough Guides include recommendations from shoestring to luxury and cover more than 200 destinations around the globe, including almost every country in the Americas and Europe, more than half of Africa and most of Asia and Australasia. Our ever-growing team of authors and photographers is spread all over the world, particularly in Europe, the US and Australia.

In the early 1990s, Rough Guides branched out of travel, with the publication of Rough Guides to World Music, Classical Music and the Internet. All three have become benchmark titles in their fields, spearheading the publication of a wide range of books under the Rough Guide name.

Including the travel series, Rough Guides now number more than 350 titles, covering: phrasebooks, waterproof maps, music guides from Opera to Heavy Metal, reference works as diverse as Conspiracy Theories and Shakespeare, and popular culture books from iPods to Poker. Rough Guides also produce a series of more than 120 World Music CDs in partnership with World Music Network.

Visit www.roughguides.com to see our latest publications.

Rough Guide travel images are available for commercial licensing at www.roughguidespictures.com

Rough Guide credits

Text editor: Andy Turner
Layout: Sachin Tanwar
Cartography: Animesh Pathak
Picture editor: Emily Taylor
Production: Rebecca Short
Proofreader: Karen Parker
Cover design: Chloë Roberts
Photographer: Eddie Gerald
Editorial: Ruth Blackmore, Keith Drew, Edward Aves, Alice Park, Lucy White, Jo Kirby, James Smart, Natasha Foges, Róisín Cameron, Emma Traynor, Emma Gibbs, Kathryn Lane, Christina Valhouli, Monica Woods, Mani Ramaswamy, Harry Wilson, Lucy Cowie, Amanda Howard, Lara Kavanagh, Alison Roberts, Joe Staines, Peter Buckley, Matthew Milton, Tracy Hopkins, Ruth Tidball; **Delhi** Madhavi Singh, Karen D'Souza, Lubna Shaheen
Design & Pictures: **London** Scott Stickland, Dan May, Diana Jarvis, Mark Thomas, Nicole Newman, Sarah Cummins; **Delhi** Umesh Aggarwal, Ajay Verma, Jessica Subramanian, Ankur Guha, Pradeep Thapliyal, Anita Singh, Nikhil Agarwal, Sachin Gupta
Production: Vicky Baldwin

Cartography: **London** Maxine Repath, Ed Wright, Katie Lloyd-Jones; **Delhi** Rajesh Chhibber, Ashutosh Bharti, Rajesh Mishra, Jasbir Sandhu, Karobi Gogoi, Alakananda Bhattacharya, Swati Handoo, Deshpal Dabas
Online: **London** George Atwell, Faye Hellon, Jeanette Angell, Fergus Day, Justine Bright, Clare Bryson, Aine Fearon, Adrian Low, Ezgi Celebi, Amber Bloomfield; **Delhi** Amit Verma, Rahul Kumar, Narender Kumar, Ravi Yadav, Debojit Borah, Rakesh Kumar, Ganesh Sharma, Shisir Basumatari
Marketing & Publicity: **London** Liz Statham, Niki Hanmer, Louise Maher, Jess Carter, Vanessa Godden, Vivienne Watton, Anna Paynton, Rachel Sprackett, Libby Jellie, Laura Vipond, Vanessa McDonald; **New York** Katy Ball, Judi Powers, Nancy Lambert; **Delhi** Ragini Govind
Manager India: Punita Singh
Reference Director: Andrew Lockett
Operations Manager: Helen Phillips
PA to Publishing Director: Nicola Henderson
Publishing Director: Martin Dunford
Commercial Manager: Gino Magnotta
Managing Director: John Duhigg

SMALL PRINT

Publishing information

This second edition published October 2009 by
Rough Guides Ltd,
80 Strand, London WC2R 0RL
14 Local Shopping Centre, Panchsheel Park, New Delhi 110017, India

Distributed by the Penguin Group
Penguin Books Ltd,
80 Strand, London WC2R 0RL
Penguin Group (USA)
375 Hudson Street, NY 10014, USA
Penguin Group (Australia)
250 Camberwell Road, Camberwell,
Victoria 3124, Australia
Penguin Group (Canada)
195 Harry Walker Parkway N, Newmarket, ON, L3Y 7B3 Canada
Penguin Group (NZ)
67 Apollo Drive, Mairangi Bay, Auckland 1310, New Zealand
Cover concept by Peter Dyer.

Typeset in Bembo and Helvetica to an original design by Henry Iles.
Printed in Singapore
© Daniel Jacobs 2009
Maps © Rough Guides

312pp includes index
A catalogue record for this book is available from the British Library
ISBN: 978-1-84836-193-5

Help us update

We've gone to a lot of effort to ensure that the second edition of **The Rough Guide to Jerusalem** is accurate and up-to-date. However, things change – places get "discovered", opening hours are notoriously fickle, restaurants and rooms raise prices or lower standards. If you feel we've got it wrong or left something out, we'd like to know, and if you can remember the address, the price, the hours, the phone number, so much the better.

Please send your comments with the subject line "Rough Guide Jerusalem Update" to ©mail@roughguides.com. We'll credit all contributions and send a copy of the next edition (or any other Rough Guide if you prefer) for the very best emails.

Have your questions answered and tell others about your trip at
® community.roughguides.com

Acknowledgements

The author would like to thank: Louise Margolin, Chaim and Anna Margolin, Mahmoud Salamat, Ali Jiddah, Jane Faure-Brac, Julian Lipman, Orel Tamuz, Ze'ev and Sharon Tamuz (Hedya Jewellers), and special thanks to Jordie Gerson for her guidance and advice. Big thanks also to Andy Turner for his staunch and patient editing, to Ruth Blackmore for her invaluable input, and to Karen Parker and Animesh Pathak for sound proofreading and typesetting.

Photo credits

All photos © Rough Guides except the following:

Introduction
View across the Muslim Quarter © John Hicks/ Corbis
Orthodox Jewish man outside a synagogue © Shai Ginott/Corbis
Damascus Gate © John Hicks/Corbis
Madaba Map © Israel images/Alamy
Praying at the Western Wall © Damon Lynch
Jewish men and Muslim children © Damon Lynch

Things not to miss
01 Church of the Holy Sepulchre © Damon Lynch
04 Woman smoking argila © Eugene Nikiforov /Alamy
08 Christmas Day in Manger Square, Bethlehem © Jon Arnold Images Ltd/Alamy
09 Hisham's Palace © David Silverman/Getty
12 Catholic pilgrims on the Via Dolorosa © Petra Wegner/Tips Images
16 Floating in the Dead Sea © Felix Oppenheim /Jupiter Images
19 Praying in the Church of the Nativity © Christian Kober/Photolibrary
20 Banksy on the Separation Wall © Dan Jacobs

The Holy City colour section
Dome of the Rock © Eitan Simanor/PCL
Orthodox Jew at the Western Wall © Eddie Gerald /Alamy
Torah book at the Four Sephardic Synagogues in the Jewish Quarter © Eddie Gerald/Alamy
Detail of the Dome of the Rock © Petra Wegner/ Tips Images

Black and whites
p.164 *King Davids Hotel* © Coutesy of *King Davids Hotel*
p.174 *American Colony* © Courtesy of the *American Colony*
p.201 Israel Jerusalem Theatre © Eitan Simanor /Alamy
p.210 Purim festival © Eitan Simanor/Alamy
p.234 The Separation Wall © Damon Lynch

Index

Map entries are in colour.

A

Abbasids 270
Abraham (biblical patriarch)
..................102, 242, 275
Absalom's Pillar............115
Abu Ghosh 252
accessibility....................34
accommodation...163–176,
233–235
Aelia Capitolina 270
"African Quarter" 77
Agnon, S.Y. (Shai)........119,
156, 286
airlines 20–22, 27
airport (Ben Gurion)...23, 27
Al-Aqsa Mosque...104, *The
Holy City* colour section
Al-Azariya (Bethany)
.............................158–160
Alexander Hospice.........71
al-Husseini, Haj Amin...107
Al-Jaliqiya......................81
Al-Kas 106
Al-Kilaniya.....................81
All Nations Church 119
Al-Wad Road 76
American Colony..........112
American football 206
Ammunition Hill 113
Anglican cathedral........111
Arabic phrases....294–298
Ariel Sharon's house.......77
Armenian Compound 52
Armenian History
Museum......................53
Armenian Quarter........47,
50–54, 93
Armenian Quarter..........48
art galleries 216–218
ATMs..............................41
audio tours 28
Augusta Victoria Hospital
..............................39, 122
Austrian Hospice....77, 165
Ayyubids.......................271

B

Bab al-Silsila.................106
Bab al-Silsila Street.......81,
106

banks...............................41
bargaining....................226
Barluzzi, Antonio 121
bars 194–198, 263
baseball 207
basketball 206
Batei Mahse 98
Baybars the Great...55, 271
beer 195
Begin, Menahem 119,
138, 143, 167
Beit Orot 123
Ben Gurion airport....23, 27
Ben Yehuda, Eliezar 132,
167
Ben Yehuda Steet.........124
Bet HaMa'alot 128
Bet Rothschild................98
Bet Sahur 239
Bet Sefer Shafitsar 131
Bethany 158–160
Bethlehem 231–240
Bethlehem....................232
Bethpage......................160
Bethseda Pools 57
Bevingrad 133
Bible Lands Museum 147
Biblical Zoo 156
Bird Observatory 148
birdwatching.........134, 148
Bloomfield Science
Museum......................148
books on Jerusalem
............................284–289
bookshops....................218
botanical garden...........122
bowling alleys...............208
British Mandate 272
Broad Wall 93
Bukharia 130
Burj al-Laqlaq................83
Burnt House 97
bus stations............23, 26
buses (intercity) 23
buses (international)
..............................20, 23
buses (local) 24–26

C

Cable Car Museum 138
cafés 181–184

cannabis 30
Cardo..............................92
cellphones 42
central souqs..................76
Chagall, Marc 147,
148, 154
Chagall Windows 154
Chamber of the Holocaust
....................................142
Chapel of the Ascension
....................................117
checkpoints....................30
children's Jerusalem.......33
Christian Quarter....61–71
Christian Quarter 56
Christianity 280–283
**Church of the Holy
Sepulchre** 63–69
Church of the Holy
Sepulchre 64
Church of the Holy
Sepulchre, original door
......................................62
Church of the Nativity ...235
Church of the Nativity
....................................236
churches........see *The Holy
City* colour section
All Nations......................119
Church of the Visitation ... 154
Condemnation 59
Dominus Flevit 119
Dormition Abbey 147
Ethiopian 132
Flagellation.......................59
Franciscan (Bethany) 158
Greek Orthodox (Bethany)
....160
Holy Sepulchre...............63–69
Lutheran............................70
Nativity (Bethlehem).........235
Nea (remains of)...............98
Our Lady of the Spasm......61
Pater Noster.....................118
Queen Helena 63
Redeemer.........................70
Russian Cathedral............135
St Andrew's.......................139
St Anne's 57
St Catherine's (Bethlehem)
....236
St Étienne.........................111
St George's Cathedral 111
St James's Cathedral.........53
St John the Baptist....70, 154
St Mark's...........................54
St Mary Magdalene..........119

St Mary's of the Gemans
(remains of) 97
St Paul's 132
St Peter in Gallicantu 143
White Russian 119
cinemas 204
Citadel 50–52
City Hall Complex 124
City of David 113–115
city tours 28
classical music ... 200–202
climate 9
clothes 9, 31
clubbing 198, 264
Coenaculum 142
combined tickets 29, 50
comedy 203
Commonwealth War
Cemeteries 122, 156
concerts (classical)
.... 200–202
Congliano Synagogue ... 125
consulates (foreign in
Jerusalem) 38
consulates (Israeli abroad)
.... 37
Convent of St Vincent de
Paul 136
Convent of the Olive
Tree 53
Convent of the Sisters of
Zion 60
costs 36
credit cards 41
crime 30
Crusaders 271
cultural centres 40
currency 41
cycling 208

D

Damascus Gate 72–75
dance performances 203
Dar al-Sitt Tunshuq 78
David (King) ... 113, 237, 267
David's Harp Bridge 129
Davidka monument 128
Davidson Center 87
Dead Sea 248
Dead Sea Scrolls 145
Deir al-Zeitouna 53
Deir Yassin 153
dentists 39
diarrhoea 38
disabled travellers 34
doctors 39
Domari Gypsies 83

Dome of the Ascension
.... 106
Dome of the Chain 106
Dome of the Prophet 106
Dome of the Rock 102
Dominus Flevit 119
Dormition Abbey 147
drinking 194–198
driving 24, 26
drugs 30
Duhovnia Building 135
Dung Gate 86
duty-free allowances 37

E

**East Jerusalem (down-
town area)** 108–112
East Jerusalem 109
East Talpiot 157
eating 177–193
Ecce Homo Arch 60
Egypt to Jerusalem 20
Ein Gedi 249
Ein Karem 153–155
Elad (settler group) 114,
115, 117
electricity 36
Elijah (prophet) 96, 103
Eliyahu HaNavi Synagogue
.... 96
embassies (foreign in Israel)
.... 38
embassies (Israeli abroad)
.... 37
Emek Tzurim National Park
.... 123
Emtza'i Synagogue 96
entertainment 198–208
entry requirements 37
entry stamps 21
Essenes 145, 249, 269
Ethiopian Church 132
Ethiopian Compound 62

F

falafel 184
festivals 209–215, 276
Field of Grey Peas 158
film 204
film festivals 215
fitness centres 207
flights from abroad 19
food 177–193, 222
football (American) 206

football (soccer) 205
forums (Roman) 60,
69, 270
Four Sephardi synagogues
.... 95
Free Polish Army
monument 143
Frumin House 128
Frutiger House 132

G

galleries (art) 216–218
Gan HaTekumah
Archeological Garden ... 98
Garden of Gethsemane
.... 120
Garden Tomb 111
Gate of Judgement ... 62, 71
gay travellers 32
Generations Center 91
German Colony 139
Gethsemane, Garden of
.... 120
Gethsemane, Grotto of
.... 121
glossary of terms .. 180, 299
Golden Gate 105
Goliath Fort 71
Gordon's Calvary 110
Government House 156
Grand Mufti (Haj Amin
al-Husseini) 107, 272
Great Synagogue 128
Green Line 7, 133
Grotto of Gethsemane ... 121
gyms 207
Gypsy community 83

H

Haas Promenade 156
Hadassah convoy
massacre 113
Hadassah Hospital
(Ein Karem) 154
Hadassah Hospital (Mount
Scopus) 39, 122
Hadrian (Emperor) 270
haggling 226
Hammam al-'Ayn 80
HaNeviim Street 132
**Haram al-Sharif (Temple
Mount)** 99–106
Haredi Judaism 131
Hasmoneans 269

INDEX

health..............................38
heat problems 38, 243
Hebrew phrases...294–298
Hebrew University 122
Hebron..........................241
Herod the Great.....88, 239, 269
Herod's Gate 82
Herodion........................239
Herodian Jerusalem, model of......................................145
Herzl, Theodor......136, 150
Hezekiah's Pool.............50
Hezekiah's Tunnel.........114
Hezir Family Tomb........116
Hill of Evil Counsel 156
Hisham's Palace (Jericho) 247
history.................267–274
holidays (public) 41
holidays 209–214
Holman Hunt, William... 132, 158
Holocaust 152
Holy Fire, miracle of 69
HolyPass 29
hospices 164
hospitals 39
hostels...163–167, 171, 173
hotels 163–176
Hulda Gates 87
hummus bars 184–186
Hurva Synagogue...........94

I

Independence Park 32, 136
insurance (travel) 39
internet access...............39
Islam 278–280
Islamic Art Museum 140
Islamic Museum 105
Israel Museum 144–147
Israelite Tower 93
Italian Hospital..............132
Italian Synagogue........125

J

Jaffa..............................261
Jaffa Gate............... 47–49
jay-walking 31
Jebel Quruntul..............246
Jebusites 267
Jeremiah's Grotto 110

Jericho................ 243–248
Jericho 244
Jerusalem Archaeological Park 86
Jerusalem History Museum 52
Jerusalem in the First Temple Period exhibition 94
Jerusalem stone .... see *The Holy City* colour section
Jerusalem Syndrome 6
Jesus 58–62, 67, 68, 142, 143, 157, 159, 160, 236, 237, 245, 269, 280
Jewish Quarter 84–98
Jewish Quarter 85
Jewish War 269
John the Baptist...118, 154
Jordan (getting to)..........27
Jordan (getting to Jerusalem from) 20
judaica..........................224
Judaism 275–278
juice bars......................197

K

Kal Grande Synagogue...95
Kara'ite Synagogue........96
Kara'ites 96, 276
kashrut...................179, 277
Kfar Etzion....................240
Khalidi Library................82
Khan al-Sultan..............82
Khan Tanqiz..................80
Kibbutz Ramat Rahel ...157, 176, 207
Kidron Valley.................115
Kikar Zion (Zion Square) 124
King David Hotel ...137, 175
King Herod's Family Tomb 137
King Solomon's Quarries 108
Knesset..........................148
kosher food 179, 277
Kotel (Wailing Wall).........87
Kotel HaQatan................80
Kursi Suleiman 105

L

LA Mayer Museum 140
language.............. 294–298

Last Supper, room of....142
laundry............................40
Lazarus, tomb of 159
lesbian travellers.............32
Liberty Bell Garden.......139
libraries............................40
light railway 25
Lion Fountain................138
Lions' Gate.............. 55–57
liquor stores..................223
Lithostratos 60
Little Wailing Wall 80
Lutheran Church.............70

M

Madaba Map 8
madrasas
  al-Baladiya 107
  al-Dawadariya.................... 58
  al-Jawhariya 79
  al-Khatuniya 79
  al-Muzhariya..................... 79
  al-Sallamiya...................... 58
  al-Tankaziya 107
  al-Taziya 81
  Rasasiya........................... 78
Magharba Quarter 86, 88, 90
Mahane Yehuda............129
mail.................................40
Malha............................155
malls 222
Mamilla 136
Mamluk architecture.......79
Mamluks..........79, 271
Mandate (British) 272
Mandelbaum Gate........133
maps................................40
Mar Elias 157
Mardigan Museum 53
markets..........................225
Mary (Virgin).......67, 68, 87, 120, 141, 237
Mary Magdalene....68, 157, 159
Mary's Spring 154
Masada 250–252
Masada 251
Masayef Synagogue.....130
Mashiah Borochoff House 128
Mazkeret Moshe...........129
Mea Shearim 129
meat market 76
media............................35
medical problems...........38
Menahem Begin Heritage Center......................138

Merrill Hassenfeld
    Amphitheatre 138,
    200, 202
midrahov 124
Mifletzet 156
Mishkan Shmuel 128
Mishkenot Sha'anim 137
mobile phones 42
model of Herodian
    Jerusalem 145
Mohammed (prophet) ... 103
Monastery of the Cross
    140
Monastery of the Temptation
    (Jericho) 246
money 41
moneychangers 41
Montefiore, Moses 137,
    240
Morasha (Musrara) 133
mosques .... see *The Holy
    City* colour section
    Al-Aqsa 104
    Chapel of the Ascension
        117
    Omar 70
    Sidi Umar 95
    mosquitoes 38
Mount Herzl 180
Mount of Olives 117–121
Mount of Olives cemetery
    119
Mount of Olives viewpoint
    118
Mount Scopus 121–123
Mount Zion 141–143
movie theatres 204
Muristan 69–71
museums
    Ammunition Hill 113
    Armenian History 53
    Bethlehem 237
    Bible Lands 147
    Bloomfield (science) 148
    Cable Car 138
    Diaspora (Tel Aviv) 260
    Eretz Yisra'el (Tel Aviv) 260
    History of Jerusalem (Citadel)
        52
    Islamic 105
    Islamic Art 140
    Israel Museum 144–147
    Italian Jewish Art 125
    Judaica 128
    LA Mayer 140
    Mardigan 53
    Museum on the Seam 133
    Natural History 139
    Old Yishuv Court 93
    One Last Day 93
    Psalms 129
    Rockefeller 110

Science 148
Shrine of the Book 145
Skirball 136
Temple Treasures 98
Ticho House 128
Tolerance and Human Dignity
    136
Underground Prisoners 134
Wohl (archeological) 96
Wolfson (Judaica) 128
music (live) 199–202
Muslim Quarter 56–61,
    72–83, 106
Muslim Quarter 73
Musrara 133

N

Nahalat Shiv'a 125
Nahla'ot 129
Nahmanides (Ramban) ... 84,
    95
Natural History
    Museum 139
Nea Church 98
New Gate 71
newspapers 35
Night Journey
    (Mohammed's) 103
nightclubs 198, 264
Nissan Bek Synagogue ... 96
Notre Dame 135

O

off licences 223
Old City quarters 6
Old Station Compound
    .... 139, 198
Old Yishuv Court Museum
    93
Olive Tree Convent 53
Omar (Caliph) 66, 70, 99
Omar Ibn al-Khattab
    Square 49
One Last Day Museum ... 93
opening hours 41
opticians 39
Orient House 112
Oslo Accord 273
Ottoman sabils (fountains)
    .... 77, 80, 106, 138
Ottoman Tombs (Omar Ibn
    al-Khattab Square) 49
Ottomans 271
Oz, Amos 288

P

Palace of Lady Tunshuq
    78
passport stamps 21
Pater Noster Church 118
Pavement of Justice 60
pharmacies 38
Phaseal Tower 51
phones 42
photography 32, 227
Pilate, Pontius 59, 146
Pillar of Absalom 115
plugs (electric) 36
police 30
pools 207
Pools of Bethseda 57
post offices 40
President's Residence ... 140
prices 36
Prime Minister's Residence
    140
Prison of Christ 61
Psalms Museum 129
public holidays 41,
    209–214

Q

Qasr Jalud 71
quarters (Old City) 6
Queen Helena's Church ... 63
Qumran 249

R

Rabbi Yohanan Ben Zakkai
    Synagogue 95
Rabin, Yitzhak 258
Rachel's Tomb 240
radio 35
Ramadan 188, 211
Ramat Rahel 157,
    176, 207
Ramban Synagogue 95
ramparts 49, 50
Ramparts Walk 50
Ratisbonne Monastery
    128
Rehavia 140
restaurants 186–192
Ribat Ala al-Din al-Basir
    78
Ribat al-Mansuri 78

Ribat al-Maridini 57
Ribat al-Nisa' 107
Robinson's Arch 87, 90
Rockefeller Museum 110
Roman Column 49
Roman Plaza 74
Romans 269
rooftop promenade 93
Rose Garden 150
Rothschild Hospital 132
Russian Cathedral 135
Russian Compound 135
Russian Mission Building
    135
Russian Monastery 118

S

sabils 77, 80, 106, 138
Saladin (Salah al-Din
    al-Ayyubi) 271
Salahiya Khanqah 70
sales tax 36
Sanhedria 131
Schick, Conrad 132
Schindler, Oskar 143
Science Museum 148
Scottish Church 139
Seam Museum 133
Secondary Cardo 86
security 29
Security Barrier 234
self-guided tours 28
Separation Wall 234
Sergei House 135
service taxis 23, 25, 27
settlements ... 117, 123, 240
sexual harassment 31
Shabbat (Jewish Sabbath)
    276
Sharon, Ariel ... 77, 101, 274
Sheikh Jarrah 112
sheruts 23, 25, 27
shop hours 41
shopping 216–228
Shrine of the Book 145
Sidi Umar Mosque 95
Siloam Inscription 114
Silwan 116
Six Day War 7, 88,
    113, 272
Skirball Museum 136
Smadar Cinema 139, 204
soccer 205
Solomon (King) 99, 110,
    137, 267
Solomon's Stables 105

Souk Khan al-Zeit 61, 75
sound and light show
    (Citadel) 52
Souq Aftimos 69
Souq al-Qattanin 80
sports 205–208
St Andrew's Church 139
St Anne's Church 57
St Étienne's Church 111
St George's Cathedral ... 111
St Helena 65
St James's Cathedral 53
St John's Hospice 70
St Mark's Church 54
St Mary's of the Gemans
    97
St Paul's Church 132
St Peter in Gallicantu ... 143
St Stephen 56, 111
St Stephen's Gate ... 55–57
St Veronica 61
St Vincent de Paul Convent
    136
Stables of Solomon 105
Stambouli Synagogue 96
stamps (postal) 40
station (rail) 24
Stations of the Cross
    58–62
Status Quo on religious
    sites 65, 88, 90
Stern House 136
Stern, Avraham 258
Street of the Prophets ... 132
String Bridge 129
Struthion Pool 92
student discounts 36
studying in Jerusalem 43
Suleiman the Magnificent
    .... 49, 56, 80, 88, 271
Sultan's Pool 138,
    200, 202
sunstroke 38
supermarkets 222
Supreme Court 149
sweets 192, 223
swimming pools 207
synagogues .... see The
    Holy City colour section
Congliano 125
diaspora (reconstructed)
    .... 125, 147
Eliyahu HaNavi 96
Emtza'i 96
Four Sephardi synagogues
    95
Great Synagogue 128
Hurva 94
Italian 125
Kal Grande 95
Kara'ite 96

Masayef 130
Nissan Bek 96
Rabbi Yohanan Ben Zakkai
    95
Ramban 95
Stambouli 96
Tiferet Yisra'el 96
Yeshurun 128
Syrian Convent 54

T

Tabor House 132
Talbiya 140
Talpiot 156
Tankaziya Madrasa 107
Tanners' Gate 86
tap water 38
Tashtumuriya 82
taxis 25
Tel Aviv 253–264
Tel Aviv and Jaffa 254
telephones 42
television 35
Temple Mount 99–106
Temple Mount 100
tennis courts 207
terrorist attacks 76, 125
theatre 202
Ticho House 128
Tiferet Yisra'el Synagogue
    96
Time Elevator 125–128
time zone 42
Tisch Family Zoo 156
tombs
    of al-Awhad 57
    of David 142
    of Jason 140
    of Jehosaphat 115
    of Lazarus 159
    of Pharaoh's Daughter
        116
    of Rachel 234
    of Simon the Just
        112
    of the Patriarchs (Hebron) 242
    of the Prophets 118
    of the Royal Steward
        117
    of the Sanhedrin
        131
    of the Virgin 120
    of Zechariah 116
Tombs of the Kings 112
tourist offices 42
tours 28
Tower of David 50–52
trains 24
trams 25

travel agents (abroad).....22
travel insurance..............39
Turba al-Sa'adiya 107
Turba of Barka Khan 82
Turba of Turkan Khatun
....................................107
TV 35
Tyropoeon Valley 76

U

Umariya School..............59
Ummayads 270
Underground Prisoners
Museum.....................134
Ussishkin, Menahem....132

V

VAT 36
vegetarian food 191
Via Dolorosa............58–62
visas 37
voltage...........................36

W

Wailing Wall............. 87–90
walking tours 28
walls (Old City) 49, 50
Warren's Gate.................92
Warren's Shaft..............115
water (tap/faucet) 38
weather............................9
websites on Jerusalem...43
**West Jerusalem (down-
town area)** 124–137
West Jerusalem....126–127
Western (Wailing) Wall
.... 87–90
Western Wall Tunnel.......91
wheelchair access..........34
White Russian Church...119
Wilhelm II (Kaiser)...........48
Wilson's Arch............81, 91
windmills...............137, 141
wine 195
Wohl Archeological
Museum.......................96
Wohl Rose Park............150
Wolfson Museum of
Judaica......................128
work................................43

Y

Yad VaShem.................151
Yad VaShem 151–153
Yemin Moshe................137
yeshivas 44
Yeshurun Synagogue
....................................128
YMCA 137, 173,
204, 207
youth hostels 163–167,
171, 173

Z

Zaltimo's Sweets 62
Zedekiah's Cave...........108
Zion (original meaning of)
............................114, 141
Zion Gate.......................47
Zion Square..................124
zoo................................156

Map symbols

maps are listed in the full index using coloured text

- - -	Chapter boundary	) (	Bridge
▄②▄	Motorway	✈	Airport
═⑤⑦═	National Highway	⊠	Gate
═══	Major paved road	⊞	Hospital
───	Minor paved road	⊠	Post office
⊞⊞⊞	Steps	♦	Point of interest
▬▬▬	Pedestrianized road	♨	Viewpoint
- - - -	Path	✡	Synagogue
───	River	⌣	Mosque
▬●▬	Railway	⚑	Monastery or convent
●- - -●	Cable car	⚐	Church (regional map)
───	Wall	✚	Church (town map)
⚑	Checkpoint	▬	Building
⅔	Rocks	⊞	Christian cemetery
⌃⌃	Mountains	⌣	Jewish cemetery
@	Internet café	Y Y	Muslim cemetery
ⓘ	Information office	▦	Park
★	Bus/taxi stop	▦	Beach

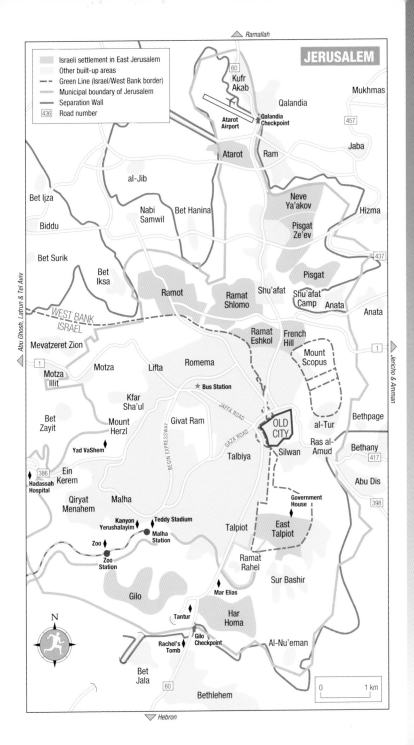

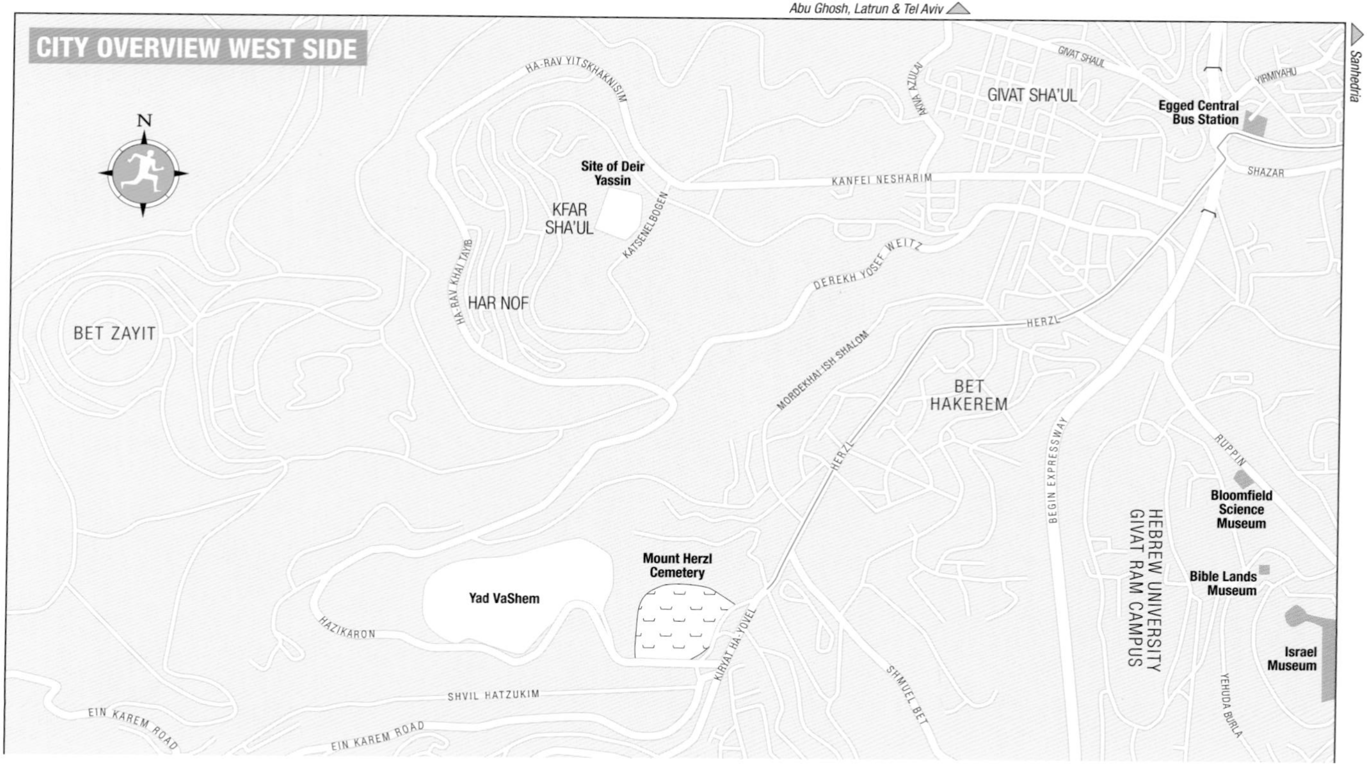

CITY OVERVIEW WEST SIDE

△ Sanhedria

Abu Ghosh, Latrun & Tel Aviv △

N

Eged Central Bus Station

GIVAT SHA'UL

Israel Museum

Bloomfield Science Museum

Bible Lands Museum

YEHUDA BURLA

HEBREW UNIVERSITY GIVAT RAM CAMPUS

RUPPIN

SHAZAR

YIRMIYAHU

GIVAT SHA'UL

AVIVA AZULAI

KANFEI NESHARIM

HERZL

BEGIN EXPRESSWAY

BET HAKEREM

SHMUEL BET

HERZL

MORDEKHAI ISH SHALOM

KIRYAT HA-YOVEL

DEREKH YOSEF W. WEITZ

Site of Deir Yassin

KFAR SHA'UL

KAISENELBOGEN

HAR NOF

HA-RAV YITSKHAKNISIM

HA-RAV KHAI TAYIB

Mount Herzl Cemetery

Yad VaShem

HAZIKARON

SHVIL HATZUKIM

EIN KAREM ROAD

BET ZAYIT

EIN KAREM ROAD

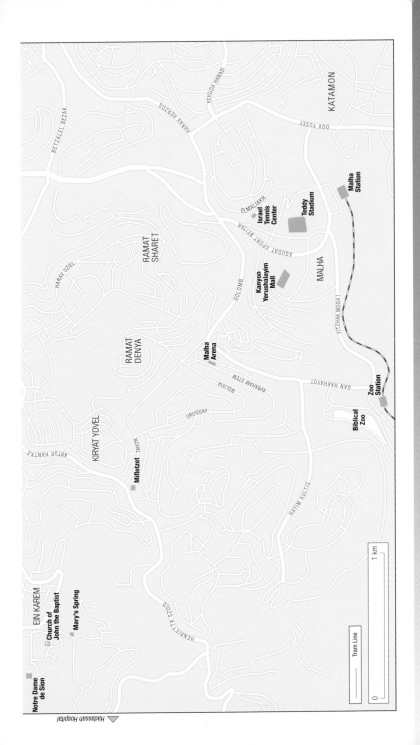

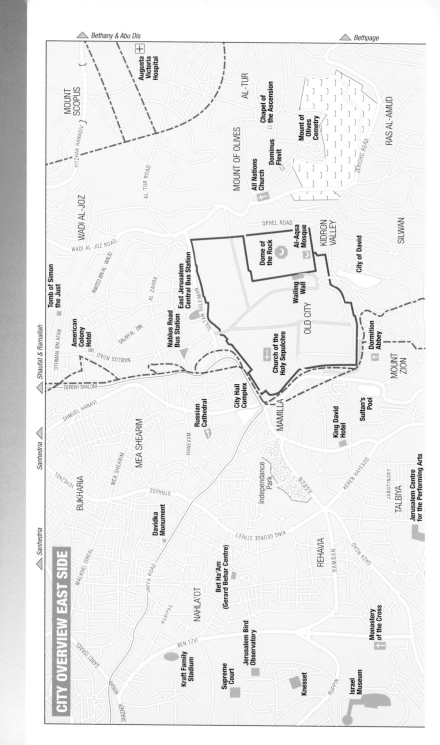

CITY OVERVIEW EAST SIDE

Bethany & Abu Dis

Bethpage

Shaufat & Ramallah

Sanhedria

Sanhedria

MOUNT SCOPUS

Augusta Victoria Hospital

AL-TUR

Chapel of the Ascension

Mount of Olives Cemetery

MOUNT OF OLIVES

Dominus Flevit

All Nations Church

RAS AL-AMUD

YITZHAK HANADIV

AL-TUR ROAD

JERICHO ROAD

WADI AL-JOZ

WADI AL-JOZ ROAD

MAYED IBN AL-WALID

AL-ZAHRA

OPHEL ROAD

Dome of the Rock

Al-Aqsa Mosque

KIDRON VALLEY

SILWAN

Tomb of Simon the Just

East Jerusalem Central Bus Station

SULTAN SULEIMAN

Wailing Wall

City of David

American Colony Hotel

Nablus Road Bus Station

OTTMAN IBN AFAN

SALAH AL-DIN

OLD CITY

NABLUS ROAD

Church of the Holy Sepulchre

Dormition Abbey

DEREKH SHALOM

City Hall Complex

MOUNT ZION

MEA SHEARIM

SHMUEL HANAVI

Russian Cathedral

HANEVIIM

MAMILLA

AGRON

King David Hotel

Sultan's Pool

BUKHARIA

MEA SHEARIM

STRAUSS

Independence Park

KEREN HAYESOD

YEHEZKEL

Davidka Monument

KING GEORGE STREET

JABOTINSKY

TALBIYA

Jerusalem Centre for the Performing Arts

SARE ISRAEL

JAFFA ROAD

MALKHEI ISREAL

Bet Ha'Am (Gerard Behar Centre)

NAHLA'OT

REHAVIA

RAMBAN

GAZA ROAD

BEN TZVI

AGRIPAS

Jerusalem Bird Observatory

Kraft Family Stadium

Supreme Court

Knesset

RUPPIN

Israel Museum

Monastery of the Cross

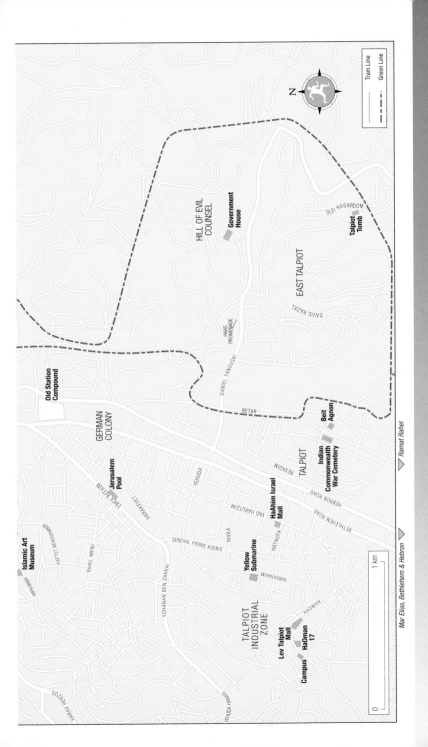

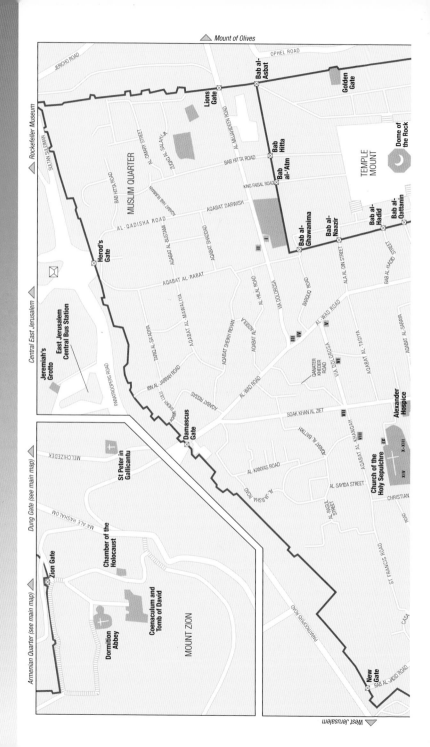

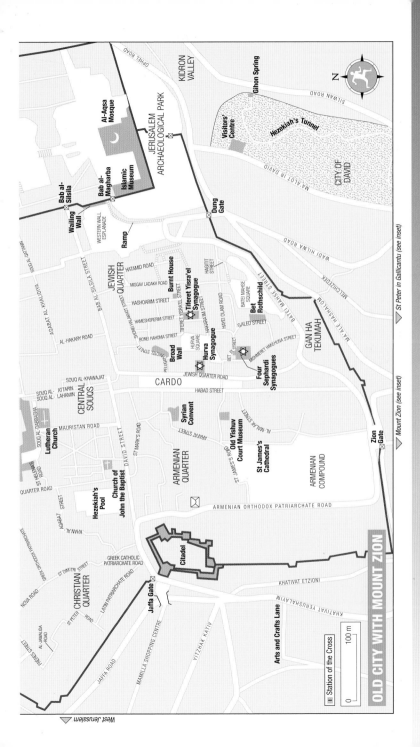

OLD CITY WITH MOUNT ZION

△ West Jerusalem

▷ Mount Zion (see inset)

▷ St Peter in Gallicantu (see inset)

N

Scale
- Station of the Cross ⊠

0   100 m

Christian Quarter / Citadel area

CHRISTIAN QUARTER

FRERES STREET

AL-JAWALDA ROAD

NOVA ROAD

ST DIMITRI STREET

ST PETER ROAD

GREEK ORTHODOX PATRIARCHATE ROAD

LATIN PATRIARCHATE ROAD

QUARTER ROAD

ST HELENA ROAD

ADABAT AL-

KHAN AL-

Hezekiah's Pool

Church of John the Baptist

Lutheran Church

SOUQ AL-DABBAGHA

CENTRAL SOUQS

MAURISTAN ROAD

SOUQ AL-ATTARIN

SOUQ AL-LAHAMIN

SOUQ AL-KHAWAJAT

CARDO

HABAD STREET

DAVID STREET

ST MARK'S ROAD

Syrian Convent

ARRAT STREET

ARMENIAN QUARTER

ST JAMES'S ROAD

Old Yishuv Court Museum

St James's Cathedral

AL-MALAK STREET

ARMENIAN COMPOUND

ARMENIAN ORTHODOX PATRIARCHATE ROAD

Citadel

GREEK CATHOLIC PATRIARCHATE ROAD

Jaffa Gate ⊠

KHATIVAT ETZIONI

MAMILLA SHOPPING CENTRE

JAFFA ROAD

YITZHAK KATIV

Arts and Crafts Lane

KHATIVAT YERUSHALAYIM

Zion Gate ⊠

GAN HA TEKUMAH

Jewish Quarter area

JEWISH QUARTER

SOUQ AL-QATTANIN

ADABAT AL-KHALDIYA

AL-HAKARY ROAD

BAB AL-SILSILA STREET

HATAMID ROAD

MISGAV LADAKH ROAD

HASHOARIM STREET

HAMESHORERIM STREET

BONEI HAHOMA STREET

PLUGOT STREET

HAYEI OLAM ROAD

SONEI HASHAD STREET

HAKARAIM STREET

TIFERET YISRAEL STREET

Burnt House

Tiferet Yisra'el Synagogue ✡

Broad Wall

HURVA SQUARE

Hurva Synagogue ✡

JEWISH QUARTER ROAD

BET EL STREET

HABGITT STREET

BATEI MAHSE STREET

Bet Rothschild

GALED STREET

BATEI MAHSE SQUARE

MISHMERET HAKEHUNA STREET

Four Sephardi Synagogues ✡

MA'ALE HASHALOM

MELCHIZEDEK

Temple Mount / Walling Wall area

OPHEL ROAD

KIDRON VALLEY

JERUSALEM ARCHAEOLOGICAL PARK

Al-Aqsa Mosque

Islamic Museum

Bab al-Magharba

Bab al-Silsila

Walling Wall

WESTERN WALL ESPLANADE

Ramp

Dung Gate ⊠

Gihon Spring

Visitors' Centre

Hezekiah's Tunnel

SILWAN ROAD

MA'ALOT IR DAVID

CITY OF DAVID

WADI HILWA ROAD

EXCURSIONS

0   10 km

Rosh Pinna

Acre

Mount of Beatitudes

Capernaum

Tabgha

SEA OF GALILEE

Tiberias

Haifa

ISRAEL

Kufr Kanna

Bet Shearim

Nazareth

GALILEE

MEDITERRANEAN SEA

N

Afula

Megiddo (Armageddon)

GOLAN HEIGHTS

Bet Shean

Sheikh Hussein Bridge

Jenin

JORDAN

Hadera

Netanya

Nablus

WEST BANK

Tel Aviv

Jaffa

Ben Gurion Airport

Lydda (Lod)

Ramla

Ramallah

Latrun   Emmaus

Abu Ghosh

Jericho

Allenby (King Hussein) Bridge

Amman

Inn of the Good Samaritan

Ashdod

Jerusalem

Qumran

Bet Sahur

Bethlehem

Herodoon

Kfar Etzion

JUDEAN DESERT

DEAD SEA

Hebron

Ein Gedi

Ashqelon & Gaza

ISRAEL

Masada

Beer Sheba & Eilat

Arad

Aqaba & Petra